C0-ASO-227

Narcissism, the Self, and Society

Also by Reuben Fine

The Personality of the Asthmatic Child (1948)
Freud: A Critical Reevaluation of His Theories (1962)
The Psychology of the Chess Player (1967)
The Healing of the Mind (1st edition) (1971)
Psychotherapy and the Social Order (editor) (1974)
Psychoanalytic Psychology (1975)
A History of Psychoanalysis (1979)
The Intimate Hour (1979)
The Psychoanalytic Vision (1981)
The Healing of the Mind (2nd edition) (1982)
The Logic of Psychology (1983)
The Meaning of Love in Human Experience (1985)
The Forgotten Man (1986)
The Psychotherapy of Men (in press)

NARCISSISM, THE SELF, AND SOCIETY

REUBEN FINE

New York COLUMBIA UNIVERSITY PRESS 1986

Library of Congress Cataloging-in-Publication Data

Fine, Reuben, 1914–
Narcissism, the self, and society.

Bibliography: p.
Includes Index.
1. Narcissism. 2. Self. I. Title. [DNLM:
1. Culture. 2. Ego. 3. Narcissism. 4. Psychoanalytic
Theory. WM 460.5.E3 F495n]
BF575.N35F56 1986 616.85'82 85-18972
ISBN 0-231-05732-6

Columbia University Press
New York Guildford, Surrey
Copyright © 1986 Columbia University Press
All rights reserved

Printed in the United States of America

This book is Smyth-sewn.

Men come together in cities in order to live; they remain together in order to live the good life.

Aristotle

Concealment and ego protection are of the essence of social intercourse.

Everett Hughes

A new political science is needed for a world itself quite new.

De Tocqueville

The descent to hell is easy
The gates stand open day and night
But to reclimb the slope
And escape to the upper air
This is labor . . . .

Virgil: *The Aeneid*

Contents

Preface

The topics of narcissism and the self have moved to the center of psychological discourse over the past few decades. Books, articles, symposia pour forth, yet no consensus is reached. The very terms are a subject of continual argument, again with no agreement.

In this book I have undertaken a conceptual clarification. While psychoanalysis first brought the question into the open with Freud's 1914 paper on narcissism, many other writers and many other disciplines have entered into the discussion. Material is available not only from psychoanalysis, but also from history, anthropology, sociology, even from neurobiology. What is most needed is a reasonable synthesis of all the available data, not a doctrinaire point of view.

The first chapter is historical, tracing the development of the concepts of narcissism and the self from the time of the Greeks. Since Narcissus was a Greek mythological figure, it is obvious that the Greeks had their own concerns with narcissism. We are told that Ovid's version of the Greek myth has through the centuries been one of the most popular of his stories, which shows again that there is nothing new about narcissism.

A review of the historical picture reveals that narcissism has been used for three different kinds of persons: rulers, the common man, and psychotics. Prior to the French Revolution it was permissible for rulers to be supreme narcissists, and they were. Afterwards the common man began to come into his own, and increasingly his/her life, interests, concerns, and welfare became matters not only for psychological inquiry but also for public regulation. It is all too often forgotten that prior to 1800 much of the world was still based on slavery, and the slave had no legitimate personality, i.e. he was devoid of the essentials of narcissism. The narcissism of the psychotic was not noted until psychiatry was well advanced.

The concept of the self came into the picture when the doctrine or doctrines of the soul left the field. In tracing the development of this concept, it was found that there are three different strands. One is the American philosophical and psychological tradition, which goes back well into the beginnings of this country. This position stressed the interpersonal configurations of the self. The second is Freud's common sense use of the term self, in its hyphenated form, such as self-esteem, self reproach and so on. The third is Kohut's more recent self psychology, which has blossomed into what many regard as a sect gathered around a charismatic figure. All three must be given their weight in a rounded theory.

The second chapter deals with the psychoanalytic theory of narcissism. The beginning of course occurs with Freud's 1914 paper, often seen as the first step in the transition from id psychology to ego psychology. While Freud made many notable advances in this paper, he also made many serious mistakes which have placed a burden on theory ever since. In particular, his theorizing in that paper led to an abstruse metapsychology involving primary narcissism, ego libido, fusion of instincts and the like which has created many headaches for psychoanalytic theoreticians. The trend today is to discard this kind of metapsychology. Ultimately the position adopted is that narcissism should be regarded as self-involvement, the simplest and the most profound of all the definitions.

Narcissism and the self are closely allied concepts. Once narcissism was brought to the fore, especially by Kohut in the 1960s and 1970s, the self did not lag far behind. An enormous body of theory has arisen about the origin, development and functioning of the self. This theory must take into account the research coming from all the social sciences. Once that is done psychoanalysis expands into a much broader theory than it has been in the past; it expands into a general psychology, with many insights into social psychology, anthropology, and other disciplines.

Again the dialogues about the self rage on, with little agreement visible. Rangell has commented that rational discourse has proved to be impossible in psychoanalysis, and he decries the cultism of groups which are excessively exclusive. In the theories of the self there is much to confirm his critical point of view.

With this background, the remainder of the book sifts various types of material from many disciplines in order to arrive at a more unified and more cogent position. To get away from the endless discussion of the question, the self is defined most readily, as William James had done in his famous chapter on the self (Chapter X of his *Principles of Psychology*, 1890) as everything that can be called me or mine. Again the common sense definition proves best.

Both narcissism and the self involve the contrast of the self with the other, or the self with the object. Chapter 4 takes up the other contrast, the individual and society. This is initially approached via the much-debated topic of neurosis and culture. Roheim's statement that every culture has its own distinctive neurosis has been amply confirmed by the subsequent research. While most interest on course attaches to our own society, data on other cultures is marshalled to show how each culture encourages certain neurotic trends, and discourages others.

This leads to the realization that the traditional psychiatric categories have little relevance to either the clinical or the social picture. Instead a distinction is drawn between the maladjustment neuroses, customarily the province of psychiatry, and the adjustment neuroses, uncovered by psychoanalysis. The realization that so many people in our culture suffer from an adjustment neurosis is quickly spreading, so that one group of sociologists is already speaking of a "therapeutic revolution." The number of people who seek out psychotherapists, largely to overcome the problems of the adjustment neurosis, is soaring. That psychoanalysis in this way becomes a philosophy of living is one of the many significant conclusions to come out of this revolution.

Chapter 5 takes up the group and the individual. Here the relationship between narcissism, the self, and the social structure is carefully reexamined. Some tension between the group and the individual is observable in all known societies; it would appear to be inherent in the nature of groups and in the nature of man.

Ordinarily the social sciences which deal more directly with groups, such as anthropology and social psychology, tend to stress the significance of the group, while those which deal with individuals, such as psychotherapy and experimental psychology, tend to stress the significance of the individual. Both are essential so that again some integration is required for the variety of material available.

The next chapter considers the relationship between the self-image and the social order. Once more every social structure lends itself to a certain self-image which is found more often in that culture than in others. But even the very concept of a self-image varies widely with the culture. It has been shown that the well-defined, narrow image of the self, with boundaries setting it off from other selves, is characteristic of our own western culture, and is not even applicable in many others. Thus it again becomes clear that the self cannot be fully understood without reference to the surrounding society. Psychoanalysis has tended to overlook this connection, while on the other hand group psychology has tended to overlook the individual origins of the self.

In chapter 7 I consider love, identity, and alienation. The problem of alienation is of course a burning issue in contemporary theory. Identity, more carefully examined, is seen to be one facet of group or groups with which he is dealing, or of which he is a member. Alienation occurs when there is no group to belong to.

However, in all this the ethos of the group must be given more careful attention. It can be a love group or a hate group, and both have been known throughout history. As I have tried to show in a recent book (*The Meaning of Love in Human Experience*, 1985) cultures can be divided into love and hate cultures, and groups can be approached in the same way. Love is the central experience of every human being's life, and no culture can be properly understood without reference to how it regulates the love lives of its members.

The next chapter considers the romance of community, the notion, so often seen in literature, that a community per se is somehow good, regardless of what kind of community it is. While man is, as Aristotle had said, a creature who lives in a polis, not all polises are alike. It is argued that community per se is inevitable, but in its own right it is neither good nor bad. How it is to be evaluated depends on whether it stresses positive or negative feelings, love or hate.

The final chapter seeks to coordinate all the previous data and present an integrative approach. This involves a combination of the Freudian and the culturalist approaches to psychoanalysis, together with addenda from all other relevant disciplines. In this way the eventual goal of one science of man can be approached more effectively.

I wish to thank Susan Koscielniak, Joan McQuary, and John Moore of Columbia University Press for their encouragement in the preparation of this work. And my debt to my wife cannot be expressed in words.

Reuben Fine

New York, July 22, 1985

CHAPTER 1
HISTORICAL INTRODUCTION

The present-day emphasis on narcissism and the self raises the question of whether this is a new phenomenon, as some maintain, claiming, for instance, that ours is the "Me Generation," or the age of narcissism, or whether it is a matter of putting old wine into new bottles. The word *narcissism*, which derives from a Greek myth, after all suggests that the concern with narcissism is anything but new. It is worthwhile to see what historical forces have led to the contemporary theories.

In Greek mythology Narcissus was the son of the river god Cephissus and the nymph Leiriope; he was distinguished for his beauty. His mother was told that he would have a long life, provided that he never looked upon his own features. His rejection, however, of the love of the nymph Echo and of his lover Ameinias drew upon him the vengeance of the gods. He fell in love with his own reflection in the waters of a spring and pined away (or killed himself); the flower that bears his name sprang up where he died. According to another source, Narcissus, to console himself for the death of a favorite twin sister, his exact counterpart, sat gazing into the spring to recall her features by his own. The story may have been connected with the ancient Greek superstition that it was unlucky or even fatal to see one's own reflection.

As usual, the myth embodies many profound psychological insights, which explains why it has been one of the most popular stories ever related and has been told over and over again through the ages. Narcissus must be there to be admired; he must never look upon himself, i.e., reflect on why he deserves so much adoration. But by rejecting the love of both women and men, he drew the anger of the world upon himself. Instead of going after other women, he lost himself in the incestuous wish for his sister. Finally, by losing himself in his own reflection or in the incestuous wish for his sister, he falls in and dies.

The myth portrays the fate of a man who withdraws from the world into himself. Yet, as Aristotle had already said, man is an animal that lives in a polis, i.e., a political creature. "He who is without a polis, by reason of his own nature and not of some accident, is either a poor sort of being, or a being higher than man: he is like the man of whom Homer wrote in denunciation: 'Clanless and lawless and heartless is he'," (Curtis 1981:64).

Aristotle then goes on to discuss the composition of the state, which is made up of households. The simplest elements of the household are that of master and slave, husband and wife, parents and children. In all of these he takes an authoritarian position: slavery is natural, the man is superior to the woman, the parents should control their children. Because of the enormous authority accorded to Aristotle in the history of ideas, these positions have wielded enormous influence—e.g., his notion of government by a well-trained elite has continued as an ideal right down to the present day, e.g., in the Soviet Union and in China.

Plato, on the other hand, stressed the character of the ruler more than the composition of the state. In a famous passage in the *Republic* he urges that philosophers should become kings:

> There never will be a perfect state of constitution nor yet a perfect man, until some happy circumstances compel these few philosophers who have escaped corruption but are now called useless, to take charge, whether they like it or not, of a state which will submit to their authority; or else until kings and rulers or their sons are divinely inspired with a genuine passion for true philosophy. If either alternative or both were impossible, we might justly be laughed at as idle dreamers, but as I maintain, there is no ground for saying so. Accordingly, if ever in the infinity of time, past or future, or even today in some foreign region far beyond our horizon, men of the highest gifts for philosophy are constrained to take charge of a commonwealth, we are ready to maintain that, then and there, the constitution we have described has been realized, or will be realized when once the philosophic muse becomes mistress of a state. For that might happen. Our plan is difficult—we have admitted as much—but not impossible. (Curtis:62)

Thus, both Plato and Aristotle already sketch the problem that has been at the core of political philosophy ever since—the gulf between the ruler and the ruled, the antithesis of the individual and society. Too much individualism breeds narcissism; too much submission leads to mindless regimentation, as in Aldous Huxley's famous *Brave New World* or George Orwell's *1984*. Arthur Koestler outlined the dilemma as well in *The Yogi and the Commissar*.

It is this tension between the individual and society that will be the main theme of the present book. It has been expressed in many different ways, yet it always comes back to the same conflict: to obey or to defy. In general, the state has demanded obedience, as blind as it can be, so that it has never really concerned itself with individual welfare. As Goode (1956) says, happiness is not a sociological variable. And, on the other side, the individual has sought to pursue his own good as he sees it, yet is constrained by the force that is exerted on him by the state. As is readily apparent, this conflict is found in all recorded societies. Its adequate *psychological* resolution through the systematic application of psychoanalytic principles is the goal that we have set for ourselves.

Since the dictates of the state take precedence over the needs of the individual, through the ages narcissism has been viewed as bad—what Zweig (1980) calls "the heresy of self-love." Incidentally, while more refined definitions will be discussed later, at this point it is sufficient to define narcissism in the simplest way, as self-involvement. This self-involvement may be either positive, as self-love, or negative, as self-hatred. Authoritarian institutions, which have almost always been in the majority, have tried to instill self-hatred rather than self-love in their subjects. Hence, self-love becomes a "heresy." The essence of Zweig's argument can be summarized here.

At the time of its zenith the Greek world was built on elitist principles. Slaves, women, children, all counted for nought. The brilliant cultural transformation of the world that came out of this elitist system has justifiably been admired, but the sordid base on which it was placed should not be forgotten. Even the homosexuality of the Greeks, as has been shown (Fine 1985), was primarily the admiration of the older man for the virility of the pubescent young boy when the achievements of the older man had already faded into the background. Nor was extreme cruelty, though not so extreme as the Roman, foreign to the Greeks (Sagan 1979).

What could the self-image of the Greek be in such a world? On the one hand, he could, regarding himself as "civilized" and all others as "barbarians," be highly narcissistic, reflecting by identification on the glory of his culture. On the other hand, such a self-image was confined to the elitist few; all others must have been filled with self-hatred in one form or another.

Thus, in the romance of Xenophon of Ephesus a homosexual boy is carried off by pirates. Aware of what lies in store for him, he exclaims: "Oh, the unhappy gift of beauty! So long kept I myself chaste, only now to yield in shameful lust to the love of a pirate! What then is left for me to live for, if from a man I must become a harlot? But I will not submit to his desires, I would rather be dead and save my chastity!" (Licht 1932:446).

The preoccupation of the Greeks with their gods was clearly a projection of their own narcissistic wish for omnipotence. Hence the elite languished in their omnipotence, while the ordinary man suffered along in his self-hatred. Already the pattern is laid down for all of subsequent history: narcissism belongs to the elite, submission to the hoi polloi. Furthermore, narcissism is associated with grandiosity and rage, while submission is tied up with self-abasement and impotent fury, often transformed into masochistic resignation. We shall see over and over how this pattern repeats itself throughout history.

The narcissistic rage of the Roman emperors, if not their outright schizophrenia, can scarcely be exaggerated. As Gibbon has already pointed out, the Pax Romana had made the empire into one vast prison, with no escape for those who resisted its authority. In such a prison the only appeal could be out of this world, away from its authority and toward some new authority whose main evidence lay not in laws, no matter how brilliantly codified, but in a certain quality of experience (Zweig 1980:4).

But a military dictatorship provides ineluctable dilemmas. In Rome everybody had to serve in the army. If the man refused, he was executed; if he joined, he had to kill or be killed. The early Christians resisted and were killed, either "gently" by crucifixion or more ferociously by being thrown to the lions. The narcissistic gratification remained with the Romans, who could, by pointing thumbs up or thumbs down, determine the fate of the victim in gladiatorial "combat."

As time went on, an increasing number of Christians refused to accept either of these two horrible alternatives, and, compromising their basic principles, they joined the army. In opposition to them there arose the numerous highly individualized sects that are commonly characterized as Gnostic. They were dangerous not only because their ethical concerns were so close to those of Christianity but also because they embodied the uncompromising individualism the Christians themselves had been led to modify in the interests of avoiding Roman wrath. The Church had to fight them, and in this fight they labeled the Gnostics "narcissists," or the equivalent in those days. The battle between the individualist, who sticks to the pure principles of Christianity, and the established Church, which is more interested in preserving order and power, runs through the ages and continues to this day. The idealistic rebels are called narcissistic by those in power, much as the dissidents in the Soviet Union today are confined to psychiatric hospitals (a psychiatrist who objected to this perversion of his science was also confined to a psychiatric hospital) (Bloch and Reddaway 1977:234–242). On the one hand, narcissism became a term of opprobrium; on the other, those in power could be as narcissistic as they wished and have it written off as necessary for the preservation of the established order.

But then again in such an atmosphere those who were truly in rebellion because of some inner emotional turmoil, not because they had any high-flown ideals, could join the bandwagon. Thus arose again the enigma of the narcissist still present in the current environment: is he narcissistic because he is idealistically unable to accept the hypocrisy of the establishment? or is he narcissistic because he is too emotionally disturbed to know what he is doing?

It is not surprising to find that no sooner had Christianity become established than heresies and revolts began to creep in. The word *heresy* itself comes from the Greek word for choice, and when men set up a dogma, others offer alternative choices. These early alternatives (in the second and third centuries) are generally subsumed under the theories of the Gnostics (Pagels 1981). The Gnostics condemned the world entirely. They were bewildered by the overwhelming presence of evil in the world and the need to account for this evil while preserving the absolute goodness of God (Zweig 1980:7). Valentinian, one of the leading Gnostics, wrote: "What liberates is knowledge of who we were, what we became, where we were, whereinto we have been thrown, whereto we speed, wherefrom we are redeemed; what birth is, and what rebirth" (Zweig 1980:7). As was to be expected, many of the early Church fathers tried to brush aside the whole mood of Gnosticism as a kind of religious madness.

According to one Gnostic author, God created primal man simply for the delight he felt in then loving His own image (Zweig 1980:11). God is love. But love cannot exist without an object. Therefore, it is in God's nature to create something separate from Himself, so that He may exist fully by loving it. This direct communication with God, without the intermediary of a church figure, was condemned by the early authorities, but the idea continually reappears throughout the history of Christianity. Self-love, since it is not directly connected with God, becomes the gateway to man's fall.

At the same time another figure appeared in the Gnostic hierarchy, Simon Magus, the saint of holy self-indulgence. Because the world is a prison, he argued, its conditions and laws are unjust. But one who has been illuminated has found in himself the spark of a higher dispensation; he is in a state of "grace" and can no longer be held accountable in ordinary terms of justice. Thus, love of God and self-deification became so closely related that the Gnostics, like the Christian mystics later, often use the language of one to express the other. The condemnation of bodily existence becomes, with the Gnostic, a masterful defense of inner freedom or narcissism. Such narcissism likewise had to be condemned by the official church.

Waves of immediate contact with God, similar to the Gnostics, repeatedly reappeared throughout the history of Christianity. In the thirteenth century the Brethren of the Free Spririt offered their initiates a prospect of self-deification, accompanied by extreme spiritual libertinism, which for centuries scandalized more timid believers. They infiltrated groups of wandering beggars known as Beghards or Beguines and in this way were able to disappear in the confusion of minor orders that prevailed during the thirteenth and fourteenth centuries.

Their elusiveness was first a response to the persecuting monolith of the Church. The very nature of their doctrine led them to live outside of society, for the doctrine embodied, essentially, a flight from social order and responsibility. The Brother of the Free Spirit was taught to assume, in and through his own exalted sensuality, a lasting communion with the highest of all authorities, God Himself. He accepted no compromise with the world. This led to a theory of mystical libertinism, in which self-indulgence and erotic freedom became signs of godliness. All of this was, of course, anathema to the Church, which accordingly branded them narcissists, although the term was not then in use.

Zweig, who describes these brethren in detail, still confuses himself because he ignores the extreme hate culture of the Church in the Middle Ages. He argues that "there is undoubtedly a kind of madness in the libertarian attitudes of the Brethren" (1980:46). No more so than those around them, who went off to murder the innocent Moslems in Jerusalem or fought savage and bitter battles all over Europe (cf. Fine 1985). As Geoffrey of Anjou during the period of the Crusades put it: "Do you not know that it is our inheritance from remote times that no one of us loves another, but that always, brother against brother, and son against father, we try our utmost to injure one another?" (Kelly 1981:213)

As the historian Friedrich Heer has commented, most of the Middle Ages can only be understood in the light of group psychosis. In such group-psychotic behavior, the underdogs, or outsiders, are labeled narcissists or "mad," while those in power are considered heroes. (If we consider the current Soviet practice of labeling dissenters "psychotic," the situation has changed little (Bloch and Reddaway 1977).

Christianity in its theology continued the age-old belief in the *soul*. It promised the believer that his immortal soul would be maintained forever (though the form was obscure), thus, as in other religions, offering solace against the horrors of the world and the fear of death. Looked at dispassionately, in this way it appealed to the *narcissism* of the believer.

Such beliefs were essential to uphold morale in an age when insane murderers like Nero (and many of the other emperors) held sway in the empire. For example, when Nero burned Rome in A.D. 65, he made the Christians scapegoats and abused them mercilessly. Tacitus, writing a generation afterward, described the Christian community as follows:

> They were called Christians. The Christus from whom the name was derived had been put to death in the reign of Tiberius by the Procurator Pontius Pilate, and the pestilent superstition was checked for a while; but it began to break out again, not only in Judaea, the birthplace of the evil thing, but also in Rome, where everything that is shameless and horrible flows together and becomes fashionable. In the first place, then, some were arrested and confessed. On their testimony a vast magnitude was convicted, not so much of responsibility for the fire as for hatred of the human race. They were put to death with mockery and insult. They were dressed in the skins of wild animals to be torn to death by dogs; they were fixed to crosses or condemned to the flames; and when the daylight failed they were burned to give light by night. Nero had granted the use of his gardens for that display, and gave a circus performance, mixing with the common people in the dress of a charioteer seated in his chariot; and so a feeling of compassion arose (though it was for guilty persons who deserved severe punishment), since they were being done to death not for the public good, but to satisfy the cruelty of a single individual. (Book xv:44; pp. 365–366)

There is certainly no ruler in history who was more narcissistic than Nero. Many others have likewise been highly narcissistic, combining it with rage and grandiosity, like Nero. But because they were rulers, their narcissism has been generally overlooked. What will appear in this discussion is that the narcissism of the average man could only come to the fore after interest in these obviously twisted minds had died down as a result of political changes.

The term *soul* has always been closely associated with such concepts as mind, spirit, or self (with which it for a while became almost synonymous), but its basic connotation has generally been life. Soul is the life of the body. Life, breath, and movement come from the soul. At death the soul leaves the body and all bodily processes cease, but the soul continues.

Varying conceptions of the nature of the soul and its relation to the body led to varying views of the afterlife. Among the Hindus the soul was believed to be reincarnated in successive existences, animal or human. Among the Christians it was held that the souls of the dead rejoin their bodies on a final day when all bodies will be resurrected, just as Christ's body was resurrected after he was crucified.

Theories of the soul remained prominent in religion and philosophy until the end of the nineteenth century. Modern rational man has in all essential respects discarded it. Generally, William James, the American psychologist-philosopher, is credited with the proof that the soul is an unnecessary and unverifiable concept, not required to undergird either the sense of personal destiny or moral responsibility. After the work of his generation the concept of the soul virtually disappeared from scientific discourse.

Within Christianity the transcendence of God means that He is absolutely free to create and to create what He will; He is not compelled to create, nor limited by existing materials or available forms. His freedom and transcendence produce an aura of mystery connected with a person whose dignity and character can never be exhaustively revealed by His activities and who therefore elicits religious awe and devotion.

Thus, God becomes Narcissist Incarnate. For the Christian, as a result, his narcissism is projected to God, and his own life on earth is a triviality. Life is but a way station to heaven, and nothing else counts. Human relations are secondary; God's will rules all.

As usual, together with such narcissism goes a considerable measure of rage and grandiosity. The pope becomes God's vicar on earth; he is infallible, thus again an absolute narcissist. And lest it be thought that Protestantism destroyed this narcissistic image, consider the following quote from Jonathan Edwards in 1723: "And if it was plain to all the world of Christians that I was under the infallible guidance of Christ, and I was sent forth to teach the world the will of Christ, then I should have power in all the world. I should have power to teach them what they ought to do, and they would be obliged to hear me" (Tracy 1980, fly leaf).

Finally, mention may be made of the current Moral Majority, who are described as prescribing "Holy Terror" (Conway and Siegelamn 1982). Their wish is to wage war on America's freedoms in religion, politics, and private lives. Again the narcissistic grandiosity reappears, together with the destructive rage, whereas the individual is reduced to an insignificant cog in the wheel, whose only duty is to obey, masochistically, whether he likes it or not. Throughout history narcissism is reserved for the classes, masochism for the masses. Again, when the average man is narcissistic, he is described as "crazy" or "eccentric," whereas when a ruler is narcissistic, he is depicted as a superman, beyond all ordinary morality and convention. Thus, here too it is seen that narcissism is nothing new; the interest engendered in it in the past twenty years refers only to the shift from the ruler to the average man.

The famous Swiss historian Jacob Burckhardt initiated a new conceptualization of the appearance of individuality (and narcissism, though of course he did not use the term) with *The Civilization of the Renaissance in Italy* (1860). Burckhardt was primarily concerned with describing the Italian between 1300 and 1530: "man suffering, striving, doing, as he is and was and ever shall be" (1958:3) Burckhardt summed up the Italian of that day as follows:

> If we now attempt to sum up the principal features of that time, as we know it from a study of the life of the upper classes, we shall obtain something like the following result. The fundamental vice of this character was at the same time a condition of his greatness, namely, excessive individualism. The individual first inwardly casts off the authority of a State which, as a fact, is in most cases tyrannical and illegitimate. . . . The sight of victorious egotism in others drives him to defend his own by his own right arm. and while thinking to restore his inward equilibrium, he falls, through the vengeance which he executes, into the hands of the powers of darkness. . . . If, therefore, egotism in its wider as well as narrower sense is the root and fountain of all evil, the more highly developed Italian was for this reason more inclined to wickedness than the members of other nations of that time. (p. 442)

Although he greatly admired the individuality of that period (otherwise he would hardly have written his memorable work), he was well aware of both sides of the picture. On the one hand, there is the prevalence of the many-sided man, what today we call the Renaissance man. The Florentine merchant was often learned in both the classical languages; the most famous humanists read the ethics and politics of Aristotle to their sons; even the daughters of the house were highly educated. A man like Leon Battista Alberti entered the life around him with the deepest of intensity. "Men can do all things if they will, was his motto" (Burckhardt 1958:150).

On the other hand, such unbridled individualism (or narcissism, we would say today) was accompanied by the most horrible kinds of violence. Even the popes of that day were as imbued with the spirit of vengeance as the lowliest cowherd.

As a typical instance of the vendetta that permeated all of Italian life, Burckhardt gives the following:

> In the district of Acquapendente three boys were watching cattle, and one of them said: "Let us find out the way how people are hung." While one was sitting on the shoulders of the other a third, after fastening the rope round the neck of the first, was tying it to an oak, a wolf came, and the two who were free ran way and left the other hanging. Afterward they found him dead, and buried him. On the Sunday his father came to bring him bread, and one of the two confessed what had happened, and showed him the grave. The old man then killed him with a knife, cut him up, brought

> away the liver and entertained the boy's father with it at home. After dinner he told whose liver it was. Hereupon began a series of reciprocal murders between the two families, and within a month thirty-six persons were killed, women as well as men.
>
> And such *vendette*, handed down from father to son, and extending to friends and distant relations, were not limited to the lower classes, but reached to the highest. (p.430)

Although he was a great admirer of the unparalleled achievements of the Renaissance in so many fields, Burckhardt was well aware that these feats were accompanied by the most incredible violence, and at the highest levels. Again, in our modern language, the Renaissance man was typically a gifted narcissist, filled with rage and grandiosity. Both elements are present in varying proportions. It could be said that the problem for later generations was to preserve the healthy narcissism, while subduing or removing the rage and grandiosity. But that is more easily said than done.

Another example could be taken from a post-Renaissance figure, Isaac Newton (Manuel 1979). Newton was a lonely, unhappy man who lived a solitary narcissistic kind of existence. His father died before he was born, his mother left him to marry another man when he was three years old, and he was brought up by a grandmother until he was eleven. It comes as no surprise that he never had an intimate relationship with a woman. In his narcissistic preoccupations he went in two directions: one great, the other grandiose. He discovered the law of universal gravitation and the calculus, which revolutionized the entire study of nature. But he also set himself to deciphering God's code for the history of the universe, an enterprise which has, of course, long since been forgotten. Once his scientific achievement was recognized, he set himself up as the dictator of British science. He was also sadistic in his dealings with his fellowmen; e.g., one of his major enemies was the royal astronomer Flamsteed, whose calculations were not quite to his liking. He accepted an appointment as Warden of the Mint, in which capacity he uncovered the counterfeiters who were debasing the currency of that day. He seems to have taken a personal delight in seeing these "clippers" tortured and at times hung. The world has been so awestruck by this phenomenal genius that it has forgotten his pathological narcissism.

Slavery and Narcissism

The intimate connection between slavery and narcissism throughout history has been obscured for several reasons. First, traditional historians have so focused on victory and how it has been achieved that they have paid little attention to the vanquished (McNeil 1982; Fine 1981). And second, the lot of the slave has been so miserable that there has often seemed to be little to relate other than a litany of agony and occasional rebellion. Yet the slave has been an essential part of all human civilizations, and to ignore his lot is to ignore a large part of the human condition.

Slaves always had to be kept in thralldom by force; as Seneca the philosopher once put it, "As many slaves, so many enemies" (Paterson 1982:339). But the narcissistic character of the slaveholder has nowhere been more clearly formulated than by Pliny the Elder in the first century. He wrote: "We use other people's feet when we go out, we use other people's eyes to recognize things, we use another person's memory to greet people, we use someone else's help to stay alive—*the only things we keep for ourselves are our pleasures*." (*ibid.* italics added)

Paterson (1982) devoted a masterful work to the history and problems of slavery, and we shall follow his account here. If the slave no longer belongs to a community, if he has no social existence outside of his master, then what is he? The initial response in almost all slaveholding societies was to define the slave as a socially dead person. Yet, if he is dead, he remains nonetheless an element of society. So the problem arises: how is he to be incorporated? Religion explains how it is possible to relate to the dead who still live. It says little about how ordinary people should relate to the living who are dead. This is the ultimate cultural dilemma posed by the problem of slavery.

Religions have frequently rationalized slavery as holding on to the "enemy within," a foreign religionist. Thus, Maimonides described the foreign slave as "like land in regard to the acquisition of title," and one who was a minor is "like cattle, and one may acquire title to him by the modes whereby title to cattle . . . is acquired" (Paterson 1982:41).

From its very early days medieval Christendom defined all pagans and infidels who resisted conversion as enemies who could justly be enslaved if taken in war. Like the Hebrews, the medieval Christian nations permitted the enslavement of their fellow Christians and denied that the conversion of slaves obliged them to manumit them.

In Islamic religious and social thought we find the purest expression of the intrusive conception of social death. The outsider was foreigner, enemy, and infidel, fit only for enslavement after the jihad, to be incorporated as the enemy within. Legally the Muslim is not permitted to enslave coreligionists, although ways were found to get around the injunction. As a cultural mode of representation, however, the image of the slave as the captured enemy and internalized outsider in a state of social death was firmly fixed in Islamic thought. The most frequent expression for female slaves in the Koran is "that which your right hand possesses." The slave is primarily "a person taken captive in war, or carried off by force from a foreign hostile country, and being at the time of capture an unbeliever" (Roberts 1925:54). One Moslem author argued that the Islamic world's conception was based on religious differences. He insisted that slavery was the result of captivity occasioned by just wars against the infidel.

An alternative view is that of the slave as an insider who has fallen, one who ceased to belong and had been expelled from normal participation in the community because of a failure to meet certain minimal legal or socioeconomic norms of behavior. The destitute were included in this group, for while they had perhaps committed no overt crime, their failure to survive on their own was taken as a sign of innate incompetence and divine disfavor. (In the United States in the late nineteenth century this dogma became popular as social Darwinism.)

A typical manner of impressing the superiority (narcissism) of the master on the unfortunate slave was in the manipulation of the slave's name. If he had no social identity, how could he deserve a regular name? Thus, in almost every slave society one of the first acts of a new master was to change the name of his slave (Paterson 1982:35). The slave's former name died with his former self. Often the new name was a badge of inferiority and contempt.

Often insult was added to injury by giving the slave a name that was ridiculous or even obscene. Among the Duala of the Cameroon slaves were given names such as Irritation, and among the Aboh of Nigeria there were names like Bluebeard and Downcast. The Nootka of the northwest coast of America, the Icelanders, and the Kachin of highland Burma are all typical of peoples who took special delight in giving to female slaves names that demeaned both their status and sex (Paterson 1982:55–62).

In Jamaica, African day names and tribal names were either selected in their pure form or adapted as English names. During the nineteenth century these African names acquired pejorative meanings: Quashee, a day name that originally meant Sunday in Akan, came to signify a stupid, lazy slave; and Cudjo, which was the Akan name for Monday, came to mean a drunkard. On some estates they were given names that ridiculed them, such as Beauty, Carefree, Monkey, Villain, and Strumpet.

In other places they were lucky to have names at all. A census taken in Colombia in 1759 showed that almost 40 percent of the slaves had only one name; 30 percent had the surname Criollo, and the remainder had African tribal or regional surnames such as Mina, Congo, Mandingo, and Caraba.

Likewise, slaves were brutally dehumanized in many other ways. In every slave society the master had the right to inflict corporal punishment. Many societies also permitted the murder of slaves by their masters, although this varied (Paterson 1982:190–191). The murder of slaves for ritual purposes was widespread. It existed at some time on every continent and in the early periods of every major civilization. Vast numbers of slaves were buried, often alive, with the earliest Chinese emperors. In Japan, between the second and third centuries, as many as a hundred slaves were buried with the empress. The legal capacity to kill one's slave is closely associated with a low proportion of males in the servile population (Paterson 1982:193). Thus, as in the widespread practice of eunuchism, the castration of boys or men, the death rate was naturally inordinately high; in the seventeenth century, on the upper Nile, only one in four boys castrated could be expected to survive (Tannahill 1980:246–251). Obviously, these were all devices to bolster the control of the ruling class over the female slaves, as well as punishment for any slave who would dare to try have sex with a woman of the ruling class. The fear that the black man would have sex with a white woman became so ingrained in the American South after the Civil War that Southerners could not realize how psychotic it was; it led to the abominable practice of lynching, found only in the United States (Dollard 1957).

It could only be expected that innumerable slave revolts against inhuman conditions are to be found throughout history, which is indeed the case. In 1854 Mommsen wrote of Rome: "The abyss of misery and woe which engulfed this most miserable of all proletariats we leave to be fathomed by those who can bear to gaze into such depths. It is quite possible that, compared with the sufferings of the Roman slaves, the sum of all Negro suffering is but a drop" (1958:27). Not only were there innumerable slave revolts, but the masters' fear of retaliation could be felt everywhere: the fear of retaliation accounted for their inhumanity. "Slavery," said Mommsen, in another famous passage, "is not possible without a reign of terror" (p. 31)

Among the Roman slave revolts the greatest was that of Spartacus, in 73 B.C., who gathered an army of 40,000 ex-slaves and within two years defeated no fewer than four Roman armies. But he was finally cornered and he and his men massacred. On the Appian Way alone 6,000 slaves were crucified.

Even when they were not worked to death, their lives were horrible (Hopkins 1978, chapter 13). Seneca, a liberal of his day, portrayed a master at dinner surrounded by slaves: "The unfortunate slaves are not allowed to move their lips, let alone talk; the birch keeps murmuring down. A cough, a sneeze, a hiccup is rewarded by a flogging, with no exceptions. Any break in silence is severely punished. They stand at the ready all night, tense and mute" (Moral Letters 47; quoted in Hopkins).

Nor did slave revolts come to an end until slavery was finally abolished in the nineteenth century. It is of interest that only in the United States did the slavocracy go to war to defend its right to brutalize its fellowmen; in all other countries the humanity and logic of the situation eventually prevailed.

Although much ink has been spilled about how "bad" American slavery was, little attention has been paid to the character of the "master race." In line with the general argument here, we would expect them to have been arrogant, sadistic, narcissistic, and reactionary. The myth of the "kind" plantation owner occasionally was to be found, but in large part it was nothing more than that, a myth (Oakes 1982). Usually, slaveholders spoke of blacks in crude racial epithets. They burst into fits of denunciation. As Alexander Stephens put it in his speech to the Virginia secession convention in 1861: "As a race, the African is inferior to the white man. Subordination to the white man is his normal condition. He is not his equal by nature, and cannot be made so by human laws or human institutions. Our system, therefore, so far as regards this inferior race, rests upon this great immutable law of nature" (Oakes 1982:135).

Another slaveholder asserted that slavery was a "moral evil" made necessary by the "condition of the negroes" (p. 135). The same kind of arguments persist today about the educability of the blacks (Jensen 1980), although they are rejected by almost all competent psychologists. The narcissism of white historians has also led to a denial of the innumerable slave revolts that dotted American history (Aptheker 1971).

The point is that throughout the ages slavery has been defended and rationalized by those who benefited from it. Unnoticed has been the extraordinary narcissism of the slaveholder, the opposite side of the coin of slavery and submission.

Whereas slavery was officially abolished in most of Europe with the disappearance of the Roman Empire, the kings and rulers who followed often lacked nothing in self-glorification. Louis XIV (1638–1715), the "sun king," is perhaps the best example. No better expression of his narcissism can be found than in his famous expression: "L'Etat c'est moi." Modesty was not one of his virtues. In his memoirs he wrote: "In my heart I prefer fame above all else, even life itself. . . . Love of glory has the same subtleties as the most tender passions. . . . In exercising a totally divine function here on earth, we must appear incapable of turmoils which could debase it" (*Encyc. Brit.* 2:1221).

Louis was as ruthless as he was arrogant. The humbling of all the great corps and estates of the realm remained his constant concern. The officers' companies were debased, humiliated, and taxed out of existence; the *parlements*, states, communes, and consulates annihilated; the arrogant nobility reduced to begging for its favors where they had once been conspirators and instigators of provincial revolts. Most of the clergy were turned into courtiers and all the ancient nobility tamed and barred from his councils, while the new lords were treated with contempt for all the cheapness of their titles. Any who persisted in untimely uprisings were massacred outright. Everlasting glory, territorial aggrandizement, and dominion abroad; at home mastery of all political and administrative life, of religion, society, and thought, and the protection of the dynasty and the succession—these he kept for his sole jurisdiction. No Roman emperor was more grandiose (Goubert 1970).

Naturally his people suffered horribly. Famine, poverty, mourning were but familiar aspects of the universal despair to which Louis was completely indifferent (like all narcissists). A famous letter to the king in 1795 reads:

> Your people, Sire, whom you should love as your children, and who up to this time have been so devoted to you, are dying of hunger. The land is left almost untended, towns and countryside are deserted, trade of all kinds falls off and can no longer support the workers: all commerce is at a standstill. . . . For the sake of getting and keeping vain conquests abroad you have destroyed half the real strength of your own state. Rather than take money from your poor people, you ought to feed and cherish them. . . . All France is now no more than one great hospital, desolate and unprovided. The magistrates are weary and degraded. The nobility, whose whole wealth is in decrees (that is, in the event of seizure) live only by letters patent. You are importuned by the murmurs of the crowd. And it is you, Sire, who have brought these troubles on yourself. . . . The very people . . . no longer rejoice in your conquests and victories, they are full of bitterness and despair. Little by little the fire of sedition catches everywhere. The people believe you have no pity for their sufferings, that you care only for your own power and glory. They say that if the king had a father's heart for his people, he would surely think his glory lay rather in giving them bread and a little respite after such tribulations than in keeping hold of a few frontier posts which are a cause of war. (Goubert 1970:220)

The Antinarcissistic Revolutions

Through the next two centuries (seventeenth and eighteenth) men slaughtered one another without qualm and without quarter. It was still the century of the absolute monarch. The narcissism of the ruler reigned supreme. Then toward the end of the eighteenth century came the two great revolutions that permanently altered the shape of the world: the American and the French. Both should be looked at in terms of the narcissism of the ruler as opposed to the narcissism of the common man.

Although the major ideas came from the French *philosophes*, the American Revolution chronologically came first. That the American Revolution did not display the terror and violence of the French no doubt can be attributed to many different causes. Perhaps the major reason was that is was more a war of national independence than a civil war. But another, and probably equally potent, reason was the horror of despotism and tyranny that dominated all the leading American intellectuals.

The rhetoric of the American Revolution stressed tyranny and slavery more than anything else. John Adams wrote in 1775: "There are but two sorts of men in the world, freemen and slaves" (Brown 1983:107). (Of course, as many have pointed out, he conveniently forgot the slaves in his own part of the world, but the awareness of black slavery eventually led to a bloody civil war in which the doctrines of the American Constitution played a vital role.)

Tom Paine insisted that it is wholly owing to the constitution of the people and not to the constitution of the government that the crown is not as oppressive in England as in Turkey (Brown 1983:124). In the Declaration of Independence Thomas Jefferson had written that all men are created equal, that they are endowed by their creator with inherent and unalienable rights, that among these are life, liberty, and the pursuit of happiness. Governments are instituted among men, deriving their just powers from the consent of the governed. All of this and more, in our present context, could be viewed as an assertion of the right of the common man to gratify his narcissism, in association with his fellowmen, like the greatest of all emperors and tyrants.

De Tocqueville, the astute French aristocrat who wrote a masterful work on America, grasped the profound significance of bowing to the will of the majority. It was, he argued, fundamentally less human reason in general that the leaders of the French Revolution were thinking of than their own in particular. They despised the crowd almost as much as they despised God. "Never has anyone shown less trust in the wisdom of the community than did these men" (Brown 1983:510).

Ben Franklin, the greatest American intellectual of the eighteenth century (apart from his political activities he made fundamental discoveries in electricity), doubted that the Constitution as presented at the 1787 convention was perfect, but he argued that "there is no form of government but what may be a blessing to people, if well administered" (Brown 1983:286). In spite of an eminent life he was modest, sincere, and devoted to democratic causes; he suggested at one point that instead of a president the country should have a triumvirate (not a bad idea, in view of many subsequent events). He even invented a form of self-analysis that was quite good for those pre-Freudian days (Franklin 1962:82ff.).

By contrast, the leaders of the French Revolution soon became embroiled in their narcissistic grandeur. Robespierre the "Just" never made a mistake, so he had a law passed that gave to the revolutionary tribunal on June 10, 1774, supreme power over all "enemies of the people"; the only penalty it could impose was death. This was the beginning of the Great Terror; it led, in Paris, to 1376 executions in a month and a half. Gay and Webb summarize: "Thus baldly summarized, the Terror seems to discredit the whole Revolution as a nightmarish orgy of madmen, a sadistic riot in the name of humanity; Robespierre and his associates seem like so many modern Caligulas, wishing that the French people had but one neck" (1973:493)

It is not surprising that after some years of this terror (which supposedly killed "only" about 35,000) (Gay and Webb 1973:494), a dictator took over who put some order into the house, though his regime was equally bloody. Violence begets violence.

The nineteenth century was dominated by the conflict of the individual with society, with monarchy and democracy in conflict all over Europe. The rest of the world (except the United States) was still caught up in the undiminished narcissism of monarchy. That the common man had the right to demand his own good, that is, in our language, to be narcissistic in a healthy way, was one of the lasting legacies of the revolutions.

But in the nineteenth century, also for the first time, attention was paid to a different kind of narcissism—that of the psychotic who withdraws from society and the world. No satisfactory explanation of such behavior could be given by the scientists of the nineteenth century until Freud came along; the others were all too immersed in organic causes: In Griesinger's famous phrase, mind disease is brain disease (many today are still caught up in this error). It would take us too far afield to trace all the vagaries of nineteenth-century psychiatry; suffice to say that before Freud even the conceptualization that the psychotic suffers from pathological narcissism was absent.

The Liberation of Women

The liberation of humankind that followed the French Revolution eventually brought every conceivable minority group under scrutiny. Why are they inferior, and why must they remain inferior? Naturally, women were among the first to obtain this attention.

The problem of women is intimately tied up with hygienic conditions and death for two reasons: first the woman has to produce children; second, until recently the mortality among children was extremely high. Shorter (1982), in his summation of the history of women's bodies, makes the following points:

1. Women were victimized by men in the form of limitless sexual access. Men's "conjugal rights" exposed women to an endless series of unwanted and unplanned pregnancies.

2. Women were victimized by their children, having to maintain large households over whose size and composition they had no control. As a result, most women among the common people were oppressed by the sheer struggle for existence, by the need to care for their own six children (the average, historically) and others. Women's exhaustion from family life appears in their greater mortality.

3. Women were victimized by nature in the form of various diseases to which men are not subject (p. xii).

It was only between 1900 and 1930 that these sources of victimization came to an end. Before then the death rates in childbirth were high, and the mortality of children was high.

According to Stone (1979), the expectation of life at birth in England in the 1640s was only thirty-two years. Between a quarter and a third of all children of English peers and peasants were dead before they reached the age of fifteen.

Under such circumstances close emotional ties between mothers and children were bound to be fragile; the woman naturally had to defend herself against the death of the child, just as more children had to defend themselves against the deaths of their mothers. Thus, it was only until hygienic conditions had improved enormously in the nineteenth century that warm ties between mother and child, which are such an integral part of modern psychology, could emerge.

The first person to sound the call for the liberation of women was Mary Wollstonecraft (1759–1797) (the mother of Mary Shelley), whose book, *A Vindication of the Rights of Women*, was published, appropriately enough, in 1792, during the French Revolution. Her life was full of tragedy. She had one child in 1794 by an American who then deserted her. Later she married William Godwin, a freethinker of his day, and had another child by him, but she died ten days after the child, Mary, was born. Later her first child, Fanny, who died a suicide, forgot all about the rights of women and devoted her life to making herself, Shelley, and her parents "respectable."

Mary Wollstonecraft's emphasis was primarily on education: "Tyrants and sensualists are in the right when they endeavor to keep women in the dark because the former want only slaves, and the latter a plaything" (*Encyc. Brit.* 10:729). However, she did not underestimate the significance of the maternal function of women.

The nineteenth century saw a consistent effort to improve women's status and to make them more equal to men. Perhaps the high point of this movement came, paradoxically, with Sigmund Freud, who was the first to show that the age-old disease of "hysteria" (derived from the Greek for womb) was understandable in light of his newer psychology. Because sexual repression made women physically ill, it became understandable that in the twentieth century, following Freud, most of the barriers to sexual equality for women were lifted. Again, in terms of the argument of this chapter, the world became convinced that women had a right to be as narcissistic as men.

In *The Subjection of Women* John Stuart Mill (1869) made one of the most eloquent pleas of the century for the equality of women. In his opinion the main factor subjecting women to men's fancies was that men wanted power; and as in all spheres where too much power was given, it was abused by the men. His book was published in America a few months after it came out in England and was used for many years as a standard series of arguments by feminists. Among other significant points that Mill made was that people do not even know what women are like. He wrote:

> To so ridiculous an extent are the notions formed of the nature of women, mere empirical generalizations, framed without philosophy or analysis, upon the first instances which present themselves, that the popular idea of it is different in different countries according as the opinions and social circumstances of the country have given to women living in it any speciality of development or non-development. (Rossi 1973:224)

This ignorance of the nature of women was soon to be remedied by the efforts of numerous social scientists, efforts that are still going on. After Freud's demonstration that women have the same sexual feelings as men, perhaps the best known of the social scientists who extended the conceptualizations of women's nature was Margaret Mead. Today it is widely recognized that while there are innate biological differences among men and women, as the 1848 Seneca Falls suffragette convention put it, all men *and* women are created equal. Careful studies of men and women have always stressed the cultural factor as the decisive one (Maccoby and Jacklin 1974). In other words, healthy narcissism is the right of both men and women.

The most recent revival of feminism was in Betty Friedan's *The Feminine Mystique* (1963), in which the argument was put forth that motherhood and domesticity had been foisted on women and that as an ideal it was wholly unnatural; women should go out in the world and do things. This seemed to be a narcissistic rebellion in which the woman maintained her right to do whatever she wanted to do, without regard for the man. Twenty years later Friedan wrote *The Second Stage* (1981), in which she came back to the age-old ideals of love and happiness within marriage. She wrote:

> If we can eliminate the false polarities and appreciate the limits and true potential of women's power, we will be able to join with men—follow or lead—in the new human politics that must emerge beyond reaction. And this new *human* liberation will enable us to take back the day *and* the night, and use the sources of our human capital to erect new kinds of homes for all our dreams, affirm new and old family bonds that can evolve and nourish us through all the changes of our lives, and use the time that is our life to enrich our human possibility, spelling our own names, at last, as women and men. (p. 343)

Autobiography

Although autobiography has always existed (March, 1951), it is really only since World War II that it has flourished to such an enormous extent. To write an autobiography requires a positive evaluation of the person's self, any individual's self, that never really existed before modern times. In that sense it represents the acme of the narcissism of the common man as contrasted with the narcissism of the rulers that dominated all previous history.

In her classic study Anna Robeson Burr (1909) described three great archetypes of autobiographer: Julius Caesar, St. Augustine, and Jerome Cardan. None of these is strictly autobiographical in the modern vein, yet each presented a certain model that many others followed.

Caesar's famous comment Veni, vedi, vinci (I came, I saw, I conquered) sums up what his book is about: he wishes to describe his exploits. In line with this model, only those who have great achievements to their credit have felt the need to put their autobiographies together; many, however, did not. But the caveat must be given that these heroic stories are more often colored by what the hero wished to have others believe than by a ruthless search for the truth.

Augustine studied himself for the glory of God. He began with the story of his sins, continued with the tale of his conversion, and concluded with an ode to the almighty ruler of the universe. His autobiography could be summed up as: I sinned (especially sexual), I saw the light, and I glory in the eternal forgiveness of God. Here too numerous copies have been made of the model. In fact, the confessions of Alcoholics Anonymous follow in this path: I was wicked (drank too much), I converted, and I glory in the great AA.

Jerome Cardan (1501–1576), in *Book of My Own Life* (*De Vita Propria Liber*) (1575), although unknown to the general public, had a far-reaching influence. Cardan was mainly concerned with describing himself. He wrote: "Speech shrill—if one may trust to the reproaches of those who profess to be my friends—and yet cannot be heard when I lecture. My gaze is fixed, as one who meditates, my color red and white, my face an oblong, though not large, my upper teeth larger than the lower" (Burr 1909:102). Yet toward the end he confesses his true passion: "Therefore it is no wonder that, thus compelled, I burned with the love of fame; rather is it a marvel that notwithstanding these reasons this strong desire persists" (p. 114).

It is in one of these three forms that autobiography has persisted and proliferated: stories of victory, confessions of guilt, and seemingly objective self-description. The first book to use the term *autobiography* was written by W. P. Scargill in 1834. But in the ensuing years innumerable others have appeared, especially in America. Stone (1982) estimates that upward of ten thousand personal histories of Americans may now have appeared. Especially since World War II no other mode of American expression seems to have more widely or subtly reflected the diversities of American experience or the richness of American memories and imaginations. Nor need it be surprising that the country that has placed the greatest emphasis on individualism should have produced the largest number of individualistic self-histories. The autobiography is par excellence an expression of the narcissism of the common man.

Nationalism

There are many reasons for the rise of nationalism in the nineteenth century. One of the most potent must be the projection of the narcissism of the ordinary person to the nation: if he cannot become great, then at least the nation can.

Nationalism and its variants had come into wide use around 1830, though no one was sure exactly what they meant. In 1835 the French Academy for the first time allowed the word *nationality* to enter the dictionary. The profound passions aroused by the concept of a nation, passions little or unknown before the French Revolution, require little further proof. Today nationalism is still one of the most powerful of all psychological forces.

Hans Kohn, one of the leading students of nationalism, attributed its force to the intellectuals. "It was the poet, the philologist and the historian who created the nationalities" (Gay and Webb 1973:669). Yet the common man had to respond to these urgings; otherwise he would never have fought and died for them in such numbers. Tennyson's famous poem "The Charge of the Light Brigade" "Theirs [is] not to reason why/theirs [is] but to do and die" captured many an imagination.

Gagliardo (1969) has traced the metamorphosis of the German peasant between 1770 and 1840 from pariah to patriot. The tendency to identify the peasant with an ideal national character was given powerful support by a new insight into the cultural significance of the "folk," the common people. Herder was one of a number of literary figures who contributed to a new definition of "nation" through the emphasis on singularity of language; he found in the peasant, by virtue of the unadultered language he used and the customs and habits that necessarily accompanied his language, the representative and preserver of pure and genuine nationality. Again, this can be seen in the projection of his narcissism to the nation: "Deutschland ueber alles" (or, in the United States, "My country, right or wrong"). Narcissism had found another outlet.

The Loss of Religion

The nineteenth century likewise saw the slow decline of religion in the minds of the masses. Today in large parts of the world religion in the old sense simply no longer exists, while even in those countries where there is an official religion (such as Sweden), it plays no significant role in the mind of the average person.

With the decline of religion came increased interest in the material world and loss of interest in the spiritual world. Particularly significant for our topic is the elimination from the scientific vocabulary of the concept of the "soul." As the joke has it, in the nineteenth century psychology lost its soul; in the twentieth its mind.

But the soul traditionally was the place where the sense of personal identity was thought to reside, in many cases, for all time. With its disappearance the questions of identity, self-image, and narcissism came to assume increasing importance. It is now to the development of scientific psychology in the nineteenth and twentieth centuries that we must turn.

The Interest in Man

In recapitulation, the topic of narcissism appears throughout history in three forms: the narcissism of the ruler, the narcissism of the common man, and the narcissism of the psychotic. As long as rulers exercised absolute authority, their narcissism could not be questioned; once their authority had been exploded by the various revolutionary currents, they were seen as the deplorable specimens of humanity they generally were. The narcissism of the common man began to dominate the field in the nineteenth century and has dominated it ever since; today we call it the sense of identity, or self-image. It resulted from the overthrow of absolutism and the recognition of the significance of the individual. The narcissism of the psychotic never really occurred to anybody before Freud. He was generally seen as suffering from brain damage, or as queer, or even (Rosen 1968) as divinely inspired in many cases (also Foucault 1973).

Historians of ideas have generally credited the switch to an interest in man in the nineteenth century to the influence of the philosophers, especially Hegel and the romantic school in Germany. In fact, Hegel is generally seen as the founder of all modern social sciences. Thus, Randall writes:

> This tendency is closely allied to a still futher attitude which, of all romanticism, most powerfully influenced the nineteenth century. If knowledge means fitting things into a larger whole, if nature is alive and growing, if the feelings that attach men to larger groups and to the past are more fundamental than reason, then human history and human traditions take on a new and vital significance . . . . Time and history are of fundamental importance. Viewed in such a light, the eighteenth century science of human nature was utterly transformed.(1926: 421)

Without depreciating the value of the philosophers, it still remains true that the new interest in the individual derived much more from the changed political situation of the nineteenth century than from any one thinker. Europe in the nineteenth century remained full of storm and stress, with revolutions, counterrevolutions, and wars following one another in quick succession. However, the United States, in spite of several wars and the prevalence of slavery in the South, was seen as the most secure home of freedom, individualism, and liberty. Even though most of the leading scholars in the nineteenth century trained in Germany and other European countries, the most powerful developments of the new sciences of man, then known as the social sciences, later as the behavioral sciences, occurred in the United States. With the later expulsion by Hitler of a large number of powerful intellects, the social sciences became virtually an American monopoly.

Walt Whitman's (1819–1892) book *Leaves of Grass* (first published 1855) represented a powerful embodiment of what we have been calling the narcissism of the common man. Foreshadowing the later analytic theory that the artist transfers his narcissism to his creation, he wrote: "This is no book. Who touches this, touches a man." He led a bohemian lefe. With his schooling over at age eleven (Untermeyer 1959; Kaplan 1980), he went to work as a jouneyman printer. His adolescence was marked by a restlessness that became a habit and drove him from one place to another. He had to work but he hated being tied down; he wanted, he said, "to just live." Wandering through various phases, he finally hit upon what he wanted most to do when he published *Leaves of Grass* in 1855. Thereafter his life centered on this book. Even though he never made any money (he did not sleep in his own bed until he was 65), he lived through his book. In his "Song of Myself" he wrote:

> I celebrate myself, and sing myself,
> And what I assume you shall assume,
> For every atom belonging to me good as belongs to you.

Nor did he shrink from pushing his own book, publicly and privately. His urge was to embrace all humankind, heterosexually or homosexually. At one point he wrote: "Sex will not be put aside, it is the great ordination of the universe . . . . Right and left [Whitman] flings his arms, drawing men and women with undeniable love to his close embrace, loving the clasp of their hands, the touch of their necks and breasts and the sound of their voices. All else seems to burn up under his fierce affection for persons."(Untermeyer 1949:565).

Proclaiming the common man he wrote:

> Of life immense in passion, pulse and power,
> Cheerful, for freest action, formed under the laws divine
> The Modern Man I sing.
> (Untermeyer 1959:577).

Untermeyer rightly called him a titanic and controversial figure: messianic, intuitive and often mistaken, rough-hewn and lopsided, but unquestioningly the most challenging writer of his time and ours (1959:577).

The enormous material changes of the nineteenth and twentieth centuries have been amply documented. In a sense it could be said to have been a revolution toward the narcissism of the common man, as we have been arguing here. And Whitman was probably its greatest literary spokesman.

The Social Sciences

The American Social Science Association was founded in 1865 (Haskell 1977:vi). A pioneer effort to institutionalize social inquiry, it was sponsored by genteel New England intellectuals and reformers who wanted both to understand and to improve their rapidly changing society. Although it died in 1909, it succeeded in spawning a large number of specialization associations, which then dominated the field from the 1890s on—American Historical Association, American Economic Association, and many others. The formation of the American Psychoanalytic Association in 1911 should also be mentioned in this context since all the social sciences have been tremendously vitalized by the doctrines and methods of psychoanalysis (Fine 1981).

Talcott Parsons, viewing the achievement of the 1890s, asked: "A revolution of such magnitude in the prevailing empirical interpretations of human society is hardly to be found occurring within the short space of a generation, unless one goes back to about the sixteenth century. What is to account for it?" (Haskell 1977:4). Parsons attributed it to the formation of a single system of what he called "voluntaristic action," which he regarded as an empirically validated foundation for all further discussion of human affairs. The essential feature of this approach is the insistence on the authenticity of human freedom. But it also acknowledged a wide range of external restraints upon human freedom. Thus, the social sciences came into being in the course of the struggle for freedom and the assertion of the rights of the individual. This too is part of the narcissism of the common man. It has remained in the forefront of the sciences of man ever since.

The Self

If individual freedom is the alpha and omega of human existence, the question naturally arises: what is the individual? In scientific psychology this has usually been phrased in terms of the self, or self-image, although the terms *individuation* and *identity* have also been used. Surprising as it may seem, some concept of the self is as old as recorded history (Roheim 1921a). But before the twentieth century it was generally seen as some substance comprising the human soul, and the efforts of philosophers and psychologists were devoted to unravelling this substance that made up the essence of the soul. Frondizi (1971) reviewed these hitorical attempts to determine the substance of the self or soul and showed how inadequate they all were.

While the concept of narcissism has only literary and some philosophical background, the topic of the self was in some directions extensively analyzed before Freud. But the analysis went in two entirely different directions. The Germans, following Hegel, stressed the unfolding of the self from an early core. Hegel, in *The Phenomenology of Spirit* (1807), writes: "The self enters into existence *as self*; the self assured Spirit exists as such for others. *Its immediate* action is not that which has validity and is actual; what is acknowledged is not the *determinate* aspect of the action, not its intrinsic being, but solely the self-knowing *self* as such "(p. 395).

Allowing for the differences in language, this passage could very well serve as a definition of Freud's primary narcissism: the self-knowing self as such.

On the other hand, the American background was entirely different. One of the major early documents was the widely read essay by Emerson, "Self-Reliance" (1841). The American philosopher's message was radically different from Hegel's. He wrote: "Life only avails, not having lived . . . . It is easy to see that a greater self-reliance must work a revolution in all the offices and relations of men; in their religion; in their education; in their pursuits; their modes of living; their association; in their property; in their speculative views" (pp. 152–155).

In German idealistic metaphysics, which was Freud's university background (Levi 1978), from the beginning of the nineteenth century on under the influence of Hegel in particular, the examination of the various aspects of the self assumed primary importance. Absolute idealism had three premises (Levi 1978): 1) the chief datum of philosophy is the human self and its self-consciousness. 2) The world as a whole is spiritual through and through, something like a cosmic self. 3) That in both the self and the world the volitional and the moral counts more than the individual. Thus, to understand the self, self-consciousness and the spiritual universe become *the* task of philosophy.

To approach this philosophical task, Hegel saw the various branches of intellect and culture as stages in the unfolding of the World-Spirit:

1. The psychological characteristics of man (habit, appetitie, judgment) representing "Subjective Spirit";

2. his laws, social arrangements, and political institutions (the family, civil society, the state) expressing "Objective Spirit"; and

3. his art, religion, and philosophy embodying "Absolute Spirit."

Thus, what began in Hegel as a metaphysics of the absolute ended by becoming a total philosophy of human culture. As might have been anticipated, this view of human culture led to different ramifications in Europe and in America.

While it is well known that Freud was not versed in traditional philosophy, its major ideas must have come down to him through a variety of applications. it should also be remembered that when Freud began his university work, in the 1870s, philosophy was still the alpha and omega of all wisdom. His shift from physiology and biology to psychology was facilitated by these philosophical assumptions.

A further consequence of the thought of the German idealists was the emphasis on alienation, which originally came from Hegel, was later taken over and given a different name by Marx, and still later by Durkheim, who called it anomie. For Hegel man's alienation is ontological, which served as a background for modern existentialism ("ontological anxiety"). It derives from the gap between the ego as subject and the ego as object; the ego as subject is alienated because it must look upon the ego as object as something outside itself.

In the idealistic dichotomy of ego as subject and ego as object, one can recognize Freud's later assumption in the 1914 paper on the narcissism of the ego libido, which remains unknown until it reaches out to objects, when it develops object libido. Freud's language actually is almost the same as Hegel's. Just as Hegel's distinction was later abandoned because it was too abstract and "academic" (as Kierkegaard claimed), Freud's was later virtually abandoned (cf. below) because it represents a juggling with words without contributing any real clinical observations.

The distinction is often made between German philosophy, which ever since Leibniz had concentrated on the inner life (Leibniz's "monads") and the unfolding of inner speculations, and British empiricism, which, following Locke, saw man as a tabula rasa formed and molded by experience. Thus, Freud, following the trend of German philosophy, eventually approached the topic of narcissism via the inner development of the individual, while British and especially American philosophers approached the topic via interaction with other people.

Among the American philosopher-psychologists who were the direct forebears to modern American psychology, Josiah Royce occupies an important position. Royce, who was also at one time president of the American

Psychological Association, held, like most American thinkers, that self--consciousness (and the self) must be connected with our relations with other people; the self, as Cooley was later to put it, is a social fact. Royce wrote in 1895:

> However you explain delusions of guilt, or suspicion, of persecution and of grandeur, however much you refer their source to altered sensory or emotional states, they stand before you, when once they are well developed, as variations of the patient's habits of estimating his relations to other selves. They involve, then, *maladies of the social consciousness*. The theoretical significance of this fact surely seems worthy of a closer consideration than it customarily receives. (Smith 1974:167)

Royce was writing at a time when the American community had been welded together by the searing experience of the Civil War, while simultaneously it was a period of enormous expansion and rampant individualism. Accordingly, his main concern was how to reconcile the community and the individual; one of his books was entitled *The World and the Individial* another *The Philosophy of Loyalty*. Community became his central idea, but a community that offered a form of life beyond the twin distortions of collectivism and of individualism. Loyalty for him was both a principle and a passion that unites many distinct selves in a community. His whole philosophy could be interpreted as the story of the cooperation and tension between individual and community.

He held that community as an identifiable form of life is to be found wherever three conditions are fulfilled: 1) There must first be a plurality of individual selves. But the "self" is what he called an "interpretation," that is, a center of meaning that is neither a datum for sense nor a universal to be grasped by reason. 2) The ideally extensible selves must be seen as genuinely distinct beings. 3) Many distinct selves, each capable of viewing themselves as creatures extending over a period of time come to acknowledge certain deeds and events of the past and certain anticipated goals in the future as their own. The shared element brings the members together in a genuine unity because each member, though distinct in his own consciousness and freedom, still identifes himself with the same past events and future hopes that form a part of the reality of all the other selves. Clearly, Royce had some inkling here of Freud's concept of the superego.

Royce even anticipated the current question Who am I? In *The Philosophy of Loyalty* he wrote:

> Here, then, is the paradox. I and only I, whenever I come to my own, can morally justify to myself my own plan of life. No outer authority can ever give me the true reason for my duty. Yet I, left to myself, can never find a plan of life. I have no inborn ideal naturally present within myself. By nature I simply go on crying out in a sort of chaotic self-will, according as the momentary play of desire determines. (Smith 1974:101)

However, Royce, for all the wealth of his ideas, remained tied to German idealism and metaphysics; in the last analysis he was more of a philosopher than a psychologist.

The next important thinker is also widely regarded as the greatest of American psychologists: William James. Like Royce, James was both philosopher and psychologist, but his most enduring contribution came in *The Principles of Psychology* (1890). The most lasting contribution is chapter 10, "The Conscious Self."

Like all American psychologists of his day, James was fully conversant with continental thinking but attempted to get beyond it in many ways. In his discussion of the self he was, as he realized, treading new ground; some have even referred to "James' theory of the self."

Like all others, James was unable to offer a clear definition of the self (nor, as will be noted, has anyone else offered such a definition once the notion of the self as soul or as something substantive was disposed of). James says, "In its widest possible sense, however, a man's self is the sum total of all that he can call his (1890 1:291). This may be called the standard definition, which has changed little, if any, since James' day. The self is everything that can be called I or me or mine.

James also saw the self as the origin and center of our thinking, referring to this as the central self, of the self or selves. He quotes a German philosopher by the name of Horwicz as follows: "Is it not the simplest explanation for all these phenomena so consistent among themselves that ego, the self which forms the origin and center of our *thinking* life, is at the same time the original and central object of our life of feeling and the ground both of whatever ideas and of whatever special feeling ensue?" (p. 326).

James also asserts most emphatically that the self can only be considered in terms of its parts. There is no such thing as the self as such. We only love or hate certain things about ourselves. Thus, he says: "An original central self feeling can never explain the passionate warmth of our self-regarding emotions, which must on the contrary be addressed to special things less abstract and empty of content.

To these things the name of self may be given or to our conduct toward them the name of selfishness. But neither in the self nor the selfishness does the pure thinker play the title role." (p. 327).

Later James considers the question of a personal identity, which he, like many other thinkers before and since, more or less equated with the self. He says: "The sense of our own personal identity then is exactly like any one of our other perceptions of sameness among phenomena. It is a conclusion grounded either on the resemblance in a fundamental respect or on the continuity before the mind of the phenomona compared"(p. 334).

James also shows that the discussion of the self goes back a very long way. Quoting David Hume, he says:

> There are some philosophers who imagine we are every moment intimately conscious of what we call our self. If any impression gives rise to the idea of self, that impression must continue invariable the same through the whole course of our lives. And the self is supposed to exist after that manner. But there is no impression constant and invariable . . . . I never can catch myself at any time without a perception. I never can observe anything but the perception . . . . If anyone upon serious unprejudiced reflection thinks he has a different notion of himself, I must confess I can reason no longer with him (p. 351).

John Stuart Mill had written: "The phenomenon of self and that of memory are merely two side of the same fact, two different modes of viewing the same fact" (quoted in James 1890 1:356). James emphasizes that all of this philosophizing revolves around the need to get rid of the concept of the soul, one of the major tasks of late-nineteenth-century philosophy.

Coming back to German philosophy again, James quotes Hegel as follows: "The self exists as one self only as it opposes itself as object to itself as subject and immediately denies and transcends that opposition"(p. 369).

James even adds an interesting quotation from Griesinger, which is also a foreshadowing of Sullivan. Griesinger wrote:

> Often their invasion into the former circle of feelings is felt as if the old self were being taken possession of by a dark overpowering might. And the fact of such possession is described in fantastic images. Always this doubleness, the struggle of the old self against the new discordant forms of experience is accompanied with painful mental conflict, with passion, with violent emotional excitement. This is in great part the reason for the common experience that the first stage in the immense majority of mental diseases is

> an emotional alteration, particularly of a melancholic sort .... The man is no longer the same, but a really new person, his own self transformed(p. 376).

In another passage James quotes Wundt, again insisting that the core of the self is the bodily feelings connected with it (as in the James-Lange theory of emotion). Wundt wrote:

> So we come to conceive this permanent mass of feeling as immediately or remotely subject to our will and call it the consciousness of our self. This self-consciousness is at the onset thoroughly sensational ... only gradually the second end of its character, its subjection to our will, attains predominance ... this consciousness contracted down to the process of apperception we call our Ego and the apperception of mental objects in general may thus after Leibniz be designated as the raising of them into our self-consciousness .... Only philosophy is fond of placing the abstract ego at the onset and so reversing the process of development ... the most speculative of philosophers is incapable of disjoining his ego from those bodily feelings and images which form the incessant background of his awareness of himself. (p. 303)

Then James likewise asserts that no amount of philosophizing can alter the conviction of the average man that there is such a thing as selfhood. It is an elementary datum. An equally elementary datum is that my own body and what ministers to its needs are thus the primitive object, instinctively determined, of my egoistic interests. Other objects may become interesting derivatively through association with any of these things, either as means or as habitual concomitants, and so in a thousand ways the primitive sphere of the egoistic emotions may enlarge and change its boundaries. This observation, that what is most central to the average person is everything connected with his selfhood, is likewise of fundamental importance.

For his own theory, James emphasized in particular the *empirical self*. Above all the empirical self was to be a subject for investigation. Thus, "personal identity" has to be taken out of the clouds and turned over to the self as an empirical and verifiable thing (p. 336). In this respect, James proves to be ahead even of many contemporary analytic theoreticians who tend to turn identity into some kind of mystical essence. This means that the person is to observe everything there is to be observed about him; thus, it serves as a heuristic principle for further investigation, which did in fact follow.

Further consideration of the emperical self reveals that it contains the material self; the social self; the spiritual self; and the pure ego. The body is the innermost part of the material self. A man's social self is the recognition that he gets from his mates. "Properly speaking, a man has as many social selves as there are individuals who recognize him and carry an image of him in their mind. To wound any one of these images is to wound him" (p. 294). This dubious proposition was later to be repeated by Sullivan. By the spiritual self James meant a man's inner or subjective being, his psychic faculties or dispositions taken concretely, thus the psychic part of him. The pure ego consists of the verifiable features in personal identity; there is nothing that can be called a "nonphenomenal sort of an arch-ego," as the idealists claimed.

Another significant contribution was made by James in *The Varieties of Religious Experience* (1902). He spoke of the divided self and the process of its unification, a topic still very much under discussion. He divided humanity into two categories, the healthy minded, who are born only once, and sick soul, who must be born twice in order to be happy. The psychological basis of the twice born he saw as a discordance or heterogeneity in the native temperament, thus essentially organic (as all disturbance was viewed in his day). He wrote:

> Some persons are born with an inner constitution which is harmonious and well balanced from the outset. Their impulses are consistent with one another, their will follows without trouble the guidance of their intellect, their passions are not excessive, and their lives are little haunted by regrets. Others are oppositely constituted . . . . Wrong living, impotent aspirations: 'What I would that do I not; but what I hate, that do I.", as St. Paul says; self-loathing, self-despair; an unintelligible and intolerable burden to which one is mysteriously the heir.(p. 238)

As Strindberg said: "Bless me, whose deepest suffering was this—I could not be the one I longed to be." James' psychological distinctions have held up well, though his notions of organic etiology have not. It is perhaps worth noting that the James family itself was saddled with crippling neuroses. Alice died young after being a neurotic invalid all her life, William suffered a deep depression in his twenties (and was thus twice born), and Henry fled his country.

James advanced the theory in many important respects. First, he offered a comprehensive picture of the self, stressing above all its empirical character. This empirical self he further subdivdied into the material, the social, and the spiritual (today we would say psychological). Second, he rid psychology once and for all of the notion of the soul, thus separating the self as a psychological fact from the soul as an abstract entity. And third, he established a line of investigation and a method of thinking about the self that has persisted to this day.

The weaknesses in James' position, from our presnt-day point of view, are, however, many. First, he does not integrate the self with the community, as Royce had done. Second, he, like all psychologists before Freud, does not deal with the unconscious. Third, although he talks about the body, he does not make the necessary distinctions to sift out the more important aspects, the libidinal drives. And finally, he does not devote enough attention to how the individual thinks about himself, i.e. his narcissism.

An important step beyond James was taken by Charles Horton Cooley, whose *Human Nature and the Social Order* (1902, revised 1922) drew all the implications of the social aspects of the self. He took the same definition as James—the self is that which I designate as me, mine, or the equivalent. But then he says:

> "Self" and "ego" are used by many metaphysicians and moralists in many other senses, more or less remote from the "I" of daily speech and thought, and with these I wish to have as little to do as possible. What is here discussed is what psychologists call the empirical self . . . the empirical self should not be very much more difficult to get hold of than other facts of the mind. (p. 168)

Cooley regarded the emotion, or feeling, of self as instinctive, doubtless evolved in connection with its important function in stimulating and unifying the special activities of individuals. Whereas we no longer think in this way, it is obvious that since the notion of the self occurs spontaneously in all known societies, there must be something about it that is inherent in the mind (Radin 1927).

Cooley's stress is on the social meaning of the self, thus continuing the distinctively American observation that the self cannot be understood except in relation to other people. He reports that he classified the first hundred I's and me's in Hamlet, encountering the meaning of bodily appearance only once (pp. 176–177).

There is an amazing foreshadowing of much of psychoanalytic thought in Cooley:

> The first definite thoughts that a child assciates with self-feeling are probably those of his earliest endeavors to control visible objects—his limbs, his playthings, his bottle and the like. Then he attempts to control

> the actions of the persons about him, and so his circle of power and of self-feeling widens without interruption to the most complex objects of mature ambition . . . we cannot deny him a self even in the first weeks. (p. 177)

His stress on the significance of other people leads him to the concept of the reflected, or "looking-glass," self. "Each to each a looking-glass reflects the other that doth pass." This seems similar to Lacan's mirror state and Kohut's mirror transference, except that again there is no concept of the unconscious.

For Cooley a self-feeling of this sort has three principal elements: the imagination of our appearance to the other person, the imagination of his judgment of that appearance, and some sort of self-feeling, such as pride or mortification. He foreshadows one of Freud's positions in his remarks on love, stating that if love closes, the self contracts and hardens (the narcissistic defense, in modern language).

He carefully observed his own children and found that he could identify the concept of the self before they were able to reason abstractly (about age two), thus foreshadowing one aspect of the work of Piaget. In its communication and growth the self-feeling is no different from other feelings and can be traced empirically. 'The fact of selective interest, admiration, presige, is obvious before the end of the second year" (p. 197). He noted the sex differences in the devlopment of the social self, stressing that girls are more social than boys. The group self, or "we," is simply an "I" that includes other persons. In discussing selfishness, he emphasizes its narrowness and inadequacy of imagination, thus agreeing with Adler's position on narcissism. An unhealthy self is at the heart of all social discontent.

While Cooley's position eventually becomes too one-sidedly social, he performs a valuable service in his demonstration that all self-feeling at some point or other is derived from experiences with other people. 'The self that is most important is reflection, largely, from the minds of others"(p. 246). Add the Ucs and the drives, and you have modern psychoanalytic theory. Cooley even has a sage comment on psychoanalysis:

> The modern study, aspiring to become a science, called Psychoanalysis, endeavors in a more or less systematic way to investigate the history and working of the self, with a view especially to understanding of its maladies and finding a cure for them . . . . The literature of psychoanalysis is suggestive and stimulating, but the more general theories to be found in it are perhaps only provisional. A sociologist will note especially the tendency to work too directly from supposed instincts, without allowing for the transforming action of social institutions and processes. (pp. 202-203)

A whole host of other psychologists followed in the footsteps of James and Cooley. Mead (1936), a philosopher, stressed the generalized other, a foreshadowing of the Freudian concept of the superego. Allport drew up a whole description of development, centering about the self, which makes very good sense. Maslow is well known for his notion of self-actualization. And finally, through the years there has been an ongoing investigation of the self-image and other empirical aspects of the self in all its aspects (Wylie 1961, 1978; Gecas and Schwalbe 1983; Suls 1982; Gecas 1982; Gergen and Gergen 1981; Mischel 1977). All of these and their related conceptualizations will be woven into the later discussions.

Thus, from the German background came the preoccupation with narcissism (in different language), while from the American side came the concern with the self. Added to these are the insights of modern psychoanalysis. Together the total integration of these points of view, first attempted after World War II, remains an important task to be performed.

The Narcissism of Psychosis

Although psychosis has existed at all times in all cultures, the recognition that it is a narcissistic disturbance did not really reach full awareness until the twentieth century, and even then with many hesitations and reservations. This fact deserves some reflection. It suggests mainly that there has been a widespread incidence of mental disorder in all cultures, most of which had gone unnoticed (as in our own).

In Plato's dialogue *Phaedrus* Socrates states that some of our greatest blessings come through madness, provided it is a divine madness and not one caused by human disease. He lists

1. prophetic madness (as in the Sibyl at Delphi);
2. "telestic", or ritual, madness (as in the Dionysiac rituals);
3. poetic madness ("inspiration"); and
4. the madness of love (Simon 1978:185).

Plato has had such a profound impact on Western thought that in the light of Socrates' view it does not surprise us that the bizarre character of madness went unnoticed for so many centuries. Erasmus, e.g., speaks of foolish persons and of the insane without clearly differentiating them (Rosen 1968:156). The latter he alleges are the happiest of all, thus subscribing to the popular notion of the happy lunatic.

From the nineteenth century on the prevailing view, held now by physicians who were for the first time entrusted with the care of the insane, was that psychotics had deranged brains. The idea that they could have retreated into a psychosis narcissistically in order to avoid the horrors of interpersonal contact rarely occurred to anybody, although today it is as plain as the nose on the face.

Primitive psychiatry has always comingled the physical and the psychological without any real attempt to differentiate them. In this sense, psychiatry today remains at the same primitive level, in spite of all the sophisticated biochemistry that is thrown into the works (Bleuler 1978).

The awareness of the narcissistic character of psychosis goes along with the realization that large numbers of persons are highly narcissistic and that they retreat into themselves because of their deep disppointments with other people. It was this that led to the designation of a "narcissistic personality disorder," following Kohut, which has since been incorporated in the Diagnostic and Statistical Manual (DSM-III) of the American Psychiatric Association. But together with all this goes the grim knowledge that psychological disturbance is widespread and dangerous, one of the major discoveries of the twentieth century, especially after World War II.

Preview

It is against this background that the questions of narcissism, the self, and society can be pursued. Narcissism is self-involvement. Three types have occurred historically: the naricissism of the ruler, the narcissism of the common man, and the narcissism of the psychotic. In Germanic countries, following the doctrine of inner causes, the emphasis eventually shifted to narcissism. In Anglo-American countries, following the doctrine of the tabula rasa, the emphasis was placed on external causes. Thus, for Freud narcissism became primary and a state of ineffable bliss. On the other hand, for the American and British psychologists the self was seen as primary and interpersonal interaction the source of human welfare.

It is to the interplay and clarification of these various points of view that we now turn.

CHAPTER 2
PSYCHOANALYTIC THEORY: NARCISSISM

After the historical introduction the next task is to review and critique the psychoanalytic theories of narcissism and the self. In this chapter narcissism will be considered; in the following chapter the self will be discussed. Although these two concepts are, of course, intimately related (thus narcissism is most simply defined as self-involvement, while Kohut's theory, which began with narcissism, ended up as a self-psychology), it is more expedient, and productive of greater clarity, if they are considered separately.

While psychoanalytic theorizing began with the 1914 paper by Freud, many of the theoretical issues concerning narcissism were discussed long before that. Freud was led to the problem of narcissism as a technical issue by his wish to understand psychosis better, an area in which therapeutic efforts had been singularly unsuccessful up to that time. He was also deeply hurt by Jung's detection the previous year (1913), which he attempted to remedy in public by demonstrating the superiority of his theoretical views to Jung's.

Actually Jung was the first analyst to tackle the problem of schizophrenia (then still referred to as dementia praecox). In 1906 he published *The Psychology of Dementia Praecox*, a pathbreaking work that first brought him to Freud's attention.

But while Jung made a significant contribution in showing that the apparent absurdities and irrationality of a schizophrenic's language could be understood psychologically in terms of the complexes or the complex associations, he held on to the image of a toxin and did not get further with the deeper psychological understanding of the topic.

At that time the distinction between hysteria and schizophrenia was still quite obscure. Psychiatrists spoke of "hysterical psychosis," a term no longer used. Sabina Spielrein (1983), who has written a revealing account of her analysis with Jung in that period, is an example; whether she was schizophrenic or not will never be known. She was admitted to Burghölzli, (in the early 1900's) where Jung was a staff psychiatrist, and improved enormously with him. The dynamics, however, remained unclear.

The next important step was taken by Abraham in 1908. He saw that in schizophrenia the libidinal cathexis of objects is lacking. The question then arises: what happens to the libido of dementia praecox patients, which is turned away from objects? Abraham gave the answer: it is turned back on to the ego, and this reflexive turning back is the source of the megalomania in schizophrenia.

Actually Abraham's observations in this paper were quite profound. He stated that the schizophrenics are still able to direct their sexual desire to a person but are no longer capable of any steady attachment to that person. Other patients cherish for years an imaginary love, which only exists in their minds; and they have probably never even seen their sexual object. In real life they keep away from any human contact. In short, there is always some evidence of their autoerotic attitude. Freud seems to take some credit for his formulations, since in his introductory lectures (1916–17) he writes: "Already in 1908 Karl Abraham, after an exchange of thoughts with me, pronounced the main characteristic of dementia praecox"(16:415).

Freud then also goes on to make the significant (and incorrect) comment that "megalomania is in every way comparable to the familiar sexual overvaluation of the object in normal erotic life" (16:415).

The next stage came with the clarification of homosexuality, on which Freud began to elucidate in the next few years. His formulation, which has since been superseded, was that homosexuality represents a fixation on the narcissistic stage and further that this narcissistic stage is a normal stage of development that lies between autoeroticism and object libido.

These formulations were offered by Freud in his book on Leonardo (1919), in his paper on the Schreber case (1911), and in the later editions of *Three Essays on Sexuality*. In the book on *Leonardo da Vinci* he states:

> The boy represses his love for his mother; he puts himself in her place: he identifies himself with her and takes his own person as a model in whose likeness he chooses a new object of his love. In this way he has become a homosexual. What he has in fact done is slip back into autoeroticism; for the boys whom he loves now as he grows up are, after all, only substitutive figures and revivals of himself in childhood—boys whom he loves in the way in which his mother loved him when he was a child. He finds the object of his love along the path of *narcissism*, as we say, for Narcissus, according

> to the Greek legend was a youth who preferred his own reflection to anything else and who was turned into a lovely flower of that name. (11:100)

It is not clear which legend of Narcissus he is referring to here. As has been seen, Narcissus in one version was totally enamored of his twin sister; Freud surprisingly ignores the incestuous implications. He also ignores the deep depression that eventually killed Narcissus.

Likewise, Freud felt that the path he described above was only one possible genesis of homosexuality; for a fuller explanation he deferred the problem.

Before 1914, then, Freud saw the course of libidinal development as proceeding from autoeroticism to narcissism to object libido. Fixation on narcissism could lead, on the one hand, to homosexuality and, on the other, as was shown in the Schreber case, to paranoia. This was one of the considerations that led him to postulate that homosexuality is an essential constitutent of the paranoid process. Why one person develops into a homosexual while another develops into a paranoiac was not clear.

It is difficult to trace precisely who contributed what idea in that early period, when ideas were flowing freely in the golden days of pyschoanalysis. What Freud called narcissism Jung called introversion. Priority is less important than the fact that the narcissistic attitude began to be investigated more closely.

The Narcissism of the Artist

The conceptualizations led to an entirely new thought about artists. Leonardo, after all, was a great artist. He reputedly had no sexual contact with either man or woman, although it was widely believed in his day that he was a homosexual. In spite of that belief, Freud though that Leonardo had made an essentially narcissistic resolution to life's problems, a resolution that at that time he thought of as conceivably healthy.

In the meantime his close collaborators Otto Rank and Hanns Sachs were devoting considerable attention to the dynamics of the artist. Their work led to the formulation that the artist is an individual fixated at the narcissistic stage.

In the first paper on artists, which was published posthumously but was known to his associates, entitled "Psychopathic Characters on the Stage" (1904), Freud pointed out that the purpose of drama is to open up sources of enjoyment or pleasure in our emotional life, many of which would otherwise be inaccesible. This is done by allowing both playwright and actor to identify themselves with a hero; however, both are also avoiding suffering by recognizing that this is only an illusion since it is "only" a play. He also made the significant comment:

> that the precondition of enjoyment is that the spectator himself should be a neurotic, for it is only such people who can derive pleasure instead of simple diversion from the revelation and the more or less conscious recognition of a repressed impulse . . . thus it is only in neurotics that a struggle can occur of the kind that can be made the subject of a drama; but even in them the dramatist will provoke not really an enjoyment of the liberation but a resistance to it as well. (7:308–309).

The basic themes about art were elaborated much more fully by some of the other analysts than by Freud. The essential theses were enunciated most clearly in Sachs' *The Creative Unconscious* (1942) and later in Kris' *Psychoanalytic Explorations in Art* (1952). The main points that the early analysts stressed were: 1) The artist is a narcissistic individual who transfers his narcissistic enjoyment to his artistic production. 2) This transfer of narcissism allows the artist to avoid the suffering, while the fact that it is a work of art allows the spectator to enjoy the revelation of the impluse. 3) At the same time there is a considerable narcissistic danger in that the artist comes close to a variety of impulses that are forbidden to ordinary men. This is why so many artists break down. The literature of psychoanalysis is replete with studies of famous artists who suffered breakdowns or nearbreakdowns.

Thus, there were four strands in the discussion of narcissism prior to the 1914 paper: 1) Narcissism is a stage of development between autoeroticism and object libido. 2) Both the homosexual and the paranoiac are fixated at the stage of narcissism. 3) Narcissism is a characteristic of both the artist and the spectator, both of whom avoid the unpleasantness attached to forbidden impulses by manipulating the artistic production. 4) Following the Schreber case (1911) and *Totem and Taboo* (1912–13), Freud postulated great similarities between the child, the dreamer, the psychotic, and the primitive, a heuristic principle that has indeed proved to be extremely fruitful.

The 1914 Paper on Narcissism

In addition to the theoretical conclusions sketched above, there was a strong personal element that drove Freud to write the 1914 paper, rightly regarded as a turning point in the history of psychoanalysis. Jung's defection from the psychoanalytic movement was accompanied by the assertion that the libido theory had broken down in the attempt to clarify psychosis; Freud was going to prove him wrong. As Jones (1953:2,304) points out, the paper on the history of the psychoanalytic movement was written at the same time as the 1914 paper, and Freud was in a rage with Jung. And Freud, like any ordinary mortal, could not think too clearly when he was in a fury. One of the characteristics of Freud's writings after 1914 was that from time to time he took critical positions against Jung and Adler, positions that seemingly had nothing to do with the matter at hand (Fine 1973). As will be seen, some of the obscurity and inconsistency of his 1914 paper derives from his frustration with his departed disciples.

The paper, "On Narcissism: An Introduction," represents Freud's first systematic shift from id psychology to ego psychology. It also involves an extension and alteration of the entire libido theory. The essential new points in it are the following:

1. He describes libido now as a quantitatively variable force, the transformations of which explain the manifestations of psychosexuality. This is the new libido theory Freud took over from the 1914 paper and included under that heading in all the later editions of *Three Essays*.

2. It contains the first systematic description of the development of object choice. This too was later incorporated into *Three Essays*.

3. It establishes various meanings of narcissism that had hitherto been ignored.

4. It makes it possible to speak of a narcissistic neurosis in which the patient is unable to establish a relationship with the analyst, in contrast to the transference neuroses in which such a relationship is established. Theoretically narcissistic neuroses were untreatable, except by a modification of technique, while transference neuroses were treatable. Later he changed his mind on this point and went back to his continuum theory, seeing the difference between transference and narcissistic neuroses as only one of degree (1953–1970, 16:421).

5. It introduces the concept of the ego ideal, later renamed superego (in 1923), thus laying the basis for the structural theory that has dominated psychoanalytic thinking ever since (id, ego, superego).

6. It has a number of important but unsystematic comments on the self, again an aspect of the personality that had previously been relegated to a secondary position or had been totally ignored.

Critical Comments on the 1914 Paper

While the 1914 paper has been extensively discussed, too little attention has been paid to its serious shortcomings, which have influenced the subsequent course of the history of psychoanalysis. For, on the one hand, Freud opened up the new areas of ego psychology and interpersonal relations (now frequently called object relations) and, on the other, he bogged down in a metapsychological jungle from which there is scarcely any escape. Thus, in her review of the literature on narcissism, Judith Teicholz commented:

> Freud's ideas on narcissism contained contradictions, inconsistencies and gaps which are still being struggled with in the present decade (Pulver 1970; Stolorow 1975). But his basic definition and formulations have been maintained by many followers with only minor changes, in spite of major theoretical advances in the rest of psychoanalytic theory. In spite of . . . theoretical complexity and sophistication . . . many leading thinkers still hold to a definition of narcissism that departs very little from Freud's original formulations. (1978:833)

At the start of the 1914 paper Freud takes what is for him an unusual psychiatric stance: he is going to discuss a perversion, narcissism, that had been introduced into psychiatric (not psychoanalytic) literature by Paul Näcke (later he said that it was introduced by Havelock Ellis). And who was Näcke? A Russian-born German psychiatrist, Näcke lived from 1851 to 1913 (Freud and Jung 1974:94) and was director of an asylum at Golditz, Saxony, exactly the kind of man for whom Freud had no regard at all. Jung wrote to Freud about him:

> In any case Näcke is hardly worth bothering about. He is a queer bird who flutters like a will o' the wisp over all the backwaters of neurology, psychiatry, and psychology . . . and has just written an exceedingly strange, altogether crack-brained "historical" monograph on cramp in the legs. (Freud and Jung 1974:94)

The notion of a perversion (which was what Näcke had described under narcissism in 1899) in which a person treats his own body in the same way in which the body of a sexual object is ordinarily treated is a strange one—a typical psychiatric error of the kind that Freud helped to banish. If he means masturbation, why doesn't he say so? If he means that the person sits around stroking his body, that is only one isolated symptom that has to be understood in light of the patient's total personality. One immediately realizes that to pick up this trivial symptom indicated that Freud was fighting with his psychiatrist–erstwhile disciple Jung; otherwise it makes no sense.

After all, numerous other strands in Freud's thought were much more important than Näcke's, who otherwise remains unknown. He is quoted as having said once: 'Unfortunately Jung has let himself be influenced too much by Freud" (Freud and Jung 1974:94).

Actually Freud had a number of avenues open to him. He could take Jung's psychiatric position about introversion of the libido; he could consider Adler's emphasis on social interest; he could review the findings of himself and his followers on the lives of primitive peoples (cf. Roheim 1921a, to be discussed below); he could consider the historical preoccupation with selflove (Zweig 1980; cf. above); or he could follow the Narcissus myth in literature and psychology, which would have been much closer to his natural bent than quoting an otherwise unknown psychiatrist. To review the psychiatric material on introversion or narcissism at that time would have been, as he knew, completely superfluous.

In the end he chose to go with Jung. (I have elsewhere tried to show that, for Freud, Jung had become the beloved friend, while Adler was the hated enemy [Fine 1974]). The new conceptualization of ego libido vs. object libido eventually culminated in the concept of the id (1923), which was virtually synonymous with Jung's undifferentiated psychic energy. The position taken in 1923 in *The Ego and the Id* derived everything from the id, instead of, as previously, dividing the psyche into the sexual instincts and the ego instincts. Hartmann had to undo this error in 1939 in *Ego Psychology and the Problem of Adaptation.*

Considerable confusion was created by the concepts of ego libido and object libido, as Jones notes (1953–57 2:302). It would have been much simpler for Freud to go along with Adler's commonsence observation that narcissism implies a turning away from other people, so that it is inherently a pathological defense mechanism. The whole argument was revived fifty years later by the Kohut-Kernberg controversy, in which Kohut took the (Jungian) position that narcissism could follow its own line of development, independent of libido, while Kernberg took the Adlerian position that narcissism was inherently a pathological formation. This has indeed been the rule taken by others, though without reference to Jung and Adler (Rothstein 1980).

Nor did future analysts always take kindly to the new ego libido theory; in fact, in general, many analysts today have discarded it, but without making their views explicit. The libido was defined in 1905 as sexual energy, and its various stages of organization at different levels of development were described and correlated with normal behavior and psychopathology. It made excellent sense and became a cornerstone of all subsequent psychiatric and psychological thought.

To do the same with ego libido requires enormous and complex detours (fusion and defusion of instincts, the whole energy theory, and the like). But above all the new libido theory, which was designed to prove Jung wrong in his assertion that it could not explain dementia praecox, implied a renunciation of Freud's beloved sexual theories. This renunciation was in its way the most remarkable of all the changes.

In an attempt to refute one point made by Jung, Freud makes an extraordinary remark about an ascetic anchorite. Such a man, he says, who "tries to eradicate every trace of sexual interest" (but only in the popular sense of the word "sexual") "does not even display any pathogenic allocation of the libido." He had hinted at such a view in his paper on Leonardo. Yet to see an ascetic anchorite as a "normal variation" would seem absurd to any analyst today. The following year, in his paper "Transference Love" Freud wrote: "Sexual love is undoubtedly one of the chief things in life; and the union of mental and bodily satisfaction in the enjoyment of love is one of its culminating peaks. Apart from a few queer fanatics, all the world knows this and conducts its life accordingly; science alone is too delicate to admit it"(12:169–70).

Surely the ascetic anchorite would qualify as one of the "queer fanatics" he refers to. This is one of the many examples in this paper where his thinking is clouded by his fury at Jung.

Both of his major disciples, Jung and Adler, had denied the preeminent role that Freud had attached to sexuality. And suddenly Freud is doing the same thing. In this sense the paper could have been an attempt to placate his opponents or it could be seen as the beginning of a depressive period in his life, which culminated in the death instinct in 1920, the most bizarre of all his theories since the early numerological speculations of Wilhelm Fliess (an early confidant of Freud's). Jones devotes a number of pages to this interpretation, which has generally been overlooked (3:278–280).

To study narcissism first-hand, he had to be in contact with psychotics, and they were not present in his practice. Accordingly, he did the next best thing and approached them indirectly. But what areas did he choose—organic disease, hypochondria, the erotic life of the sexes? This is indeed a peculiar combination.

Why not art, which had already been the subject of much research? Why not ordinary social living, which had been discussed by many psychologists (cf. the American school, above). Since he had met William James in America in 1909, he must have had some familiarity with the American's famous chapter on the self. But this would have led him into Adler's territory, and he had so much inexplicable contempt for Adler that the younger man's theories were completely discarded. Unfortunate, indeed, since the ego psychology of interpersonal relations, which Adler had pioneered, later became one of the richest sources of psychoanalytic theory and knowledge.

In the discussion of narcissism and love Freud again opts for a retreat from sexuality. Distinguishing the anaclitic from the narcissistic types of object choice, he first states that the narcissistic is to be observed in disturbed individuals. Then he goes on to say that both types of object choice are open to each individual. Again sexuality no longer plays such a dominant role in interpersonal relationships.

A further weakness of "Transference Love" is that Freud saw narcissism as the chief characteristic of the psychotic, ignoring the underlying anxiety. In this respect he was simply going along with the conventioanl psychiatric "wisdom" of his day, which held that in psychosis there is no anxiety. It might be said that such a view is due to Freud's inexperience with psychotics, but that would not hold water. After all, in "The Defense Neuropsychoses" (1894) he had already cited a case in which the ego fended off an incompatible idea through a flight into psychosis. There he also wrote:

> I have only very few analyses of psychoses of this sort at my disposal. But I think we have to do here with a type of psychical illness which is very frequently employed. For no insane asylum is without what must be regarded as analogous examples—the mother who has fallen ill from the loss of her baby, and rocks a piece of wood unceasingly, or the jilted bride who, arrayed in her wedding-dress, has for years been waiting for her bridegroom. (3:60)

Besides, the continuum theory that there is only a quantitative difference between normality and psychosis, not a qualitiative one, was familiar to him and had been his position from the very beginning; it remained his position throughout his life. Even in his distinction of the transference and narcissistic neuroses, one of the contributions of the present paper, he later qualified his view: "the concepts which we arrived at during our study of the transference neuroses are adequate in helping us to find our way about in the narcissistic neuroses which are so much more severe in practice. The conformities go very far; at bottom the field of phenomena is the same" (16:421).

Finally, even in his consideration of self-esteem (translated by James Strachey as self-regard), he held on to the idea that somehow narcissism may be a perfectly normal state of affairs. He says:

> Applying our distinction between sexual and ego-instincts, we must recognize that self-regard has a specially intimate dependence on narcissistic libido. Here we are supported by two fundamental facts: that in paraphrenics self-regard is increased, while in the transference neuroses it is diminished; and that in love relations not being loved lowers the self-regarding feelings, while being loved raises them . . . Further, it is easy to observe that libidinal object-cathexis does not raise self-regard.(14:98)

The course of analytic history has contradicted Freud on both of the above accounts. In schizophrenia (his term was *paraphrenia*, but this never caught on and has disappeared) self-esteem is basically shattered, regardless of the front that the patient puts up. And his notion that there is a negative relationship between loving someone and being loved, so that self-love diminishes the love for others, is likewise incorrect. Actually, at another point in his 1914 paper he reverts to his more familiar stance when he says "we must begin to love in order not to fall ill, and we are bound to fall ill if, in consequence of frustration, we are unable to love" (14:85).

Thus, the inadequacies of "The Defense Neuropsychoses" stem primarily from the new concept of ego libido and its concomitants, replacing the older image of libido as sexual energy. This newer theory is closer to the Jungian notion, though the discussion is couched in such complex language that this has not been observed. What is more important is that the analyst today (and in ensuing years) could choose between the libido theory of 1915 (when it was incorporated into *Three Essays*) and the libido theory of 1905. I indicate over and over throughout this book that the 1905 theory makes much more sense than that of 1915, and in fact, the 1915 theory is the root cause of much of the confusion that has followed.

Freud himself did not come back to the term *narcissism* or to the concept of the self. Even the concept of a narcissistic stage of the libido was dropped when in 1924 Abraham systematized a much more sensible way of tracing psychosexual development, fully in accord with the 1905 position. Instead of narcissism he spoke of narcissistic libido or of the narcissistic individual, using narcissistic now as either self-involved or self-loving. As an adjective narcissistic remained the usual form (see Schafer 1976), until Kohut revived the whole question in the 1960s and 1970s.

Post-Freudian Developments

Even though the word *narcissism* was little used prior to the 1960s (Bing, McLaughlin, and Marburg 1959), a number of lines of thought in the paper were followed up. However, the proper understanding of these ideas requires a reexamination of the history of psychoanalysis, which I have done in *A History of Psychoanalysis* (1979a). Here I can only allude to the main findings.

1. The concept of the ego ideal eventually became the superego (1923). Intermediate in this transformation lay the discovery, or rather the elaboration, of the introjection of early persons (objects) as a crucial factor in the development of personality (*Mourning and Melancholia*, 1917).

In the 1920s Melanie Klein began her contributions in which the internalization of persons significant in a child's environment was given the highest emphasis. However, she herself was rather confused about certain aspects of this internalization. Were they inborn or did they come from frustration, or were they precipitated by the parents? In conformity with the more classical formulations of Freud, she tended to avoid speaking of mother and father (although that is what she meant), referring mainly to part and whole objects.

While her ideas were ridiculed for a long time, especially in the United States (although there was bitter opposition within the British society as well), particularly because of her disregard of the usual time table of mental development and, in therapy, her direct plunge into the deepest material without regard for transference complications, eventually it became clear that Klein had made some valid points. Today the notion of early introjection (primitive internalized objects or the like) is generally accepted, but still often without the clarification that what is referred to is the mother or father, an omission that creates some mystification on the part of the student. Her emphasis on the defenses of splitting and projective identification have also been accorded a warmer welcome in recent years, though unfortunately with insufficient reference to the overpowering anxieties that set these defenses off.

Because of her concern with these early internalizations and the earliest kinds of mental experience, her theories were particularly suitable to the analysis of psychotics. She and her followers made a number of significant contributions in this area (see Rosenfeld 1965).

2. The division into transference and narcissistic neuroses proved to be

extremely rewarding but had unexpected consequences. Eventually it turned into the question of the treatability of schizophrenics, a field in which Freud himself had actually done no work at all, though he did make some theoretical contributions to the dynamics of schizophrenia.

It soon became obvious that Freud's commonsense view that schizophrenics are too narcissistic to be analyzed (a point that, as noted above, he himself later doubted) had to be considerably modified after World War I when hospital psychiatrists for the first time began to apply the concepts of psychoanalysis to psychotics. As Arlow pointed out in 1952, "In the light of our newer knowledge concerning the defensive functions of the ego, we should reexamine the concept of narcissism in schizophrenia which, as Dr. Fromm-Reichmann had pointed out, proved for so many years a pitfall in the path of analysts" (Brody and Redlich 1952:115).

In other words, actual observation showed that schizophrenics were by no means as narcissistic as they seemed to be (Searles 1965; Bleuler 1978; Karon and van den Bos 1981). Many psychiatrists had noted this fact through the years (Boyer and Giovacchini 1980), but for the vast majority of hospital psychiatrists, untrained in psychoanalysis, the schizophrenic proved unapproachable. Whether it is the lack of training of the psychiatrist, as Sullivan (1962) maintained, or the inherently organic character of the schizophrenic illness that justifies the widespread use of tranquilizing drugs, as practiced today, remains a moot point. It is noteworthy that some recent authors have stated that even with drugs the outcome of the treatment of the schizophrenic has not changed in a hundred years (Cancro 1982; Rodgers 1982; Tissot 1977).

3. The concept of the self-image, which Freud touched on only briefly in the last portion of the paper, underwent extensive development and rediscovery. It was eventually realized that the term *self* lends itself more readily to English than the German *Ich*, which is the ordinary German word for I, and that the self-concept had long been in use in American psychology and psychiatry, even before psychoanalysis was discovered (cf. above). Roheim (1921a; writing now in German) published an article in *Imago* showing that some concept of the self was to be found in every culture known, even the most primitive. No one any longer doubts the importance of the concept, but many controversies about it still remain.

4. Unmentioned in Freud's 1914 paper, but related to it, is the concept of *identity*, extensively analyzed by Erikson in the 1950s, which has since become an essential part of the psychoanalytic vocabulary.

5. The question of object choice was widened into the broader topic of

interpersonal relations. Here a curious historical detour has taken place. The term *interpersonal relations* was first emphasized by Sullivan and his school (though Sullivan himself felt no conflict about it with Freud). But because of the political turmoil in American psychoanalysis (Quen and Carlson 1978), Sullivan had to be avoided by the more orthodox Freudians. Instead, it was belatedly discovered that the British had a middle group, which was then dubbed the object relations school or the British school. Since object means person in this context, it really makes little sense to speak of object relations rather than of interpersonal relations, yet the term has become entrenched in spite of its obscurity.

Further, the topic of interpersonal relations was much more extensively examined by the whole culturalist school; this is its major contribution. Group theory, family structure, the individual and his society, the relationship of individual psychology to the structure of culture, all of these and many other questions were carefully examined. Technically, the whole topic was first raised by Adler, but he failed to tie up social interest with drive theory. Later the major bridge building occurred through the study of the mother-child relationship (from Spitz on), which Freud had surprisingly neglected.

6. The libido theory propounded in the 1914 paper led via the *Pleasure Principle* (1920) and *The Ego and the Id* (1923) to some of the most arcane and incomprehensible doctrines of metapsychology. Later it was discovered that in his theorizing of that period Freud was reverting to some of the ideas of the abandoned project of 1895. But commentators failed to appreciate that this represented a weakness in Freud's thinking, not a strength. The repeated attacks on such concepts as ego libido, psychic energy, neutralized energy, and the like have made the second libido theory the weakest link in Freud's theorizing. Few have noted, however, that as has been shown, this dubious version of the libido theory was first introduced by Freud in 1914 in order to refute Jung's contention that the libido theory did not explain psychosis. As will be shown later, however, had Freud stuck to his original libido theory, his explanations would have been much more incisive.

7. Finally, the concept of narcissism, except in the case of the artist (and later the scientist as well), fell into disuse until it was revived by Kohut in the 1960s and 1970s. The sequence of autoeroticism-narcissism-object relatedness was given up when Abraham formulated his 1924 theory of psychosexual development. Kohut's position will be examined more carefully below. Eventually, the separation-individuation paradigm of Mahler entirely replaced the older formulations, in spite of its own weaknesses.

Thus, while it remains true that the 1914 paper opened up whole new areas of psychoanalytic observation and theorizing, it failed to resolve them in any significant way, and today little value can be attached to Freud's exact formulations there. In light of all the work done subsequently, what does require clarification are the many questions still seemingly unanswered.

Briefly, my contention is that some theoreticians have fallen back on Jung's views in that period, some on Freud's, and some on Adler's. Freud himself tried to reconcile all three with the tripartite structure: the id was much like Jung's undifferentiated energy, the ego was Adler's stress, the superego came from the American Putnam. It has persisted because of the profound insights that it offers, but still as an amalgam it leaves much to be desired, which explains why the attempt to force everything into it (as Hartmann and Jacobson, e.g., have tried) has not succeeded very well.

Once the significance of transference and resistance was appreciated, after World War I (which was not true of either Adler or Jung—neither understood the transference concept nor could use it), the field bifurcated into those who stressed the intrapsychic and those who emphasized the interpersonal. In order to achieve a full psychoanalytic psychology in the true Freudian sense, it is essential to offer a synthesis of the intrapsychic and the interpersonal points of view. Such is the main thrust of the present work. In order to do this, the above topics, thus far only mentioned in brief outline, will have to be elaborated much more fully.

After World War II Heinz Hartmann emerged as the major theoretician of the Freudian school, which he remained until his death in 1970. At the same time the political events of the time cannot be ignored. The large-scale split between the Freudians and the culturalists began to take shape after World War II and reached its climax in the formation of the Academy of Psychoanalysis in 1956 and the concomitant reorganization of the American Psychoanalytic Association, where adherence to Freudian concepts became a requirement for membership (this had not been the case before). Accordingly, the major thrust of Freudian theoreticians, led by Hartmann, was to force everything into the mold of the structural theory (even though Hartmann with his 1939 paper on the ego had already corrected Freud's careless overestimation of the id in *The Ego and the Id* in 1928). About narcissism Hartmann wrote in 1950:

> In turning now to questions of ego cathexis, the second point I have singled out for presentation today, we are confronted with the many-faceted and still puzzling problem of narcissism. Many analysts do not find it altogether easy to define the place which the concept of narcissism holds in present analytic theory. This, I think, is due mainly to the fact that this concept has

> not been explicitly redefined in terms of Freud's later structural psychology. I shall limit my remarks to those points that are essential if we want to avoid possible misunderstandings of what I want to say about ego cathexis. Many aspects of narcissism have been reformulated by Federn in a series of searching papers (1929, 1936). I shall not discuss this reformulation because in the course of his studies Federn came to modify the concept of the ego in a way which seems to me not altogether convincing. I would prefer to integrate Freud's early formulations on narcissism into his later views on mental structure, rather than to change any of the main aspects of the latter. (1964:126).

Thus, the main outline of the subsequent argument was laid down by Hartmann, whose authority was enormous. But the investigations then changed from an examination of narcissism to an attempt to fit narcissism into the structural theory. By this time American analysis was dominant, and Hartmann stated that: "In analysis a clear distinction between the terms ego, self and personality is not always made," a statement that is not entirely accurate. Then he went on to define narcissism as "the libidinal cathexis of the self" (1964:127) in contrast to Freud's definition of narcissism as the libidinal complement to the ego.

However, the definition of narcissism as the libidinal cathexis of the self, if looked at more closely, is merely a tautology. If narcissism is self-involvement, then it is by definition the libidinal cathexis of the self, only here the term *libidinal* is used more in the broad sense than in the narrow one of sexual. Hartmann is also saying no more than William James did (and others) with the observation that those matters connected with the self are always of prime concern to the individual.

Kohut and the Current Situation

Before Freud wrote his paper, he was faced by two exactly contradictory attitudes toward narcissism by his two chief disciples. Jung, who explored the inner life in the greatest of detail, saw the introvert (a term he contributed to the literature) as one of two main types, both equally healthy in their own way (introvert vs. extravert). Jung viewed introversion as genetically determined and even warned that any attempt to change an introvert into an extravert through psychotherapy could have serious consequences. Adler, on the other hand, saw no problem at all in narcissism: it was the antithesis of social interest and hence per se pathological.

Before Kohut there was one other contribution of significance, that of Paul Federn. Federn's views have been obscured because of his idiosyncratic language and should really be read without reference to his own metapsychological propositions. His main points can be summarized as follows:

1. Healthy narcissism is employed as countercathexis to the object strivings and for their support (e.g., hope, ambition) but not as their substitute. The more narcissism functions as a substitute, the more pathological it becomes.
2. The ego boundaries are resistant to normal narcissism; the ego is sufficiently stable due to the adequate narcissistic countercathexes.
3. The affects are resolved without sentimentality, though without intensity, that is, without renewed investment of narcissism.
4. The level of forepleasure satisfaction resulting from the narcissistic cathexes is not too high; whereas the level of such forepleasure inherent in the permanent ego feeling is in general as high as possible.
5. The satisfaction in conscious and unconscious narcissistic fantasies is conditional on real object libidinal discharges, although the converse conditionality is not lacking. In pathological narcissism the latter predominates (i.e., object libido depends on narcissistic fantasies).
6. The contents of conscious and unconscious narcissistic fantasies are more in accord with reality, less infantile, and cathected by fewer perverse infantile components.
7. The last point is further confirmed by the fact that the promise magically established in these fantasies becomes more and more grandiose and more impossible in the same measure as the contributory narcissistic attitude deviates from normality.

Federn's views were taken over by many other analytic authors, often in different language. E.g., Erich Fromm (1939) stated that love of others and self-love are not alternatives; on the contrary, an attitude of love toward oneself will be found in all those who are capable of loving others.

But the great stimulus to the rearousal of interest came with Kohut. His first paper on the topic, in 1966, "Forms and Transformations of Narcissism," received relatively little attention. As he correctly observed, the reason narcissism has been ignored is that it carries an unfavorable connotation (thus ignoring Federn). Its contributions to health, adaptation, and achievement have not been treated extensively. While he does mention Federn in a footnote (1966:244), he leaves out Sachs, Rank, Sharpe, and others who had described the positive features of artistic and scientific productivity.

In tracing the further development of narcissism, Kohut first emphasizes that primary narcissism bifurcates in the preoedipal period into the narcissistic self and the idealized parental imago. (Later he changed the term *narcissistic self* to *grandiose self.*) These he regarded as age appropriate and recognized that the cognitive image changes with the maturation of the child's cognitive equipment.

Kohut then describes five later states, which he regarded not only as transformations of narcissism but also as attainments of the ego and as attitudes and achievements of the personality: man's creativity; his ability to be empathic; his capacity to contemplate his own impermanence; his sense of humor; and his wisdom. Although he did not yet see narcissism and object love developing along different lines, he came close to it by arguing that an achievement of any of these various transformations of narcissism should be rated as "a more genuine and valid result of therapy than the patient's precarious compliance with demands for a change of his narcissism into object love" (1966:270).

In evaluating this paper, it is not really clear how he gets to his conclusions. Creativity was always regarded as related to narcissism. But empathy involves the capacity to sense another person's feelings. Why is this narcissistic? It seems rather to be the opposite. The contemplation of one's own impermanence is the fear of death, which has always been a terror to mankind. Humor was profoundly analyzed by Freud in his book on jokes in 1905 (which Kohut does not mention, referring only to Freud's later addendum to the topic in 1927). As far as wisdom is concerned, why should that be narcissistic? It is not surprising that this 1966 paper of Kohut's was generally disregarded.

When Pulver came to summarize the disparate views in the field, he began by saying: "In the voluminous literature on narcissism, there are probably only two facts on which everyone agrees, first that the concept of narcissism is one of the most important contributions of psychoanalysis; second that it is one of the most confusing" (1970:319).

In reviewing the literature, Pulver found that narcissism had been defined in a number of different ways:

1. Clinically, to denote a sexual perversion.
2. Genetically, to denote a stage of development.
3. In terms of object relationships, to denote two different phenomena: a type of object choice and a mode of relating to the environment.
4. To denote various aspects of the complex ego state of self-esteem.

Pulver argued, like others, that Freud's concept of narcissism was highly productive and useful in its time but was now incomplete and at times misleading. He urged that the concept be given the elaboration in ego psychology that it so richly deserves.

The definition of narcissism that Pulver found most satisfactory is from *Glossary of Psychoanalytic Terms* (Moore and Fine 1968): narcissism is a concentration of psychological interest upon the self.

Kohut: The Analysis of the Self

While Kohut's earlier paper attracted little attention, his first book, *The Analysis of the Self* (1971), started a virtual revolution; many even spoke of the "Kohutian revolution." Eventually a society for self-psychology, inspired by the Kohutian ideas, was formed in the early 1980s. At the same time there was wide criticism of his various positions. Hanly and Masson stated that "no single work in psychoanalytic literature on this subject, since Freud, has had a greater impact on the psychoanalytic community" (1976:49). Nevertheless, they rejected his position, insisting that narcissism cannot be separated from object relations.

Kohut offered a new definition of narcissism: "Narcissism, within my general outlook, is defined not by the target of the instinctual investment (i.e., whether it is the subject himself or other people) but by the nature or quality of the instinctual charge. The small child, for example, invests other people with narcissistic cathexes and thus experiences them narcissistically , i.e., as self-objects" (1971:26).

The concept of self-object, the new definition of narcissism, the types of transference in the narcissistic patient, which he described as idealizing and mirroring, the assumption that narcissism and object love develop along independent lines, and the diagnostic category of narcissistic personality disorder were all novel and accordingly aroused an enormous amount of discussion and controversy.

In *The Analysis of the Self* the stress was still on the narcissistic personality disorders, though of course the notion of the self (to be discussed below) had to be included. In his second book, *The Restoration of the Self* (1977), the focus had shifted almost entirely to his new conceptualization of the self.

The term self-object refers to objects that are not experienced as separate and independent from the self. He argued that patients with narcissistic personality disturbances have in essence attained a cohesive self and have constructed cohesive idealized archaic objects. Separating them from the borderline states, he considered them analyzable. They are recognizable chiefly through their transferences (idealizing and mirroring). Further, he felt that the state of the grandiose self, reached at about three years of age, was a normal stage of development and that from there on narcissism follows an independent line of development. Kohut's position was strongly challenged by Kernberg, who felt that narcissism of the kind described by Kohut was pathological, just as the grandiose self was not a normal stage in development (as simple observation of children could demonstrate). This Kohut–Kernberg controversy for a while attracted much attention but has since been eclipsed by other considerations.

In *The Restoration of the Self* Kohut focused almost entirely on the self and attempted to elaborate a new kind of self-psychology. He felt that this new self-psychology could conceivably replace the whole edifice of psychoanalytic theory. In one sense this was a bold step, since he recognized (without saying so) that traditional drive theory and self-psychology are not easily reconciled, so that he thus avoided many of the contorted locutions that others had ventured. But in another sense he was throwing out the baby with the bath, since libido theory (in the original 1905 sense) has so much to offer. Kohut, going to extremes, wrote: "I trust I have succeeded in demonstrating (see Chapter Two) the relevance and explanatory power of the hypothesis that the primary psychological configurations in the child's experiential world are not drives, that *drive experiences occur as disintegration products when the self is unsupported*" (1977:17; italics added).

Kohut's notion of the bipolar self and his classification of the self disorders will be discussed in the next chapter.

Rothstein (1980), in trying to make sense of the diagnostic category of the narcissistic personality disorder, goes along with Kohut up to a point. Elaborating on Kohut's ideas, he takes the position first of all that all people are narcissistic, which is obvious enough. He further agrees that a differentiation must be drawn between the investment of the libido in the self-representation and its investment in the object representation. For the former he sticks to the term *narcissistic personality disorder*; for the latter he suggests *suppliant personality disorder*.

As characteristics of the narcissistic personality disorder he enumerates: poor anxiety tolerance; poor frustration tolerance; poor impulse control; use of projection, denial, and splitting; imcomplete superego and ego ideal structuralization; disappointment in life; painful, often disorganizing affects; rage and defiance; fear of losing the self representation; separation seen as a fantasied act of self-destructive murder; latent homosexuality; refrains from seeking analytic help; presence of both oedipal and preoedipal conflicts; and the personality of the parents (particularly the mother) is the single most important factor in the genesis of the disorder.

In general, Rothstein's description fits in with that of others. E.g., Kernberg (1975) defines *borderline* as the patient who is neither typically neurotic nor typically psychotic and who shows further: typical symptomatic constellations; a typical constellation of defensive operations of the ego; a typical pathology of internalized object relationships; and characteristic genetic-dynamic features.

Several further comments are in order here. The definitions of *narcissistic disorder* and of *borderline* are not particularly different from the general definitions of neurotic personality structure given in psychoanalysis since its inception. The major differences lie in the addition of new theoretical insights, such as harsh introjects. The same pattern has been given different names by different investigators. This fact shows the weakness of current diagnostic categories; nor need it cause any surprise that the DSM-III of the American Psychiatric Association, the official diagnostic bible, has been revised about every ten years since its inception in 1917, nor that the new 1981 version is already under major revision.

A second point is even more important. If all people are narcissistic, as is clear, then at what point do we call a person a "narcissistic disorder"? Since it becomes a quantitative rather than a qualitative question, in agreement with Freud's fundamental continuum approach from the very beginning, where do we draw the line? None of the theoreticians involved has considered this crucial question seriously.

As a result of this confusion, that is, whether narcissism is healthy or pathological (and when), every author seems bent on giving his own definition of narcissism. Freud orginally defined narcissism as the libidinal complement to egoism (1953–1970, 14, chapters 1–3). Hartmann changed this to the libidinal cathexis of the self. Both statements are juggling with words, not clarifying concepts. Kohut's definition of narcissism (1971:26) is none too clear and was dropped in his later work. Stolorow (1975) defined narcissism as the structural cohesiveness, temporal stability, and positive affective coloring of the self-representation; this omits the negative aspect (self-hatred) and other features of narcissism, such as its connection with psychosis. Bach (1977) argued that the narcissistic state of consciousness is characterized by mood swings, which patients variously describe as feeling manic, depressed up, or down, alive or dead, together or disorganized, excited or dull, interesting or boring, etc.: "Although patients may talk about these mood swings as either depressions or elations, they in fact bear a qualified resemblance to the classic cyclothymic states both descriptively and dynamically, being characterized by limited duration and rapid vacillations, with relative maintenance of insight and the general integrity of the personality" (1977:224). This introduces an entirely new element, confusing narcissism with mood swings. Rothstein defines narcissism as a felt quality of perfection (1980:17). The idea of perfection, or narcissistic perfection, should encompass the libidinal concept primary narcissism, the object representational concept self-object duality, and Andreas-Salome's (1921) "deep identification with the totality." This overemphasizes the grandiose characteristic of some narcissistic experiences.

Surely one word cannot possibly have so many different connotations. The fact that every writer feels free to offer a new definition serves to show only that the term is too vague to have precise connotations. There is still no better definition than that found in the Moore-Fine glossary: narcissism is self-involvement.

Furthermore, the whole Freudian notion of primary narcissism (rephrased by Mahler as infantile autism) has come under severe attack from the infant researchers, and properly so. The image of the infant as "narcissistic" or living in a state of "narcissistic bliss" has to be abandoned (Lichtenberg 1981, 1983; Chiland 1982; Pine 1981).

Lichtenberg states:

> Our view of the newborn infant has accordingly changed from that of "blooming, buzzing confusion" or existing in an undifferentiated state or a *tabula rasa*, to one whose internal states and capacities for behavioral regulation are rather complex. From the documentation provided by the new research, the neonate emerges as much closer to the tiny replica of self that delights his parents than to the not yet psychologically meaningful tension-discharging organism that often has been postulated by classical analytic theory. (1981:35)

And Chiland, drawing on the newer information about the significance of the father from the earliest stages of life, maintains that a mother-child couple does not exist without a father somewhere: "Thus we may state that in the extreme there is no dyadic relationship" (1982:377). She concludes: "The concept of a purely dyadic relationship between infant and mother is now as unacceptable as the concept of a stage of normal autism" (1982:377).

In the early days Freud was concerned with the biologically determined stages of development, and his delineation of them in *Three Essays* (1905) remains a permanent contribution. The notion of a narcissistic stage (though it came later) fitted in with this kind of thinking. But it was not nearly as securely anchored as the other concepts, so it has been buffeted about interminably.

The work of the culturalists from the 1930s on and the body of clinical experience accumulated combined with more recent experimental work on the first few years of life (Greenspan and Pollock 1980; Lichtenberg 1983; Call, Galeson, and Tyson 1983; Field et al. 1982; Emde 1981) have led to the emergence of a different orientation. While there are biologically determined phases, what happens in them depends very heavily on the environment, particularly the parents, in the early years. Hence, the watchword has become *interaction*. From an astonishingly early period (and perhaps prenatally as well, the evidence is now accumulating) the child remodels itself in accordance with the responses it receives and then plays an increasingly active role in its growth. E.g., as early as the first postnatal day the infant has been found to move in precise synchrony with the articulated structure of adult speech (Condon and Sander 1974). Infants aged twelve to twenty-one days can consistently copy facial and manual gestures made by adults. Many researchers (Lichtenberg 1983) are now speculating that the infant is programmed to seek out stimulation and respond to it because it is needed for neural growth. Thus, e.g., the infant looks from an early stage. When his favorite stimuli are offered, rather than withdrawing into quiescence, the newborn will prolong his alert period.

Thus, the notion of narcissism, as far as the infant goes, has to be replaced by cognitive incapacity on the one hand and by the interactions with mother and other adults on the other. Freud failed to make this essential distinction, and almost none of the other theoreticians have done so. In using the adjective narcissistic, which becomes preferable to the noun narcissism (Schafer 1976), a distinction must be made between reactions that are cognitively inadequate and those that are more truly self-centered. The term narcissism can be retained with its original (and still best) meaning of self-involvement, not with any positive or negative connotation. The narcissistic individual, like any other, can be understood analytically wherever we choose to draw the line. When these considerations are kept in mind, much of the current argumentation about narcissism turns out to be a war of words.

Nor is it in any sense true that narcissism is the problem of our times; it is merely the concern of certain theoreticians of our times. In its more enduring connotation of the "self" (see chapter 3) it has always been close to the center of psychological theorizing. As has been shown before, three types of narcissism can be distinguished: the narcissism of the ruler, the narcissism of the psychotic, and the narcissism of the ordinary man. It is only in the past two centuries, when the ordinary man has become the focus of attention, that the theorizing of modern psychology and psychoanalysis could be tolerated.

In his paper Freud was caught between the Jungian notion of introversion and the Adlerian notion of social interest. Because of Freud's strange dislike of Adler, he tended to ignore the younger man's thought and to move closer to Jung. It was for this reason, as noted above, that he made many of the mistakes he did in the paper; prime among these is the misconceived notion of ego libido. Neither the self nor narcissism can be understood properly without reference to both the intrapsychic and the interpersonal, including the social. Thus, again, it is by a combination of Freudian and culturalist positions that we can arrive at the best approximation of the truth.

Identity and Identification

The concept of identity is indissolubly linked with the work of Erik Erikson. This concept occurs in Freud, but only in the sense of equality: thus, he speaks of perceptual identity in dreams ("Wahrnehmungsidentitaet"). Erikson brought it to the attention of Freudian analysts at much the same time as interest in the self was evoked, and the reactions were similar. Many were sharply critical of his work and placed him outside the bounds of "true" analytic theory, which was defined as the structural theory. This is both incorrect and unfair. Here too, as will be seen, the structural theory is inadequate and must be enlarged.

Before getting to identity, it is necessary to discuss *identification*, a concept that preoccupied Freud from the very beginning. For him identification always involved other people; i.e., identification was always identification with another person (Laplanche and Pontalis 1973: 205–208). In the early days Freud evoked it in connection with hysteria: "Identification is a highly important factor in the mechanism of hysterical symptoms. It enables patients to express in their symptoms not only their own experiences but those of a large number of other people; it enables them as it were, to suffer on behalf of a whole crowd of people and to act all the parts in a play single-handed (4:149)."

At another point he commented that the common element is a fantasy; e.g., the agoraphobic woman identifies unconsciously with a streetwalker, and her symptom is a defense against this identification and against the sexual wish that it presupposes. Lastly Freud noted at an early date that different identifications can exist side by side. Had his thought moved in that direction, he could have elaborated on the concept of introjection at an early date, since it is obviously implicit in the above remarks.

Later, after World War I, when he came to consider the ego in more detail, he placed great importance on identification. Here his main formula was that object cathexes regress to identifications; thus, in the oedipal period the cathexes of the parents are abandoned and identifications take their place.

In *Group Psychology* (1921) Freud distinguished between three modes of identification: the primal form of the emotional tie with the object; the regressive replacement for an abandoned object cathexis; and in the absence of any sexual cathexis of the other person the subject may still identify with him to the extent that they have some trait in common.

With the investigation of the oral stage, which began in the 1920s, various authors created distinctions, embodied in the terms *incorporations, introjection, internalization,* and *identification*; incorporation was assumed to be the most primitive. However, the clear differentiation between these various processes has always been a theoretical puzzle.

For most writers identification seems to pose no special problems. Thus, Meissner says:

> Identification is a process of internal organization and synthesis within the ego which is carried on essentially as a modelling and self-organizing process in which the object representation is left intact and no translation of object elements into the self-organization takes place. Thus, while incorporation and introjection can be understood as defensive measures and ways of dealing with the intolerable threat of separation from or loss of the object, in identification the object is left totally intact and distinct and its inherent separateness is not only tolerated but preserved. (1981a:53)

Nevertheless a few pages later (p. 59) Meissner says that "identification is a process of structure formation in the internal world of the psychic apparatus. . . . The process of identification provides one of the major mechanisms of ego development. Early in the course of development, the organization of the inner world is dominated by introjective processes, but identification nonetheless takes place in more or less partial and global ways." When he speaks of "identification with the introject" (1981a:63), the confusion is complete, and one rightly begins to suspect that the twistings of this abstruse metapsychology have lost touch with clinical realities. Here lies one of the dangers arising from Freud's exceedingly cumbersome theorizing in his later period; they are absent from the earlier work (before 1914).

On reexamining the material, it appears that Freud used identification in much the same way as introjection was used later. It was Ferenczi who introduced introjection in 1909 and Freud adopted it. The course of analytic history accentuated the importance of the concept; it did not create a novel situation.

The crucial question with introjection, as with identification, is whether the object world (the other person) is internalized as it is or through the distortions of the inner lens. Merely posing the question suggests the answer: both take place (see Freud's three types of identifications above). In many passages Klein writes as if the introjects were largely of the child's own fabrication, but she never clearly tackles the question of where they originate. As a matter of fact, the early criticism of Klein (e.g., Kernberg 1969) was that she made these introjects too internal, not allowing sufficiently for the effect of the parents and the external world. This was also the root of her historic argument with Anna Freud about the presence or absence of transference in child analysis: if the introjects are there early, as she maintained, then they can be released and transferences can take place and be analyzed; if not, Anna Freud was right and the external world plays the fundamental role, with little or no transference in child analysis.

Thus, again, the shift in language from identification, as in Freud's writings, to introjection, as in the contemporary literature, is primarily a shift in terminology rather than in conceptualization. The major question is: when and how does introjection take place? The process has been pushed back further and further. Thus, as noted above, infants twelve to twenty-one days of age can consistently copy the facial and manual gestures made by adults (Condon and Sander 1974); can we say then that they introject these adults? Had she been familiar with these data, Klein might well have said yes. But with our newer knowledge of the constant interaction process between mother and child (of which perhaps she had some notion in her cycle of introjection-projection-reintrojection-reprojection, etc.), the introjection begins shortly after birth, then the introject must move around a lot before it settles down to its definitive form. No doubt, with the burgeoning of infant research, the question will eventually be answered on an empirical rather than a theoretical basis. Nor can there be any doubt that the answers will vary from infant to infant; individual differences are great (Chess and Thomas 1977).

With the question of *identity*, however, a different problem arises. The term *identity* is used in two different ways, as equivalent to the self, "one's true identity" (what William James called the "self of selves") and as a significant atrribute of the self. In this latter sense identity is essentially an identification with a group: e.g., he is an American, or he is a businessman, or she is a housewife. Erikson seems to use it in both senses.

As noted before, Erikson's classic work on identity has been regarded as nonanalytic by many analytic authors because he does not fit it in neatly into the structural theory, which, since World War II, has become an essential dogma for any analyst who wishes to call himself Freudian. In spite of this rejection, his scheme of psychosocial development may be regarded as one of the fundamentals of psychoanalytic theory.

Erikson himself does not pay sufficient attention to the group aspect of the identity crisis and identity formation. Like many other Freudian authors, he regards individual development as more fundamental, even though Freud himself (*Group Psychology*, 1921) had commented that individual and social psychology are essentially the same. But the study of group psychology has never been actively pursued by analytic theoreticians in spite of Freud's excellent beginning in 1921. Mitscherlich (1971) has pointed out that because of this overemphasis on the individual, analysts have not been able to make any significant contribution to the psychology of large groups.

Nevertheless, the relationship of the individual to the group (community, society) has been extensively discussed in many disciplines. Freud's point that man is a horde animal, not a herd animal, has been confirmed over and over but has not been given sufficient weight in theoretical formulations. This is the weakness pointed out (cf. below) in works such as Jacobson's (1964) *The Self and the Object World*: while she pays careful attention to the development of the self, she has very little to say about the object world.

Again it becomes a matter of theoretical clarity and conceptualization. If everything emanates from the id, as Freud postulated in 1923, how can we possibly get to the group? Thus, the empirical question of what groups are about has been shunted to one side, in favor of the theoretical question of how identity can be fitted into the structural theory. Since no one has found a suitable way of doing so, identity has been ruled out of analytic theory, while group formation and behavior have been largely neglected by classical Freudians. For example, the term *identity* is not even found in many compendia, such as Laplanche and Pontalis (1967) or the *Psychiatric Glossary* (1975). Obviously such a state of affairs blocks empirical investigation in favor of a theoretical dogma and should not be allowed to continue.

Toward Theoretical Clarification

In order to reach theoretical clarification, it is necessary to reexamine Freud's original formulations in his 1914 paper. To arrive at the concept of ego libido, he uses the following argumentation:

> Patients of this kind (i.e., schizophrenics) display two fundamental characteristics: megalomania and diversion of their interest from the

> external world—from people and things. In consequence of the latter change, they become inaccessible to the influence of psychoanalysis and cannot be cured by our efforts. . . . A patient suffering from hysteria or obsessional neurosis . . . has by no means broken off his erotic relations to people and things. He still retains them in fantasy. . . . It is otherwise with the paraphrenic. He seems really to have withdrawn his libido from people and things in the external world, without replacing them by others in fantasy. . . .
>
> The question arises: What happens to the libido which has been withdrawn from external objects in schizophrenia? The megalomania characteristic of these states points the way. This megalomania has no doubt come into being at the expense of object-libido. The libido that has been withdrawn from the external world has been directed to the ego and thus gives rise to an attitude which may be called narcissism. . . .
>
> This extension of the libido theory . . . receives reinforcement from a third quarter, namely, from our observations and view on the mental life of children and primitive peoples. In the latter we find characteristics which, if they occurred singly, might be put down to megalomania. (14:74–75)

It is doubtful that one can find any comparable passage of Freud's in which there are so many errors. This statement is, of course, not made to disparage him. Rather, because of the undue weight attached to every word he wrote, the errors became the basis of the subsequent confusion.

First, the major characteristics of schizophrenics are not megalomania and withdrawal of interest. The latter is, of course, true, but megalomania is by no means a constant characteristic of the psychotic; many go to the opposite extreme and consider themselves "evil incarnate" (see Fine 1979b).

Furthermore, the withdrawal of interest is just a surface manifestation, as Freud actually said in earlier publications. In his 1896 paper on the defense neuropsychoses he wrote:

> One is therefore justified in saying that the ego has fended off the incompatible data through a flight into psychosis. The process by which this has been achieved once more eludes the subject's self-perception as it eludes psychologico-clinical analysis. . . . The ego breaks away from the incompatible idea, but the latter is inseparably connected with a piece of reality, so that, insofar as the ego achieves this result, it, too, has detached itself wholly or in part from reality. (3:59)

To explain the situation further, it is necessary to call attention to an error in descriptive psychiatry that prevailed until fairly recently. It was assumed by

Kraepelin, and those working in his framework, that the schizophrenic had no anxiety, in contrast to the neurotic. This dogma was so firmly established that if the patient displayed any sign of anxiety the conclusion was immediately drawn that he was not "really schizophrenic." As a result of persistent psychoanalytic investigation, it gradually became evident that exactly the opposite was true: that the schizophrenic experiences panic where the neurotic feels anxiety. In other words, the anxiety of the schizophrenic is so great that he cannot tolerate it and so escapes from reality in order to avoid it. Freud had virtually said so in the above passage, but then he forgot it and reverted to the more usual everyday psychiatry of Kraepelin and the man in the street: the schizophrenic has no anxiety about what he is doing. For some strange reason (perhaps brain damage), he has simply adopted another personality or moved off into another world. The notion that anxiety is at the root of *all* emotional disturbance, which was so fundamental for Freud and has since been confirmed by all observers, was put aside.

With regard to the megalomania, his explanation likewise falls wide of the mark in terms of present-day concepts. First, as mentioned, not all schizophrenics exhibit megalomaniac ideas; there are innumerable variations. Today we would say that the megalomania, when it occurs, is a defensive posture against the feelings of murderous threat and annihilation that assail the patient. It is, in our terms, the narcissism of the ruler: to avoid being a slave, he imagines himself a ruler.

> A literal example of this was seen in a patient in a mental hospital who said that he was the king of Siam. He dressed meticulously, and would come down to breakfast every morning to order his ministers and servants around. He would announce what was to be done that day, and would then retire to his chambers to spend time with his wives, since he knew that the king of Siam had a harem. As is usually the case, nothing could budge the man from his delusional system.

Further, the megalomania of primitive peoples, such as the omnipotence of thoughts Freud cites (described first in *Totem and Taboo*), is explained readily enough as part of the magical beliefs of those who are terrified by the world, whether primitives or children or psychotics or dreamers. Magic, too, is a defense against extreme danger, as, e.g., in primitive societies where there is no such thing as a natural cause of death. As soon as someone dies, various magical devices are invoked in order to take revenge or to ward off further threats of murder.

His statement that the schizophrenic cannot be cured by our efforts has also undergone considerable modification. In *Glossary of Psychoanalytic Terms*, Moore and Fine state:

> Originally it was felt that "no transference" relationship could develop in such cases because of the degree of narcissism; however, a more accurate description is that quite intense and distorted transferences (sometimes described as transference psychosis) develop which have to be handled and resolved with great care since they often represent the patient's initial and very tenuous efforts to reestablish a genuine object relationship with another human being. (1968:82)

Eventually it appeared that Freud's view that the schizophrenic was untreatable was primarily a personal reaction, a countertransference. In a letter to Hollos in 1928 he remarked: "I finally confessed to myself that . . . I do not like those patients, that they irritate me, that I find them foreign to me and to all that is human" (Frosch 1983:3). And finally he asked: "Is it the consequence of an ever increasing preference for the primacy of the intellect, the expression of animosity toward the id?" (Schur 1972:134). Thus, he was mainly annoyed by the psychotic's release of uncontrollable urges the normal individual has to restrain (e.g., incontinence).

Next, the notion that the schizophrenic does not replace the lost object by fantasies, like the hysteric, is contradicted by his own statements in the 1894 paper.

A young girl is jilted by a man whom she loves, and falls into a psychosis. Freud describes it as follows:

> When all the trains by which he could arrive had come and gone, she passed into a state of halluncinatory confusion: he had arrived, she heard his voice in the garden, she hurried down in her nightdress to receive him. From that time on, she lived for two months in a happy dream, whose content was that he was there, always at her side, and that everything was as it had been before . . . she was happy so long as she was left undisturbed. . . . This psychosis, which had been unintelligible at the time, was explained ten years later with the help of a hypnotic analysis (3:60)

In this passage he recognized that the psychotic girl has not given up the object; in fact, she remains fixed on it. As is known today, when the psychotic (or neurotic) does seem to give up the object and retreat to a fantasy, it is always the fantasy of some other object, ultimately the mother.

Finally, there is the question: what happens to the libido, which has been withdrawn from the external object in schizophrenia? No set answer can be given because the possibilities are so numerous. It may be transformed into hatred; it may be punished by the superego and experienced as constant anxiety or terror; it may be projected to other people, as in paranoid fantasies; it may be denied; it may be split off, etc. Freud's own explanation that the libido is focused on the ego, which then creates the megalomania, is not a dynamic explanation that would carry any weight today.

How then are we to explain the dynamic characteristics of schizophrenia in terms of the first (1905) libido theory? At that time (1914) he still had not penetrated into the oral stage, he still saw aggression largely as a result of frustration, and he was not familiar with many of the ego mechanisms that are common currency today (the psychotic defenses). Still, as he himself observed just a few years later, the essential explanation runs along the same lines as in neurosis.

Although there is still much that is unclear about schizophrenia and other psychoses, and even analysts differ considerably among themselves in many important particulars (Frosch 1983), there is ample reason to believe that the original libido theory is sufficient to explain the major phenomena of the psychoses. Such a point of view is most clearly set forth on the current scene by Arlow and Brenner (1969). They describe the differences between the psychoses and the neuroses in the following terms:

1. In the psychoses, instinctual regression tends to be more severe and more pronounced than in neuroses. Prephallic fixations and conflicts over derivatives of these drives are particularly prominent. This, however, does not preclude the fact that typical phallic conflicts may play an important role in the psychoses.

2. In the psychoses, conflicts over aggressive impulses are more intense and more frequent than in the neuroses. Because of these impulses, the patient has a special need to protect the object from his own aggression. As a result, serious disruption in the patient's relationship with external objects and the environment are likely to be prominent.

3. In the psychoses, disturbances of ego and superego functioning are much more severe than in the neuroses. This is perhaps the most important distinguishing feature of the psychopathology of the psychoses. The disturbances of ego and superego functioning may be due to faulty endowment, maldevelopment, or regressive deterioration as a consequence of conflict (Arlow and Brenner 1969:10).

In one of his later papers (1924) Freud stated that "the aetiology common to the onset of a psychoneurosis and of a psychosis always remains the same"

(19:151). Although he offers his famous formula that neurosis results from a conflict between the ego and the id, while psychosis is the analogous outcome of a similar disturbance in the relations between the ego and the external world, he adds to this statement: "There are certainly good grounds for being suspicious of such simple solutions of a problem" (p. 149). On the next page he states: "The ego has come into conflict with the id in the service of the superego and of reality, and this is the state of affairs in every transference neurosis" (p. 150). Subsequent research (as Freud says earlier, we require "a profitable return from grey theory to the perpetual green of experience") has shown that the same thing is essentially true of the psychoses, or narcissistic neuroses; the difference is only one of degree.

But if the difference is only one of degree, then the far-reaching changes in the libido theory introduced in 1914 were totally unnecessary. He could have let the 1905 theory stand, added later the oral stage, the role of aggression (which becomes stronger when love is weaker) and also requires no new complex theory, such as that in *Beyond the Pleasure Principle* (1920), the superego and the self-image, the introjects (introjection-projection), and the role of culture, and we have a comprehensive modern theory of psychoanalysis without the tortured and convoluted theorems of the later metapsychology that have aroused so much controversy.

Thus, the problem of narcissism becomes a pseudoproblem, a large-scale war of words. All people are narcissistic; the difference is only one of degree. Naturally there are also differences in the manner in which the psyche handles the narcissism. The concept of a narcissistic personality disorder requires a quantitive element that is always lacking, and hence it should be discarded. The excessively narcissistic attitudes displayed by many people can easily be analyzed in terms of their libidinal stages and their past histories. In a sense Kohut recognized this when in his second book (1977) he switched from a prime concern with narcissism to a prime concern with the self.

Healthy and Pathological Narcissism

A more important distinction than that between the narcissistic individual and the nonnarcissistic (which is only one of degree, not of kind) is that between healthy and pathological narcissism. When can the narcissistic manifestations be said to be "healthy" and when can they be said to be "neurotic"? Federn (1929) had already directed attention to this topic, but as mentioned, his formulations were couched in such unusual language that they never won wide acceptance. In his first paper (1966) Kohut had indeed performed a service by pointing out that a certain amount of narcissism could be psychologically healthy, but his conceptualization of what narcissism could turn into ("forms and transformations") was wide of the mark. In the famous Kohut-Kernberg controversy Kohut insisted that the narcissism could be completely normal, while Kernberg stressed its pathological aspects. This argument has now passed into history with the recognition that both may be right. But a further clarification is needed (Ornstein 1974).

In order to make meaningful distinctions between healthy and pathological narcissism, it is first necessary to examine the vast body of empirical data that has accumulated since Freud originally wrote his paper in 1914. These data can be subsumed under two main headings: the narcissism of the schizophrenic and the data from infant observation

The Narcissism of the Schizophrenic

It has already been observed that the schizophrenic is not as narcissistic as he appears to be. Perhaps one reason that Freud accepted this trait of narcissism so readily is that in European psychiatry the term *schizophrenic* referred mainly to the most deteriorated patients, while in the United States, particularly under the impact of psychoanalysis, the designation has been considerably broadened.

Freud was not a hospital psychiatrist, as a result of which he had little access to hospitalized schizophrenics. After World War I, when hospital psychiatrists began to become familiar with the principles of psychoanalysis and tried to apply them to their patients, the first and major discovery was that the patients were not really as narcissistic as had been thought. For example, Federn wrote:

> It may sound paradoxical but is nevertheless in accordance with our theoretical knowledge when I assert that it is precisely in the case of the psychotic whose reason is impaired, that our treatment must address itself to his reason, in such measure as he retains it, and, similarly, that the transference is even more important than in a transference neurosis. (1934:210)

Federn had begun to treat schizophrenics as early as the 1900s, but few others did so. In the 1920s reports began to be more optimistic. Kempf, an early American pioneer, had reported a successful case in 1919. It may be noted here that the optimism of the American psychiatric scene in general has played a considerable role in the attitude toward schizophrenia. Waelder (1924) suggested that certain schizophrenic patients might benefit from psychoanalysis without gross modifications, and Brunswick (1928) supported this stand. Landauer (1924) wrote of this procedure in treating schizophrenics, stressing the beneficial results of passive techniques.

But the first great breakthrough in the treatment of schizophrenics came with Harry Stack Sullivan (1892–1949). Writing at a time when the attitude of psychiatrists toward the therapeutic amelioration of psychotics was one of almost total helplessness ("impenetrable narcissism"), Sullivan reported in 1931 on the more or less elaborate investigation from 1923 to 1930 of 250 young male schizophrenics seen at Sheppard and Enoch Pratt hospital near Baltimore. Of these, he chose 100 of the first 155 serial admissions for more careful statistical study, relating onset to outcome. In these 100 the onset was insidious in 22, acute in 78. He reported that 48, or somewhat over 61 percent, of those with acute onset showed marked improvement: "in a considerable number, the change has amounted to a recovery from the mental disorder" (Sullivan 1962).

Sullivan made a number of other statements relevant to our topic of narcissism. He stripped the concept of schizophrenia of the connotations of inevitable chronicity and deterioration, which virtually all psychiatrists of that day, following Kraepelin, had assumed, and insisted that recoveries are by no means infrequent. Although he used different language, he was essentially in agreement that the difference between the schizophrenic and the neurotic was only one of degree, not of kind, that the schizophrenic (cf. Arlow and Brenner above) essentially reacted with greater anxiety to situations of frustration and deprivation. In other words, rather than describe him as narcissistic, Sullivan saw the schizophrenic as highly vulnerable, or easily hurt by other people.

Another vital contribution that Sullivan made was that the illness itself was less important than the total interpersonal situation in which the patient found himself. In particular, the standard members of the medical profession were peculiarly unfit to treat schizophrenics. He wrote:

> The graduate of our medical schools, for somewhat different reasons, is so detached from a "natural" grasp on personality that it usually takes him from 12 to 18 months residence on the staff of an active mental hospital to crack his crust to such effect that he begins to learn "what it is all about." The graduate nurse, however, harassed as she is by upstart interns, inefficient physicians, utterly unmoral male personnel, etc., etc., seems usually too preoccupied ever to make this beginning. (1962:263–264)

In an earlier paper he had written:

> An improvement from seclusive, self-contained or pent-up attitude with lack of the ability to use available outlets for the expression of distressing content, to one in which the patient was relatively open and able frankly to discuss some of his life problems, was generally observed. Even in the group who came out of their psychosis with a decidedly paranoid adjustment to reality, there had been a change from an obviously ineffectual adaptation to one in which the social contacts of the individual caused him much less profound discomfort; emotional introversion and brooding gave way to the less individually destructive projection of discomfort and hate (1962:14)

The significance of this comment, as well as his special selection of ward personnel for the patients, is that the narcissism was now seen as part of a special relationship with some other person, which might not necessarily apply at all to a different person. In other words, it was not that the patient was narcissistic; rather he was simply afraid or reluctant to talk to Dr. X but was quite willing to talk to Dr. Y. This observation of the transference-countertransference dimension has since become standard information about the therapeutic process.

A striking instance of this limited communication is seen in a case described by Kubie and Israel (1955). The patient was a five-year-old girl confined to a hospital because she could not "talk." Kubie heard her saying faintly: "Say you're sorry." Accordingly, he gathered a number of professionals around a conference table, with the child at one end, and had everybody say "I'm sorry." A week later the allegedly mute child was talking.

From an opposite, but equally important, point of view, it had long been noted that ordinary hospitalization, where the patient is completely isolated from human beings with whom he can communicate, leads to a notable worsening of the condition. As a result, much of schizophrenia (and narcissism) has been relabeled *iatrogenic*. This is one of the many factors that has led to the discharge of most schizophrenic patients from hospitals (Talbott 1984).

But if the schizophrenic is not narcissistic, what is he? Here the work of Bowlby is relevant. During World War II Bowlby had an opportunity to observe many children in London who were removed from their mothers. The reactions to this separation he described in three steps: protest, despair, detachment. The final stage of detachment signifies that the child has given up all hope of ever seeing his mother again. A similar sequence can be ascribed to the schizophrenic.

He is in a state of detachment or, at best, despair about ever having meaningful relationships with other human beings.

Instead of narcissism, then, the schizophrenic is essentially in a state of despair. Life holds nothing for him, hence why should he talk, or wash himself, or even go to the toilet. Further, the sense of abandonment has made him furious, so that he wishes to destroy the world and everybody around him. With such unreasonable rages he is likewise unable to communicate, so again he falls back on himself. But here, too, the underlying problem is the sense of despair about life.

Thus, the surface narcissism covers up inner states of despair and rage. These states explain much of the symptomatology that surfaces. On the other hand, it is highly important to note that the narcissism is of the pathological type. As a matter of fact, it is usually difficult for the schizophrenic to be alone in any meaningful sense (Hartog, Audy, and Cohen 1980); his aloneness is a frightened retreat rather than a positive attempt to do something with his time.

Much has been made of the physiological concomitants of schizophrenia, but these have rarely been interpreted dynamically. E.g., the theory of excessive dopamine usually fails to consider the fact that excessive stress leads to a release of dopamine (Bellak 1979:61), so that even if the dopamine hypothesis were substantiated, which it has not yet been, it would still remain an open question whether the dopamine causes the schizophrenia or the schizophrenia causes the dopamine release. To discuss this topic further would take us too far afield. In any case, there is adequate basis for regarding much of schizophrenic symptomatology as psychogenic. E.g., Lippman et al. (1983) used pulse rate to assess the severity of psychosis: the more psychotic the patient, the higher his pulse rate. Since pulse rate is chiefly a manifestation of fear, it is clear that they were measuring the degree of fear. Upon discharge the schizophrenic patients had had their pulse rates markedly reduced.

Another line of evidence comes from therapeutic experiences with schizophrenics. Usually psychiatrists are unable to do much with them. One reason for this apparent untreatability is the alteration of extreme narcissism (withdrawal from the therapist) with outbursts of rage and despair (the underlying emotions). These become so difficult to manage that many therapists themselves become filled with rage and despair and simply give up. Those who do not are much more likely to succeed.

In another paper (Fine 1984) I have pointed to the analytic triad—the patient, the therapist, and the important other person in the patient's life. One thesis expounded there is that the transference of the schizophrenic becomes so intense that he has to be seen in a triad situation (i.e., with two transferences) in order to be helped. Many of the leading therapists who have treated schizophrenics have noted this, though without referring to the triad. E.g., Sullivan (Perry 1982) often saw the patient in the presence of someone else. Sperling advocated the simultaneous analysis of mother and disturbed child. Family therapy (McFarlane 1983) has often been successful with schizophrenics, precisely because the patient does not have to face the one-to-one situation with the therapist. Thus, here too the narcissistic vulnerability of the schizophrenic is so great that it can only be handled by having a third party present to act as a cushion.

Infant Development and Interaction

Another important line of evidence comes from the recent startling discoveries about very young children (Lichtenberg 1983). Here the newer material divides itself into three bodies of information: 1) the activity of the infant; 2) the infant-mother interaction; and 3) the infant-father interaction.

1. The older image of the neonate as a totally helpless creature has been completely exploded. Here are some typical findings (Lichtenberg 1983:18ff.): There is now substantial evidence of the existence of organizing, orienting, and controlling functions from birth on. The infant's sensory apparatus is far ahead of its motor apparatus, which explains why the first year of life involves organizing the sensory experiences, while increasing the capacity of the motor experiences.

Odors are identified as unpleasant prior to any training (Bower 1971). Newborns will turn their eyes correctly toward the source of a sound. When a breast pad is placed on either side of eight-day old neonates, one from the mother and one from another woman, the infants reliably smell the difference and turn toward the mother's pad (MacFarlane 1975). As early as the second week, infants will reach for an actual three-dimensionsal object rather than a photograph of the same object. On the fifth day numerous trial attempts were made before the thumb entered the mouth. By the tenth day, bringing the thumb to the mouth was a successfully executed pattern (Murphy 1973).

Newborns show appreciable ear-hand coordination. They will reach out to grasp objects they can hear but not see. This ability normally disappears at five or six months when vision takes over as the primary perceptual mode. The infant consistently shows diminished responsiveness to repetitions of visual, auditory, and painful stimulation (Bridger 1961). Infants respond in different ways to unpleasant stimuli. They seem to have some capacity for making time estimates, as indicated by their responses in social interactions, especially in the rises and falls in their excitement as the caretaker talks, sings, or clucks to them in various beats. Stern believes that the newborn is equipped with one method for timing intervals of less than half a second and another method for estimating social behaviors longer than half a second.

From birth, motor organization appears as a more or less coordinated unit. Brazelton's (1973) Neonatal Behavioral Assessment Scale measures flexion, extension, and smoothness of movement; ability to hold the head erect; amount of spontaneous and elicited motor activity; and intensity and rapidity of skin color changes both spontaneously and in relation to stimulation. The newborn can even perform a kind of "walking." If properly supported, a newborn will march along a flat surface. This ability normally disappears at about eight weeks, but it does not appear to be a random activity pattern, without significance. If an infant practices walking at the very early phase, the experience will accelerate the appearance of walking later (Bower 1976).

2. Ideally, from the beginning of life mother and infant are synchronized. Thus, with split-screen photography mother and infant can be observed to perform a repertoire of eye widening, mouth opening, and vocalizings with temporal gradients of speeding up and slowing down. These suggest an experience of "being with" rather than a "you and I." When a stranger attempts to introduce a similar response sequence, the fit is not likely to be as great (Lichtenberg 1983:58).

Still another set of behaviors can be observed in play intervals, the pattern of which involves establishing a causal sequence. Experiments show infants activating lights or recording of voices or mobiles by turning their heads, kicking, or sucking at certain rates. In these examples infants initiate a movement sequence of their own to cause a result perceptually outside themselves. Grasping, mouthing, sensory exploration, hitting, kicking, all are play activities that operate in a sequential mode, but at a different rhythm and with different coordinations than in the social exchange.

Of particular importance to our topic of infantile narcissism is the pattern of attachment and disengagement, which begins very early in life. For a few minutes infants who have been fed, when placed in their cribs, will play on their own. Increasingly it develops complex action patterns that lead to an increasing disengagement from the mother. Here lies one of the basic roots of narcissism—when the infant has all its major needs satisfied, it moves out to seek other stimuli. Justifiably this has been called by Furer the "love affair with the world." This love affair begins early and continues for a long time.

In order to facilitate this love affair with the world (which as will be seen is the origin of healthy narcissism), the mother must be "in tune" with the infant;

this has led to sudies of mother-infant attunement (Beebe and Sloate 1982). This capacity is based in large measure on the mother's ability to differentiate her child's needs from her own and maintain an appropriate level of stimulation and need satisfaction for her infant. The mother must not stimulate her infant too much, nor should she stimulate the infant too little. The "attunement' leads to an optimal kind of stimulation, which in turn is optimal for healthy growth.

So much for the ideal. What is the reality of mother-child interaction? If the mother is warm, empathic, in tune with the child, engages in reciprocally gratifying interactions, the child grows properly. But how vulnerable is the infant? Very vulnerable.

Beebe and Stern (1977) carried out a "visual violation" experiment in which the mother fixed her gaze above the infant's eyes, keeping her face expressionless and immobile. Infants will first attempt to recapture the mother's expected response by trying to meet her eyes, moving their hands and eyes, reaching with their arms, legs, indeed their entire bodies. When this is unsuccessful, the infants collapse into an attitude of withdrawal. The cycle of attempt at contact followed by collapse is then repeated, with increasing evidence of distress.

The psychoanalytic hypothesis that psychosis often derives from extremely frustrating situations with the mother is borne out by numerous clinical and experimental studies. Bleuler (1978), in his long-term study of schizophrenics, found that every one of them had had a "horrible" childhood, though he could not generalize about the kinds of horrors that they had gone through. Massie (1978), studying ten cases by home movies of the children, found that the interaction between mother and infant in these movie sequences followed one form or another of the protest-aversion behaviors described by Beebe and Stern (1977), including dodging, inhibition of responsiveness, and escape to the environment. In one case, when the mother tried to engage her baby, at times looming over the infant and tugging at him with increasing frustration, the four-month-old infant averted his eyes, ducked his head, moved his body back, turned, or pulled away. Increasingly this chase-and-dodge interaction resembled a fight, with the infant lapsing more and more into nonresponsiveness.

In the above case an experimenter was present who could pull the infant out of his nonresponsiveness. But ordinarily no such person is present. What then? The nonresponsiveness becomes internalized, and we have the roots of later neurosis and psychosis. Beebe and Stern summarize as follows:

> The model of what is internalized thus includes mutually regulated sequences of maternal-infant actions with a particular temporal patterning. It is important to note that since the infant is in a dyadic system in which

> the behaviors or action-schemes are potentially so intimately meshed with the mother's, one aspect of what becomes internalized in the first object-relation is a "time-frame of connectedness" or of mutual responsivity . . . .
>
> Although the "chase and dodge" interaction in itself . . . cannot be construed as pathological, if chase and dodge were heavily characteristic of the interaction, it might well have pathological implications . . . . It is interesting to speculate as to whether the organization or behaviors . . . - might be the earliest prerepresentational origins of the persecutory object. It is a mode of interaction in which the infant stays acutely tuned to the mother through peripheral visual monitoring, locked into the object relation temporally as he, at the same time, avoids her posturally and visually. (1977:53)

In this respect the older analytic literature in which the pathology of mother-child interactions was explored in greater depth and detail should not be ignored or forgotten. One thinks of Fromm-Reichmann's (following Sullivan) concept of the schizophrenogenic mother, of Levy's overprotective mother, of the ubiquitous "rejecting" mother in one form or another, of the abusive mother, of the phallic-narcissistic mother, and so on. In all these cases the child has great difficulty coping with the maternal hostility.

Even apart from clinical material, Senn and Hartford, studying eight "normal" families in New Haven who were having their first child, concluded with an apology for the pathology encountered:

> The readers, like the research team, may be concerned about the degree of neurotic and emotional problems seen in this random selection of normal Americans. In a way, it is a sad commentary on the emotional health of people generally and on the state of our society and its culture. On the other hand, equally impressive is the resilience and the effectiveness of psychological defense mechanisms which permit people not only to survive but even to rise above stressful circumstance. (1968:526)

Likewise, Brody and Axelrad (1978), in their normative study of average children, found a close correlation between the warmth in the mother-infant relationship and the child's intellectual development. This correlation was, however, obliterated in the oedipal period, where, evidently, the emotional turmoil is so great that every child simply passes through an emotional crisis (as Freud had once pointed out, though he erroneously limited himself to middle-class children). These investigators likewise single out neglect as one of the cardinal errors committed by parents whose unconscious (or conscious) hostility to the child is too great for them to manage:

> Were we to single out a cardinal contribution to unfavorable development in the child we should, with knowing simplification, name *neglect*. We mean neglect that, intentional or not, that appears in seemingly benign forms in *ignorance*—in an inability to recognize uneasiness, distress or age—inappropriate behavior in the child; in *intolerance*—in overhasty judgements of the child's motives, leading to erratic or excessive expectations of behavior, which are incongruent with the child's capacities; in *disinterest*—in a reluctance to repond or to act on behalf of the child's emotional states, curiosities, and other age-adequate needs; in *excessive indulgence*—in a failure to nourish the child's capacity for delay or for frustration tolerance; and in *carelessness* in a failure to protect the child from excessive stimulations, gratifications, and deprivations, from aggressive acts or libidinal seductions physical or psychic, or from threats of such experiences. (Brody and Axelrad 1978:553)

It may be asserted here that the recent research relates more to cognitive development than to the older issues of emotional interaction, although this too is included. But the older position that the infant, in its interactions with mother, responds with either love or hate remains unchanged, though necessarily made somewhat more complex. If the child has such a large repertoire of reactions, and if it is so vulnerable to the frustration of any of these reactions, then it is more likely to feel unloved, to become depressed, and to feel angry. That is, as Jones (1929) put it, the outcome of early childhood experience is a weak ego, which may then develop in a number of different directions.

For the present discussion there are several important conclusions to be drawn about narcissism. "Primary" narcissism in the sense of Freud's 1914 paper or Mahler's "autistic" stage is not found. Instead, what is found is first a love relationship with mother, which then is frustrated and moves in a variety of different ways. After a short time the development becomes so complex as to defy easy summarization, except for the generalization that a warm loving mother makes for a secure child, who then attaches and disengages in a positive narcissistic direction.

Then two types of narcissism can be distinguished: healthy narcissism, deriving from the disengagement with a loving mother and the clinging, anxiety-laden, reassurance-seeking narcissism, deriving from the overattachment to or disengagement from a hostile unloving mother. Naturally, innumerable mixtures of these two will be found. The first type is the healthy narcissist, the second the pathological one. This distinction is more fundamental than that between primary and secondary narcissism (Freud). It is also better established than Kohut's view of narcissism, developing along lines independent of object relationships, a view that psychoanalysts and psychoanalytic psychologists had long since rejected when it came from Jung.

3. To summarize the nature of the infant-father interaction is far more difficult than to summarize that of the infant-mother for the major reason that we are in the midst of a sociopsychological revoltuion with regard to men. Thus, when Spock published the edition of *Baby and Child Care* in 1946, he advised: "It doesn't make sense to have mothers go to work and have them pay other people to do a poorer job of bringing up their children." By 1976 he had reversed himself completely, writing that "both parents have an equal right to a career if they want one . . . and an equal obligation to share in the care of their children" (Lamb 1981:96–97).

It has long been facilely assumed that mothers are for obviously biological reasons much more important to their offspring than fathers. Even this assumption has to be questioned in the light of newer findings on males. Thus, Redican and Taub, after reviewing the empirical evidence on male parental care in monkeys and apes, sum up as follows:

> The range of behaviors directed toward immature conspecifics by nonhuman primate males is impressive. They have been observed to assist during the births of neonates; to premasticate food for infants; to carry, sleep with, groom and especially play with young; to defend young virtually without exception; to provide a refuge during periods of high emotional arousal; to interact with young in a quasi-didactic fashion; to promote motor development, to interrupt potentially destructive agonistic interactions among young; to become primary caretakers of orphaned infants; and to use infants in triadic interactions with other males. They may ultimately contribute to the infant's welfare less directly by defending a territory, the troop, or the mother from predators and conspecifics, and their frequent role as troop leaders may enhance the likelihood of infant survival in the long run. At the opposite extreme they may also threaten, attack, kill and eat infants, but the more severe of the behaviors have been documented relatively rarely. (Lamb 1981:242)

Thus, the old cliches about the inherently greater aggressiveness of males, their dominance, their wish to hurt, and the like all have to be given up. It has become obvious that in spite of the biological underpinnings the similarities among males and females are far greater than the differences and that the differences have been culturally determined. Since they are culturally done, they can also be culturally undone, the situation in which we now find ourselves (Fine 1986).

Research on neonates (Chiland 1982) shows that the neonate is aware of the difference between mother and father virtually from birth. Just as there is no such thing as a baby without a mother, there is no such thing as a mother-infant dyad without a father. The question is: how is the narcissism of the infant affected by the relationship with the father?

Again, going back to the material on schizophrenics, the overattachment to the mother may and should also be seen as the underattachment to father. In the developmental process the child remains excessively fixated on mother, either because the father is too threatening or unapproachable or because the mother keeps the child from father. Since the schizophrenic presents pathological narcissism, the inability to reach father is one powerful element in this orientation.

However, the cultural norm is still that of the mother taking care of the child while the father goes out to work. Hence, in the nature of things, the father will have less contact with the child than the mother. This lack of contact is frequently exacerbated by the desertion of the father from the family picture. Historically, this has generally been the case. Katz and Konner (1981), reviewing five primitive cultures of widely differing types, found that in 90 percent of the sample societies the mother was the "principal" or "almost exclusive" caretaker of infants. In only 4 percent of the sample cultures was a regular close relationship apparent between fathers and infants, and in only 9 percent between fathers and young children. It can also be taken for granted that the oedipus conflict is universal (Spiro 1982); only its details vary. Likewise the father-son relationship in most societies has been an occasion for the father to release a great deal of hostility against the growing boy, especially when he reaches puberty (Herdt 1982). In a few cases the initiation rituals for pubescent boys are so violent that some of them actually are killed (Tuzin 1982).

Thus, any generalizations made about the relationship to the father would have to be seen as guidelines for the future rather than as exact descriptions of the present. Using Mahler's separation-individuation framework, it is generally assumed today that relationships after the mother will follow a similar pattern: attachment, separation (hatching, practicing, rapprochement, and object constancy), followed by eventual independence and autonomy.

Herzog (1982) has suggested that there is a strong father hunger in children that, if ungratified, increases their aggressive drives, especially in boys between the ages of eighteen and sixty months. How the narcissism that the little child has built up in relation to the mother will fare in the subsequent relationship with father depends on many different factors, but particularly on how this father hunger is frustrated or gratified.

Summary: Healthy and Pathological Narcissism

The decisive question that theory and clinical observation must concern itself with is whether the narcissism of the child, which is a universal phenomenon, is healthy or pathological. Healthy narcissism is an outgrowth of a loving relationship with the mother. It begins with episodes of attachment and disengagement, when the "fuel" provided by the satisfying attachment to the mother serves to underwrite the child's forays into the outside world. By contrast, when the narcissism is pathological, it derives from an angry despairing relationship with the mother, in which all that the child wants is to be left alone or to regress and cling to her in a more infantile fashion. This is the kind of narcissism that Hermann (1936) described.

In all the neurotic (including psychotic) conditions the narcissism is pathological, though many times a secondary narcissism is set up and becomes automomous, which enables the individual to function in the real world. E.g., in the Schreber case, Schreber, in spite of his paranoid delusional system, was able to function as a judge. (It would be interesting to see what kinds of decisions he handed down.)

That secondary narcissism can be structuralized and function autonomously has been known for a long time. In some cases it can sustain the individual for a lifetime; most of the time, however, there are various degrees of neurotic disturbance. And not infrequently the narcissistic defense (Modell 1975) breaks down, and the person can no longer manage his life or manages it in a self-destructive way.

The relationship between narcissism and society will be considered in a later chapter. In this chapter my goal was simply to offer a conceptual clarification, since it is only by means of such clarifications that progress is made in the field of psychology.

CHAPTER 3
PSYCHOANALYTIC THEORY: THE SELF

The psychoanalytic theory of narcissism is too complex (and, as we have seen, too contradictory) to be made easily intelligible to either professional or lay readers. It is quite the opposite with the self. All cultures have recognized the existence of some entity such as the self and have woven various kinds of theories about it. As was seen in the historical introduction, for most of history up to the nineteenth century the self was often seen as a subordinate entity guiding the activities of the individual, and generally called the "soul." With the disappearance of the soul from scientific discourse, the question is again reopened: what is the self, and how does it relate to the remainder of the psyche?

Lyons (1978) confirmed that the concept of the self received an enormous impetus in the eighteenth and nineteenth centuries, though he does not connect this increased interest sufficiently with the political and social changes following the French Revolution. It became clear, both in German philosophy, with its Hegelian emphasis on self-consciousness and the subject-object dichotomy (which Freud took over), and in American philosophy, with its pragmatic emphasis on the self as the resultant of interpersonal interaction, that the self as a concept could no longer be disregarded. The individual had moved into the center of the stage, and how he viewed himself moved into the center of psychology.

For Wundt (Robinson 1982), with his predominantly materialistic orientation, the self-concept offered a mystery. It could not be approached experimentally, and its materialistic basis could not be ascertained. What then to say about it? For him, as for Hume, the self was nothing more than our awareness of the interconnections among our own experiences. He wrote:

> It is in this way that the concept of the self ("I") arises: a concept which, taken of itself, is completely contentless, but which, as a matter of fact,

> never comes into the field of introspection without the special determinations which give a content to it. Psychologically regarded, therefore, the self is not an idea among other ideas; it is not even a secondary characteristic, common to all or to the great majority of ideas; it is simply and solely the perception of the interconnection of internal experience which accompanies that experience itself. (1894, 15, section 6)

It would, however, be an injustice to Wundt to maintain that everything in psychology can be solved by experimental methods; on the contrary he was quite explicit that there were many areas of psychology where experimental methods were entirely inappropriate and unlikely to yield any real progress. These areas are generally what we call today the clinical-social field. In accordance with Dilthey and others in the German tradition, Wundt accepted the notions of two kinds of science, one explanatory (*Verstehende*), the other causative (*Erklaerende*). He wrote:

> fortunately for the science, there are other sources of objective psychological knowledge, which become accessible at the very point where the experimental method fails us. . . . The results of ethnic psychology constitute, at the same time, our chief source of information regarding the general psychology of the complex mental processes. In this way experimental psychology and ethnic psychology form the two principal determinants of scientific psychology at large. (*Ann. Rev. Psych.* 1979:13)

In spite of such explicit disclaimers, Wundt was generally interpreted as meaning that all psychological problems should be approached experimentally. Hence, his chief followers, the experimental psychologists, generally ignored the concept of the self until fairly recently, and even now they only approach it peripherally or, as will be seen, in terms of aspects of the self that are not of crucial importance.

Jung and His Concept of Introversion

Jung stressed introversion (narcissism) as an inherent trend in certain individuals; he even warned therapists not to try to change it when it existed.

He was the first within psychoanalysis to speak of the self. But what he said had more of a metaphysical and religious connotaion than a psychological one. He saw the self as the totality of all our psychic existence, a supraordinate concept. The self is our life's goal, for it is the most complete expression of that fateful combination we call individuality, the full flowering not only of the single individual but also of the group, in which each individual adds his portion to the whole. We can say nothing about the contents of the self; thus, Jung really still equated the self with the soul (as his later works make clear). The ego is the only content of the self that we do know. The individual ego senses itself as the object of an unknown and supraordinate subject. Thus, Jung should also be given credit for being the first to speak (though in a somewhat different sense) of the concept of self-actualization that has become so popular since World War II. However, his language is frequently so full of allegory and historical allusions that his meaning becomes unclear. Thus in 1935 he said:

> The city as a synonym for the self, for psychic totality, is an old and well-known image . . . . the city with the four gates symbolizes the idea of totality; it is the individual who possesses the four gates to the world, the four psychological functions, and so is contained in the self. The city with the four gates is his indestructible wholeness—consciousness and the unconscious united. (1935:137)

At another point, in *The Religious and Psychological Problems of Alchemy*, he wrote of the self as an archetype, "a term on the one hand definite enough to convey the essence of human wholeness and on the other hand indefinite enough to express the indescribable and indeterminable nature of this wholeness" (1938:448-449).

Adler and Social Interest

For Adler social interest was the strongest expression of health and lack of social interest the most prominent feature of neurosis. Thus, narcissism for him represented no problem: it was inherently bad. He used terms such as egocentricity and hypersensitivity.

However, Adler did not go on to make any special statement about the self. In part this had a linguistic basis, since as will be seen with Freud, the German word *Selbst* has connotations that are in many ways different from the English *self*. In part, it was his lack of interest in the self-absorbed. But for Adler it was already clear that a healthy family life could not produce a withdrawn narcissistic individual who, like the hero in the myth, spent his life looking at his own (or his sister's) reflection, and eventually drowned in it.

Freud's Concept of the Self

It is frequently held that Freud had no theory of the self, and subsequent writers who have introduced various conceptualizations have started from that premise. It is also often stated that the German word *Ich* can at times be indifferently translated as ego or as self. Even though authorities as learned as Hartmann and Kernberg have made this statement, specific evidence for it is lacking.

If we look at Freud's work directly, and its philosophical background, it becomes clear that the concept of ego (German "Ich") was of enormous philosophical import for him. The German concept of the self, on the other hand, Selbst, had no such philosophical connotations. Hence, it is understandable that Freud would concentrate on the Ich, the ego.

On the other hand, the German Selbst is used in a number of combinatorial phrases, as in English, such as self-analysis, self-observation, self-esteem, and the like. In the index to the German edition of Freud's works, which is more complete than the English index, the following headings for Selbst (self) are listed: self-analysis, self-reproaches, self-sacrifice, self-preservation wish, independence wish, self-control, self-observation, self-damage, self-punishment, self-consciousness, self-deception, self-destruction, self-exposure, self-maintenance, self-maintenance drive, self-knowledge, self-image, self-esteem (Strachey translates this term, *Selbstgefuehl*, as self-regard), self-adequacy, self-conversation, self-criticism, self-love, self-distrust, suicide (self-killing), attempted suicide, self-damage, self-overestimation, self-underestimation, self-betrayal, self-perception, self-destruction (certainly a formidable number of entries). In addition the reader is referred to headings under Ich.

Thus, one reason for the ever greater concern with self-psychology since World War II has been the simple fact that the major language of psychoanalysis has changed from German to English. It would be easy enough to show that before the immigration of many top analysts to the United States and England, the term *self* was rarely used by Freudian authors in an independent sense; afterward it became an important source of theoretical discussion.

A second major reason for the increased importance attached to the self-concept is that Freud really did not have a comprehensive notion of the self-system, in whatever sense that term is used toady. What he did have was a number of empirical observations on various aspects of the self, what James called the empirical self. In spite of his apparent naiveté, however, Freud should be credited with a notion of the self, the same kind of commonsense notion found in James and other writers. This meaning of self I shall call the Freudian self. It appears mostly, as in Freud, in hyphenated form. What comes out eventually, as will be seen, is that this apparently unsophisticated notion is one of the keys to the real meaning of self.

At this point it is appropriate to give some weight to the political feuds within psychoanalysis. When the center of psychoanalytic thought shifted from Europe to America, the large-scale battle between the Freudians and the culturalists assumed ever-increasing significance. In this battle the Freudians (as was seen before with narcissism) tried to understand everything within the explanatory framework of the structural theory (ego, id, superego), while the culturalists, following Sullivan, had a clear-cut approach to the self as a system. Nor could anyone blink the obvious observation that the self-concept was an exceedingly useful one, applicable not only to psychosis but to many other situations as well. The Freudian focus on the self (as on identity) then took the form of trying to fit it into the tripartite system. In this they were singularly unsuccessful, which eventually led to Kohut's formulations and to other seemingly deviant approaches. Even today, a leading exponent of the Freudian tripartite approach, like Brenner (1982), does not list self in the index to his most recent book, as though it were not really a major part of analytic theory. The battle then has become one between those who wish to explain the self in terms of ego-id-superego and those who do not. Where this has led we shall see.

Roheim's Clarification of Animism

A very important publication in the Freudian literature on the self has been almost completely neglected: Roheim's (1921a) paper published in *Imago*. In view of Roheim's extraordinary erudition and the presence of this paper in one of the major psychoanalytic publications, it is little short of astounding that it is never mentioned. It is listed in the bibliography to Fenichel's (1945) work *The Psychoanalytic Theory of Neurosis*, but so far as I have been able to discover Fenichel does not refer to it in the body of the text. Because this paper is virtually unknown, and because it has a great deal of valuable material, even though it was based on what was known in 1921, I shall summarize the major points.

The article runs to 166 pages, thus a true monograph, though it was never published independently. It is divided into four parts: The magical meaning of the human body; the essence of things; eidolon; and the outer soul. As usual in German-language publications of such a scholarly nature, it is subtitled: a preliminary communication.

The Magical Meaning of the Human Body

Roheim begins with the question: can the magico-religious actions and ideas of primitives be given some adequate explanation in terms of the libido theory? Although this question, which was so central to the thinking of the early analysts, especially after the publication of *Totem and Taboo* in 1913, was often raised, the problem still remains. It cannot be shifted to a theoretical "systems approach" or "functional anthropology"; data are presented, and they call for clarification.

Roheim considers each libidinal drive in turn, beginning of course with the oral. He notes that sucking is constitutionally determined, that the infant sometimes sucks until three, four, or even five years of age. The mother, he notes, does not want to give up the pleasure.

As a result of the continuation of the oral drive, the saliva acquires a magical meaning, as well as its derivatives. This magical meaning involves the power to project the libidinal impulses into the supernatural.

Other aspects of the drive are taken up, with instances from numerous cultures. Breath-magic, magic or oral utterings, singing, food, and even pregnancy may regress to oral eroticism.

For the anal zone there are relatively few instances of magic. In one, burning the feces of another person represents destruction magic. In skin eroticism tattooing scares off bad spirits, while jewelry represents projections of the erogenous zones into the outer world. Likewise, blood, urine, semen, and other body parts acquire magical power and meaning. Thus, in New Guinea if you bury the hair of another person he will die.

Roheim's overall formula is: the magic of a body part is its erogeneity, its capacity to release pleasure, so that the magical power of the body parts is a projection of them to the supernatural.

The Essence of Things

In this section Roheim discusses the concept of the soul, which derives from the projections of the body parts. As Tylor had already put it: "The act of breathing so characteristic of the higher animals during life and coinciding so closely with life in its departure has been repeatedly identified with the soul or life itself"(Roheim 1921a:144)

Again the soul is interconnected with the magical meanings attached to the body parts. Thus, the Malay have an auxiliary spirit, which they call a Polong. They cut themselves in a finger once a week, so that the Polong can suck. In the same or similar ways all parts of the human body can become seats of the soul. The concept of a second ego, or self, can come out of the active and passive magical apperceptions of the body parts.

The formula here emerges (Roheim 1921a:159–160) : Everything that in vaguer form appears as "luck," "essence," magical power," in more precise terms becomes the "soul"; all of this is a transformation of libido. Thus, if the soul becomes attached to drops of blood, then it is an attachment to skin eroticism, if to body dirt, then to anal eroticism, if to food remnants of oral eroticism, etc.

The first glimmer of a unified personality now begins to shine through. The organ soul is organ pleasure, the body soul is the summation of the erogeneity of the erogenous zones. The unification of the partial instincts leads eventually to the image of a personality.

Eidolon

Eidolon is defined in the dictionary as an unsubstantial image, a phantom, or an ideal; Roheim uses it here in the sense of the first glimmer of the self, seen particularly in self-doubling, or the image of the double, which many anthropologists had described. The notion of a double, or likeness (eidolon), is a step in the liberation of the psychosexual libido from the body; it is also what we would call today a step in individuation. The double also guards against the threat of death, since the primitive so frequently assumes that the body may die but the double, the soul, will go on forever (Rank 1914).

This notion that the soul will go on forever is obviously extremely widespread; it lies at the base of the Indian theory of reincarnation and is present in many other religions as well. Among the Banjang a chief expressed the idea in this way: "I can see my soul every day, all I have to do is put myself against the sun, the shadow is my soul, it disappears with death, for as soon as one is dead he does not cast a shadow anymore" (Roheim 1921a:313).

Doubles and likenesses arise from the psychic act of self-observation. Roheim is pointing here to a phenomenon later described in the analytic literature as "mirroring"—e.g., Lacan's mirror stage, Kohut's mirror transference, or the actual experience of the child in looking at his reflection in the mirror (Amsterdam 1972). Kohut's concept of the self-object is another expression of this primitive mirroring experience.

The double is the origin of the self-image and is directly described that way among many cultures. E.g., the Mafulu say: every human being has "during life a mysterious ghostly self in addition to his bodily, visible and conscious self, and this ghostly self will on his death survive him as a ghost" (Roheim 1921a:313). One native, when he was shown a mirror, said he had seen the spirit world.

Roheim offers many examples of the mysterious and magical power attached to the double, the self, or the soul. Thus, he quotes Codrington: "The power of the spirit, vui, could lay hold on a man by a fragment of his food, the shadow being in a way another person of the man. But that the shadow was the soul was never thought." Roheim comments: not yet, but the road there has been set out. E.g., in Hawaii if the shadow of a common man falls on the chief, the common man must die. In Roheim's opinion the origin of the double lies in the striving of the libido toward the ego as object (1921a:339).

The primitive dualism is not only a contrast between body and soul but also a split in the soul part of the personality. His soul is he, but also something else, whose attachment to him he feels. Soul, libido, unconscious, infantile can all be equated (this follows one of Freud's formulas in the Schreber case). The size of the soul is often estimated to be that of the finger or has the shape of a finger, and the finger is a symbolic phallus. The formula he eventually arrives at is the following:

> From a comparison of phylo- and ontogenesis we reach the conclusion that the narcissistic-animistic developmental phase is a compromise between the libidinal drives attached to the partial instincts and the resistance. The summation of the libidinal drives (body soul), which arises because of the diffuse erotogeneity and is the basis of the sense of self (ichgefuehl) leads to the construction of a second non-corporeal ejected ego (eidolon, likeness-soul). These ejected ideas and feelings are easily attached to ideas that are objectively provided by the outside world, so that the person who is looking for his likeness finds it in shadows and in mirror-like images. Because the unconscious can be satisfied by substitute objects, man incorporates his hate and love in the crudely formed image and acts accordingly. But the real reason for every ejection is an inhibition, either outer or inner, An outer inhibition arises when, e.g., the enemy cannot be found, so that one has to be satisfied with the likeness. An inner inhibition would be the intrapsychic resistance which turns the positive libidinal strivings into negative ones as a result of psychic bipolarity. But it is this resitance that sets up the wall between conscious and unconscious. That which is ejected because it comes up against resistances is therefore the libidinal drives, but also the unconscious. The soul is the unconscious, the split of the world into bodily and spiritual arises from the split of the individual into conscious and unconscious and corresponds to the contrast

> between the reality principle (body-conscious) and pleasure principle (soul-unconscious). The endopsychically perceived manifestations of the unconscious in presentiments (Ahnungen) and dreams are therefore rightly regarded as expressions of the soul, the pleasure principle. As the pleasure principle the soul appears in the thumb-form (phallic symbol). Since the repressed consists of material from childhood, the soul has the form and speech of a child. Now we shall see how this duplication of the person relates to the outside world. Naturally the outside world must double itself to please the person. (1921a:347–348)

The External World

This section begins with a Peruvian saying: "all things in nature have a spiritual essence or counterpart." The Chuckchee say that "of such objects the Chukchee sometimes say that they are having a master but more often they call them having a voice implying that they are endowed with life, which, however, is not separable from them" (1921a:457). Since the doubling of external objects is available to the human, there are some cases in which the invisible living essence of an object offers itself to a person as his guardian (1921a:458).

The first manner in which the person grasps the external world is certainly an attempt at devaluation, since he has the world of his animistic wishes to which he gives preference over reality. But he has to maintain his interest in the external world, which stands for reality, so he introjects a part of it, usually an animal. Thus, he has an external soul (the man in the animal), and an internal soul (the animal in the man), the animal usually or often being seen as still alive. This also leads to various doctrines of metamorphosis.

The key to these metamorphoses lies in the objectification of the inner capacity for transformation of the varying dominance of particular psychic complexes. Eventually the external soul and the animal in man can be traced back to the fetus in the womb.

However, the decisive event for the definition of the ego occurs in puberty. Ego libido becomes sexual libido, following sexual object choice. The parallel between libido theory and animism is reinforced by the observation that the choice of a guardian spirit or an external soul is a puberty rite.

Coming back to his main question, whether the libido theory (as formulated by Freud in 1914 in the paper on Narcissism) corresponds to the ethnological material, Roheim offers the following answer (1921a:502):

The autoeroetic phase with its erogenous zones and libidinal cathexes of the body corresponds to the active and passive magical meaning of these erogenous zones. The magical meaning is erogeneity, the summation of the partial instincts is the soul. The self-duplication of the narcissistic phase corresponds to the ejection of the drives ejected in an eidolon, the soul liberted from the likeness of the man. In this way the duplication of the world in body and soul arises. This is nothing more than the objectification of an inner split between the pleasure principle and the reality principal. The third step, object choice, corresponds a) according to the narcissistic type, to the projection of the personality into a guardian spirit and external soul and the introjection of part of the external world in the complex "animal in man"; b) according to the anaclitic type, to the rediscovery of the father-imago in the guardian spirit and the search for the projection of the external soul in the mother (tree, etc.). However, psychic development is a continuum, and behind all the ideas we find one driving force of the pairs of opposites pleasure-unpleasure.

While Roheim's brand of id psychology is no longer popular, either among psychoanalysts or among anthropologists, his unusually extensive discussion of the topic of the genesis of the self should be regarded as an important, if overlooked, contribution to the topic. We are not concerned here with the accuracy or inaccuracy of his anthropological field data or with the position that current anthropologists have taken toward this kind of interpretation. Harris (1968) dismisses magic, religion, and myth with a few sentences, viewing everything as fitting within a certain social system. This can explain some customs but fails to explain others (Fortes 1977). Acutally most of Roheim's material has simply been disregarded because it does not fit in with the Zeitgeist. Yet his fundamental assertion that "totemism is the belief in the existence of a specific magico-religious connection between a human group and a natural species" (1921a:157) is one way of looking at the diverse findings regarding magic and religion, nor is there any compelling reason to believe that the alternative explanations, which are largely sociological, are more correct. The fact is that human beings do employ magic, especially in religion but also in ordinary life; the only question is to what degree. In any case, while the overemphasis in the Roheimian approach may lead to wild guesses, the underemphasis on it, which is so characteristic of the present scene, impoverishes the field of psychology. Today, when so much research on the early development of the self is going on, his views may be particularly relevant. Just as Klein's delineation of the early mental life of children was at first dismissed as too "speculative," only later to be embraced as a stroke of genius, the more careful study of the mechanisms of magic, projection, and introjection in primitive cultures à la Roheim could also prove extremely fruitful.

Sullivan and the Self-System

Sullivan, who was more familiar with the work of Cooley and Mead than that of Freud (Perry 1982), continued the thinking of these psychologists on the self-system. However, his great achievement lay in the demonstration that schizophrenics could be successfully treated by psychotherapy at a time when Kraepelin and others were saying that perhaps 70 percent of the schizophrenic patients in hospitals were incurable (Frosch 1983). To clarify his success in the treatment of schizophrenics, he evolved a different theory, which has been called the "interpersonal theory of psychiatry." In this theory the self-system plays a prominent role.

As with all investigators who have studied the schizophrenic, Sullivan's attention was drawn to the self-image because the patients so frequently developed psychotic identifications, losing all awareness of themselves as real persons. Some explanation was called for.

Sullivan argued that the schizophrenic condition came about through the dissociation of the self, which in turn was set off by the need to block off unacceptable impulses. Essentially, this sounds like Freud's repression of unbearable ideas. However, the self for Sullivan was more complex.

The essential elements in the self for Sullivan were experiences of praise and blame and the need to ward off anxiety. He put it as follows:

> The self dynamism is built up out of this experience of approbation and disapproval, of reward and punishment. The peculiarity of the self dynamism is that as it grows it functions, in accordance with its state of development, right from the start. As it develops, it becomes more and more related to a microscope in its function, Since the approbation of the important person is very valuable, since disapprobation denies satisfaction and gives anxiety, the self becomes extremely important. It permits a minute focus on those performaces of the child which are the causes of approbation and disapprobation, but, very much like a microscope, it interferes with noticing the rest of the world. When you are staring through your microscope you don't see much except what comes through that channel. So with the self dynamism. It has a tendency to focus attention on performances with the significant other person which get approbation or disfavor. And that peculiarity, closely connected with anxiety, persists thenceforth through life. It comes about that the self, that to which we refer when we say "I," is the only thing which has alertness, which notices what goes on, and, needless to say, notices what goes on in its own field. The rest of the personality gets long outside of awareness.

> Not only does the self become the custodian of awareness, but when anything spectacular happens that is not welcome to the self, not sympathetic to the self dynamism, anxiety appears, almost as if anxiety finally became the instrument by which the self maintained its isolation within the personality. . . .
>
> Not only does anxiety function to discipline attention, but it gradually restricts personal awareness. The facilitations and deprivations by the parents and significant others are the source of the material which is built into the self dynamism. (1939:20ff.)

Essentially, then, as this passage shows, Sullivan was equating the self with the superego. Although in theory he did not leave out the id (he called it the "dynamism of satisfaction"), in practice the effect was to focus on the parents and other people and thus to ignore the impulse life of the individual. Although he did set up a journal and a school, there can be little doubt that Sullivan was not a sufficiently systematic thinker to replace the entire body of psychoanalytic knowledge that has been so carefully assembled over the years.

However, many of his ideas are sufficiently novel and penetrating that they have had a wide influence. E.g., his concept of participant observation to describe the therapeutic situation could be, if properly employed, a means of eliciting both transference and countertransference material. His emphasis on interpersonal relations, although in itself largely a reformulation of Freudian hypotheses, called attention to some aspects of the personality that were otherwise neglected. And his emphasis on the self continued the fruitful American tradition, deepened this tradition with a notion similar to the unconscious ("dissociation"), and could have saved a lot of time and energy if it had been applied more directly when it was offered. On the whole, however, these and other ideas have to be incorporated into the mainstream psychoanalytic tradition rather than set up as a "system" in their own right.

The Self and the Tripartite Structure—Hartmann, Jacobsen, et al.

Hartmann (1946 on) pointed out that in analysis a clear distinction between ego, self, and personality was not always made. Hartmann also made clear that in ego psychology there has been a "near complete neglect in psychoanalysis of that important chapter of psychology," referring to narcissism and the self (1964:286).

But his own efforts to clarify the situation did not lead far. He saw the self as the person, or the whole person, the traditional statement. His view that narcissism is the "libidinal cathexis of the self" is, as pointed out above, a tautology.

A major reason for the confusion in this area lies in the injection of politics into the scientific discourse. The American school, in which Sullivan was then most prominent, had always discussed the self and the self-image but had not tied it up with drive theory. Yet the concept of the self, and later identity, were clearly relevant, important, and explanatory. The problem then became not one of understanding the concepts and the empirical data better but the more political one of fitting these new concepts and the new data into the tripartite structure. Yet, as has been seen over and over, it simply cannot be done. The result, I shall argue later, is to set up a broader theoretical position in which ego, id, and superego are not the only factors to be weighted. But anybody who tried that in the 1940s and 1950s committed political suicide. So the discussion hinged around a very narrow range.

The ambivalence about the concept of the self is illustrated in a remark by Dr. Wolf at a panel meeting of the American Psychoanalytic Association in 1979. There he opened with the remarkable statement that this was the first panel on the psychology of the self ever held at a meeting of the American (*JAPA* 1981:29), thus disregarding years of thought and work on the topic. It is clear that a good part of the problem lies in using the self-concept as a base from which to establish a theoretical position rather than as a method of exploring the concept and its ramifications.

Before the 1970s the most comprehensive Freudian approach to the topic of the self was to be found in Jacobson's *The Self and the Object World* (1964). Tuttman says of this book:

> Here was the first attempt to trace within a strictly psychoanalytic framework the development of the self—a term introduced into psychoanalysis by Hartmann (1950) to signify the whole person as a subject in contrast to the surrounding world of objects . . . . It is my belief that Edith Jacobson's contribution is the most encompassing and integrative work dealing with human development within the context of modern ego psychology. (1981:81–100)

It is of course absurd to state that Hartmann introduced the concept of the self in 1950; it had been there long before. Even in the strictly Freudian corpus, as we have shown, it was extensively discussed by Freud and given a special place in his 1914 paper.

Kernberg states: "I believe that the most important contribution of Edith Jacobson to psychoanalysis is her development of a comprehensive, developmental and psychostructural model that includes an integrated object relations theory, a sophisticated model that provides a clearly circumscribed, yet broad frame of reference for psychopathology and normal development" (1981:103).

This statement likewise has a strong partisan ring. As I shall show, Jacobson's book is not so novel; rather it is an attempt to fit the new psychology of the self into the older and then more dominant ego psychology, in other words to show how it articulates with the tripartite structure.

Jacobson's definition of the self reads as follows:

> The term "self," which was introduced by Hartmann (1950), will, in agreement with him, be employed as referring to the whole person of an individual, including his body and body parts as well as his psychic organization and its parts. As the title of this volume indicates, the "self" is an auxiliary-descriptive term, which points to the person as subject in distinction from the surrounding world of objects. (1964:6)

Tuttman presents her work under the categories of drive-energetic factors, structural concepts, and their reciprocal impact on the development of object relations. The most speculative and hypothetical areas of her project deal with the neonatal state (she does not consider the research material available at that time).

Then, basing herself on the mother-infant dyad, she describes a series of processes and stages in answer to the question: how does development progress from the primitive, infantile amorphous matrix in which self and object are fused to the transitional, reversibly fluid boundary state of beginning ego and superego identifications of the self as distinct from other and the emergence of a coherent, ongoing sense of self delineated and apart from an awareness of others. As the second year of life begins, there are signs of a gradual transition toward individuation and ego autonomy. Vital factors are the concept of a future and the developing ability to distinguish and compare single features of objects and self. She stresses the critical role of parental influence in stimulating the growth of the ego (but does not discuss it in any detail).

She describes the formation of a sense of sexual identity, a most significant component of personal identity (this has since been formulated as gender identity, see below). She then makes the surprising statement that "identity formation and the feelings of personal identity are not quite as dependent upon the heterosexual position as one might imagine" (1964:73).

In her description of the superego, often considered the most valuable part of her work, she credits the mature autonomous superego with many functions: signaling fears; expressing self-critical and self-rewarding effects; guiding and enforcing principles and demands; motivation via guilt feelings; modifying the ego's cathectic conditions and discharge processes; influencing self-esteem stabilization by regulating narcissistic and object cathexes; and governing factors on behalf of mood regulation.

Although Jacobson's monogrph has been widely praised, subsequent discussions have shown that most of the problems connected with the self have remained unresolved. In a panel of the American Psychoanalytic Association held in 1972 (Marcus 1973) the chairman, E. James Anthony, commented that "the self had entered the analytic field and was there to stay, along with other elements of the system, such as identity." What he really meant was that the self and identity were important concepts that could no longer by neglected by Freudian theoreticians, but that it was not yet possible to incorporate them within the main body of the tripartite structure.

The most cogent critique of the concepts came from Schafer, who concluded that "self and identity express basic problems in Freudian theory" (Marcus 1973:159). Schafer enumerated several reasons why self and identity have become popular terms: First, there has always been a tendency toward personification of terms in Freudian theorizing. Second, ego psychology brought the concept of representation to new prominence. third, there was need for a concept that would serve two purposes: it would stand for the adaptive, executive undriven regulation of one's being and yet not reintroduce the personified ego. Fourth, there was a readiness to accept and use theoretical concepts that seemed to be closer to actual experience and actual clinical work. Finally, a number of prominent analysts have tried to introduce self and identity concepts into traditional metapsychology (Jacobson, Kohut). But Schafer felt that they would be in a better position if they began speaking of self or identity as a structure, as a dynamic or forceful psychic organization, and as a determinant of behavior, fantasy, and feeling. Schafer's negative reaction was counterbalanced by the partial acceptance by Spiegel and the full acceptance by Furman in terms of integration of the self-concept into classical theory.

Thus, there was exhibited neither clarity nor unity about the self-concept, and again it became manifest that what was at stake was not so much the self-concept as such but how to integrate it into the traditional structural theory.

In his review of Jacobson's book Searles made two critical comments. First, he said that her insights, though highly creative, were expressed through a Procrustean bed of technical jargon. Her book is in fact almost devoid of clinical material, so that in many passages one is not sure what the clinical referents are. Second, Searles felt that she showed an essentially fearful attitude toward symbiosis. In this sense she misses the constant battle against a clear identity and a cohesive self that goes on throughout the child's life. he says: "Probably the greatest reason why we tend to rebel against our developing identity is because we feel it to have come between, and to be becoming increasingly between, ourself and the mother with whom we once shared a world-embracing oneness" (1965:531).

Menaker (1960) made a somewhat similar point, seeing the self-image as a defense and as a resistance.

But the greatest weakness of Jacobson's work is really that only half of the picture is seen. The title is *The Self and the Object World*. While she says a lot about the self, she says almost nothing about the object world. The term *object world* is in itself misleading, since what is meant is other people; thus, it should be interpersonal world, but this terminology was avoided for obvious political reasons, that is, to reassert the differences between the Freudians and the culturalists. Yet, as has been seen, ever since the concept of the self had come under discussion, it had been noted that self implied other people and that the self could only be understood in its social context. Thus, again, the true synthesis that we are looking for is synthesis of the Freudian theory of the drives, the intrapsychic, with the culturalist theory of human relations, the interpersonal.

Kohut's Theory of the Self

Aware of the failure of other theoreticians to fit the self-concept into the structural theory, Kohut was clever enough to abandon the attempt altogether and instead try to build a new psychology of the self with little or no reference to the older concepts. He wrote: "Having thus shed the ballast of taking into consideration the various concepts and theories used by other researchers, I trust that my own viewpoint will emerge clearly in the present work" (1977:xxi).

In addition to claiming a new psychology of the self, Kohut goes so far as to maintain that he is revolutionizing all of psychoanalysis. He writes: "the psychology of the self . . . shifts our basic outlook to such an extent that we can no longer speak of psychoanalysis, but must, however reluctantly, admit that we are now dealing with a new science" (1977:208).

Since Kohut's formulations have aroused such a strong reaction, both pro and con, his views on the nature of the self require closer examination.

First, Kohut admits that he cannot offer a more exact definition of the self. He writes:

> Let me in this context refer in particular to a feature of the present work that might appear to some as a serious defect. My investigation contains hundreds of pages dealing with the psychology of the self—yet it never explains how the essence of the self should be defined. The self . . . is not knowable in its essence. . . . Demands for an exact definition of the nature of the self disregard the fact that the "self" is not a concept of abstract science, but a generalization derived from empirical data. (1977:310–311)

This position is strange indeed. Why is the self not knowable in its essence, any more than ego, or superego, or anxiety, or any other concept? And even granted that it is only a generalization derived from empirical data (which is true of all scientific concepts), then why is it imposssible to define this generalization more clearly? Kohut after all is talking about the empirical self, as William James had described it a hundred years earlier. If pressed for a definition, he would have had to agree with the standard one that the self is the sum total of everything I call mine.

In his classification of the primary disturbances of the self, Kohut includes five psychopathological entities: the psychoses; borderline states; the schizoid and paranoid personalities; the narcissistic personality disorders; and the narcissistic behavior disorders. He then maintains that only the last two are in principle analyzable. As a rationale for this statement, he claims that only in the last two does the diseased self enter into limited transference amalgamations with the self-object analyst—the working through activities concerning these transferences constitute for him the very center of the analytic process (Kohut 1984).

With this classification, somewhat gross and not entirely novel, Kohut disregards a great deal of psychoanalytic history. First, he reverts to Freud's 1914 distinction of the transference neuroses vs. the narcissistic neuroses, with the peculiar twist that the narcissistic neuroses are considered to have workable transferences. Freud's qualification that there is no essential distinction between the transference and the narcissistic neuroses is disregarded, as is the work of thousands of devoted analysts who through the years treated and helped all kinds of patients, including severe psychotics (Frosch 1983). Further, his claim that the narcissistic behavior disorders, under which he includes perversion, delinquency, and addiction, are in principle analyzable because they form workable transferences flies in the face of all analytic experience. These conditions (perversion, delinquency, and addiction) are precisely those that are most refractory to analytic help; e.g., every analyst knows that drug addiction is extraordinarily difficult to treat by analytic means, if not entirely untreatable without some form of behavioral manipulation.

The two most original concepts introduced by Kohut are the self-object and the bipolar self. The self—object is defined as "objects which are themselves experienced as part of the self" (1971:xiv). Here he reverts to Freud's confusion between lack of emotional development (as in the infant) and cognitive inadequacy, the same confusion noted about Freud's notion of primary narcissism and Mahler's notion of the autistic stage. He does not refer to Federn's perceptive delineation of ego boundaries nor to Klein's formulation of projective identification; his concept of self-object is similar to both.

He argues, as do many others in this tradition, that the small child invests other people narcissistically, i.e., as self-objects (1971:26–27). The expected control over such (self-object) others is then closer to the concept of the control a grown-up expects to have over his own body and mind than to the concept of the control he expects to have over others. Here he disregards the traditional Kleinian material on the powerful emotional cathexes of the infant, which lead to a circle of introjection and projection, as well as the more recent infant-observational material already touched upon before. The confusion between self and others, or between subject and object, goes back to Freud's differentiation of ego libido from object libido, which in turn goes back to Hegel's notion of alienation resulting from the fact that the ego is both subject and object to itself. It is again a juggling with words rather than a clear observation of the clinical or developmental realities.

Toward a definition of the bipolar self Kohut says the following:

> the child has two changes as it moves toward the consolidation of the self—self disturbances of pathological degree result only from the failure of both of these developmental opportunities.
>
> The two changes relate, in gross approximation, to the establishment of the child's cohesive grandiose-exhibitionistic self . . . on the one hand, and to the establishment of the child's cohesive idealized parent-imago . . . on the other. The developmental move frequently proceeds . . . from the mother as a self-object . . . to the father as a self-object . . . exceptional circumstances in the environment may occasionally force a child to turn to his parents in the reverse order. . . .
>
> The definition of the bipolarity of the nuclear self and the correlated

> outline of its genesis is no more than a schema. Yet, although it is an abstraction . . . it permits the meaningful examination of the empirical material the psychoanalyst observes in his clinical work. (1977:183–184)

Thus, the bipolar self involves the relationship with both parents. Put this way, it hardly sounds novel at all; rather it has always been an essential aspect of psychoanalytic theory—only the words are new. In a panel discussion on the bipolar self in 1979, Kohut's protagonists and antagonists presented their positions. Ornstein, one of Kohut's foremost followers, presented the theory as entirely novel. Wallerstein, a skeptical conservative, wondered whether the new terminology was any better than the old, or whether it allowed us to do better work. At the end the conclusion was:

> In the main, there seemed to be agreement among all panelists of the importance of self-psychology and its ultimate need to be integrated into the main body of psychoanalysis. The main disagreement was whether the self should be viewed as a superordinate concept of the bipolar self, or whether the self should be viewed as a content of the mental apparatus. (Meyers 1981:158)

It is understandable that in such a framework of novel and dubious terminology that Kohut's views have come under sharp and extensive discussion. But instead of clarity there has ensued a strong polarization of views, with a division into warring camps, as has happened so often before in the history of psychoanalysis (Fine, 1979). In his review of *Advances in Self Psychology*, edited by Arnold Goldberg, Jacob Arlow states:

> At this late date, what more can one add to the already voluminous discussion of self psychology? Kohut's books have been widely read and intensively discussed. All the leading psychoanalytic journals have published articles by adherents as well as by critics of his views. The issues, theoretical and technical, have been weighed by some of our most distinguished colleagues. Recently, for example, an entire issue of the *Journal of the American Psychoanalytic Association* was devoted to the subject of the self. In it is a comprehensive and masterful summary by Rangell (pp. 863–891). Certainly no one can say that Kohut has been disregarded or that his ideas have not been given their day in court. . . . Self psychology espouses a very specific image of man which tends to evoke a sympathetic response . . . in those who emphasize in their concepts the subjective, creative, experiencing aspect of the psyche. (1983: 445–446)

In view of the fact that this issue of the *Journal of the American Psychoanalytic Association* (no. 4, 1982) sufficiently summarized the views about the self by a number of leading analysts, it is worth examining the papers critically and in detail.

The first paper, by Mahler and McDevitt, considers primarily the emergence of the sense of self in the first fifteen months of life. They begin by saying that "the development of the sense of self is an eminently personal internal experience that is difficult, if not impossible, to trace to its beginnings by observational studies or by reconstruction in psychoanalysis" (*JAPA* 1982 30:827). Then they go on to trace it through sensations from within the infant's body, especially by proprioception. The evidence for this view is not given. They agree that activity is the most important trigger of the developing sense of self; but if proprioceptive sensations are the chief source, how can activity be so important? The core of the self is the body self, which is also the core of our personal identity.

In this essay the authors are rather contradictory, since first they say that the sense of self cannot be traced, then they trace it. Furthermore, they made the error of assuming that the sense of self has to be laid down in earliest childhood. Like Jacobson and many other Freudian analysts, they largely disregard the effect of the surrounding world on the developing sense of self, this in the face of all the evidence and theorizing that the differentiation of self and object is intimately connected with the interpersonal world.

The second paper, by Ticho, deals with the alternate schools and the self. He correctly points out that if the alternate schools are studied, Kohut's notion of the self is not as new as it seems to be.

Ticho engages in the customary linguistic discussion of the translation of Ich and the use of the term self. He goes along with the fashionable myth that Freud used Ich ambiguously, this in the face of the fact that Ich is an ordinary German word, the word for I, and that it has a long psychological and philosophical history attached to it. He is, however, the only one that makes the correct observation that the alternate schools prefer the word self and that in German Selbst sounds awkward and is rarely used. In the current German literature, ironically, Selbst appears more and more frequently, a result of the fact that German literature contains many translations of papers from America and England. As Jespersen (1922) pointed out in his classic work on language more than sixty years ago, the conquered nation frequently takes on the language of the conqueror or changes its own language to suit the conqueror. (see Ernest Jones' 1920 discussion of English.)

While Ticho makes some trenchant comment about the alternate schools, he commits some of the customary errors found in the Freudian literature in his misunderstanding of their theories. Thus, he says that they are strongly opposed to theories that stress internal conflicts—this in the face of the fact that every one of their theories is a conflict theory. Horney even titled on of her books *Our Innter Conflicts*, while one of Fromm's best-known works is *Escape from Freedom*, i.e., the inner conflict about freedom. He also argues incorrectly that they all reject a dynamic unconscious. To some extent this was true of Adler and Jung, who never really grasped Freud fully, but it is certainly untrue of the later revisionists, all of whom were trained in the classical tradition. He is misled by their language. Too much of his commentary centers on Jung rather than on the current culturalist theories, which are much closer to the Freudian position.

The third paper, by Rangell, is the most critical of the Kohutian and other contemporary theories of the self. He is the only one to note that much of the current controversy derives from the splitting up of the analytic community into warring groups that propound their slogans without examining either the slogan or the empirical basis carefully. Rangell writes:

> What is to be noted most and is generally overlooked in a shift of this magnitude in theory and practice is the failure of the responding psychoanalytic public to judge these changes rationally and promptly. . . . This phenomenon will not be bypassed in this presentation. It is an observation made not as criticism or lament, but as a datum itself to be focussed upon and understood. Psychoanalysis studies affective distortions. I have recently turned my attention to distortions brought about by groups, and believe it is relevant to apply this thinking to psychoanalytic groups as well. (1982:864)

Rangell stresses throughout that the empirical basis of the various theories has never been carefully considered. Thus, quoting Kohut to the effect that "I could find no place (within classical mental-apparatus psychology) for the psychological activities that go by the name of choice, decision and free will—even though I knew that these were empirically observable phenomena" (Kohut 1977:244), Rangell points out that this comment is simply incorrect. These questions have repeatedly been discussed in the course of psychoanalytic history, either under the same rubric or under a different one. Thus, in the index to the first five volumes of Grinstein, covering the early history of psychoanalysis, there are at least twenty-five entries for these topics directly and a large number of others indirectly. Thus, the topic of will was generally handled under the rubric of compulsion or compulsive behavior.

Again and again Rangell returns to his major criticism that there is no rational discussion in this field, merely the flat assertion of contradictory opinions. Thus he says:

> To the multitude of questions that have been brought up, a main observation I wish to make is that a satisfactory discourse has not been engaged, rational in the sense of a resolution of conflicts, or of actions on the basis of arguments presented. No less deserving of attention is the gulf between any convincing demonstration of new data or more applicable theory and the group swell approaching cultist proportions clamoring for a new paradigm and feeling that it has found one. Extreme enthusiasm and extravagant claims continue as though nothing had been pointed out or opposed. This discrepancy, which is a datum in itself, is not disputed but is alluded to privately and jocularly, not publicly. . . . Social and cultural processes seem to accelerate with time; everything is more inflated now. (1982:870)

He shows in detail that the self concept per se is not new, that there is a search for some all-powerful authority figure, that neither the self nor narcissism has specifically been linked to early states. One of his conclusions is:

> Obscurity of language and imperviousness to criticism, which often accompany such theoretical systems, turn out not to elicit rational critique, but ironically and empirically, to enhance an image of invincibility and of a durability of self which is identified with and vicariously joined. . . . Whether in parts of this country or . . . in South America, audience responses demonstrated . . . "group think," mystical union, results by shock rather than by reason—in psychoanalysis no less than in social or poltical life or even art. (1982:884)

Otto Kernberg begins his discussion with the oft-quoted remarks that Freud's term Ich has been mistranslated, in that at times it means ego and at times it means self. This is untrue, since, as noted, Ich has a special place in German philosophy and psychology, which Selbst does not have. He notes that in the index to Freud's writings under the heading Selbst, it says "s. Ich" (see ego). He neglects to point out that (see above) there are a large number of entries under Selbst that have nothing to do with Ich or ego, and that likewise under Ich there are a large number of entries that have nothing to do with Selbst. All that the index indicates (as does the ordinary German dictionary—cf. Cassell, which translates Ich as ego or self) is that on some occasions Ich and Selbst may be used synonymously, but this is a far cry from saying that the two terms are commonly used in the same sense. Furthermore, he totally ignores the well-established historical fact that as long as Freud was alive, no one dreamed of translating Ich as self; this came only after Freud was dead, and after numerous alternate schools had analyzed the concept of the self exhaustively. Kernberg also ignores the linguistic differences between the German Selbst and the English self, which Ticho had pointed out, as well as the philosophical backgrounds from which the different schools derive.

It is entirely untrue that Freud was ambiguous about the meaning of Ich. It must almost always be translated as ego. If ego is a Latin word essentially and Ich is an ordinary German word, there is good and weighty reason for using ego in English rather than I. For example, in one passage that he quotes relating to the analytic pact in which the analyst makes a pact with the healthy part of the patient's ego to combat the sick part (*JAPA* 1982 30:894), the English construction in terms of ego reads very well; if the word I were introduced, it would be confusing to say, e.g., the "sick part of the I."

Furthermore, there is a perfectly good German word for self, and that is Selbst. Freud uses this word innumerable times, as indicated above, as do all others. Had he wished to say self, he would have used Selbst instead of Ich. The linguistic argument serves to obscure the political struggle pointed out by Ticho: all the revisionist schools did extensive work on the self-concept, with impressive results. The Freudian schools did not. In order to bring the self into Freudian theory, they then retrospectively began to speak of the double meaning of Ich, a fact that had never been mentioned before.

Coming to a direct discussion of the self, Kernberg then proposes to eliminate the use of the concept of self as opposed to object: "This concept of the self leads to psychosocial descriptions and to confusing psychoanalytic with sociological concepts, a confusion found, in, for example, some of Erikson's writings" (*JAPA* 1982, 30:898). Instead he proposes to reserve the term self for the sum total of self-representations in intimate connection with the sum total of object relations. What the sum total of self-representations is and what the sum total of object representations is is not readily intelligible either to a child or to an analyst. This is an example of the obscurity of language and imperviousness to criticism that Rangell describes (cf. above).

Kernberg sees the normal self as something that emerges naturally as the tripartite intraphysic structure is constructed and integrated. "From both clinical and theoretical viewpoints, we can thus define the self as an integrated structure that has affective and cognitive components, a structure embedded in the ego, but derived from forerunners of the ego—intrapsychic substructures that predate the integration of the tripartite structure" (*JAPA* 1982 30:914–915). Kernberg's most original contribution is his view that control over the self is maintained by repressed internalized object relations, libidinally and aggressively invested, that strive for reactivation through invasion of the self's intrapsychic and interpersonal field.

The crucial question in Kernberg's position is whether these internalized object relations derive from actual experience or from some genetic or other source. If they are derived from actual experience, his position does not differ from Kohut's or any other of dozens of mainstream psychoanalytic theoreticians. The self, in other words, derives from the internalization of what mother and father have done to the child, or more precisely, of how the child has interpreted what mother and father have done. But what the internalization is is never too far from what has happened.

A paper by William Grossman (*JAPA* 1982) entitled "The Self as Fantasy: Fantasy as Theory" views the self as a personal myth, in the sense in which Kris used it, a myth of which everyone has his own more or less original version. This engaging theory need not detain us further.

Arnold Richards (*JAPA* 1982) takes up the crucial question of the superordinate self in psychoanalysis and in the self-psychologies. He is opposed to the concept of a superordinate self, which he claims (and rightly) has played too great a role in the self-psychologies. Kohut's major contribution, he feels, has been clinical; he has sharpened our sensitivity to our patients' perceptions of what we say and how we say it, as well as our awareness of our patient's vulnerabilities.

Harold Blum (*JAPA* 1982) discusses these contributions. His conclusion stresses the same point that has been made here over and over again: the self-concept is an important one, but it has defied integration into the classical theory of the tripartite structure. He says:

> Insofar as "self-concept" is an abstraction, it remains ill-defined and itself subject to recurrent tendencies to reification as metapsychological concepts. However thoughtful, stimulating, and imaginative analytic concepts of the self (not to be confused with self-representation) have been, they have so far defied compatability with metapsychological assumptions and the

tripartite structural hypothesis; nor have they enlarged analytic exposition and explanation. (*JAPA* 1982 30:976)

Subsequent to Kohut's death, his work has been continued by a number of enthusiastic admirers. Their work is contained in a volume edited by Lichtenberg and Kaplan (1983) and in a posthumous book by Kohut (1984) on technique. No particularly novel insights are offered by these works, so that the theory of self-psychology, as Kohut formulated it, remains substantially in the same state in which he left it.

Thus, neither the attempt to coordinate the concept of the self with the structural theory nor the attempt to abandon classical Freudian theory altogether and strike out on an entirely novel line has met with any signal success. No one author or point of view has gained general recognition in the theory of the self. My thesis has been all along that to understand the self properly there must be a synthesis of the classical Freudian and culturalist points of view.

Developments in the Culturalist School

In spite of his emphasis on the self, Sullivan did not write too much about it. He described the self as the core of the personality but did not tie it up with the drives or other internal experiences. In schizophrenia he saw the self dissociated; in more normal behavior the self could expand or contract with praise or blame. His view that the self controls the anxiety experience seems to leave out the early anxieties, which have been so eloquently described by so many others. By and large, as noted, his view of the self is not far from the Freudian concept of the superego.

The formulations of Sullivan aroused a strong positive response among many psychologists, sociologists, and social psychologists, more so than among his psychoanalytic followers, who generally felt that he had discarded too much of Freud and classical psychoanalysis. For example, Arieti criticized Sullivan for viewing the self as a passive reflection of the parental appraisals. "The mechanism of the formation of the self cannot be compared to the function of a mirror" (1974:87). Arieti also stressed the importance of conceptual thinking; from adolescence on he thought that the image of the self will consist mostly of concepts. The image of the self varies through the life cycle. After several transformations in adolescence it consists of remnants of previous images, but predominantly of concepts. On the whole, however, Arieti did not have any fundamental disagreement with Sullivan.

Winnicott, who is generally classed with object relations theorists, added several important observations. One aspect of neurosis for him is the existence of a "false self." In the course of treatment the patient works through to a true self, which gives him a new sense of satisfaction and of the progress that meant true growth. As Roheim had pointed out (1932:103), some sense of the true (private) self and false (public) self is present even in the most primitive of men. As Winnicott put it:

> A principle might be enunciated, that in the False Self area of our analytic practice we find we make more headway by recognition of the patient's nonexistence than by a long—continued working with the patient on the basis of ego—defence mechanisms. The patient's False Self can collaborate indefinitely with the analyst in the analysis of defenses, being so to speak on the analyst's side in the game . . . recognitions of important fact, made clear at the right moments, pave the way for communication with the True Self. (1975:xv)

Of course, Winnicott was British and was trained as a classical analyst. If he is classed with object relations theorists, it is only because he reached conclusions similar to theirs. Thus, there is his famous remark that "there is no such thing as an infant, meaning, of course, that whenever one finds an infant one finds maternal care, and without maternal care there would be no infant" (1975:xxvii). In more formal language he was saying that there is always a mother-infant dyad. Today this is a truism; in 1940 it was a startling novelty. It is similar to Sullivan's phraseology of the "personified person I," referring to the fact that the individual builds up a fantasy of what he is really like.

Finally, in this context there is Winnicott's notion of the "holding environment," which has been particularly useful in understanding the therapeutic situation. This goes back to a positive mother-child relationship. As he puts it:

> Although many types of experience go to the establishment of the capacity to be alone, there is one that is basic, and without a sufficiency of it the capacity to be alone does not come about; *this experience is that of being alone as an infant and small child, in the presence of mother.* Thus the basis of the capacity to be alone is a paradox: it is the experience of being alone while someone else is present. (1975:xiv)

A similar pattern was described earlier in the section on narcissism: healthy narcissism starts as a series of attachments to mother, followed by disengagement when the child is (temporarily) free to do whatever he wants to do. Thus, the mother provides a holding environment that makes the child feel safe and secure, even though she may literally be doing nothing but being there.

In 1954 Ronald Fairbairn published *Object Relations Theory of Personality*. Ever since, this view, pursued by a number of British and American analysts, has been called the object relations theory of personality. Guntrip later became strongly identified with it and wrote the description of the school for the *American Handbook of Psychiatry (vol. 1, 1974)*. Guntrip also independently authored a number of other books expounding his views.

Guntrip explicitly identifies object relations theory with the interpersonal theory of Sullivan and the American culturalists, though there are certain differences. He claims that object relations theory "is the emancipation of Freud's psychodynamic personal thinking from its bondage to his natural-science, impersonal, intellectual heritage" (1973:20).

This brings us to the other side of the coin, the misunderstanding of Freud displayed by many of the culturalists. Guntrip writes:

> This [1908 paper] presented in an uncompromising way the classic psychoanalytical "Instinct Theory" that all our troubles are due to the repression of instincts, and that since sublimation (or diverting instinctive energies to socially approved goals) is so hard, most of us are doomed to be either neurotic or criminal, that is, antisocial. (1973:4)

Actually, in the paper that Guntrip refers to ("Civilized Sexual Morality and Modern Nervousness," 1908) Freud refers not to the instinct theory as such but to the sexual repression that was the hallmark of the times. Since then Freud's point that severe sexual repression leads to neurotic illness has been almost universally accepted, by the object-relations school as well. Furthermore, Guntrip, when he speaks of the libido theory, refers to the 1914 theory, not to the earlier 1905 one; like so many others, he does not realize that Freud changed theories. To throw out instinct theory altogether, as Guntrip seems to want to do (1973:34), is to deny the indisputable realities of biology.

Guntrip states that he does not regard object relations theory as a new school of psychoanalysis (1973:21). In contrast to the American culturalists, the British school also adopted Klein as their first great theoretician. This is a most remarkable switch. Klein, whom Bibring (1947) had already described as the originator of the British school of psychoanalysis, out-Freuded Freud in her glorification of instinct. Reading her works leaves the strong impression that people have nothing to do with the powerful internal currents that rage through the young infant: at best they can modify some of the reactions.

It thus becomes clearer that there is a personal quarrel going on between the object relations interpersonal school and the Freudian classical analytic view. The culturalists hammer away at Freud's instinct theory without understanding it or really quoting it properly (as Horney, e.g., had done in her 1937 book *New Ways in Psychoanalysis*), while the Freudians insist that the culturalists deny the dynamic unconscious and inner conflict.

Actually, each side has made certain important points. Instincts, however defined (and there is considerable redefinition going on, especially in the light of the advances made in ethology), are our biological heritage: to deny that they exist makes no sense. On the other hand, the explanation of interpersonal activity in terms of projections and transformations of drives, as at times Freud wished to do and even more emphatically some of his more enthusiastic followers tried (e.g., Fenichel, Roheim), misses out on the more mature functions of the individual, expressed in such concepts as healthy narcissism, the self, identity, culture, and so on. Since both the instinct and the interpersonal are important, they must be combined to reach a complete theory of human nature: to divorce one from the other is to have an imcomplete or truncated theory.

The culturalists have, perhaps more than the orthodox Freudians, stressed the positive, aspiring wishes of the human being with such theories as Maslow's self-actualization, Laing's divided self, Winnicott's true self vs. false self, Masud Khan's private self, and the like. They have also dealt in therapy in a more active way with the patient, hoping in this way to bring out his positive feelings more directly (Alexander and French 1946). However, this technique in turn stumbles against the inevitable resistances, and in criticism of it, Freudian theorists have labeled it supportive rather than analytic. To trace the arguments further would take us too far afield. At the moment my main goal is to reach conceptual clarification.

Other Views

Because the self is such an easy concept to manipulate, it has been a favorite topic of social psychologists for many years. Their tradition, as noted, goes back to William James and Charles Cooley but also is beginning to take note of the psychoanalytic positions. Recently Jerry Suls has edited two volumes on current perspectives in the field, which will be briefly summarized here.

In the preface Suls says:

> Social psychology has had a critical role to play, as it seems clear that the self has significant social underpinnings. One major change in thinking brought

> in part by the work of social psychologists has been the appreciation that "to know thyself" means "to know one's fellows." Theoretical and empirical work reinforce the notion that self-knowledge stems from the reciprocal relationship between ourselves and our social group. Conceptions of our traits, abilities and options grow out of the reaction of others, and how we compare to them. In short, the self is made of social cloth. (Suls et al. 1982:vii)

In the first paper Albert Bandura discusses the self and the mechanisms of agency; this relates to whether and how people exert some influence over what they perceive and do. Next Hazel Markus and Keith Sentis discuss the role of the self in social information processing. William McGuire and Claire McGuire discuss significant others in self-space: sex differences and developmental trends in the social self. Jerry Suls and Brian Mullen take up the topic of self-evaluation across the life span, making the relevant and important point that "an individual may . . . have as many selves as seasons through which he passes" (Suls et al. 1982:121). Kenneth Gergen takes up the topic from self to science: what is there to know? He argues for a reconsideration of the valuational criteria in the enterprises (Suls et al. 1982:146). Anthony Greenwald reviews the implicit assumption of personal unity in social psychological theory and finds much evidence for it. Mark Snyder and Bruce Campbell consider the question: Of what consequences are self-conceptions for what individuals subsequently think, feel, and do? They find the manifestations pervasive. Robert Wicklund considers how society uses self-awareness; he finds that it checks the deviant and promotes conformity. Edward Jones and Thane Pittman offer a general theory of self-presentation. They distinguish five kinds of self-presentation: ingratiation, intimidation, self-promotion, amplification, and supplication.

The second volume in the series emphasizes the personality perspective in addition to that of social psychology. First, Abraham Tesser and Jennifer Campbell outline their self-evaluation maintenance model (SEM). Next, William Swann discusses cognitive and behavioral strategies that ensure the stability of self-conceptions. Third, Robert Eicklund and Peter Gollwitzer outline their theory of symbolic self-completion and its relevance to the validity of self-reports about attitudes, capabilities, and traits. Yaacov Trope discusses the role of self-assessment in achievement behavior. Michael Scheier and Charles Carver emphasize the distinction between two forms of self-awareness: attention to the public self, the kinds of things from which social impressions are made, and the private self—personally held feelings and attitudes. Sixth, Jav Hill and Richard Carver present a model that links self-awareness to alcohol consumption. They argue that alcohol reduces self-awareness by interfering with the cognitive encoding of self-relevant material. N. Kuiper, M. Macdonald, and P. Derry provide a review of a research program examining the self in depressed individuals. Seymour Epstein reviews his cognitive self-theory of personality. This is the only chapter that tries to link up with any psychoanalytic views, since he postulates three conceptual systems, corresponding roughly to the conscious, preconscious, and unconscious. Jonathan Cheek and Robert Hogan are critical of contemporary psychological theories that emphasize the instability of the self and situational influence.

There is so much published along these lines that some summary and evaluation is called for. The most extensive examination of the experimental work is by Ruth Wylie (1974, 1961). She is highly critical of the experiments, arguing that they are often conceptually faulty and empirically involved in inappropriate or misleading kinds of measurement. As the reasons for the weak state of current measurement in this field she offers the following (1974:326–329):

1. In some quarters there has apparently been little or no appreciation of the problems connected with adequate instrumentation.
2. In large part the conceptual difficulties and ensuing discouragement may stem from the continuing poor state of self-concept theories.
3. Relatively little prestige is attached to the activity of building and refining a valid instrument for measuring a personality construct.
4. Most persons interested in self-concept theory are insufficiently versed in conceptual and technical principles of measurement of personality constructs.
5. Work on the most studied instruments is widely scattered and is thus not easily available to researchers.
6. Proper instrument development implies that nothing less than a program of research must be carried out.
7. Most researchers who use self-concept variables seem to be interested in getting on with substantive research, even when they recognize that suitable measuring instruments are not at hand.
8. Disturbing questions about the potential value of the entire enterprise of trying to measure inferred "traits," or "states" (including self-concept variables), are raised by the generally quite limited success in using trait or state measures to predict behavior within any situation or across situations.

Inasmuch as the self cuts across the individual and the social dimensions, it has understandably received considerable attention from sociologists. Perhaps the best-known work in this field is by Goffman: *The Presentation of the Self in Everyday Life* (1959). Goffman took a careful look at the surface interactions, omitting any consideration of deeper motivations. As he puts it:

> The perspective employed in this report is that of the theatrical performance; the principles derived are dramaturgical ones. I shall consider the way in which the individual in ordinary work situations presents himself and his activity to others, the ways in which he guides and controls the impressions they form of him, and the kinds of things he may and may not do while sustaining his performance before them. (1959:xi)

When Cooley wrote of the "looking-glass self," he had more in mind than the surface impressions people make on one another, though he had only a glimmering of the unconscious forces that could be at work. Goffman, however, stays very close to the surface. When that is done, it is more proper to speak of the role that the individual plays rather than the self, which implies more of an inner participation. And, in fact, Goffman's use of the theatrical analogy emphasizes that he is studying primarily roles. I shall discuss the nature of the role later (Biddle 1979); it will suffice here to point out that Goffman does not deal with any of the more dynamic issues concerning the self.

A much more sophisticated approach is adopted by Rosenberg in *Conceiving the Self* (1979). Here too, however, he has to begin with the remark that "the self-concept, in its full complexity, is still not adequately understood" (1979:56).

Rosenberg discusses three aspects of the self—the extant self, the presented self, and the idealized self. As a definition of the self he more or less agrees with William James and sees it as "the totality of the individual's thoughts and feelings having reference to himself as an object" (1979:7).

Under the extant self he considers four areas: first, the parts (contents of the self); second, the relationship among the parts (structure); third, the ways of describing both parts and whole (dimensions); and finally, the boundaries of the object (ego extensions). By the ego extensions he more or less meant what William James called the empirical self.

Even though Rosenberg has a number of useful insights, his theoretical bias is so strongly in favor of the social dimension that he omits virtually all the inner psychological factors that have been so extensively discussed by the psychoanalysts. Thus, the terms *sexuality* and *aggression* are not even found in the index, as though they were not really central to every person's self-image.

Most of his book is devoted to consideration of various quantitative studies of various aspects of the self-concept. Yet the strictures offered by Wylie (cf.

above) on such quantitative work are applicable here as well. On the whole, the various studies teach us little that was not already known and add little to our knowledge of the deeper problems. Rosenberg comes to the same conclusion when he says:

> In sum the burden of these observations is that there is a great deal more to the self-concept than self-esteem, and that most of it has been neglected in research. Today self-concept research seems to be spinning its wheels, unable to get untracked. All the important sociological variables that might be expected to account for it—age, race, social class, birth order, sex, ethnicity, religion—are found to explain remarkably little variance in it. (1979:286)

The psychoanalytic critique of work of this kind is that it omits the significant variables that make people tick. When he agrees with Mead's assertion that "we are more or less unconsciously seeing ourselves as others see us," he ignores such defensive maneuvers as projective identification, projection and denial, as well as powerful libidinal and aggressive forces that color our perception of ourselves as well as of others. For example, the role of envy in evaluating others is certainly powerful, yet it is nowhere given either practical or theoretical weight.

Summary

In this survey of analytic and nonanalytic studies of the self, it has been seen that the major difficulty lies in the proper definition of the self-concept. The Psychoanalytic Glossary (Moore and Fine 1968) adopts a commonsense definition: "The total person of an individual in reality, including his body and psychic organization; one's own person as contrasted with 'other persons' and objects outside one's self. The 'self' is a common-sense concept; its clinical and metapsychological aspects are treated under self image, self representation, etc. See ego, identity, narcissism" (1968:88). In spite of strenuous efforts to do so, none of the authors cited has really improved on this commonsense definition.

Freud discussed the self in various reflexive forms, as common sense does; thus, he spoke of self-esteem, self-destructiveness, self-love, self-hatred, and so on. In so doing, he distinguished self from the more technical term ego, which had a long linguistic and philosophical history in German thought. He never considered the self as a superordinate system, as many authors today wish to do. In the two passages in which he speaks of the self most explicitly, in *Narcissism* (1914) and *Instincts and Their Vicissitudes* (1915), he consistently uses the term Selbst in one section and person (1915) in another. Thus, it can reasonably be said that the distinction between ego and self was fairly clear in his mind, even though at times the two meanings may merge.

Roheim, in his exhaustive summation of the anthropological evidence of his day, likewise used the self in a commonsense way. He was able to show that some notion of the self is present in all cultures, no matter how primitive, which also distinguish between what today is called the public self and the private self: all cultures recognize that the person puts up one front to society and another to himself. In addition, Roheim was able to draw extensive parallels between the anthropological material on animism and the psychoanalytic material on libido development. He laid a foundation for the growing awareness of the self as a result of projection of body parts and functions, together with an introjection of the outside world. This sequel of projection and introjection was later to receive a more systematic treatment by Klein. In spite of intense opposition, especially in America, Klein's views have in their essence now been incorporated into the main body of psychoanalytic theory.

In line with a different linguistic and philosophical background, the American school of philosophy and psychology, as represented by men like Royce, James, Cooley, and Mead, saw the self as the result of an interplay with other people, other selves. James in particular (1890) is of great importance because he formulated the concept of the empirical self and eliminated the notion of soul from scientific discourse. James' theories still exert considerable influence. If we add to them the unconscious and the development of drives, we get to a reasonable approximation to the current psychoanalytic notions of the self.

In line with this orientation social psychologists have studied the self extensively and tried to quantify it. These efforts have met with little success, largely because the self-concept remains poorly defined and because the unconscious affective bases of the self are generally omitted by psychologists working in an academic tradition.

In psychoanalysis the American tradition was continued by Harry Stack Sullivan, who probably had some personal contact with Cooley and Mead during his early years (Perry 1982). For Sullivan the self-system was designed to ward off anxiety, and its increase or diminution made it the core of the personality. Since Sullivan's greatest contribution lay in the demonstration that schizophrenics are treatable by psychotherapy, his conceptualizations carried particular weight with those who were working with schizophrenics. However, Sullivan ignored the appearance of anxiety before the self-system is formed, as well as numerous other aspects of its psychoanalytic derivation.

In general, the culturalist school, following Sullivan, stressed the self as the unifying element in personality. They say conflict in terms of the true vs. false self (Winnicott), divided self (Laing), self-actualization (Maslow), and the like. In so doing, they extended the notion of the self to the wider social structure, showing that the self cannot be properly understood without some reference to this wider structure. However, they too were constrained to minimize the role of the unconscious and the drives, though they recognized these factors in theory.

Kohut's doctrine of the bipolar self presented a curious mixture, if looked at in its historical context. From an initial interest in narcissism, he replaced this concept by the self as the key doctrine in personality and wrote of self-objects and the bipolar self. His views have aroused strong reactions, pro and con. Upon closer examination, however, his thinking is not as novel or as sound as it seems to appear. In many ways he has repeated the position of the culturalists, especially with his later insistence that the drive theory be dropped as an independent system and replaced by the development of the nuclear self, which in some measure is present from birth.

A symposium on the self, in which many of the leading theoreticians of the American Psychoanalytic Association participated in 1980, led to no consensus among the discussants. Rangell argued that there was a kind of "group neurosis" at play, in which cult formations developed around charismatic figures such as Kohut and Kernberg, while disregarding the evidence of their own clinical experience. The only conclusion to be drawn from the symposium was that the self is an important concept, that it is not, or not easily, integrated into the structural theory, and that an adequate definition and a theoretical rationale for it remain to be found.

In sum, it can be said that there are three different views of the self vying for theoretical recognition on the current scene: the Freudian self, a commonsense notion embodying the various ways in which the term is used in ordinary discourse; the social self, examined largely by theoreticians of the American and culturalist schools; and the Kohutian self, which theorizes that there is a superordinate entity guiding the individual's destiny throughout life. Each of these views has its partisans. What has to be done now is to reexamine them in light of the total body of psychoanalytic knowledge and theory.

The many difficulties involved in the clarification of these basic concepts have to be understood first in light of the problems of psychology as such and second as a consquence of the rather authoritarian manner in which psychoanalytic psychology has progressed. For it is by now obvious that Freudian theoreticians, instead of dealing with these questions directly, have sought to compress them into the framework of the tripartite structure and have failed to do so; culturalists, on the other hand, have extended their inquiry to the larger questions of interpersonal relations and society in general but have paid too little attention to the libidinal and aggressive wishes inherent in man. Both groups have also missed an essential characteristic of these topics in that both have more or less ignored the changes that occur in them throughout the life cycle. For example, the narcissism of the neonate whose life is beginning is certainly qualitatively different from the narcissism of the old man whose life is ending, while both in turn differ from the narcissism of the adolescent who is breaking away from his parents. So it need not cause us any surprise if the definition of narcissism has caused such immense difficulties, since it comprises an attempt to compress many different kinds of life experiences into one rubric.

A further problem arises in that all psychological matters necessarily have a normative element attached to them. Humankind is always seeking happiness, even if people define happiness in different ways. Hence there is always a positive or negative connotation attached to narcissism, as well as to self or identity. Theory should take this normative component into consideration: it has failed to do so up to now.

The theme and variations of this book can now be clarified. The main task is to offer more satisfactory clarification of the concepts of self, narcissism, and identity. All involve a tension between the individual and the group. Hence I shall systematically illuminate the major tensions that have been described between individuals and groups. Theoretically, for this purpose, I should also offer a more systematic approach to the social structure, but that topic, it need hardly be said, is in as much of a state of disagreement as psychoanalytic theory. It will be sufficient for my purpose to refer to different kinds of societies or cultures rather than work out some theoretical dry-as-wood definition.

CHAPTER 4
NEUROSIS AND CULTURE

The first area in which the tension between the individual and the group can be examined is that of neurosis. The naive definition of neurosis is that of an individual who deviates too much from the culture, thus embodying the notion of a tension between the individual and the group. The course of psychoanalytic thought has virtually destroyed this notion in its entirety. Thus, a reconsideration of the concept of neurosis is bound to shed a great deal of light on the individual-group conflict, as well as on the concepts of the self, narcissism, and identity.

When the DSM=III of the American Psychiatric Association was issued in 1981, the category of "neurosis was omitted. Instead there is a note: "NEUROTIC DISORDER: These are included in Affective, Anxiety, Somatoform, Disassociative and Psychosexual Disorders" (APA 1981:375). Similarly, when Dohrenwend and his associates (1980) undertook to determine the prevalence of various kinds of mental disorders, they used the term "demoralization disorder" rather than the more usual "neurosis." Again, when the Michigan Legislature in 1975 revised its code for legal commitment, the legislature was unable to sort out the conflicting definitions and omitted a definition of mental illness from its new code (Dohrenwend and Dohrenwend 1980:2). These are but a few instances of the dilemmas that experts encounter when they try to define neurosis and psychosis more precisely.

The glossary of psychiatric terms issued by the American Psychiatric Association states under neurosis:

> Neurosis (psychoneurosis): An emotional maladaptation arising from an unresolved unconscious conflict. The anxiety is either felt directly or modified by various psychological mechanisms to produce other, subjectively distressing symptoms. The neuroses are usually considered less severe than the psychoses (although not always less disabling) because they manifest neither gross personality disorganization nor gross distortion or

PROPERTY OF WASHINGTON
SCHOOL OF PSYCHIATRY
LIBRARY

> misinterpretation of external reality. The neuroses are classified according to the predominant symptoms. (1975:106)

Laplanche and Pontalis, in their examination of the language of psychoanalysis, define neurosis as a "psychogenic affection in which the symptoms are the symbolic expression of a psychical conflict whose origins lie in the subject's childhood history" (1973:266). Then they add:

> The task of trying to define neurosis, as revealed by clinical experience, in terms of the comprehension of the concept of neurosis, tends to become indistinguishable from the psychoanalytic theory itself. . . . It is scarcely possible to claim that an effective distinction has yet been established between the structures of neurosis, psychosis and perversion. (p. 269)

In discussing the subject historically, Karl Menninger stated:

> "The word 'neurosis' has come to mean too many different things to mean anything. Neurosis once meant a disease of the nervous system; then it came to mean a severe illness, then a mild illness, then a feigned illness" (1963:176).

In his most recent book Charles Brenner does not even list the terms "neurosis" and "psychosis" in the index and makes no attempt to define them (1982). Thus, the weight of expert opinion is that the terms "neurosis" and "psychosis" are extremely difficult to define, if definable at all. Yet people glibly, keep on using the terms as though they had a clear-cut meaning.

These considerations can be applied to the notions of mental health embodied in the concepts of narcissism, self, and identity, which form the main subject of this book. In each there is an effort to focus on one aspect of the personality or illness and to omit the rest, thus creating a one-sided picture of the difficulties involved.

Kohut proposed a diagnostic category of "narcissistic personality disorder," which has since become incorporated into the DSM III. He differentiated this state from the "ordinary" transference neuroses as follows:

> In uncomplicated cases of transference neurosis the psychopathology does not primarily reside either in the self or in the archaic narcissistic self-objects. The central psychopathology concerns structural conflicts over (incestuous) libidinal and aggressive strivings which emanate from a well-

> delimited cohesive self and are directed toward childhood objects which have in essence become fully differentiated from the self. The central psychopathology of the narcissistic personality disurbances, on the other hand, concerns primarily the self and the archaic narcissistic objects. These narcissistic configurations are related to the causative nexus of psychopathology in the narcissistic realm in the following two ways: 1) they may be insufficiently cathected and are thus liable to temporary fragmentation; and 2) even if they are sufficiently cathected or hyper-cathected and thus retain their cohesiveness, they are not integrated with the rest of the personality and the mature self and other aspects of the mature personality and are deprived of a sufficient or reliable supply of narcissistic investments. (1971:19)

Later he observes that the essential genetic trauma is grounded in the parents' psychopathology, in particular on the parents' own narcissistic fixations (1971:76). Again, he comments that in the analysis of the transference neuroses we aim at achieving an expansion of the (pre)conscious ego (1971:94–95), while in the analysis of the narcissistic personality disorders the strivings are ultimately brought under the dominance of the reality ego.

These statements, hard enough to grasp in themselves, go along with the repeated assertion that while oedipal conflicts were prominent in Freud's times, self-conflicts are the predominant ones today. Classical theory, he states, emphasized guilty man; his theory stresses tragic man. But then again he goes on to state that seen from the point of view of classical analysis (1971:238), the oedipal phase is par excellence the nucleus of neurosis, while seen from the point of view of the psychology of the self, in the broad sense of the term, the oedipus complex, whether or not it leaves the individual beset by guilt and prone to neurosis, is the matrix in which an important contribution to the firming of the independent self takes place, enabling it to follow its own pattern with greater security than before.

This attempted clarification leaves the reader more confused than ever about what is novel in his position. It was always known (as shown above in the listing of the self-concept in Freud's works) that the oedipal resolution gave the child an adequate sense of self-esteem, which is the same as Kohut's firm sense of self, or self-cohesiveness, while oedipal conflicts interfered with the self-esteem. Why Freud's views should lead to the image of a guilty man, while Kohut's lead to tragic man, is not explained; it would appear to be rhetoric without substantial content. In fact, the usual accusation against Freud is that he was too pessimistic and stressed the tragic unresolvable elements in man's fate too strongly, as in his extreme position on the death instinct.

When we examine Sullivan's papers on technique and his formulation of the self system, it becomes clear that while he was still writing about his technical modification, which produced such good results with schizophrenia, he scarcely deviated from orthodox psychoanalytic formulations. In his major paper "The Modified Psychoanalytic Treatment of Schizophrenia" (1931) he begins by saying that he employs a procedure with schizophrenics that is "rather intimately related to the psychoanalytic method of Sigmund Freud." He subscribes to Freud's one-genus postulate that the difference between schizoid and schizophrenic is wholly one of degree and not one of kind. (Ernest Jones in 1929 had also made the same point in the paper he read at the opening of the Columbia University Psychiatric Institute.) Sullivan did insist that schizophrenia is meaningful only in an interpersonal context, but this was in no way contradictory of standard psychoanalytic theory at that time (or at the present). He viewed the schizophrenic as living out a dream, a point Freud had also made the other way around, by saying that the dream is everybody's nightly psychosis. He stressed that the only procedures that justify enthusiasm in the treatment of schizophrenia are the psychoanalytic and the sociopsychiatric program he had evolved from them; then he adds that any achievement with the schizophrenic requires the establishment of a transference. The schizophrenic is to be treated as a person among persons. Energy must be expended in reconstructing the actual chronology of the psychosis. Essentially he saw his treatment as consisting of two parts, first with a view to adequate socialization and second by more fundamental reorganization of personality.

In all of this Sullivan did not deviate in any marked fashion from psychoanalytic theory and technique. Others had done the same (Frosch 1983), but he did it more carefully and more adequately. The injection of the self system as the core of the schizophrenic disturbance came later. At that time his explanations remained within the standard psychoanalytic views.

Erikson, who had less of a need to be a charismatic personality than either Kohut or Sullivan, offered his formulations of identity as a continuation of standard psychoanalytic thought. He stressed particularly that the identity crisis and role diffusion that are so common in adolescence have a long background in the psychosocial development of the individual, which he described in considerable detail. Although he argued that identity is as crucial a problem in our time as sexuality was in Freud's, he ascribes this fact to the shift in focus of the analysts rather than to a shift in the cultural situation (in contrast, e.g., to the argument that oedipal disorders are not as prominent in our day as they were in Freud's). Erikson writes:

> The study of identity, then, becomes as strategic in our time as the study of sexuality was in Freud's time. Such historical relativity in the development of a field, however, does not seem to preclude consistency of ground plan and continued closeness to observable fact. Freud's findings regarding the sexual etiology of the neurotic part of a mental disturbance are as true for our patients as they were for his; while the burden of identity loss which stands out in our considerations probably burdened Freud's interpretations as well as ours, as re-interpretations would show. Different periods thus permit us to see in temporary exaggerations different aspects of an essentially inseparable whole. (1950:242–243)

Thus, the attempt to clarify neurosis by reference to one major concept, such as narcissism, self-cohesiveness, or identity crisis, is necessarily an oversimplification. What then is the nature of neurosis? To answer this question, a historical detour is necessary.

The term "neurosis" appears to have been first used by the Scottish doctor William Cullen in a medical treatise published in 1777 (Laplanche and Pontalis 1973:267). Subsequently, nineteenth-century authors used the term neurosis in a rather vague way, covering conditions that today would be classified as neurosis, psychosomatic conditions, and/or neurological affections. However, everything about the concept was vague and poorly defined. Thus, Axenfeld, writing in 1883, said: "The whole class of the neuroses has been founded on a negative conception; it was born the moment pathological anatomy, which had been enjoined to explain illnesses by the deterioration of organs, found itself face to face with a certain number of morbid states whose raison d'etre escaped it" (Laplanche and Pontalis 1973:269).

Until fairly recent times most psychiatric textbooks, such as Kraepelin's standard work, had virtually nothing on neurosis. What they did include, if anything was included, was a brief description of the most severe forms of hysteria and obsessional neurosis.

The term "psychosis" was introduced by Feuchtersleben, dean of the University of Vienna Medical School, in 1845. For him it denoted mental illness, whereas neurosis denotes affections of the nervous system—only some of which may be expressed through the symptoms of a psychosis. "Every psychosis," he writes, "is at the same time a neurosis, because without an intervention of nervous life no modification of the physical is manifested: but every neurosis is not necessarily a psychosis" (Laplanche and Pontalis 1973:372).

In all this it must be realized that the vast majority of conditions now listed under neurosis in the textbooks were entirely outside the purview of the average psychiatrist before psychoanalysis was born. Such problems as marital conflict, alcoholism, drug addiction, work problems, failures in school, dissastisfaction with life, and many others were simply ignored, or handled by age-old techniques of religious inspiration or magical remedies.

Only against this historical background can the achievements of Freud be understood. He came up against a vague, ill-charted field, where the symptoms were obscure, the etiology unknown, and the treatment haphazard. He brought considerable order out of the chaos. First, he established that neurosis was a psychological problem worthy of study and not a form of hereditary degeneracy or malingering, as had been hitherto believed. (Charcot, his teacher, e.g., was the first to establish that hysteria was a psychological illness and was severely attacked for doing so—most of his contemporaries thought that it must be organic.) Second, he reformulated the disparate symptoms that his predecessors and colleagues had described, dividing them into two major clinical entities—obsessional neurosis (the term itself stems from Freud) and hysteria. Hysteria was further subdivided into conversion hysteria and anxiety hysteria; both designations stemmed from Freud. Third, in terms of the libido theory (1905) he established what could be regarded as the normal course of development and showed how neurosis could be made intelligible by reference to such normal development. Fourth, he demonstrated that neurosis and normality differ only in degree, not in kind, and thereby restored the neurotic (and even more so the psychotic) to a place in society. Fifth, he established that these neuroses are amenable to psychoanalysis and that psychoanalysis is the best treatment for them. The analyzability of these patients rests on the fact that they form transferences, which can then be worked through.

Once his experience had grown, Freud offered a new distinction on a therapeutic basis in his paper on narcissism (1914). There he divided the neuroses into transference and narcissistic neuroses. However, as seen above, he did not hold on to a sharp line between these two conditions; from the very beginning and until the end of his career he espoused a continuum theory, which Sullivan perhaps put most tellingly in his famous phrase: We are all more simply human than otherwise. Or as Freud put it at one point: nothing human is foreign to me.

From his earliest dynamic papers (1894) he saw the fundamental conflict as that between the ego and the id, what he originally termed the "neuropsychoses of defense," in which the person defends himself against unbearable ideas. This was reformulated in various ways until the id-ego dichotomy became the standard one in 1923.

In defining with more precision the characteristics of the two major types of neuroses, Freud included the following: sexual conflicts, emotional outbursts, transformations of sexual conflicts into somatic symptoms, somatic symptoms without any organic base, anxiety, denial of anxiety, inability to love, rage, low frustration tolerance, doubt, obsessional brooding, overconcern with death, lack of development, regression, fixation at early stages of development, perverse actions of all kinds more characteristic of childhood (the "child is polymorphous perverse"), masochism, the wish to suffer, inability to accept the move from the principle to the reality principle, self-damaging activities, lack of self-esteem, narcissistic regression, etc.—the list could go on almost indefinitely to include every neurotic symptom ever known or described. How the could the neuroses really be differentiated from one another? And even more important, how could the neurotic be differentiated from the normal?

In considering the types of onset of neurosis Freud wrote in 1913:

> It remains to say a few words on the relation of these types to the facts of observation. If I survey the set of patients on whose analysis I am now engaged. I must record that not one of them is a pure example of any of the four types of onset. In each of them, rather I find a portion of frustration in operating alongside a portion of incapacity to adapt to the demands of realities; inhibition in development, which coincides, of course, with inflexibility of fixations, has to be reckoned with in all of them, and as I already said, the importance of quantity of libido must never be neglected. I find indeed, that in several of these patients their illness has appeared in successive waves, between which there have been healthy intervals, and that each of these waves has been traceable to a different type of precipitating cause. Thus, the erection of these four types cannot lay claims to any high theoretical value; they are merely different ways of establishing a particular pathogenic constellation in the mental economy . . . but this situation . . . does not come as a novelty to mental life and is not created by what is spoken of as a "cause of illness." . . . The importance in the causation of illness which must be ascribed to quantity of libido is in satisfactory agreement with the two main theses of the theory of neuroses to which psychoanalysis has led us: first, the thesis that the neuroses were derived from the conflict between the ego and the libido, and secondly, that there is no qualitative distinction between the determinants of health and those of neurosis, and that, on the contrary, healthy people have to contend with the same tasks of mastering their libido—they have simply succeeded better in them. (12:236–237)

Thus, Freud has succeeded in defining two major types of neuroses, but then he found that the most common was a mixed type and that these neuroses differed only in degree from the normal individual. The notion that neurosis involves a conflict between ego and id (here still libido) was further expanded in the 1920s (when the concept of the superego was formulated) to the formula that neurosis is a conflict between ego and id, psychosis between ego and reality and the narcissistic neurosis (depression) between the ego and the superego. However, this was one of Freud's facile formulas that has not stood the test of time; the difference between normality, neurosis, and psychosis is only one of degree; the same or similar dynamic factors operate in all of them (Bellak et al. 1973).

With the outbreak of World War I two momentous changes in psychoanalytic theory occurred. One was the introduction of hostility or aggression as an independent drive, not in the form of the death instinct as originally proposed by Freud, which was rejected by almost all of his followers, but in the form of a dual instinct theory, as later most explicitly formulated by Hartmann, Kris, Loewenstein, and Brenner. From here on all the formulations about neurosis and normality had to consider the role of aggression. Implicitly this had always been done—since when there is no love, there must be anger—but now it became explicit.

The Training Analysis

The second momentous change came with the institution of the *training analysis*. Prior to World War I any person who wished to become an analyst could do so, and many did. Then when formal training began at the Berlin Institute in 1920, it was generally agreed that those who wished to practice analysis should undergo a "preparatory" analysis themselves. While this was an innovation at that time, eventually it became an indispensable requirement: every person who wished to become an analyst had to undergo analysis.

This is so commonly understood today that its revolutionary import has been obscured. The candidates for analytic training are drawn from the ranks of physicians, psychologists, persons with university degrees, of substantial education, many with considerable accomplishment in life. Why then should they have to undergo an analysis? In what sense can they be considered neurotic? How does this alter the traditional image of what neurosis (and psychosis) is?

By contemporary standards the training analysis at Berlin, which created the model that all other institutes since have followed, was brief indeed. Horney wrote: "The length of the training analysis depends on the personality of the candidate: in the experience of the training institute it can be estimated to last at least for one year of daily sessions." (Maetze 1970:51).

The very term training analysis has in itself caused numerous disputes. The German term is *Lehranalyse*—learning analysis. Only gradually did it become apparent that the analysis was in every sense a therapeutic analysis, in that the candidate did not differ in any essential respect from the patients whom he was going to treat.

Eventually all analytic institutes openly stated in their bulletins that the training analysis was in no respect different from a therapeutic analysis. Thus, the *Bulletin of the New York Psychoanalytic Institute* states:

> The preparatory analysis is a requirement for the training in psychoanalysis. Its therapeutic goals are not different from those of a therapeutic analysis. Its educational goal includes freedom from personality factors which would interfere with the ability to conduct psychoanalytic treatment independently. Therefore, no fast rule can be applied to the duration of this preparatory analysis which is determined by the analyzing instructor. It will be seen that any statement of a definite number of hours of analytic treatment is incompatible with this concept. (1983-84:11)

Hanns Sachs, one of Freud's closest adherents and the first training analyst, wrote that what analysis needed was a novitiate like the religious orders and that this novitiate was to be provided by the training analysis: "What is at stake is that the future analyst must learn somthing which other people, easily, willingly and permanently overlook, and that the analyst must be in a position to maintain this capacity for observation, even where the results are decidedly contradictory of his own wishes and feelings" (in Maetze 1970:53).

Thus, for Sachs and the other brilliant organizers of the Berlin institute, the training analysis served as both indoctrination and entrance to an inner world denied the ordinary mortal. This state of affairs has continued ever since. Yet it is anything but easy to apply in ordinary practice. After all, the potential analyst wants, like any other professional, to get through his training, to make a living, to set himself up as an equal member of the profession. In no other field is there anything like a training analysis (the religious novitiate serves the purpose of indoctrination much more than that of enlightenment). It is a requirement that is self-evident to the insiders but very puzzling to the outsiders.

The training analysis is the core of all the conflicts that have erupted (and there have been many) in psychoanalytic societies, and the problems connected with it are far from resolved. In his survey of fifty-seven institutes all over the world, in which only half replied, Wallerstein (1978) posed three questions:

1. How do you attempt to encompass the dual goals of training competent practitioners for the profession of psychoanalysis and of educating people to comprehensively understand and advance our knowledge of the science of psychoanalysis?
2. What is the kind and degree of personality alteration that you expect psychoanalytic training to achieve with your candidates?
3. How does the training sequence (of personal analysis, of formal curriculum, and of supervised analytic work) organized in relation to those educational goals and these expectations for personality alteration foster these goals and expectations?

The replies received from the twenty-seven institutes that did reply attested once more to the wide variety of opinions that exist within psychoanalysis.

When in conclusion he takes up the question of whether the International Psychoanalytical Association can now be a shaping body for analytical institutes, his answer is essentially negative. He writes:

> I think that it is reasonable to conclude on the basis of this survey that our expectations in this regard need to be somewhat modest at this point in time. In its training philosophy and practices, psychoanalysis world-wide is clearly a most richly variegated, always vigorously opinionated, and often sharply disputatious body . . . . We have in full view now a range of experiments in training. (Wallerstein 1978:503)

If there is such a wide range of disagreement about the training analysis, what does this say about the psychoanalytic views of normality and neurosis? Clearly there must also be a wide range of disagreement on these topics as well, for every training analysis seeks to move the patient toward an image of normality that ideally should be shared by patient and analyst.

Normality and Neurosis

Freud was never really content with his technical elucidation of the problem of neurosis. It did not take him long to realize that he was dealing with universal human conflicts, not just those of his time and place. This led to the recognition that all mankind was his patient. That in turn meant that he was a social reformer as well as a psychiatrist.

It was the promptings of others that led him, however, to deal with the social reforms suggested by the findings of psychoanalysis. If sexual frustration plays such a huge role in illness, why not change the sexual arrangements of society? The philosopher von Ehrenfels in 1907–08 tried to do so, but Freud temperamentally was unfit for a practical reform movement, however much he might encourage it in others.

It was the American neurologist James Jackson Putnam, an eminent American professor who turned to analysis late in life, who stimulated him most strongly to look at social reform more carefully. But his answer, as before, was: leave it to others. In 1914 Freud wrote:

> I comprehend very little of philosophy and with epistemology (with, not before) my interest ceases to function. I quite agree with you that psychoanalytic treatment should find a place among the methods whose aim is to bring about the highest ethical and intellectual development of the individual. Our difference is of a purely practical nature. *It is confined to the fact that I do not wish to entrust this further development to the psychoanalyst.* (Putnam 1971:170; italics mine)

In his work after World War I Freud began to state more explicitly that psychoanalysis was destined for more than purely therapeutic purposes. In *Civilization and Its Discontent* (1930) he wrote: "If the development of civilization has such a far-reaching similarity to the development of the individual . . . may we not be justified in reaching the diagnosis that under the influence of cultural urges, some civilizations, or some epochs of civilization-possibly the whole of mankind—have become 'neurotic'" (21:144).

Nor did he shrink from the idea of creating a new profession that would ameliorate the burdens that civilization placed on so many. In the *Question of Lay Analysis* he wrote:

> Our civilization imposes an almost intolerable pressure on us and it calls for a corrective. Is it too fantastic to expect that psychoanalysis in spite of its difficulties may be destined to the task of preparing mankind for such a corrective? Perhaps once more an American may hit on the idea of spending a little money to get the "social workers" of his country trained analytically

> and to turn them into a band of helpers for combating the neuroses of civilization. (20:249–250)

The broad view here of neurosis as part of the burden of civilization, together with the idea that whole civilizations can become neurotic, epitomized the far-reaching expansion of the whole idea of neurosis that he had built up in such a painstaking way for forty years. The culture imposes intolerable demands on the individual, demands so great that in the effort to accede to them the individual falls into neurotic conflicts on one kind or another. This point of view was quite common in the thirties and early forties.

If civilization makes us neurotic, what is normality? Love and work was his simple answer; or to be more precise, in his own terminology, achievement and pleasure (*Leistung* and *Genuss*) (1953–1970, 16:457). And how can love and work be reached as goals? Either by therapy or by education. By 1939, the year he died, Freud's vision was reasonably complete (Fine 1981). But the world was also in a shambles. At that point it was a purely utopian vision.

In the meantime another technical development had taken place that illuminated many of Freud's insights. Anthropologists for the first time went out into the field after World War I armed with Freudian ideas to see what they could see in primitive tribes. And they saw what Freud had described—sexual conflicts, aggressions, different modes of handling sexuality, different modes of rearing children (some better, some worse), and different belief systems (some more sensible than ours, some less). Anthropology was the experiment of nature. There were good alternatives to the severe repressions and hatreds endemic in Western culture—they were viable, they did not cause debilitating neuroses, they had much to teach us. Many anthropologists went into analysis, and some even became lay analysts (Labarre 1961).

Then came the outbreak of World War II, with its enormous toll of neurotic illness and mass murder and its extraordinary expansion of therapeutic services of all kinds, especially in America. In the crucible of World War II a new profession was born, what Freud had once referred to as "lay curers of souls, who need not be doctors but should not be priests" (Freud and Pfister, p. 126).

Following World War II the psychoanalytic movement, though still very small, became infinitely more powerful—and infinitely more aggressive. Split followed split, until someone could seriously write a book about "136 therapies." But the biggest split of all was that between the culturalists and the Freudians. The culturalists maintained that problems were basically due to the culture in which we had been brought up; the more orthodox Freudians insisted that neurosis was inherently a biological phenomenon. Paradoxically, Freud's drive theory, never clearly formulated after 1905 by Freud and never adequately formulated by his followers (cf. Fenichel's disagreements with Freud, 1945, as well as Jones, 1953–1957) became the shibboleth on which banners were unfurled, and in defense of which or against which the two sides went to war. The hope that a better world could be created by the united efforts of all psychoanalysts was doomed even before it got under way.

Apart from the battle between the culturalists and the Freudians, which reached a head in 1956 with the formation of the American Academy of Psychoanalysis, two new professions emerged from the war—clinical psychology and psychiatric social work. Both studied psychoanalysis and its offshoots, practiced analysis and therapy, and grew at a fantastic rate. In opposition to Freud the American psychoanalytic movement had strenuously fought the practice of psychoanalysis or psychotherapy by any person who was not an M.D. In spite of this antagonism, lay analysts and therapists of all persuasions flourished. By the 1980s psychotherapy was more of a nonmedical discipline than a medical one.

In addition to the nonmedical therapist, within the ranks of the physicians, another split developed. After the discovery of thorazine in the mid-1950s, psychiatrists claimed they had a miracle drug cure for schizophrenia and shortly thereafter formulated the dopamine hypothesis, according to which schizophrenia is due to an excessive release of dopamine (reason unknown). This was one of the earliest claims of biological psychiatry, which then became increasingly forceful in its insistence that all of psychoanalysis and all of psychodynamics were almost entirely irrelevant. They went back a century to Griesinger, the German psychiatrist who said flatly: Mind diseases are brain diseases. However, these claims were greeted skeptically by the medical profession as a whole. The evidence for the familiar social-psychological genesis of emotional disturbance was too immediate and too convincing.

What becomes of the concept of neurosis and of diagnosis in general in this context? Considerable confusion. The DSM, deriving from the first American system of psychiatric classification, of 1917, issued officially in 1952 after World War II, has changed twice since, and a third revision has already been announced. In spite of all the technical improvements, the clarification of neurosis and mental illness is severely limited by the lack of an overall theory. As noted before by Laplanche and Pontalis, the definition of neurosis is actually tantamount to the definition of psychoanalytic theory, and such a definition is subject to the various political pushes and pulls that have been described.

Throughout psychoanalytic history, various aspects of the personality have been singled out as the cause (or approximate cause) of neurosis: sexuality, infantile sexuality, anality, castration anxiety, pleasure vs. reality principle, ego vs. id, superego vs. reality, fixation, conflict, masochism, borderline states, momism, ego psychological considerations, object relations deficiencies, self-cohesiveness, identity crises, and so on. Each of these has pointed to one feature of human existence that many persons are unable to handle. By and large, however, when looked at more closely, these designations demonstrate a considerable similarity, differing only in degree from psychosis. What is really at issue is not some startling new idea but a clarification of psychoanalytic theory as a whole. Such a clarification has been seriously impeded by the political quarrels in the field.

Without depreciating his followers in any way, at one point or other Freud anticipated the emphases on various neuroses that came later: masochism, ego deficiencies, identity crises, self-depreciation, etc. All have been extensively studied and either loosely or strictly incorporated into what is called Freudian theory (e.g., in Fenichel). The one aspect of neurosis that has not been adequately appreciated by the classical Freudians is the role of culture. So much evidence along those lines has been accumulated that it is essential to summarize it and tie it up with the more common notions of conflict, fixation, and the like.

A number of lines of evidence have to be integrated at this point: epidemiological studies of various disorders; therapy in other cultures; social class differences within our own culture; the continuity of the definition(s) of neurosis with the dominant values of varius cultures; a proper evaluation of the findings with Freudian-oriented psychotherapy over the past hundred years; and the evaluation of our own culture in the light of the analytic ideal.

Epidemiological Studies

Murphy (1982) has recently published an excellent summary of the numerous studies of the incidence of various disorders in contemporary cultures, with some historical data as well. He notes that psychiatrists are still reluctant to look at their own (1982:v). We shall have more to say about this later.

Schizophrenia. There is considerable variation in the incidence of schizophrenia. It is clear that "social factors affect the risk and character of the disease" (Murphy 1982:88). The highest rates are found among the Irish and the Croations, the lowest among the Hutterites, Tongans, and Taiwanese. With differing politicosocial circumstances, a marked shift among the Achienese (Dutch Indies) and Tallensi (African) were found. Although he tends to minimize the differences, the fact that rates in one culture are sometimes four times as high as those found in another seems particularly meaningful.

Three factors seem to be especially important in the incidence of the illness: internalized social expectations that conflict; obstacles to the attainment of rewards implied in the foregoing expectations; and the absence or excessive complexity of rules and guidelines for action.

An important addendum to Murphy's work is a recent paper by Warner (1983) who shows that psychoses have a briefer duration in the Third World and that there is virtually no evidence to show that such illnesses have a worse outcome anywhere outside the Western world. These facts he attributes to the greater sense of community in Third World countries, an observation with which Murphy would be in essential agreement. Warner writes:

> In the third World, by contrast, the psychotic is more likely to return to a useful working role and to retain his or her self-esteem, a feeling of value to the community and a sense of belonging. These are things which four billion dollars does not buy the schizophrenic in the United States or elsewhere in the Western world. Such differences may account, perhaps, for the superior outcome from schizophrenia in the developing world. (1983:210)

Acute reactive psychoses. While different names are attached to them, these are conditions found in many societies, e.g., amok, puerperal psychosis, *bouffée délirante*, etc. There is again wide cultural variability. As common grounds for the appearance of these reactions Murphy enumerates the following: dependency; separation from the community on which dependency has focused; and lack of education. Although he is reluctant to commit himself fully, he does consider that temporary psychosis may be a manipulative device: "Becoming temporarily psychotic may, in terms of survival, be a reality-oriented act, and in some societies there are many more graduations in the process than in others" (1982:114).

Affective disorders. The main etiological findings here are that in societies where there are more affective disorders there is also: a) more individual striving and competition; and b) a higher level of individual need or expectation for emotional support. The common American division into endogenous vs. exogenous, or unipolar vs. bipolar, is not borne out in his studies.

Suicide and parasuicide. Here there is so much variability that Murphy does not regard suicide as a unitary entity. He finds, in general, a lack of social integration; a lack of availability of psychic energy for aggressive purposes; an ego-superego conflict—e.g., without one, even when daily life is miserable, suicide is rare; that variety of types is the most important factor; and a close connection between the wish for power and suicide.

Alcohol and drug abuse. Again there is wide cultural variability. Both are a side effect of men's efforts at responding to certain types of social demands and pressures. Both are either the consequence of an inability to live up to a certain ideal or a disguised form of suicide.

Psychosomatic disorders. Murphy's emphasis here is on pluricausality. E.g., national cultures can change quite markedly over time, and the physiological predispositions to disease can change quite markedly as a result. Weiner (1977), in his exhaustive survey of the western literature on seven major disorders considered to be psychosomatic, again and again emphasizes both the psychological and the physiological factors involved. The older explanations (e.g., Alexander 1950) are found, but they cannot be extended to all cases.

Neuroses. Murphy emphasizes the social relativity of neurotic symptomatology—there cannot be distinct neuroses but only a vast variey of ways of malfunctioning and coping with this malfunctioning. He comments on the content, structure, and purpose of neuroses as follows: the content comes from the symbolic tradition; the structure comes from the coping style that the patient has learned from his society; and the purpose depends on the pains and rewards to which the patient is exposed by society and on the ways in which he has been taught to perceive them.

Finally, with regard to therapy, Murphy states that the form developed in the patient's own society is apt to be more effective than one developed elsewhere.

Therapy in Other Cultures

Contrary to the image of the "happy savage," which goes back to Rousseau, all cultures ever studied diplay some persons with neurotic malfunctioning (in their terms) and have developed forms of therapy to deal with these deviants. Note, however, that they deal with deviants, not with the average person in the culture. Kiev (1964) has edited an interesting volume with descriptions of a variety of "primitive" therapies. Some examples follow.

American Indian tribes. These have developed individual confession to a surrogate for the supernatural and ritual public confession sins. For example, the Chol Maya would confess to their chiefs when sickness afflicted a member of the family, holding the belief that the sickness would end in death unless confession were made by son, father, husband, etc. Should the whole community be suffering from plague or sickness, the confession of a serious sin would lead to the shooting of the sinner with bow and arrows. The Inca of Peru, after confession of guilt, bathed in a nearby river and repeated the formula "O thou river, receive the sins I have this day confessed unto the Sun, carry them down to the sea, and let them never more appear" (Kiev 1964:38). In Nicaragua confession was not permitted until the time of puberty and traditionally came within one day of the fault, lest evil meantime befall. As with the modern psychiatrist, the old man is not permitted to disclose what is told to him. The Huichol of southern Mexico confess their sexual sins at the time of the pilgrimage to the north to obtain hikuli or peyote for their religious rituals. The reverse is also found: among the Blackfoot, as among other tribes, there was a ceremonial avowal of innocence.

Among the Winnebago there is a pattern of confessing guilt and then asking for forgiveness; this is induced by smoking peyote. At about midnight the peyote begins to affect some people. These generally rise and deliver self-accusatory speeches, after which they go around shaking hands with everyone, asking for forgiveness.

Cults among the Yoruba. Among the Yoruba in Africa (Nigeria) cults serve many purposes, one of which is healing. Two common kinds of Orisa cult are characterized by "possession" and "masquerade." The possession cults are chiefly for women and the masquerade cult for men.

In the Sopono cults there is a magic designed to ward off evil spirits, who are similar to "smallpox spirits," Although the Soponos were blamed for about 10 percent of the cases in the informant's series, only three were initiated into the cult as part of their treatment. The others were merely required to sacrifice to Sopono during their stays in the treatment center and received routine treatment for "Sopono madness."

The Gelde is a male masquerade cult that protects its members from witchcraft. Men join the cult because of impotence, because their wives are barren, or because of other diseases or misfortunes caused by witchcraft. During the annual festival the men masquerade as women, wearing women's clothes and flaunting prominent bulletlike breasts. Some look grossly pregnant, others carry wood carvings of children on their backs. All wear grostesquely carved wooden masks, some of which are frightening. It is obvious that this cult offers an outlet for homosexual strivings. The informants said to one anthropologist: "Gelde is the secret of women. We the men are merely their slaves. We dance to appease our mothers."

The Apaches. The description of Apache healing is written by L. Bryce Boyer, a California-based psychoanalyst. According to Boyer, the basic personality type of the Apache fits the Western diagnosis of hysterical and impulsive character disorder. The psychosis of "choice" is one or more of the goup of schizophrenias. It appears that women are more secure than men, for the latter suffer from severe problems related to latent homosexual drives. The typical Apache is capable of only shallow emotional relationship to love objects.

There is a strong belief in witches. A person is diagnosed as a witch principally through his actions and personality. As a rule, he will be more than sixty years old. Any person is suspect if one or more of his forebears have been known as powerful witches. If a person points at people with his finger rather than his lips, is afraid to sleep indoors with others, eats only his own cooking, dances naked in the woods, is paranoid, a braggart, or a miser, or above all "talks mean," he is considered a sorcerer.

Witches have three principal methods of operating: magical words and gestures, calling upon their supernatural powers, and controlling the actions of ghosts. Sorcerers can use silent or spoken curses to harm individuals or entire tribes. Witches have traffic with ghosts of dead humans.

In general, according to Boyer, the narcissistic attitude of Apache mothers toward their infants stunts id-ego differentiation and constitutes the fundamental factor of greatest importance in their psychosexual and psychosocial unfolding. The typical Apache retains faulty id-ego differentiation throughout his life, a phenomenon that must contribute to the specific kinds of psychic breakdown to which these Indians are subject: variants of the group of schizophrenias. In the case of the males, a fourth serious psychic injury is provided by the absence of an esteemed masculine role with which to identify. A final psychological trauma of far-reaching consequences has been provided by confinement to reservation existence. There is no doubt that the female is the strong figure in the household and that the role of the woman is more consistent and respected in Apache society than is that of the male.

With regard to shamanism, in the past all events influencing the lives of these Indians were ascribed to the actions of bosses, ghosts, or witches, i.e., all malevolent persons. The spirits and sorcerers could be influenced by ceremonies, of which the major ones were the possession solely of shamans. The roles of the shaman and the witch are easily understood as displaced representatives of the good and bad parents, in the final analysis the mother, and of projections of portions of the individual. Within this framework, Apache psychiatry as carried out by the shamans coincides with faith healing.

In general, as Kiev points out, five beliefs are commonly found in non-Western groups: soul loss; breach of taboo; disease sorcery; object intrusion; and spirit intrusion. In the more logical and more rational person of today, there are analogies to these beliefs expressed in different form. Thus soul loss is self-conflict, breach of taboo is guilt about some violation of the norms, disease sorcery is infection by some noxious agent, object intrusion is contagion from some wicked person, and spirit intrusion is an internalization of the persecutor or bad object. Thus, in a very real sense the same determinants of neurosis are found in all cultures; only their distribution and intensity and expression vary.

Social Class Differences in Our Own Culture

One of the major surprising findings of the 1950s to which too little attention has been paid by conventional psychiatry is that emotional disturbance varies with class. In the Hollingshead-Redlich survey at Yale (1958) schizophrenia was nine times as frequent in the lowest socioenconomic class as in the more affluent. A century earlier Edward Jarvis, the leading American psychiatrist of the nineteenth century, had found mental illness (then not yet designated as schizophrenia) to be 64 times as common among the poverty-stricken classes as among the more affluent. Jarvis wrote:

> Poverty is an inward principle, enrooted deeply within the man, and running through all his elements; it reaches his body, his health, his intellect, his moral powers, as well as his estate. . . . Hence we find that, among those whom the world calls poor, there is less vital force—a lower tone of life, more ill health, more weakness, more early death, a diminished longevity. There is also less self-respect, more idiocy and insanity, and more crime, than among the independent. (1971:52)

In modern times it took a while for professionals to appreciate the devastating psychological effects of poverty, largely because the psychological effects of wealth seemed to be equally devastating. However, there is a vast difference. Poverty has throughout history literally meant a difference of life or death.

In a famou essay the anthropologist Oscar Lewis (1966a) coined the term "the culture of poverty." He distinguished four major features:

(a) The lack of effective participation and integration of the poor in the major institutions of the larger society.
(b) Poor housing conditions, crowding, gregariousness and above all a minimum of organization beyond the level of the nuclear and extended family.

(c) On the family level the major traits are the absence of childhood as a specially prolonged and protected stage in the life cycle; early initiation into sex; free unions or consensual marriages, a relatively high incidence of the abandonment of wives and children, a trend toward female- or mother-centered families and consequently a much greater knowledge of maternal relatives; a strong predisposition to authoritarianism; lack of privacy; verbal emphasis upon family solidarity, which is only rarely achieved because of sibling rivalry; and competition for limited goods and maternal affection.

(d) On the level of the individual the major characteristics are a strong feeling of marginality, of helplessness, of dependence, and of inferiority.

Although Lewis' description has been questioned, as has everything in this much-disputed field, there can be little doubt that poverty is one of the major contributing factors in all mental and emotional disturbances. This is best explained by the assumption that emotional disturbance derives from a sense of futility about life, and such futility is strongly exacerbated by the terrible living conditions that stem from poverty (see also Krieger 1970).

Another important finding from the Yale studies is that psychiatrists are divided into those who favor the organic-diagnostic approach, which they call DO, and those who lean toward the analytic-psychotherapeutic approach, which they call AP. The DO psychiatrists do not believe in psychotherapy and practice it very little. By contrast, the AP psychiatrists are resistant to the use of drugs and other physical interventions and stay away from them as much as possible.

Neurosis and the Dominant Values of the Culture

Enough has been said to illuminate this point. Thus, if the culture has a strong belief in witches, then neurosis arises with the conviction that a person has been attacked by witches who made him ill ("bewitched"). Similarly, if there is a strong competitive drive in the culture, the neurotic reaction is one of a feeling of failure, an inability to live up to the demands made upon the individual; much of this is relevant to our own society.

Results of Freudian-Oriented Psychotherapy

Without reviewing the statistical findings in great detail, it suffices to say here that psychotherapy, as conceptualized and practiced by Freud, has been singularly successful with the wide range of disorders labeled neurotic but less so with those labeled psychotic. It has also opened the door for the first time in history to the therapy of the "normal" in our society, who turn out to have all kinds of inner conflicts in spite of their outward normality. That psychotherapy can effect a significant change in individuals carries considerable weight in our definitions of neurosis and psychosis.

Evaluation of Our Culture and the Analytic Ideal

Perhaps the most important of all the findings in this field in the past century has been the recognition that in light of the analytic ideal our culture is singularly disturbed. If our history is looked at more objectively, this need not cause so much surprise: wars, massacres, slavery, brutality, and exploitation have been the order of the day for centuries. Love has been conspicuous by its absence. I have made this point in much more detail elsewhere (the reader is referred to the more detailed arguments in *History of Psychoanalysis, 1979a, The Psychoanalytic Vision*, 1981, and *The Meaning of Love in Human Experience*, 1985).

We come back then to the essential question of this chapter: what is neurosis? In primitive psychiatry a neurosis is something that has been inserted into the person or harmed him or bewitched him in some mysterious way or it may be that some part of his body has gone astray or he has lost touch with his soul. All of these notions characterized Western psychiatry before Freud, even though in the nineteenth century it pretended to have a scientific cast.

There are many critics of psychiatry on the current scene; the tendency to dismiss them as "cranks" or "lunatic fringe characters" is too strong, even though in some cases it may be true. The problem is rather that given the medical model that has been upheld for several centuries, tremendous confusion reigns. Freud, in his first significant publication, *The Interpretation of Dreams*, in 1900, stated that those who cannot interpret dreams should not try to help people; this included virtually everybody in his day. Harry Stack Sullivan complained in his time that psychiatry was neither science nor art, but sheer confusion.

A recent critic of psychiatry, Jonas Robitscher, himself a psychiatrist, psychoanalyst, and lawyer, has made even more serious charges in *The Powers of Psychiatry*. Sexual abuse, manipulation of patients' funds, and sheer quackery are all too often the order of the day. He says:

> It is the thesis of this book that psychiatric authority is a recent addition to the scene, that it comes to us with the imprimatur of science, although it is not always scientific, that it carries the weight of medical authority

> although it is only occasionally truly medical, and that its power and influence are constantly growing. (1980:xiii)

After listing a large number of serious breaches of the Hippocratic oath, Robitscher states that "as of today there is little indication that psychiatry is concerned enough with the proprieties of psychiatric practice to devote time and energy to . . . a housecleaning effort" (1980:433). Deploring the excessive power entrusted to psychiatry, he concludes that "until a new, less authoritarian breed of psychiatrists emerges, psychiatry will continue to exert too much power over too many people" (1980:483).

My concern here is not with the abuses, though that is serious enough, but with the scientific and theoretical misconceptions that dominate the field. The primitive notion that neurosis is a "thing" of some sort that has to be driven out of the patient is still with us in disguised form.

The most effective theory deriving from Freud but augmented and changed by many other leading minds is that neurosis and psychosis both refer to certain types of universal human experiences. Three types in particular can be distinguished: conflicts inherent in human existence; the maladjustment neuroses; and the adjustment neuroses.

Inherent Conflicts are Inescapable

Death, sickness, frustration, and natural calamities over which man has no control. These conflicts are universal and account for the fact that some anxiety must be present in any human society. This, however, should not blind us to the fact that these conflicts can either have their effects softened, or postponed, or, as with many illnesses, even overcome by rational inquiry.

The Maladjustment Neuroses

Maladjustment neuroses represent the deviant groups and individuals whom psychiatry has dealt with from time immemorial. It is only since Freud and the development of his theories that they have become intelligible and, to some extent, manageable. Traditionally these are known as the neuroses and the psychoses.

One of our major concerns in this book has been to understand the roles that narcissism, the self, and identity play in neurosis and "normality." Freud had already established a number of intense conflicts that are found in these experiences: the id-ego conflict, the pressure of the superego, the urgency of the drives, the strength or weakness of the ego, and so on.

After Freud's death in 1939 the numerous schisms in the field crystallized into two major groups: the Freudians and the culturalists. The split was further accentuated by the fact that analysts were for the most part psychiatrists looking for patients, so that they geared their writings as well as their theoretical orientations on the one hand to the group to which they belonged and on the other to the general public to clarify their malaise.

In this process a number of revisions were introduced into the classical Freudian position: Hartmann's ego psychology, Mahler's separation-individuation paradigm, Kernberg's theory of borderline conditions, Kohut's self-psychology and, if we go back a way, Melanie Klein's elucidation of early infantile experience are the most important. Object relations theory, as Guntrip frankly admits, is simply a British name for interpersonal theory.

In these revisions of Freudain theory there is one glaring omission: the role of culture. That schizophrenia, e.g., varies with the culture in incidence, in symptomatology, in available treatment, and even in the attitudes of the psychiatrists who do the treatment is all beyond dispute. Yet it is never mentioned. In all the current hullabaloo about the "effectiveness" of the new tranquilizing drugs (new since the mid-1950s), little notice is ever paid to the feeling of most competent authorities that the most effective approach to the schizophrenic must involve long-term reconstruction of his socio-interpersonal environment (Talbott 1984). Drugs alone will not do the trick. And even then many claim that even under the best of circumstances, with orthodox drug treatment the effectiveness of the therapy has not changed in 100 years (Rodgers 1982).

Furthermore, if the culture is brought in, the dynamics of schizophrenia and other disorders comes out much more clearly. In all the severe personality disorders the patient is unable to liberate himself from the family. That means that he cannot become an individual in his own right. Thus, the excessive narcissism is once again not due to a withdrawal from others but to a retreat to the mother or a mother substitute. The cohesive self of Kohut results from an intact family structure, while the divided self, or disintegrating self, is a sign that the individual is unable to leave the family and move out into the outside world. Finally, the person who cannot find his own identity (alienated) is unable to move on to a group beyond his own family.

But in all these cases the family is also isolated from the larger culture. The son holds on to the mother, or becomes enmeshed with her (in the language of the family therapists), because she holds on to him. Likewise, the narcissist comes from a family that cannot relate to the outside world.

When the culture is brought in, the need to "supersede" classical theory vanishes. In all the severe disorders there is not only an overattachment to the family and a problem in moving to the outside world but also a fear of the instinctual impulses, which are aroused or activated by the outside world. Thus, e.g., in Schwaber's sample case in *Advances in Self Psychology* (Goldberg 1980) the first problem that crystallizes in the transference is detachment. But the patient comes from a detached family and is also unable to relate to girls.

In Freud's 1914 paper it was seen that he could easily have solved the problem of narcissism within the confines of the original libido theory. Likewise, the nuclear self can best be understood within the confines of the libido theory, since especially in infancy the most important constituent of the self is the bodily component. In fact, if the situation is examined more dispassionately, both Sullivan and Kohut make too much of a fuss about the self. As William James had observed long before, everybody knows what his self is. The trouble is that when it is set up as a supraordinate entity, as many Kohutians wish to do, interminable difficulties arise.

In a more commonsense way it becomes obvious that the self, like narcissism and identity, is one aspect of the personality that is not present at birth but that matures as the individual gets older. Furthermore, as we have pointed out before, it not only matures but also continues to change over the life span, so that the self-image of the old man is quite different from that of the neonate or that of the adolescent, although there are some elements in common.

In his view that self-psychology cannot be attached to the structural theory in a simple way, Kohut is undoubtedly right. But that does not mean that the two are incompatible; several papers in Goldberg (1980) show that it is. It merely means that the development of the self after the early years has to be traced more carefully and should be tied in with the narcissistic gratifications, as well as the libidinal, aggressive, and other aspects of the personality.

On the other hand, the difficulty that Hartmann, Jacobson, Kernberg, and others have had with the self-concept does not stem from the concept but from their insistence that somehow it must be made part of the tripartite structure; as Kernberg says, the self is embedded within the ego. But this makes little sense. The self is an essential aspect of interpersonal relationships, deriving from the differentiation between self and object as the person grows. This differentiation, how it is effected, and what comes out of it clearly depend very heavily on the surrounding evironment. While the parents are the major influences in early childhood, they in turn are subject to the pressures of the surrounding culture, and as time goes on, new persons become increasingly important. Kohut's concept of the self-object merely gives expression to the attempt of the child to merge with the parent and/or the inability of the child to cognitively separate himself from the parent. As the ego grows, the self-object recedes into the background; as indicated earlier, the concept itself is unnecessary, since it is already contained in the older formulations of merger, fusion, projection, projective identification, and the like.

Many therapists on the contemporary scene have found that schizophrenics respond more positively to family therapy than to individual. After the theoretical discussion above, this need not come as a surprise. Family therapy straightens out some of the conflicts within the family but does not force the patient to assume some individuality beyond the family, which individual therapy would do. It is the very inability of the schizophrenic to reach some stage of independence that makes him more amenable to the family therapy situation (McFarlane 1983).

In sum, the maladjusted individual (maladjustment neurosis) is one who remains so attached to the group of origin that he cannot achieve any real personhood in his own right. The self does not develop beyond the family; hence, even in adult life he is still strongly affected by the tachistoscopic presentation of "mommy and I are one" (Silverman, Lachmann, and Milich 1984). But this in no way negates his equal inability to accept his sexuality (which after all does imply a relationship outside the family), or his aggression, or his low frustration tolerance, which makes anxiety even more frightening to him than to others. In short, the explanations of schizophrenia in terms of the tension between the individual and the group and the one in terms of the weak ego, harsh superego, fear of id impulses, and excessive anxiety (all the classical explanations) do not in any way contradict each another, so that they do not in any way call for new formulations or new terms.

A further addition to analytic theory that comes out of this discussion is the proper appreciation of the role of the group in the life span. For growth proceeds not only by successive libidinal drives, succesive love objects, and stages in the self-development but also by successive moves from one group to another. Identity, as will be seen in more detail later (chapter 8), involves group belonging. The person's identity is made up of the various groups to which he belongs or had belonged in the course of life from the family of origin on.

The vital importance of the group has also been overlooked or ignored by classical analytic theory, again for largely political reasons because group therapists, some of whom at first were analytically trained (e.g., Wolf, Ackerman), gradually moved more and more away from analysis and set up group therapy as an "idealized" therapeutic modality in its own right. This severance of the therapeutic modality from the basic analytic paradigm is quite frequent. At first the practitioners are analysts who hope to get results that are better than those achieved by classical analysis. They add some modality, such as the group or the family. Then they attract followers who are not trained analytically and who do not have the same understanding of analysis. These followers then discard the analysis, latch on to the new therapeutic modality, and build that up out of proportion. Again, this is a political rather than a scientific maneuver. After a while, as today, the various fields of group therapy, family therapy, psychoanalytic therapy, and pure psychoanalysis are so far apart that no reconciliation seems possible, although a closer look at what is going on does indicate that the contradictions are not nearly as great as they may seem.

The Adjustment Neuroses

The maladjustment neurosis, usually designated deviance, has been known from time immemorial and in every culture ever studied: there are always some deviants. But that there is also an adjustment neurosis is a discovery that was made by psychoanalysis, the first psychological theory to give the theoretician the conceptual tools with which he could approach the problems that the average person has to face in his culture. As will also be seen, this notion of the adjustment neuroses has already taken a strong hold on the average American and promises to become more and more important as time goes on.

The adjustment neurosis can best be understood in light of the analytic ideal (Fine 1981). This is an outgrowth of Freud's definition of normality as the capacity to love and work. These two requirements have been expanded as follows: man achieves the greatest degree of happiness when he a) loves; b) has pleasure; c) has sexual gratification; d) has feeling yet e) is guided by reason; f) has a role in a family; g) has a role in the social order; h) has an adequate sense of self-esteem; i) has creative outlets; j) can communicate with his fellow men; k) can work; and l) is free from psychiatric symptomatology. Each of these merits more detailed consideration.

Love. Love has the capacity to make men happy (Fine 1985). Here the unfortunate break in the history of psychoanalysis between the early Freud, who examined the love life of his time, and the later Freud (after 1914), who focused much more strongly on aggression, has had pernicious consequences. Love has been forgotten so competely that the very term is not listed in the official *Glossary of Psychoanalytic Terms* (Moore and Fine 1968), nor is it listed in other official compendia, such as the *Psychiatric Glossary* or Laplanche and Pontalis' *The Language of Psychoanalysis*. This is also the more astounding when it is recalled that in 1908 Freud suggested to the Viennese Psychoanalytic Society that they set up an Academy of Love. Up to 1914 Freud always emphasized the inability to love as the crucial factor in neurosis; and even in the 1914 paper, where he introduced profound changes in theory, he could still write that "we must begin to love in order not to fall ill, and we are bound to fall ill if, in consequence of frustration, we are unable to love" (14:85).

In a previous book I have differentiated between love cultures and hate cultures (Fine 1985) and tried to show that western civilization has since the time of the Greeks been a hate culture. In this hate culture love becomes more a refuge than anything else. Ideally, love involves a strong affectionate feeling, mutual reciprocity, physical gratification of some kind, and the chance to experience it within a love culture. This ideal is rarely achieved though it is not unknown or impossible. One of Freud's major points should not be forgotten: sex without love is possible, though not as gratifying as some think, but love without sex or some capacity for physical gratification is a psychological impossibility. The insistence that love should be sexless, which was so characteristic of the nineteenth century, can be seen as the root of many of the neurotic disturbances that Freud analyzed and that we still analyze today. A fuller discussion of love will be found in chapter 7.

Pleasure. The pleasure principle not only dominates human behavior but does so quite rightly. There is not the remotest reason, other than perverse neurotic gratification, why suffering should be preferred or even exalted. Yet throughout history we find that suffering has been placed on a higher ethical plane than pleasure: as among saintly ascetics who mortified the flesh, or flagellants who deliberately beat themseles or had others beat them, or the Russian Skoptzi who castrated themselves, or the African tribes who impose horrible mutilations on little girl's genitals (Hosken 1979) so that she will not enjoy sex later on in life, or the contemporary sadomasochism (SM) enthusiasts, some of whom see SM as the "last frontier" (of what?). It is of course true that an indiscriminate abandon to any kind of pleasure will in the long run prove harmful, especially if the pleasures are of a physical kind, the effects of which wear off after a while; but this is no reason that a more reasoned and temperate acceptance of pleasure should not be accepted as a sensible way of life.

Sexual Gratification. Sexual gratification is again an aspect of the hate culture that has been the cause of much needless distress. As with pleasure, there is no reason for the excessive sexual taboos that dominated the world of Freud a century ago. And in the course of the century more and more of the old taboos have been relinquished: premarital sexuality, sex in the teens, the right of both men and women to enjoy sex to the fullest, the recognition that sexual problems exist in both sexes and are correctible, the shedding of excessive clothing, even to the point where nudity is acceptable in many parts of the world, all are desirable outcomes of the sexual revolution that Freud started. He showed that sexual repression leads to physical illness, a startling thesis that many of his contemporaries, who also urged greater sexual freedom, had overlooked. If sexual frustration causes illness, why maintain it at such a high price?

On the other hand, again as with pleasure, indiscriminate gratification can have all kinds of undesirable consequences: venereal disease, unwanted pregnancies, excessive jealousies leading to violence, and the like. But again, as with pleasure, there is no reason that a moderate acceptance of sexuality cannot be a source of enormous happiness to the average couple. In view of the central role of the family, marital sexuality will no doubt remain basic, but the anthropological evidence shows that for many people extramarital sexuality, if it does not interfere with the marital relationship, can also become a happy part of life. The hate culture has blinded us to such an extent that the promise of a good life still remains very frightening.

Feeling. This is again one of the desiderata of the good life. In general, the WASP personality, with its strict avoidance of feeling and spontaneity, has been the dominant image in American society for a long time. This has led to a variety of repressions, which, as Freud showed, in time break through to form symptoms or make life miserable in other ways.

But once again excessive emotionality can become a source of pain. The problem becomes more one of release of negative emotions, such as hatred, jealousy, envy, revenge, and the like, than of positive emotions, warmth, love, affection, enjoyment. The degree to which our civilization has for centuries been built on wishes for revenge is deplorable. Whole countries, such as Britain and Ireland or the various Lebanese factions or blacks and whites in America carry on feuds that last for decades, if not longer. To this day the American South will not admit that it engaged in a civil war but insist that it was a "war between the states." Textbook publishers who wish to sell their books in the South are compelled to conform.

Reason. Reason remains one cornerstone of the good life. Paradoxically, psychoanalysis, which has explored man's seeming irrationality so thoroughly, comes out with the conclusion that man is never really irrational; he merely shifts the rationality to an unconscious level. This realization has allowed astute clinicians to understand the verbalizations of schizophrenics and others and has also uncovered the secret of dreams, peculiar gestures, slips of the tongue, and other seemingly bizarre actions and words.

The capacity of the human being to reason clearly is limited by two factors: his given intelligence and his emotional prejudices. So far as we can see, all human beings or all cultural groups have the same basic intelligence, so that the outcome in terms of capacity to think clearly depends more on cultural factors than on anything else. As far as emotional prejudices are concerned, these take a long time to overcome; however, as Freud once said, "the voice of reason is weak, but it persists until it gets a hearing."

Role in the Family. As Margaret Mead once observed, communes come and communes go, but somehow the family returns. The family is in fact a specifically human achievement, although many animal species do have elementary families. But with the human, there is a role for a father because of his psychological attachments, and the united family can provide a degree of security and affection that cannot be obtained anywhere else. All human societies have been built around the family in one form or another; Murdock (1949) presents evidence that the nuclear family is universal, though it may, and often does, extend in various directions.

The family, with the mutual forms of gratification offered by the various family members to one another, is uniquely qualified to make the human being happy. In contrast, the older image of an originally promiscuous group, which many saw as an ideal at that time, as an antidote to the repressions of the family has since been abandoned as historical fact, and as an alternative life style, it becomes increasingly less appealing. Regardless of the culture, persons without a role in the family invariably show a much higher incidence of all kinds of physical and emotional disturbances. In our society, e.g., the highest suicide rate is found among single men over the age of forty-five.

Even though the family is in many ways an ideal arrangement, it can, and does, lead to terrible conflicts. Again here, as with pleasure, sexuality, emotion, and so on, some moderation is essential. Modern experiments to abolish the family, such as communes, the early Soviet experiments, or the Israeli kibbutzim have all failed and gone back to the family structure. Improvement of the psychosocial interior of the family makes more sense than its abolition.

Role in the Social Order. Just as the family is universal, the social order is too. Many types of social orders have been described, and it hardly seems to matter which one is chosen by a particular group, although obviously a lot depends on the material conditions with which they are faced. Without some social order the human being is lost, even if the social order is as widely dispersed and as isolated as, say, among the Eskimos.

In animals the dominance-submission pattern has been described as the mechanism by which order is kept. Among humans there is no such built-in mechanism, and social orders tend to deteriorate in various ways. Some people become too powerful, some too sadistic, some too murderous. The rational management of society is a problem that is always present but one that can be handled.

Sense of Self-Esteem. To be happy, the human being has to be able to value himself; we call this a sense of identity or self-esteem. This self-esteem drives from all the experiences described earlier—love, sexuality, pleasure, family role, feeling, etc. It is easy enough to see how any individual's self-esteem is built up in a given society; it is harder to order that society in such a way that everyone can feel well about themselves.

Children are especially vulnerable to damage to their self-esteem. Children learn to love by being loved. If they are exposed to violence, separation, abandonment, mistreatment, or the like, their self-esteem lowers considerably.

The self-hatred of the blacks in the United States has been the subject of much study and discussion. The famous desegregation order of the U.S. Supreme Court in 1954 took cognizance of the highly deleterious consequences of this self-hatred and tried to correct it by desegregating the schools. According to some studies, there has been some success in that direction. Obviously, however, much more remains to be done. In general, the tendency of some dominant group to lord it over inferior groups, whether as an inferior race or in actual slavery damages the self-esteem of the inferiors.

Creative Outlets. The ability to live creatively rather than in repetitive stereotyped situations is one of the major hallmarks of mental health. This creativity relates to inner growth, not to outer achievements. Many studies have shown the severe mental problems associated with achievers in all walks of life; some theoreticians have even urged that the stress on achievement on our society produces more conflicts than it resolves.

Communication. One of the essential human requirements is to be able to communicate with one's fellow beings on an adult meaningful level. Inasmuch as so much of mental life exists in the unconscious, communication becomes extraordinarily difficult. Freud's elucidation of the dynamics of dream mechanisms in 1900 paved the way for an understanding of all unconscious communications, which follow the same principles as dreams.

Repression of anxiety-arousing material into the unconscious is a major defensive process and occurs in virtually all people much of the time. As a result, many persons are not in touch with the situations or stimuli that really arouse anxiety in them. Often enough, the defensive structures acquire secondary autonomy, so that a person may live out his whole life in a defensive manner without really ever becoming aware of the underlying conflicts; in fact, this is more the rule than the exception.

Work. Work should be a source of graification rather than a burden. Since the weakening or even disappearance of the Protestant ethic, people have been looking for a different kind of psychology to justify their immersion in work. The theory of work satisfaction has by now expanded into a study of the quality of life, so that looking for more satisfaction in work is equivalent to looking for more satisfaction in life. The rationalization of the work place is one of the most exciting of the recent developments in the mental health field.

Freedom from Psychiatric Symptomatology. Psychiatric symptoms are extremely disabling, ranging all the way from mild discomfort to total incapacity, including the unwillingness to live. Some psychiatric syndromes may have organic roots; if they do, they should be classified as neurological rather than psychiatric. The basic explanation for most psychiatric disability is psychological.

This formulation of the analytic ideal, a natural outgrowth of mainstream psychoanalysis from Freud on, can form the basis for further discussions of neurosis, psychosis, mental health, and related issues. Health can only be grasped in relation to sickness, and as long as sickness was defined as deviance and health as cultural normality, the most grievous errors resulted. But if health is defined in terms of the ideal, then sickness can be defined as the distance that the individual is from this ideal and, in a large measure for the culture, as the distance the culture in general is from the ideal. In that way, for the first time psychoanalysis presents a conceptual framework within which to gauge the mental health or sickness of any culture, just as normal physiology presents a framework within which to gauge the physical health of the members of any society. The argument that something is "normal" because it is commonly found in a given culture must be dropped in both the mental and the physical fields.

If neurosis is thus looked at as the distance from the analytic ideal, the historical developments of the past century in the growth of the mental health professionals make sense. Thus, when Freud discovered the sexual malaise of his generation, it first came to light in the case histories of his patients, who were after all deviants. Then, enlarging upon his newly found knowledge, he realized that sexual conflicts were endemic in his society; in 1898 he speculated that it would take mankind 100 years to overcome their sexual disabilities. The Kinsey reports (1940s-1950s) confirmed on a statistical basis much of what the psychoanalysts had discovered on a clinical basis. Consequently, the previous acceptance of sexual frustration, which had been considered normal, was now revealed to be an aspect of the culture. And since man had made it, man could also unmake it. Hence, the urge for overcoming sexual problems was shifted from the therapeutic (i.e., confined to deviants) to the educational (i.e., for the normal individual) realm.

Similar developments have occurred in all components of the analytic ideal. First it is uncovered in the clinical environment; then the question is asked: what is the difference between this clinical picture and the way in which the average person behaves or feels? When the answer is that there is none, then the question shifts again from the therapeutic to the educational. In this way, gradually psychotherapy and psychoanalysis become avenues to social reform.

It is, of course, fully recognized that the above is an ideal picture and far from everyday realities. These everyday realities are so bad that at the meeting of the World Mental Health Congress in 1983, Soedjamoko, the rector of the UN University in Tokyo, made the following gloomy statement:

> The world is at the brink of madness, as aberrant as any disturbed individual. The state of the world makes almost a mockery of mental health . . . . It is difficult to raise people with the mental strength to be peace-loving when they have been brought up surrounded by violence. How can they grow up sane in an insane world? (APA Sept. 1983:8)

The only exception that I would take to his statement is to the "brink of madness," which he describes has never been any different; the world has always been more insane than sane. In light of these discoveries, it is superfluous or misleading to think up ever-new categories of neurosis and/or mental disorders. If how people live and behave is compared with the analytic ideal and with the social-cultural institutions that are available, then a sufficent perspective is created to understand inner conflict and disturbance and to find means to treat it and to overcome it.

Thus, the search for the meaning or definition of neurosis shifts from a technical to a broader cultural-social level. However, in this process the technical discoveries should not be ignored or dropped or forgotten. the social-cultural malaise can best be understood by comparing what is ideally possible for the human being with what is practically available.

The Psychological Revolution

There are two entirely different levels at which the development of psychoanalytic theory has intersected with the surrounding society: the technical one, in which the mental health professionals are engaged, and the broader impact of psychoanalysis on the average cultured individual.

After reviewing some of the basic concepts that have been offered—narcissism, self, and identity—and the battles surrounding them, the conclusion is inescapable that these battles are much more politically than scientifically motivated. It is often said that psychology has had its Newton but has not yet found its Einstein. This, together with the Nobel prize complex from which many intellectuals suffer, leads, especially in this complex field, to the proliferation of ever more new and newer theories. Yet when they are looked at in the cold grey light of history, they represent at best only small additions to the basic structure bequeathed to us by Freud, a structure for which I have suggested the term mainstream analysis.

There really need be no *theoretical* argument about narcissism, self, and identity. They are all commonsense notions, easily fitted into the main body of mainstream analysis. What attracts attention, however, is when they are lifted out of the mainstream and set up as a "new paradigm" that resolves all the old problems. Actually, such an activity creates more problems than it resolves. Thus, while narcissism is easily understood as self-involvement and excessive narcissism as excessive self-involvement, the various technical definitions of narcissism that have been offered are so obscure as to make the subject incomprehensible; further, many of them are simply incorrect. Similarly, the notion of the self, which any child can and does understand, is suddenly catapulted into a "supraordinate" entity, thus reactivating the older notion of the soul, which the scientists of the nineteenth century had dispensed with once and for all. There is no end to the arguments about the theoretical meanings of these concepts because they all begin with the same error of avoiding the basic commonsense meaning.

Another source of error and confusion is the attempt to force everything into a rigid theoretical framework. Thus, the Freudians have attempted to fit self into the tripartite structure and have failed to do so; nevertheless, they continue to try. The reasonable conclusion is that the tripartite structure should be expanded to include the notion of the self, which is what has always gone on in practice. As I showed earlier, Freud used the self-concept at many points in a commonsense way, without losing himself in any terrible theoretical argument. And when he did start fooling around with the notion of narcissism in the 1914 paper, the result was chaotic. Occam's razor is still a valid guide for scientific method in psychology.

Thus, the real issue becomes the empirical one of clarifying the clinical and observational data. There are many narcissistic individuals; what is there about their lives and about the social order that makes them so narcissistic? People are concerned with various aspects of the self; how are these concerns to be formulated and investigated? Everybody has some identity; where does it come from, how does it function? These and similar questions make up the real subject matter of psychoanalytic inquiry, far more than the sterile arguments about theory that have filled the journal pages for so many years. I agree with Rangell (cf. above) that these theoretical arguments represent cult phenomena and that it is not necessary to change standard theory in any appreciable way to explain the phenomena. It is, however, necessary to state more clearly what standard theory is, since Freud was always changing his mind about many important issues (Fine 1979).

In *The Inner American* and *Mental Health in America* Veroff, Douvan, and Kulka (1981a, b) there is ample evidence that the psychological revolution introduced by Freud has had an enormous impact on American culture and that the technical arguments with which we have had to be concerned here are of little consequence. In general, the concept of the analytic ideal is easily grasped and accepted by an increasing number of people. Their books are worth more extended discussion.

The Inner American and its companion piece on therapy, *Mental Health in America*, present findings from two national studies of the American population that focused on questions of well-being and satisfaction, life experience and performance in major roles, psychological stress, and the methods people use to manage the stresses that life presents. The studies permit an assessment of life experience of Americans at two points in time: 1957, when the first study was conducted, and 1976, when it was replicated.

To consider the question of the subjective mental health of the American people, six topics were examined in more detail: feelings and sources of well-being; self-perceptions; marriage; parenthood; work; and symptom patterns. Beyond the traditional assessments of psychological adjustment, the surveys added four special emphases: a multiple-criteria approach, the analysis of psychological experience for positive as well as negative feelings, evaluation of the salience and experience in social roles, and measurement of people's psychological involvement with their own experience. Though somewhat different language is used, it is clear that what they are looking for is how people shape up in terms of the analytic ideal.

In summarizing the state of subjective mental health in 1976, Veroff, Douvan, and Kulka (1981a) note the following:

1. General sources and feelings of well-being: we seem to be a happy society

although we are somewhat worried about the future. Our happiness seems to be largely contingent upon interpersonal issues. Contentment in marriage is a very strong basis of well-being.

2. Self-perceptions: as a people we are fairly confident about our own efficacy. Most of us are willing to talk about our strengths. When we do so, most of us talk about personal rather than external qualities and conditions. In talking about our weaknesses, however, we are also more alerted to internal matters than to the external bases of difficulties.

3. Marriage: We are a family-centered society. Family roles—marriage and parenthood—yield high value for most people; compared to work or leisure activities they are clearly more central to self-definition. Most married people invest in marriage and derive both support and satisfaction in the relationship with their partners. They report their marriages to be happy, and they feel reasonably adequate in their own performance as husbands and wives.

4. Parenthood: Parenthood, like marriage, is very important in the life view, identity, and values of people who choose to become parents or who blunder into parenthood. Norms about parenthood are neither strong nor rigid.

5. Work: As a people, we are surprisingly committed to and satisfied with our work. Very few people admit to being dissatisfied, ambivalent, or even neutral about their jobs. Most people say that the work they do is challenging and interesting when asked to think about the issue.

6. Symptoms: A minority of American men and women in our society report a high frequency of physical, psychological, or psychosomatic symptoms. More women than men report a high frequency of symptoms that would unmistakably be coded as indicating distress.

7. Coping with problems and social supports: our dominant mode of adapting to worries or periods of unhappiness is talking to someone about our troubles. We are a very social people who rely on interpersonal contacts with others to help us cope with life's problems.

In terms of therapy, Veroff and his co-workers found that more than a third of the American population had turned to professional help for some kind of personal problem at some time in their lives.

On the whole, the study presents perhaps too rosy a picture of the degree of mental health; had the interviews continued, or probed more deeply, much more might have come out. But there is little doubt that the persons interviewed value the analytic ideal as one of the major guidelines to living. Although the overall degree of anxiety was about the same in 1957 as in 1976, people were obviously looking inward rather than outward for answers.

Thus, the notion that the technical categories of neurosis are holdovers from the past and that neurosis is looked at most fruitfully as the distance from the analytic ideal has ample evidence to support it. This distance is a function of the culture as much of the individual. Few individuals can overcome their culture entirely, although many try.

CHAPTER 5

THE GROUP AND THE INDIVIDUAL

The group is an essential part of human existence. Because of sharp (and unnecessary) theoretical splits, the literature in the field generaly deals with either the one or the other, rather than with the interaction of the two. For the individual, psychoanalytic psychology has been the dominant theoretical frame of reference; for the group a behavioristic sociology-psychology has served that purpose. The two must be integrated to provide a complete picture.

Ever since the loss of domination of the Church after the Middle Ages, modern society has been fiercely individualistic, much more so than other cultures, either contemporary or historical. Nevertheless, the individual develops within a group. Human existence could in fact be described very well in terms of the groups through which the individual passes in the course of life, from the family to the larger society. How the self-image grows out of this process and interaction is the question posed in this and the next chapter.

Perhaps the best approach is that first presented by the Dutch-French sociologist Arnold van Gennep in 1908, which he named the rites de passage—the rites of passage. Van Gennep viewed these rites as universally valid for the transition of a person from one group to another, a transition that goes on throughout life. In this transition he delineated three stages: separation, transition, and incorporation. To form a self, the child must separate from the family, go through a transition stage, and then incorporate himself into a new group (or the family at a higher level).

Although the language varies widely, all students of human development have incorporated these three stages into their thinking. The family therapist Murray Bowen speaks of the undifferentiated family ego mass—a conglomerate emotional oneness that exists in all levels of intensity, from the family in which it is most intense to the family in which it is almost imperceptible (Bowen 1981).

Freud spoke of the progression from narcissism to anaclitic dependency to object relatedness in his description of the development of object relations (1914). Mahler et al. (1975) describe the stages as separation, rapprochement, and object constancy, a different formulation but not a different idea. Piaget speaks of accommodation and assimilation, the two tied together by circular reactions, again a similar idea. Thus, there is virtual unanimity about the stages of the growth process, which moves from the group to the individual.

My interest, however, is only in certain aspects of the self, the self-image, and self-esteem. How these develop, the influences brought to bear on them, what leads to health and what to sickness—these are the major questions that I will seek to answer here. Understandably the literature has concentrated much more heavily on cognitive aspects of the self, more easily observed and more easily measured. However, in keeping with the psychoanalytical frame of reference, the emotional aspects of self-development will be my main concern.

The First Eighteen Months

During the first year and a half of life the infant cannot yet verbalize any statement about the self. However, a careful perusal of his behavior shows that some notion of the self, however fuzzy and however unformulated or poorly formulated, is present. This awareness of the self emerges in all modalities, developing slowly in accordance with the emotional and cognitive growth of the child.

The most striking emergence of self-awareness comes with the reaction to the mirror image in the second year of life (Amsterdam 1972). Amsterdam noted the presence of a variety of self-conscious behavior, including embarrassment, coyness, showing off and clowning, starting at about fourteen months of age. In the first year of life infants responded to their mirror images with unrestrained enthusiasm and delight. In the second year of life, children no longer respond to the mirror with naive joy, but they withdraw and become wary of their images. Self-conscious behavior follows and continues through the period when children show objective recognition of the image starting at eighteen months. These observations lead one to conclude that some change in the feeling about oneself has occurred in this second year of life, so that the question arises: what is this change and what significance does it have?

The inner change in the child at this time has been described in various ways. Spitz (1965) emphasized the appearance of the capacity to say no. Mahler et al.

(1975) stressed the rapproachment phenomenon, moving back and forth from and to mother. Freud and his early disciples (Fenichel 1945) pinpointed the anal problem and the appearance of an obsessive-compulsive personality structure. Piaget saw the change as that from sensory-motor thought to preoperational thought. He characterized the preoperational child's thought as midway between socialized adult thought and the completely autistic and egocentric thought of the Freudian unconscious (Piaget 1923; Flavell 1963). Galenson and Roiphe (1981) clarified that the time around eighteen months is roughly when sexual awareness develops, with positive feelings in boys, somewhat negative and apprehensive in girls.

While all of the above observations are valid and useful, they omit another central feature of the child's development: the move into group awareness and activity. Traditionally, it has been assumed that the child is only tied to the mother at this time, that other people will come later. Greenspan (1980, 1982) postulates a move from the dyadic to the triadic at around two and a half years old. Fine (1984) has urged that a triadic awareness, however dim, may be noted in the infant from birth on; among the more classical theoreticians Klein (1948) essentially agrees with such a position, though her stress is highly individualistic and virtually ignores the social surroundings.

Many have speculated about why the earliest period in life has been so impenetrable. Schachtel (1947) feels that the dividing line is the capacity for language; the earliest age is the prelinguistic, sharply divided as inner experience from the later linguistic stage. This is a plausible hypothesis, but still ignores the social environment. As is well known, Freud had already discovered that the amnesic barrier, before which nothing is recalled, occurs at about two years of age; this observation has been verified innumerable times since. Thus, we reach the puzzling conclusion that the experiences of the first two years are of vital importance for the child, yet they cannot be recalled or brought to light by any known means—unrememberable and unforgettable.

Since there seems to be such a strong probability that "the child is the father of the man," so that the first eighteen months or two years are of great significance, a number of studies have attempted to find out whether later personality formation can be inferred from any of these earliest events.

Perhaps the first of these studies was that by Shirley (1933). She studied twenty-five babies from birth to two years of age using standardized developmental tests as well as behavioral observations. She then wrote personality sketches of each baby. Fifteen years after the original study, Neilon (1948) interviewed and tested nineteen of the original subjects, and gathered complete data on sixteen subjects. The follow-up included two personality tests, independent ratings by subjects and their mothers of twenty-three personality traits and six specific abilities, interviews with each of the subjects and their mothers, and rating scales and ability scales mailed to the fathers. Personality sketches at age seventeen were then written without knowledge of the matching infancy descriptions. Boys and girls were analyzed separately. Ten judges were asked to match six female infant sketches to five adolescent sketches, and five judges were asked to match thirteen male infant sketches with ten sketches at adolescence. For the females, the mean number of successes for all judges involved was 3.2, which significantly exceeded chance. The largest number of successful matchings, achieved by three of the ten judges, was four of the six subjects. For the males, the mean number of successes was 2.6, again exceeding chance.

Numerous other studies were conducted at various research centers in the postwar period. Some of the most important are Gesell and Ames (1937), Bell, et al. (1971), Thomas, Chess, and Birch (1968), Escalona (1968), Escalona and Heider (1959), Kagan (1971), Honzik and MacFarlane (1963), Jones (1960), and Moss and Kagan (1964). While suggestive findings were obtained here and there, as in the Shirley study, little of any significance was definitively established. As Bell et al. stated: "Newborn behavior is more like a preface to a book than a table of its contents yet to be unfolded. Further, the preface is itself merely a rough draft undergoing rapid revision" (1971:132).

Freud, of course, always emphasized that the first five years of life were the major determinants of the individual's personality, and this has been a core psychoanalytic hypothesis ever since, with some variations. According to Fisher and Greenberg (1977), for some aspects of this theory the empirical evidence is moderately supportive. Annemarie Weil (1970) spoke of the "basic core" laid down in infancy, which changes little in the course of life, referring mainly to activity and passivity types. Engel (Viederman 1979) published a 25-year follow-up study on a woman who had had an esophageal fistula as a child, and for that reason was followed up at the hospital; she emerged as a rather passive-dependent woman. However, beyond this point the evidence is more clinical than conclusive. Fries (1977) presented findings from her own 43-year-old longitudinal study. Four cases were studies from prenatal state to parenthood. She particularly emphasized the constitutional factors in theory; in practice, however, in the case presented in the most detail, the eventual outcome was clinically surprising, emphasizing that even with all the resources in the world, prediction is very difficult. In addition, precisely what is carried over from infancy is hard to determine.

With regard to the basic questions I have been asking about narcissism and the self, the following could be said about their emergence and functioning in the first eighteen months or two years of life. Inherently, the infant is cognitively inadequate rather than narcissistic in the pathological sense. He is endowed with various capacities that he takes delight in developing (e.g., seeing, eating, touching, moving, etc.). In this sense it is narcissistic, deriving pleasure from his own activities, but not in the adult sense that he prefers these activities to human interactions. The infant can easily lapse into a defensive narcissism when the maternal care is inadequate.

The self-image develops gradually. Some self-awareness exists from birth, perhaps prenatally. It is not verbalized in this early period, and perhaps for that reason it is much more flexible and much more likely to change with more or less favorable circumstances. Psychoanalytically, these circumstances are primarily connected with feelings of love and hate (good mother–bad mother) that are experienced in the environment (Fine 1985). The clinical evidence that points to feelings of deprivation and frustration from earliest infancy also points to the continuation of these frustrations throughout life. When they are changed, the child tends to change (Goldfarb 1974).

The Oedipal Period (18 months to 6 Years)

The family is a universal human institution. Though its immediate form varies widely (polygamy, extended, nuclear, etc.), at its core there is always a nuclear group composed of mother, child, and father (Murdock 1949).

Freud focused on the oedipal complex rather than the total family structure as such. In *Three Essays* (1905) he wrote:

> It has justly been said that the Oedipus complex is the nuclear complex of the neuroses, and constitutes the essential part of their content. It represents the peak of infantile sexuality, which, through its aftereffects, exercises a decisive influence on the sexuality of adults. Every new arrival on this planet is faced by the task of mastering the Oedipus complex; anyone who fails to do so falls victim to neurosis. (7:226, footnote)

While Freud's emphasis on the oedipal conflict has been considerably broadened and deepened, first by himself, later by others, it still leaves unstated that the oedipal conflict lies at the heart of family structure. It is only within this family structure that the crystallization and subsequent development of the self can be understood.

In spite of the self-evident nature of the above remarks, the field has bifurcated, with consequent misunderstanding and confusion. In continuation of Freud, the more orthodox psychoanalytic theoreticians have virtually ignored the family as a structure, though paying close attention to its individual parts (cf. Greenspan and Pollock 1980, where the family is scarcely mentioned, or Fenichel 1945, where again the emphasis is highly individualistic). On the other hand family theorists, while exploring the family in imaginative depth, have generally ignored the manner in which the individual interacts with the family, falling back on the common sociological assumption that social forces will generally override psychological factors, or perhaps more accurately, that sociological forces are more basic than psychological. Hence, there is one group that studies identity and the self from an individual point of view (Kohut remains in this category too), while another stresses the group, the family, and society, almost ignoring the identity crises of the individual. For a full picture to come out both points of view have to be integrated.

In the nineteenth century many anthropologists (most of whom had never been out in the field) cherished the romantic notion that originally society consisted of communal bands with no structure, and that families formed out of this mass. Subsequent research has established this as an illusion. The family is universal, with some aspect of the nuclear family always present, and has a definite biological basis.

The biological basis of the family derives from three aspects of human existence: the woman's shift to regular menstrual cycles instead of the less frequent estrus of nonhuman females; the feelings of affection and love that require expression and that are expressed most easily within a family; and the greater capacity of the human being to remember his past and to meditate about his future, which leads in particular to the need to give the family a definite form in which the father will play a clear-cut role. The role of the father is highly variable in subhumans because of their inability to function at the same psychological level; thus, the mother-infant bond may be as strong as in the human, but then once the infant is weaned neither party remembers much, if anything, about it. Thus, for sound biological as well as psychological reasons the family is always one of the pillars of human existence.

The self reaches a new level at about eighteen months, when the toddler is able to recognize itself in the mirror, and when the earliest verbalizations of me, mine, or the like begin to appear. But thereafter it does not stand still. There is throughout childhood, and actually all of life, continual examination and reexamination of the self-image, except that the changes in childhood are more dramatic.

Because the influences brought to bear on the self image are so complex, no simple formula will do justice to the situation. Instead, much as Roheim had to do with the anthropological data, the child's growth must be carefully charted through the numerous developmental lines into which they may be divided for purposes of clarification. Nevertheless, the younger the child, the more effect the parents have on his growth; part of the oedipal struggle is to attach oneself to the parents and then to free oneself. Thus, in its broad connotations not its specific referents, Freud's formula, cited above, still remains valid.

Throughout life the love-hate dichotomy remains basic. We can speak of love cultures vs. hate cultures, of loving families vs. hating families (Beavers 1977), of loving people vs. hating people (Fine 1985). No cognitive aspect of the personality can be properly understood without proper reference to its bearing on love and hate.

The dichotomy of self vs. object that begins to take more concrete form at about eighteen months, has been explored in great depth. However, what has been given insufficient attention is that there is an ongoing dichotomy of the individual vs. the group as well. Ideally, the course of life can be seen as moving from one person to another; it can also be seen as moving from one group to another. Because this developmental process of group belongingness has not been adequately appreciated, I wish to discuss it at greater length.

Even in the Narcissus myth there is reference to the family; mother tells him he is the most beautiful man on earth but never to look at himself; sister becomes his passion; so even Narcissus is not completely narcissistic.

Likewise, in the child in the oedipal period the narcissism always has to be seen in relation to the surrounding people (this is why I rejected the notion of narcissistic personality disorder earlier). Narcissism is at times healthy, as in the child's love affair with the world or it is defensive because the child feels hurt and retreats into himself. Healthy narcissism is a sign of a healthy ego; defensive narcissism is the hallmark of the weak ego, even if, as in many artists, it leads to extraordinary productions.

There can be no doubt that the presence of so many different variables impinging on the formation of the self-image accounts for the difficulty of predicting the later behavior from early data. Even in a relatively "calm" index like the IQ, Bayley (1955) found wide variations in the first eight years, which had never been suspected to exist before.

Likewise, the traditional emphasis on the parents has to be broadened to account for all the findings. Gunnar, Senior, and Hartup (1984), studying the exploratory behavior of eighteen- and thirty-month-old children, found that peer presence facilitated leaving the mother. Thus, developmental changes occurring in the second and third year include the increased salience of age mates in supporting separation from the mother and exploration of the environment in the context of sustained social interaction.

As Brazelton (1976) points out, the contemporary neonatal research stresses particularly *interaction* and *quality of life*. Neither one is easy to single out or to measure, yet both are vital to a clarification of the whole scheme of development and of course the formation and growth of the self-image and self-esteem.

Looking more closely at this period in childhood, the self-image changes rapidly, especially since the major concern of the child until puberty is growth and his uncertainty about what he will be like a year hence. This is why no matter how young the child, and even when demonstrable organic damage is present, remedial measures almost always prove to be of help, if properly conceptualized and carried out (Fraiberg 1980; Tjossem 1976).

While self-awareness grows, it can never be said to be complete, even in the healthy adult; there are always areas in the personality that are denied, distorted, or simply unavailable to even the most sophisticated individual, as psychoanalysis always shows. Thus, the self-description "I am normal" is largely a denial of what is really going on inside; in this connection Sullivan's phrase "the personified person I" (Perry 1982) is illuminating. Furthermore, self-awareness is a function of the degree of disturbance, of the particular function involved, and of the cultural values impinging on the child.

Careful investigation has revealed no such entity as the "nuclear self," which Kohut and his followers have stressed so strongly (Kohut 1977, 1984). This, as pointed out in an earlier chapter, is a resurrection of the centuries-old idea of the soul.

Rather, as the child grows, there is a series of conscious and unconscious self-evaluations in the many different aspects of the personality: toilet training, sexuality, interpersonal relations, aggression, linguistic, competence, peer interaction, and many others. Roheim's (1921a) work is relevant for the earliest years.

What the nuclear self really refers to is a self-evaluation, the sense in which Sullivan used the term self (1939). The child believes himself to be "good" or "bad" or "competent" or "incompetent" in various areas, and this self-evaluation tends to take on a global character in the more disturbed individual, though the healthier one will be able to say I am good at this but not so good at that.

Mahler's conceptualization of the rapprochement crisis beginning at eighteen months and ending roughly at three years also has to be questioned. As she sees it (Mahler et al. 1975), the toddler moves away from mother and then back to mother, for "refueling." This ignores the fact that the toddler is also moving toward other people, father, peers, siblings, in many cases grandparents (Cohler and Grunebaum 1981). The eighteen-month old is already able to join in a group, although at a modest level; the thirty-month old fully. Thus, there is first of all the family group, and second the next group away from the family, the peers. This peer group now becomes important and remains important for the rest of the person's life, though its composition will vary all the way.

Finally, self-esteem in this age period depends most heavily on the amount of love and/or hate received from the parents and other significant persons in the environment. This love/hate will vary all over place, depending on the functions involved and the cultural environment in which the child is living. Thus, socioeconomic status turns out to be a powerful determinant of self-esteem, generally favoring the "rich, powerful and well-born" in any society. Had his thinking been different, Freud could in fact just as well have begun with the innumerable faces of Victorian cruelty (Pearsall 1975) as with the frustrations of Victorian sexuality.

Latency (6 years to Puberty)

In his earliest formulation of psychosexual development (1905) Freud divided childhood into three periods: early infantile sexuality to oedipal complex, latency, and puberty. In latency, he held, sexual manifestations were quiescent, only to be resumed in full force at puberty. This he felt corresponded to a biologically determined growth pattern. Yet, he later maintained that it can give rise to a complete interruption of sexual life only in cultural groups that have made the suppression of infantile sexuality a part of their system: "This is not the case with the majority of primitive peoples" (1953–1970, 20:37, footnote). Thus, he was saying that while latency is a biological fact, its manifestations depend on the cultural environment.

Subsequent analysts have on the one hand agreed with Freud, in seeing a diminution of sexual activity in latency (or a total absence), and on the other disagreed with him to stress other factors. Sarnoff (1976) sums up the later views as follows: In general latency can be divided into two parts, the early phase from six to eight and the later phase from eight to twelve. The early phase is marked by the child's preoccupation with himself. There is an inhibition of masturbation. Fantasies are frightening. The superego is strict and brutal. Real objects are denied to the child as outlets. Fantasy is the primary means of adjusting to emotional stresses. The child uses reality only to disengage himself from untenable and unfulfillable drives and fantasies (Bornstein 1951, 1953).

The second phase is marked by an increasing availability of the outside world as the source of objects through which fantasies can be gratified. Masturbatory activity becomes less proscribed. Fantasies contain figures that resemble people. He can accept his oedipal urges a little more, and so can represent parents with symbols that are a little less disguised. There is an overall diminution of the strictness of the superego. As a result of maturation, the child becomes more aware of the world, his place in it, and his relationship to the future.

In this orthodox view, which has been explored in depth by numerous other authors, the role of the group is virtually ignored, to be admitted only as a way of gratifying the impulses. Yet, as common observation shows, from the time the child enters school he spends more time with his peers than with his parents. Furthermore, this gap constantly increases, so that by the time adolescence is reached some children shun their parents entirely. Surely such an overwhelming attachment to peer groups must be more significant than merely gratifying impulses. Sarnoff himself says: "latency, like a crystal held to the light, has facets unsuspected till it is viewed from another angle" (1976:84). I propose to view it from such another angle, that of successive group formations.

Again this is part of my fundamental thesis, that the child moves from one group to another throughout the course of life and that this group movement must be coordinated with the individual movement to get a full picture of its dynamics.

In spite of the obvious fact that children from an early age live in groups, this group behavior has received little dynamic scrutiny after the pure family period ends, usually with the move to school. One of the few authors who has written about the dynamics of the group in latency is Edith Buxbaum:

> The peer group becomes increasingly more important for the child. He feels alone and unhappy if he doesn't have friends. The group serves a number of functions for the latency child. The school group which is the choice of the parents licensed, ie., sanctioned by the State, is supposed to introduce the child into the knowledge and mores of his society. The knowledge which he is taught is censored, i.e., it is selected by the educators who decide what he should or should not learn. The child is being indoctrinated. That word is usually reserved for those regimes who are teaching the children an ideology which may or may not be in agreement with that of the parents. Yet teaching with the system or against the system has in common that in either case it is an authority figure who superimposes

> his ideas upon the child. However, the child uses the group in ways that do not serve that purpose alone. By joining or making a children's group within the school group or outside of it, he gets into a group which has a life of its own, unsupervised or directed by adults. In such subgroup he may recreate the world as he sees it: play house, or school, break into houses, and terrorize younger children. In either case, the children devise their own rules and organizations, decide what is or is not permissible within their group. It is the subgroup which allows the child to think differently from his parents: the subgroup's judgment may supercede the parents' judgment and strengthen his own. Depending on his own strength or weakness, he may go from being dependent on his parents to being dependent on the group or making himself independent from both if he feels secure enough to do so (1980:133–134)

Even here, the feeling comes through that the group serves a defiant purpose, as in her comment that the children can "terrorize" younger children. There is still insufficient stress that the child starts to live with groups, and remains with them for the rest of his life, moving from one group to another, following Van Gennep's formulation of rites of passage: separation, transition, incorporation. It is this process that combines with individual inner psychological development to produce a full and happy person. Since the focus in the literature is almost entirely on groups of disturbed children, or experimental subjects (e.g., Strain 1981; Goodman 1972), I shall concentrate more on the values inherent in group formation for the positive growth of its members.

It is well known that the child's initial reaction to school depends on how similar or dissimilar the school is to his home environment (Jencks et al. 1979). When the relationship is negative, understandably there is considerable friction and frustration. But when it is positive, it introduces the child to a whole new world. In some cases such a world would be available to the child anyhow because of the high professional attainments of the parents. But in many others, probably the majority, what counts most is the attitude of the parents toward school, not their own educational level. Here the child, supported by the parents, moves into a world where he will eventually surpass the achievements of the parents. Traditionally, this has been quite common in the American system.

According to Bowlby (1973), most school phobias center around the child's fear that mother will die or be hurt while he is at school. But most children do not develop school phobias, though it may often take a little time to get used to the new situation. What most children whose families are positively related to the school experience is, for the first time in their lives, camaraderie with a group of like-aged children. As yet, this group spirit is educational not unisexed (that will come shortly). There are of course many different affective reactions involved: learning, obedience to or defiance of the teacher (authority), freedom from the mother and the home for the first time in life, etc. But the overwhelming *new* experience is that of group solidarity in a peer group.

The relationship between the solidarity with the peer group and the intrapsychic reactions have a profound effect on the sense of identity and the self-image. If the child falls too far behind, it falls out of the group; if it forges too far ahead, it also falls out of the group (it is often even isolated). Hence a conflict arises between the individual self-image and the self-image imposed by the group. In one form or another this conflict will come up for the rest of the life span.

What are the psychological benefits derived from the group experience? Many analytic authors see the group as an arena in which individual needs can be projected and handled via the projections. Yet, if the child is not put into such a group, there are other consequences.

Furthermore, these heterosexual or coeducational groups are universal, found in all cultures. It should also be considered that group behavior is characteristic of almost all animal species, so characteristic in fact that a different word is available for each animal group—a pride of lions, a gaggle of geese, a flock of sheep, a herd of cows, etc. Thus, it can be inferred that in animals as well there is a profound need for the group experience. The mechanism of dominance-submission (the "pecking order") guarantees that the group will not be disrupted by undue violence, and provides a mechanism to subdue such violence if it should occur (Moss 1982).

It is natural to think that behavior found in most animal species and in virtually all human cultures has some instinctual basis, even if it is not the direct expression of an instinctual drive. Thus, we are driven back to the notion of some kind of gregarious instinct, even though such an idea has been almost universally rejected.

The need would appear to be understandable in the light of the concept of rites of passage. After participating in one group (the family) for many years, the child is separated, has a short period of transition, which may or may not be accompanied by anxiety symptoms which as a rule pass quickly, and then is reincorporated into a new group. The nature of the new group will be different at some point, although if the same group stays together all through the school years (Spiro 1965) a greater sense of security results.

In the early part of the century everything was ascribed to instinct, following Darwin's extraordinary discoveries in evolution. Freud's role was to focus first on the sexual instinct, then the aggressive, but above all on the intricate psychological ramifications that occur because the instinct cannot be directly gratified. In reaction to Freud and the early psychologists (e.g., William James) behaviorism in the period between the two world wars insisted that there are no instincts at all. This extreme behaviorist position has now passed into history. There are obviously unlearned drives, or instincts, if you wish, and many ways of modifying these instincts. But what are they? Apart from love, hate, and fear, which virtually all agree upon, there must also be some need for group cohesiveness.

However, this group cohesiveness is not as unitary a need as the other drives, with which it may also interact. It is rather a maturational sequence, the manifestations of which appear at different ages and in somewhat different forms.

Anyone who has ever seen the enormous pleasure that children take in their play groups, or in their school groups if they are positive, cannot doubt the enormously positive rewards that the children derive from them, and would question the notion that group formation is essentially defensive. This does not alter the fact that the nature of the group will show considerable variation as the child grows.

The self-image of the six-year old thus embraces membership in a group as an essential constituent. Group membership in turn interacts with membership in the family group, but not yet with membership in the wider social order. On the other hand there is also the individual self-image, formed out of the superego, which embodies the mother and father, and the personality of the teacher, a new outside authority on whom the superego is projected. Again, the amounts of love and hate in these individual aspects of the self-image will interact with the group to make the child feel great self-esteem or considerable self-hatred.

In this situation as well individual differences become more important than before. The handicapped child feels left out of it, emerging with a negative self-image because he cannot live up to the standards set by the others. The gifted child soon learns that he is superior to most of the others and begins to wonder how to handle these superiority feelings. Special talents also come to play a role at this age—the ability to dance, engage in athletic sports, or handle other tasks that become part of the competitive race. For clinical experience teaches us that in an achievement-oriented society like ours, a profound sense of failure may dog the tracks of virtually everybody because they are prodded by parents ("you can learn anything") or teachers ("you can do better") who set up standards they cannot reach.

Something can be said here too about the bias produced by the socioeconomic situation. There is abundant evidence that the lower classes will generally do worse, even in the first grade (Jencks et al. 1979). Thus, the lower-class child, whose self-image has already been badly battered by his home environment, now moves on to a new group in which he will be made to feel inferior or will find himself inferior. That this will lower his self-esteem is inevitable. And in addition the groups that he forms will be negatively toned rather than positively. They will move toward harassment of others, toward defiant, frequently illegal activities, toward aggression and stagnation instead of toward love and growth. This has become such a truism that innumerable remedial programs have been initiated in the past two decades to change the "child at risk." The general opinion is that these "head start" programs produce temporary benefits which then disappear in the long run because the special conditions provided in the beginning (i.e., increased stimulation and care) are taken away. Thus, the self-esteem of the child in the lowest socioeconomic groups begins to fall at an early age and remains negative throughout his life.

The early coeducational group of the first grade soon changes into a fiercely sex-segregated group, which continues to predominate more or less until puberty. This implies both a change in the self-image of the child and a change in the orientation of the group. From now on boys will play only with boys, girls only with girls; the situation changes markedly only in adolescence.

This turning against the opposite sex requires some theoretical clarification. Evidently, it is connected with the need to avoid sexual temptation, yet why does it take such a pronouncedly hostile form? Added to the sexual temptation is the fear of disturbing the positive benefits derived from association with the group. Sometimes this comes out directly later in life, when a young man will be reluctant to marry because that would mean giving up his "evenings with the boys." Thus, the group predominates over the sexual interests.

If the group is so central, what happens to the child's narcissism at this stage? In order to belong to a group, there must be some, at times considerable, abandonment of the narcissistic position and gratifications. It does not come as a surprise then when we discover that in problem children the narcissism breaks through and becomes a prominent feature.

> Little Hans, one of the classic cases of psychoanalysis, is a good illustration. Hans was a five-year-old boy who developed such a fear that a horse would bite him that he refused to go out of doors. The child's father was an adherent of Freud's who came to him with the problem. Freud treated the child through the father, and saw the boy only once.
>
> The dynamics of the phobia were traced by Freud and tied up with the

> Oedipal situation. The father brought the various productions of the child to Freud who interpreted them, and these interpretations were then given back to the child by the father.
>
> Today technique of course would be entirely different, but here we are interested only in the psychodynamics. It turned out that the phobia had started after the birth of a sister when little Hans was three and one-half years old. This started the child on a train of thought about where babies come from, the difference between the sexes and related questions. Hans was much preoccupied with his penis, which he called his "widdler," and with castration fears. These eventually led to the horse phobia. The phobia was directly derived from the Oedipus complex; the horse was equated with the father who, Hans thought, would castrate him for wanting mother. For protection Hans stayed home with mother.
>
> The therapeutic result was excellent. The child got over the phobia completely. His interest turned to music, which was his father's profession.
>
> Hans was followed up for the rest of his life. Eventually he became a professional musician, like his father. Among his other accomplishments he became an assistant director at the Metropolitan Opera Co. in New York. (SE, 10)

Although it is not usually looked at in that way, Hans' phobia also represents a breakthrough of his narcissism. He gives up the outside world (evidently he was not yet in school at the time his phobia broke out), stays home with mother, avoids father, whom he fears. That this also means a retreat from the group at that age is an observation that psychoanalysis had not yet reached at that time.

The prime task of the latency period is to consolidate ego, superego, and self-cohesiveness. It is for these reasons that libidinal drives have to be subordinated and are, with certain exceptions, not strong enough to upset the balance. Group formation favors the consolidation of ego and superego and provides a base from which identifications, of such great importance in the latency child, can be drawn. Thus, story books, movies, and other fantasy outlets play a great role for the school-age child (Blanchard 1953; Eidelberg 1945; Peller 1958).

While narcissism has to be suppressed, it emerges in sublimated form in the identification with the numerous heroes and heroines of the latency-age child. Superman, Supergirl, Tarzan—one has only to look at the names and activities to recognize the grandiosity projected into them by the child.

The changes that arise in this situation come about because of overwhelming eruptions or libidinal or aggressive drives, either physiologically or culturally determined. The first such eruption, virtually universal, is that of sexuality around age eight. As Yehudi Cohen (1964) has shown, there are various physiological changes, real though much less noticeable than the later ones, that occur around age eight. These changes lead to a heightened sexual drive. All cultures have to take this heightened drive into consideration. Since drives are nondiscriminatory, this tends to increased incestuous wishes between brother and sister. To handle this incestuous drive, cultures resort to two devices: brother-sister extrusion or brother-sister avoidance. In brother-sister extrusion it is usually the boy who is taken out of the home and placed with a relative or close friend; sometimes he is adopted. Brother-sister avoidance is obviously the solution that our own society has traditionally chosen. The predominance of unisex groups, which increase at this age (eight on), such as cub scouts, girl scouts, and the like, serve to underline the hostility between the sexes and have profound implications for sexual behavior in later life. It is here that the real crux of the differences between love and hate cultures (Fine 1985) is most solidly established.

Collective aggression has been one of the most fearful and most discussed phenomena of the twentieth century. However, it would appear that it has always existed; in fact, in many cultures aggression is fully justified and even considered perfectly "normal."

That people will do things in groups they will not or rarely will do individually is an old observation going back to the French sociologist Le Bon. He wrote: "In the life of the isolated individual it would be dangerous for him to gratify these instincts while his absorption in an irresponsible crowd in which in consequence he is assured of impunity gives him entire liberty to follow them" (1903:57).

Experimental data also indicate that groups will often act more sadistically than individuals (Jaffe and Yinon 1983). The decisive factor seems to be anonymity (Mathers and Gest 1975). This likewise seems to have been decisive in the Nazi and Soviet atrocities.

Anonymity means that the individual is absorbed into the group; he derives his identity from the group rather than from his family, or some other more usual source. It follows that the aggression of school-age boys and girls is fostered by their anonymous identifications with "boys" and "girls," who are expected to tease, fight, bully, and be bullied by one another. On the other hand, belonging to the group can also cover up as an excuse for the otherwise unresolvable wish to hurt others.

As the child gets older, group belonging becomes increasingly important and frequent. In their well-known Middletown study the Lynds (Lynd and Lynd

1929) found a proliferating system of clubs that touched the life of the city in all its major activities. During 1924, a total of 458 active clubs were found, or roughly one for each eighty people (1929:285). A similar canvas of the city in 1890 revealed 92 clubs, or roughly one for every 125 people; thus the importance of the club for the city had grown.

Of course, the Lynds merely counted; they did not explore psychodynamics, though they do say that "most Middletown clubs apparently offer people not an extension of their customary activities but a way of escape from them" (1929:286). This does not go very deep. Here I am focusing on the activities of school-age children. Evidently, these social activities in groups offer a number of gratifications: outlet for hostility, repression or channelization of sexuality, a new source of identity, heroes and heroines whom it is acceptable to admire, disguised or sublimated homosexual gratifications (as Kinsey had shown, the incidence of homosexuality in childhood and puberty is suprisingly high; Kinsey et al. 1948, 1953).

Thus throughout, narcissism is confronted with group belongingness in which narcissism has to be reduced, often to the point of anonymity. This creates a problem for many children who prefer to hold on to their individuality (healthy narcissism) in some way. The theoretical point being made here is important: narcissism cannot be properly understood without considering how the individual is relating to the group.

As far as the self-image is concerned, throughout childhood it varies, growing, changing with each new year. Growth is after all the preeminent fact of childhood, so that the child tends to look forward to the future rather than focus on the past. Many experts tell the parents that a child's problems will be "outgrown," and the parents tend to go along with this easy resolution. Though the seeds are sown in childhood, a definitive self-image does not crystallize until adolescence, or often later.

Adolescence

In adolescence the conflict between the individual and the group becomes most apparent and most acute. For this there are two major reasons. First, the dramatic bodily changes of puberty signal the birth of a new person, radically different from anything that went on before. It is only with Freud that the continuity of life was discovered; yet Freud tended, perhaps because of the need to overturn earlier convictions, to overestimate the significance of childhood.

And second, the adolescent, because of his growth and independence, now moves toward leaving the family and joining entirely new groups. For it is one of the ironies of development that the process of separation-transition-reincorporation leads from the family as the group of origin to a "psychosocial moratorium" of varying duration, then to reincorporation into some other group. Even in cultures that traditionally stress the need to be individualized (such as India with its Buddhist and Yogi traditions), these persons tend to congregate in groups rather than move off completely on their own.

Just prior to puberty there is a move toward a close friendship with a person of the same sex—the preadolescent chum. Sullivan (1939) in particular placed the heaviest emphasis on this experience, claiming that persons who did not go through it were more prone to becoming schizophrenic later in life. While there is some truth in his claim, it is contradicted by the voluminous evidence that the origins of schizophrenia lie much earlier in the mother-child relationship and are only brought to light later on with the cessation of growth. (Frosch, 1983).

Although the physiological changes are biologically determined, they exhibit a considerable degree of variability. The most reliable source of information is still Kinsey and co-workers (1948, 1953). Sexual differences are of course of vital importance here.

Among boys about 90 percent ejaculate for the first time between the ages of 11 and 15, inclusive. At the end of the seventh grade about 37.5 percent are adolescent; by the end of the tenth grade nearly all of them are (96.5 percent). The mean age of first orgasm resulting in ejaculation is 13.88 years (Kinsey et al. 1948:186–187).

For females, the age of first menstruation ranges from 9 to 25 years, but the median was 13.0 years. There was a lapse of 8.4 months between the onset of pubic hair and breasts and the age of first menstruation for the median female (Kinsey et al. 1953:123–124).

The secular trend has been noted by many observers. It would appear that in the last 50 to 100 years children have been maturing in the physiological sense at progressively earlier ages. It is not certain that this is a worldwide phenomenon, but it is agreed that it is potentially likely to become one as the more technically backward and underdeveloped nations become more prosperous. In some societies it seems that puberty is reached by as much as five years earlier than a century ago. Since about 1900 children have increased in height, by age five to seven, by 1 to 2 centimeters (0.4 to 0.8 inch) each decade and at ages ten to fourteen by 2 to 3 centimeters (0.8 to 1.2 inches) each decade. Body weight has also gone up proportionately. Only temporary disruptions of normal life caused by war, famine, or economic crisis seems to have halted this trend (*Encyclopedia Britannica* 19:1091).

Since educational and other social arrangements depend on exact ages, these secular trends (which apparently are greater in the case of girls than in boys) create a conflictual situation that further complicates the already complicated dynamics of adolescence. For each individual child it means coming to grips at an unforeseen time with the most dramatic changes he or she will ever undergo (apart from pregnancy in women). Further, since menopause occurs in women at around forty-five to fifty years, and does not seem to vary much, while the male's sexual capacity does not really diminish until about twenty years later, a further cause of conflict is rooted in another biological fact.

Both boys and girls reach full growth some time in adolescence, which gives them both the feeling and reality of much greater independence from the parents and other family pressures. Separation from the parents (what analysts have called the second individuation process, but it is also the second group process) is followed by a transitional period of varying duration and then by reincorporation into new groups. Few people, if any, avoid the extrafamilial group experience, though for many the transition from the family to the outside world is fraught with enormous difficulties and frustrations. Thus, the adolescent will either move toward a new group and stay there (or to new groups), or fall back on the original family, which is essentially what we mean psychologically by schizophrenia.

Inherent in all this is the ongoing conflict between the individual and the group. To join a group, the individual has to give up some of his narcissism; he may also project it to the group and attempt to gratify it that way, but still not by direct means for himself. This conflict between the group and the individual, which has been going on all through life, is highly accelerated in adolescence and remains a focus of conflict until the very end of life (e.g., in how to be buried and how to be memorialized by the next generation).

Puberty Rituals

The onset of puberty is so dramatic that all societies (except for the modern unromantics) have devised rituals to celebrate the event. Naturally, there are different rituals for boys and girls. Their existence serves to highlight the profound meaning that every change in the life cycle has for both the individual and the group.

Rituals have been studied both from a sociological and an individual point of view. Sociologically, Paige and Paige (1981) have contributed the most extensive study, based on a sample of 108 societies. They found that in societies in which there are stable and valuable economic resources, strong fraternal interest groups are likely to develop, and the dilemmas posed by the major events of the human reproductive cycle are responded to by surveillance rituals, a form of ritual bargaining. In other words, the larger society always has a profound interest in what happens to the child at puberty, and dictates how it should be handled.

The Paiges argue that in strong fraternal interest group societies the elders try to control their sons by circumcision, a substitute for castration which is too severe an action (though practiced in other groups, cf. Tannahill 1980). A circumcision ceremony, they say, is a surveillance ritual by which members of a strong fraternal interest group, particularly the most influential members, assess and minimize the likelihood of fission by requiring a public demonstration of loyalty of any man who has a son. Thus, for maximum efficacy it must be performed at a time when it can be dangerous to the growing boy, that is, around puberty.

For girls menarche represents not only the time when a woman is of maximum value in a marriage bargain but also the beginning of a period in which she will become especially vulnerable to seduction and rape. A father's dilemma at menarche is his choice between marrying off his daughter at or shortly after menarche without being able to take advantage of the best economic and political conditions or running the risk of losing his daughter's marriage value through her seduction, loss of reputation, or depreciation over time. In the light of these social considerations, the various menarche rituals can be understood. Primarily, they involve control of the daughter's virginity, varying from secluding her to such barbarous customs as infibulation, still practiced in parts of Africa (Saadawi 1982). In the birth of children, rules of social avoidance and seclusion facilitate the surveillance and control of the mother and her kin and potential competing claimants to paternity rights.

Psychodynamically, the classic analytic study of puberty rites (Reik 1919) clarifies the way in which the pubescent boy is terrified of his sexuality. Among the Arunta the youths, after their circumcision, are given a number of moral precepts and prohibitions regarding food, the nonobservance of which means death. Among the Luritcha the chief utters the following exhortation to the young people after the subincision: "You are always to go about with young men; you are not to go after girls or married woman; you are not to have any intercourse at all with the 'beautiful sex' . . . If we hear that you go after women and girls we shall cast you into the fire" (1919:129). In girls guaranteeing unambiguous paternity rights to a husband by giving him a virgin bride is crucial in marriage bargains. While fathers in most societies attempt to prevent seduction of an unmarried daughter by supervising her conduct and restricting her contacts with men, this surveillance is most effective in strong fraternal interest group societies since it requires the assistance of many people, who protect the father's interests as their own. In these societies kinsmen may guard the daughter so strictly and continuously that no man can gain access to her. Among the Riffians of Morocco, e.g., the time between the signing of the betrothal agreement and the wedding is considered an extremely dangerous period for all parties to the bargain. The betrothed daughter is hardly ever allowed to leave the house. When she does go out, she must be accompanied by a group of companions. The disastrous effects of such severe restrictions on the personality of the girl are beautifully brought out by the Egyptian doctor Nawal el Saadawi (1982), who lived such a life until she was an adult.

How can these rituals of more "primitive" societies be generalized to our own more permissive style of life? The onset of puberty creates a profound upheaval in both the boy and girl. This upheaval is handled either by the considerate affection of the caring of the parents, or by the willful defiance of obstreperous adolescent groups. In either case the adolescent goes through a terrible period of storm and strife before settling down, although the storm and strife can be considerably reduced by careful psychological measures (Offer and Offer 1975).

Alternatives in Modern Society

What are the alternatives offered to the adolescent in modern society and how does he or she handle them? This is a continuation of the crucial question posed throughout this book—the individual or the group (the yogi or the commissar). The high incidence of mental disorder and milder emotional disturbance shows that the adolescent tends to swing too far in one direction or the other.

Along the *dimension of individuality* various possibilities are encountered. Many gifted persons go their own way, even though it is at considerable cost to themselves. Mozart is one of the best examples in history. Considered by many to have been the most gifted musician that ever lived, he was a prodigy at five. In childhood his father took him around Europe to give concerts and amaze the noble and the humble.

Deprived of a normal chance to play and relax in childhood, Mozart grew up to be an arrogant, narcissistic genius who lacked the capacity to get along in conventional society. The world of his day was still dominated by arbitrary tyrants whose will was law. Mozart could not get along with them, so that in spite of his extraordinary abilities lesser men managed to get ahead of him. As he grew older his personal responsibilities became ever more pressing. It is most remarkable that through these troubled times he was still able to turn out such an extraordinary amount of music, outstanding both quantitatively and qualitatively. But his personal troubles became so great that his income dropped, his health worsened, and he died at the early age of thirty-five, to be buried in a pauper's grave because no one would raise the money to give him a more decent burial (Davenport 1979).

Without the great gifts of someone like Mozart, many narcissistic adolescents in the present-day world move in the direction of schizophrenia. Physical growth has stopped, ending that fantasy outlet for the child. He has come to grips with himself as moving to the world of adulthood. In terms of the analysis offered here, this means separation from the family, transition, and reincorporation. All of these are so difficult that he bogs down in one or the other. Schizophrenia may be seen as a sense of despair about ever getting into another group that offers more adult gratifications, particularly sexual ones.

A cultural example is the case of Ireland, which has the highest incidence of schizophrenia in the world. Evidence of this high rate of psychosis dates from the nineteenth century. By 1911 the proportion of the population in asylums was 50 percent higher than in England, and in the United States the Irish immigrants had a psychiatric admission rate four times that of the U.S. born and double that of other immigrant groups (Murphy 1982:65).

Messenger (1969) and Scheper-Hughes (1979) both presented voluminous evidence for the extreme cultural and sexual deprivation that the Irish experience. Inis Beag (an old Irish folk community) is described as one of the most sexually naive of the world's societies. Sex is never discussed in the home when children are present. Boys are supposed to be better informed than girls, but the boys learn about sex informally from older boys, and the men from observing animals.

Menstruation and menopause arouse profound misgivings among women of Inis Beag because few of them comprehend their physiological significance. The ethnologist (Messenger) reports that his wife was called upon to explain these processes more than any other phenomena related to sex. When they reach puberty, most girls are unprepared for the first menstrual flow and find the experience a traumatic one, especially when their mothers are unable to provide a satisfactory explanation for it. And it is commonly believed that the menopause can induce "madness." In order to ward off this condition, some women have retired from life in their mid-forties and in a few cases have confined themselves to bed until death.

The incidence of unmarried persons is extremely high (Scheper-Hughes 1979). As the title of her book (*Saints, Scholars, and Schizophrenia*) indicates, Ireland is a country where all men withdraw from sex and the ordinary affairs of the world. Because of the high degree of sexual frustration, the escape valves of drinking, alcoholism, disputes, and pugnacity are everyday occurrences. Even "dirty jokes" are largely taboo, and in dancing little bodily contact is allowed. (A fuller discussion of the dynamics of rural Ireland will be found in chapter 8.)

Opler and Singer (1956) comment that anthropological investigation reveals that the central figure in the Irish family is the mother. Fathers, especially in straitened economic circumstances, are frequently by contrast shadowy and evanscent. "An Irish male patient beset with anxiety and fear of female figures early in life, and lacking possibilities of firm male identification with a father, would later experience the sexual repressions and socio-religious definitions of marriage and sexuality for which his culture, with its high celibacy rates, protracted engagements, and sin-guilt emphases is justly famous" (Messenger 1969:25).

On the other hand, all of this should not be taken to deny that there are also many healthy narcissists, who function well within their spheres and do not suffer profound emotional disturbances. The artist and the scientist often fall into this category, as well as many other ungifted people who find happiness and contentment within themselves.

As far as those who veer too far toward the other extreme, group living, these are often people who have so little access to their inner life that their narcissism is completely repressed so that they seem to have no identity other than that of the group to which they belong. These are the people for whom Riesman (1961) coined the term "other-directed," and whom he described as a "lonely crowd." Abrams (1979) has depicted the psychological problems of persons with such excessive "groupiness" and virtually no access to the inner life. It is little wonder that such persons take to drink, adultery, or any form of sensation to relieve the tedium of their lives and the abscence of any real inner feeling.

On the other hand, extreme emphasis on group experience can also lead to extraordinary outbursts of violence. Yablonsky (1970), who made a special study of violent gangs, described the members as almost paranoid in their distrust of adults and authority figures. The clichéhas become 'Never trust anyone over thirty." Like classical paranoid personalities, many rebellious youths relate to adults and authority in a manner that produces "establishment" behavior that reinforces and validates their distrust. Like violent gang members, youths on the new scene constantly test the rules to see the response of the authorities.

With regard to black groups, Yablonsky found many parallels between their behavior and that of the near-group members. Hence the violent gang has over the years been for many black youths their only source of identity, status, and emotional satisfaction. Ill-trained to participate with any degree of success in the dominant white middle-class world, they construct their own community. The demands of the white world are confusing, those of the violent gang on the other hand readily adaptable to his personal needs. He can belong one day, quit the next without submitting any formal resignation. Some boys say that the gang is organized for protection and that one role of a gang member is to fight. How, when, with whom, and for what reason he is to fight are all unclear. In any case it is clear that the gang offers him a socially acceptable outlet for his rage, and he is familiar with the comment of James Baldwin that to be a Negro in this country is to be in a rage almost all the time.

To Yablonsky's excellent analysis can be added some comments about the superego and the binding of libidinal ties. The violent gang member, who usually comes from a broken home, has a deficient superego formation that leaves him rather helpless in solving life's problems; the gang makes it up to him, also giving him a new identification (Eagles, Black Cats, Egyptians, Black Muslims, etc.). Further, there are strong homosexual ties; the members are all "blood brothers," much as in the blood covenants of yore. It may indeed be questioned whether these gangs, in spite of the dissimilarity of the social structures, are so different from the blood brotherhoods and blood covenants described in so many primitive societies.

With regard to heterosexuality, on the surface at least there is often a kind of indifferent promiscuity among these violent gang members. On deeper analysis, however, the quality of their love life turns out to be intensely sadistic. The ties to girls are in fact so tenuous that they are often abandoned relatively early in life. True love relationships would involve leaving the gang kind of formation, and are thus rarely seen.

Yet, as Yablonsky showed in *Synanon: The Tunnel Back* (1971), the cohesiveness can often be put to a socially useful purpose in spite of the underlying rage. Closely knit groups such as Synanon have proved to be one of the most effective means of combating the life-threatening despair of the drug addict. In this case the "delinquent," defined here as a member who resorts to drugs again, becomes the target of the group's hostilities, and in order to get back into the good graces of the group he gives up the drugs. This is an excellent example of the interplay between narcissism and the group: to take the drug is to regress to pathological narcissism, to give it up means going to the group and abandoning narcissism.

Thus, here too we see that while there is a counterpoint between the individual and the group, whether what is involved is a love affair or a hate affair makes the decisive difference. Neither narcissism nor group belongingness are per se pathological; what has to be considered in addition is whether these attitudes derive from constructive (love) or destructive (hate) impulses.

Sexuality and Love

Finally, the all-important questions of sexuality and love, so vital in the psyche of the adolescent, have to be considered. Figures about sexual behavior could be cited here but would be misleading since the picture seems to be changing all the time. There is no question that with penicillin, the pill, sex education, and the permissive attitude a sexual revolution began in the 1960s. Still, the inner meaning of this sexual revolution has to be carefully considered.

There can be no doubt that even though many deplore the new openness in sexual relationships, and the problems they bring (herpes, teenage pregnancy, etc.), a new morality is in the making for many adolescents. Sorensen, in his survey of adolescent sexuality, comments:

> A new kind of love is being worked out by American adolescents in a strongly sexual context. Mutuality and belongingness are emphasized by many young people in describing what love means to them . . . . One result of this greater emphasis on mutuality in love has been a lessening need to require sex as a fundamental condition of a love relationship. 82% of all adolescents denied that the most important thing in a love relationship is sex, with the intercourse-experienced (82%) no less firm in their conviction about this than the virgins (81%). (1973:108)

Yankelovich (1981), who combines psychodynamic sophistication with virtuosity in sampling and statistical techniques, found that about 80 percent of Americans are now committed to one degree or another to the search for self-fulfillment at the expense of the self-denying ethic of earlier years. For them the older ethic meant conformity to a group-oriented way of thinking that denied them any real individuality or in the alternative to narcissistic aggression and rebellion against excessive authoritarianism, such as the Vietnam war, which caused so much upheaval in this country. With the emphasis on mutuality and love, which both Sorensen and Yankelovich describe, it can be said that many adolescents are trying at least to find a happy meeting ground where both healthy narcissism and healthy group activity can be combined. How far they will succeed is another question only the future can answer.

Adulthood

Because of Freud's early conviction that the essentials of the personality structure are laid down in the first five years of life, for many years analysts took little note of what happened afterword, concentrating on what aspect of infantile experience was being repeated. However, Freud himself changed his mind to some extent; in the *Outline of Psychoanalysis* he wrote that the superego in the course of life receives contributions from later successors and substitutes of the parents, such as teachers and models in public life of admitted social ideals. Later in the same work he stated that the superego takes up a kind of intermediate position between the id and the external world; it unites in itself the influences of the present and the past (23:146). "In the establishment of the superego, we have before us, as it were an example of the way in which the present is changed into the past" (1953–1970, 23:207).

Other authorities have taken a similar view, often in sharper disagreement with Freud. Hartmann, Kris, and Loewenstein write:

> The development of personality is not concluded at this point (with formation of superego) and we feel that the potentialities of its transformation throughout latency and adolescence have for some time been underrated in psychoanalytic writings. But it seems that the basic structure of the personality and the basic functional interrelation of the systems have been fixed to some extent. The child does not stop growing and developing, but after that age both growth and development modify an existing structure. (1946:34)

Empirical research (Clarke and Clarke 1976) has shown that the modification of existing structure begins virtually at birth, so that development always proceeds in terms of the interaction between the existing personality structure and the new elements. But, of course, it goes without saying that the younger the child, the more plasticity he demonstrates. However, much of the alleged fixity of the personality derives from the persistence of the same environmental influences; when these change, the child can change accordingly. Indeed, if this were not so, psychotherapy would be impossible.

By now a considerable literature has appeared on the course of life in the adult years, much of it analytically oriented. This literature includes both statistical surveys, longitudinal studies, and case histories. I shall organize the discussion around the major topic of this book, the tension between the individual and the group.

When adolescence ends and adulthood begins is of course a moot point. But it is reasonable to take marriage as a starting place. In spite of all the talk about singles, most people still get married and see marriage as the central focus of their lives.

The notoriously high divorce rate has made many young people skeptical of the value of marriage, so that the incidence of "live-ins" becomes increasingly frequent. Accordingly, the high incidence of singles has been noted. Even palimony has been awarded, though later overturned. Nevertheless, as Veroff, Douvan, and Kulka (1981a) found in comparing the inner American in 1976 with 1957, while there is a significant increase in people's awareness of marital stress and of the fact that family roles involve problems and burdens, yet there has been an *increase* in marital happiness over the twenty-year period in which the two studies were conducted. (Compare Samuel Johnson's witticism: "Marriage has many pains, but celibacy has no pleasures.")

Ideally, as most educated people see marriage today, there has to be a considerable degree of mutuality to make it happy; when there is, it is the most desirable state. This means that there has to be some abandonment of narcissistic pleasure, as well as some diminution of the pressures for group activity; both more easily said than done.

Many young couples have a romanticized view of marriage. Lederer and Jackson (1968) call this the utopia syndrome. While people believe that they are marrying for love, unconscious needs for sex, nurturance, and approval may predominate. These authors view the attributes of a good marriage as tolerance, respect, honesty, and the desire to stay together, usually between people with similar backgrounds, interests, and values.

The revolt against marriage has been fueled by the contemporary women's liberation movement, which has stressed particularly the subordinate position in which the woman is placed who centers her whole life around marriage. Ehrenreich (1984) has argued that it is men, oppressed by the heavy demands made on them by marriage, who really led the revolt. Yet Betty Friedan (1981), whose *The Feminine Mystique* (1963) sparked the current wave of women's protests, has finally come around to the conclusion that a happy marriage is still the best solution for a woman.

It is a truism that marriage involves a recapitulation of the oedipal situation; thus children of happy marriages tend to make happy marriages themselves; children of unhappy marriages fall into an oedipal trap. In the oedipal period the conflict lies between oral regression and oedipal reality; if the parents are unhappily married, the child chooses some form of oral regression, ending up unable to make a happy marriage.

The first and most persistent problem that always comes up in a new marriage is that of fidelity. Throughout all cultures there is a virtually obsessive concern with infidelity, and numerous social arrrangements have been constructed to cope with it. Within our own culture, the double standard has been the norm for centuries, changing only in the past fifty years, since the end of World War II.

While men have always felt that it is permissible to have an occasional sexual fling outside the marriage, women have accepted this, to the extent that they have, only fairly recently. One young woman, a 24-year-old student, said: "I have a roving eye and sometimes I give in to it . . . . If it's time that doesn't take away from Walter's and my time, I'll let it happen. I consider myself a very sexual person, and I need an adventure from time to time. And I think he does too. But that's all it is—fun and a little bit of an ego thrill" (Blumstein and Schwartz 1983:282).

Such an attitude is a far cry from that prevalent in the days of the Kinsey report, just barely a generation ago. Kinsey and his staff found that adultery was quite common, and a source of great concern to all involved. They also found many difficulties existing in marital sexuality, as did Masters and Johnson in their studies (1966). It may well be that sexual satisfaction is greater today (Veroff, Doucan, and Kulka, 1981b) because of the sexual revolution, the attitudes of the women's liberation movement, and the generally greater acceptance of psychoanalytic ideas. However, our clinical experience warns us not to be too sanguine about external changes; the internal conflicts may remain unaltered or may manifest themselves in different outlets.

The problem may again be conceptualized as the tension between narcissism and group experience. In marriage each partner is required to give up some of his/her individuality, which often leads to resentment and frustration. Furthermore, the transition from same-sex pursuits (being with the boys) to a heterosexual family, thus involving a shift from one type of group to another, is by no means easy. In persons with strong childhood conflicts, there is often a *regression in the service of the spouse.*

If the two marriage partners are involved in what has been called mutual parentification (Eisenstein 1956), each will subtly try to mold himself/herself to the demands of a parent rather than to the more mutually gratifying demands of an equal. Thus, they become children again in an effort to please the spouse. Traditionally, this has occurred more with the women who give up their independence, their outside activities, even their original names, and remain as housewives; for the extreme of these Freud coined the term "housewife psychosis." Not infrequently these regressions may take the form of a severe depression or an outright psychosis; the traditional "involutional melancholia" is a striking example since it has been shown that it is merely another form of depression in an inadequate personality and not the result of the biochemical changes brought about in the menopause.

Here are some clinical examples.

When her husband died, Mildred was 75. Only then did it become clear that she was almost totally disoriented. She had not worked since she married. Her husband had dominated her completely. Her own mother had committed suicide, roughly at that age. Mildred had regressed into senility without being noticed by anybody.

Sylvia and John met on a subway and were married shortly thereafter. The honeymoon period was a happy one and brought two children. Then came the regressions, on both sides. Sylvia felt too depressed to do the housework. She attempted suicide a number of times, the last one inflicting severe brain damage, although she did not die. John, a free-lance photographer, would rather masturbate than have sex with Sylvia. His fantasy life centered around "making it" with other women, which he did on rare occasions. He could not work adequately, relying on his wealthy parents to help in his support.

In the honeymoon period the couple would engage in infantile games, such as showing one another their stools after they had been to the toilet. After a while this disappeared, and they engaged in endless quarrels.

In spite of their deep disappointments in life, and their obvious difficulties, the two stayed together all their lives. Both attempted therapy, but left because they could not face the severe problems that were uncovered.

It is to be noted that in a statistical survey this couple could easily have been found to have had a "happy stable marriage."

The Parental Stage

Again Freud's erroneous assumptions about the overwhelming importance of childhood tended to restrict investigation of parental behavior. In the paper on narcissism he wrote:

> If we look at the attitude of affectionate parents towards their children, we have to recognize that it is a revival and reproduction of their own narcissism, which they have long since abandoned . . . . Parental love, which is so moving and at bottom so childish, is nothing but the parents' narcissism born again which, transformed into object-love, unmistakably reveals its former nature. (14:90–91)

As a result, the serious investigation of parenthood did not really take off until the 1940s, after Freud died, although there were of course many astute observations earlier. All aspects of the life cycle of relationships between parent and child have been considered. Here again the emphasis will be placed on the relationship between parental narcissism and the wish to belong to a group, or to develop individually, away from the child.

Helene Deutsch (1945) had already pointed out that *pregnancy* involves first and foremost an identification with the mother; the fate of this identification determines the course of pregnancy, and in fact whether the girl will become pregnant at all. The ego of the pregnant woman must find a harmonious compromise between her deeply unconscious identification with the child, which is directed toward the future, and her indentification with her own mother, which is directed toward the past. The fetus may thus become a hostile parasite or a blessing that will rescue her from a world of misery.

Grete Bibring (1959), in an extensive investigation of pregnant women, thought it most fruitful to regard pregnancy as a crisis that affects all expectant mothers, no matter what the state of psychic health. The various measures and educational procedures designed to help future mothers have concentrated much more on the physical fears than on the psychological conflicts.

Benedek coined the term "the parental stage" (Benedek and Anthony 1970), although she related it more to the mother than to the father. Parenthood is timeless; yet it is, like any living process, under the inescapable domination of time. Time means change and change requires adaptation. With parenthood, this implies continuous adaptation to physiological and psychological changes within the self of the parent, parallel to and in transaction with changes in the child and his expanding world. To describe parenthood as a psychological process throughout the life cycle, as it has to be, presents an overwhelming problem. The easiest way to handle it is by limiting oneself to pertinent remarks about the critical periods in a child's life. It should be noted that the literature up to now has focused mainly on the mother; it is only recently that the father's role has been examined more closely (Fine 1986; Ross et al. 1982; Lamb 1981).

Theoretically, the child has to be helped to socialize into its culture; in this process the chief role is that of the parent. If the parent is too narcissistic the outcome will be a sadistic denigration of the child, either directly or by innuendo ('I never had it so good as you"). If the parent is too group oriented, the child is subordinated or even sacrificed to the needs of the parents to maintain their status in the community. This becomes particularly apparent in the adolescent period when the child's rebellion may first become manifest. Separation from the child is also a continual trauma, since the child first becomes a focus of the parental social life (group behavior) and then gradually has to be allowed to outgrow his dependency.

The attitude of parents toward their children may be viewed from two poles: intrusive and detached. The intrusive pole does not allow the child to be an individual, e.g., it frustrates his narcissism. The detached does not form an adequate group atmosphere; it leaves the child isolated. In both cases extremes lead to schizophrenia or schizophrenic spectrum disorders.

Whether the parents will be intrusive or detached at a point in the life cycle depends on their own histories, their own personalities, and on the kinds of interaction that are imposed on them by the family situation. In infancy the classic study of intrusiveness is David Levy's *Maternal Overprotection* (1943). The studies on detachment are well summarized in Bowlby's work on loss (1980). In the anthropological literature an excellent study of detachment is Linton's work on the Marquesans, where the pursuit of sexual pleasure led to an extremely low birth rate (Kardiner 1939:138).

Nor is it to be supposed that the attitudes of the parents will remain the same throughout the chid's life. Kris (1953) initiated a fruitful study of variations in parental attitudes, arguing that this problem deserves more attention than it has hitherto found. Because of this variability, generalizations tend to be extremely difficult. Certainly throughout life the child's need to separate and the parental wish to hold on make for constant friction. To develop this topic further would require extensive case histories, which go beyond the province of this work.

My main concern has been to show that narcissism and group activity (the family, later other groups) are the foci around which parent-child relations gravitate. Even in extreme old age the parents may attempt to hold on by manipulation (one man who had been left a trust fund, which he was to acquire when he was forty used to visit his parents' graves periodically and dance there; he was bitter that they had not left him the money outright) or the parents may give up, lapsing into senility (Erikson's contrast of integrity and despair).

Stages in Adult Development

While the process of change has been voluminously documented for the early part of life, once people get married it is as though scientists agree with the wedding ceremony that they will "live happily ever after." Naturally, nothing could be further from the truth; life always has its ups and downs and some theoreticians hold that the mind is always in conflict (Brenner 1982).

More recent research has attempted to penetrate beyond the veil of cultural conformity to see what really happens to people later in life. Levinson et al. (1978) have contributed a classification, deriving from Erikson, but going beyond him, of the adult life cycle based on intensive case histories: childhood and adolescence, 0–22; early adulthood, 17–45; middle adulthood, 40–65; and late adulthood, 60–?. Throughout there is the same tension that we have described over and over: between being one's own man (narcissism) and fitting into the larger society (group belonging).

Early adulthood. On the basis of the case histories, Levinson et al. comment further that in early adulthood a man is faced with tremendous burdens, as he attempts to form an occupation, start a marriage and family, meet heavy financial demands, modify his ties to the preadult self and world, and integrate his life as an adult. Age thirty is frequently a time of crisis. Just when he is getting more settled, many of his relationships, goals, and values come into question. As this transition ends, settling down begins, and he must make crucial choices. For some men just when they are coming into their own they find the independence intolerable.

Midlife Crisis. This is the period in the adult life cycle that has been examined most extensively. In the psychoanalytic literature Jung was the first to point to the major differences between the first part of life and the second. Following Freud again, the analytic tradition stipulated that psychotherapy could not be successful with men over fifty, but this has since been questioned and it is believed today that there is no period in life when psychotherapy could not be of some value.

At midlife (40 approximately) a man's bodily and mental powers, though somewhat dimishished, are still adequate for an active full life. The instinctual drives also tend to pass their maximal level and are somewhat reduced. The central conflict at this stage centers around the realization by the man that he is not so old that he cannot undertake something new, while he is not so young that he can devote years to the effort. Changing physiology, e.g., diminishing muscular capacity, provides the first intimation that life can come to an end.

At midlife most men undergo a change in style of work and living. Other qualities can ripen: wisdom, judiciousness, philosophical perspectives on life. This is also a period when the children are growing up (if not grown up) and leaving him. This produces the "empty nest" syndrome, which is so painful to people in their later years, who have oriented their lives for some twenty years about the family and their children. Not unnaturally breakdowns frequently result.

Once the midlife crisis is past, both men and women have to come to grips with what they are going to do for the rest of their lives. Maas and Kuypers (1974) reviewed the later lives of men and women who had been in the Berkeley guidance studies, thus persons whose earlier lives were reasonably well known from direct information and did not have to be reconstructed de novo, as would otherwise be the case. They broke the life events down into about a dozen areas of daily living in which they sought and discovered patternable similarities and differences in the life-styles of the persons. There were four major dimensions along which these life-styles varied: interaction, involvement, satisfaction, and perception of change.

Among the fathers they found four life-styles: family-centered, hobbyists (independent), remotely sociable, and unwell-disengaged. Among the mothers six life-styles were differentiated: husband-centered, uncentered, visiting, work-centered, disabled-disengaging, and group-centered. On the whole they found their subjects to be in good health and satisfied with life; however, the study did not attempt to go below the surface.

What does all this tell us about the concepts of narcissism, the self, and the group, which have been the main focus of this chapter? Narcissism will vary all over the lot, both inter-individually and intra-indivdually. A man or woman may be narcissistic in one area, group-centered in another. Certainly little of this material fits into the psychoanalytic descriptions of narcissism, which tends to confirm my thesis that narcissism may be an analytico-genic fabrication. Seen as self-involvement, some people are narcissistic at certain times or in regard to certain people but not narcissistic with regard to others.

There is always a group to which the individual belongs, either the original family or some substitute for it. As these studies of adult development show, all people move from group to group, with wome peripheral groups (Bott 1971); some may shift to different groups. But the group is just as important to the individual as his own needs and interests (narcissism), so that there is always some tension between the individual and the group.

With regard to the self, the self-image will vary throughout the life cycle, depending on age, socioeconomic circumstances, health, wealth, and many other factors. No evidence accumulates empirically that there is such a thing as the nuclear self which begins at birth and lasts until death. The truth would appear to lie more in the earlier Freudian formulations of self-consistency, self-esteem, self-reproach, an the many other hyphenated aspects of the self-image. Self-esteem will depend on the superego and the external environment, particularly on the relationship between the two.

Thus, without taking both aspects into consideration, narcissism and the group(s) in which a person lives, human behavior cannot be properly understood.

CHAPTER 6

THE SELF-IMAGE AND THE SOCIAL ORDER

Because of the way in which theory has been written, the intrinsic connection between the self-image and the social order has largely been overlooked. The self is either regarded as an individual phenomenon, as in much of psychoanalytic theory, or as a group phenomenon, as in much sociological theory. But the interrelationship between the two, as seen in the previous chapter, is an essential part of the phenomenon. "No man is to himself an island intyre" is John Donne's famous phrase. Likewise the commonly heard question "Who am I?" is an effort to find some individuality in a world where social conventions and forces seem to rule the roost.

As noted earlier three stages in the evolution of the self may be distinguished: 1) the preverbal (to one and one half years) in which while the self exists it cannot be verbalized—yet it remains unforgettable and unrememberable; 2) the growth in childhood—the self, in the bosom of the family, undergoes constant change, influenced at first almost exclusively by the family, later, and with increasing emphasis by the social surroundings; 3) the adult, whose self-image is largely defined and gives definition to the culture in which the person lives. In these various stages the relationship between the self and the social order, while always there, differs.

In reality, as we have seen, there are changes all through life. Adult development is just as real as childhood development, even though it is not as obvious. But events do move more slowly. There is not the constant physical change that makes life so exciting and forward looking for the child. There are social changes, many of them independent of the individual, with which the person must deal, with better or worse results for the self-image. As a result the self-image remains constant for longer periods of time. But sooner or later it undergoes a variety of transformations. For the person for whom this does not occur we speak of excessive rigidity.

It is also necessary to distinguish conscious from unconscious images of the self. Like much of what goes in personality functioning, a good many self-observations are made at an unconscious level, yet have a vital effect on conscious functioning. By and large this will also vary with the degree of pathology in that one definition of mental illness is clearly lack of self-awareness; hence the preoccupation of therapists working with the schizophrenic with the self-image (e.g., Sullivan, Federn). Consequently, material from studies of neurotic and psychotic illness as well as the careful investigation of other cultures both offer the possibilities of profound insights into the self.

Loss of the Self: Three Instances

To most people in our culture maintaining a cohesive sense of the self is a vital desideratum of healthy living. It is therefore all the more surprising to discover individuals for whom this is not the case. Three examples can be cited and sifted for their theoretical value.

The Japanese Suicide Pilots in World War II

While heroic deaths occur in all wars (the first in World War II was actually an American pilot, who was about to die and ended his life by crashing his plane into a Japanese ship), there was no record in modern warfare of men deliberately sacrificing their lives for the glory of their country. Even the fanatical Nazis and Communists could not summon their subjects to such a pitch of self-sacrifice. It was therefore all the more remarkable that toward the end of World War II the Japanese could muster thousands of young men who deliberately crashed their planes into American ships (Hoyt 1983). It has been argued that theirs was the sacrifice of a religious mania, but this does not hold up for a modern nation like Japan.

For the military regime toward the end of the war it was a godsend. By the end of 1944, when the United States recaptured the Philippines, Japan was obviously finished. Suddenly, the kamikaze defense appeared. In the Philippines alone 1198 pilots sacrificed their lives in suicide attacks. Later many more were to do so; there was no shortage of pilots, only a shortage of planes. It is true that the Japanese high command grossly exaggerated the losses inflicted on the Americans; all military commands do that in time of war. But the fact was that the American high command was quite worried by the new turn of events. It was one of the factors that led to the use of the atomic bomb the next year, since it was anticipated that the suicide attacks would continue and cause heavy damage. But the figures on the readiness of the Japanese were staggering. By the end of June 1945, 340 suicide squadrons had been orgainized. By August production was back up to two thousand planes a month. Altogether the army still had 6,150 aircraft at its disposal. Standing by were 6,150 pilots with another 2530 in training. The army also had 2.3 million soldiers in the home islands who were prepared to die to the last man (Hoyt 1983:291).

It is highly paradoxical that with most of the country prepared to die during the war, that after the war Japan should have reached a pinnacle of unexampled prosperity. Evidently the same kind of self-sacrifice and group spirit that led to suicide in the war has led to increasing success in the economic field after the war.

But while self-sacrifice for the sake of industry is comprehensible, since it requires hard work but not death, the extent of the suicide defense remains incomprehensible. One man wrote a song that became the symbol of his squadron:

> Insignificant little pebbles that we are,
> The degree of our devotion does not falter,
> As for our country we move toward our final rest. (Hoyt 1983:118)

Another pilot left a farewell message in which he said that "after all, the body is only an attachment of the spirit" (Hoyt 1983:287).

While there was no shortage of suicide pilots, there were others who would not go. The suicides were called "the madmen" by the nonsuicides. The suicides in their turn called the nonsuicides "the lechers" because they wanted life and pleasure.

Little has been published on the kamikazes, and what there is does not explain the psychology of so many thousands of pilots. That a few men might give up their lives for their country can be understood in terms of pathology, but that so many were willing to die remains incomprehensible. It shows however that even in a modern nation, the self can be completely submerged to the point of death in favor of a communal undertaking.

Mass Suicide of the Peoples Temple in Guyana

In 1978 a bizarre religious cult came to light. Led by Rev. James Jones, about 1200 Americans emigrated to Guyana, leaving all their belongings behind in the

United States. There they set up an isolated community in which Jones had complete control. Among other matters, Jones was the only one permitted to have sex (Yee and Layton 1982). After receiving complaints from some of his constituents about the kidnapping or brainwashing of their family members, Congressman Leo Ryan left for Guyana to look at the situation first hand. He was shot. Then came the most gruesome news of all. At Jones' command 908 members of the community committed suicide by drinking poison. Jones shot himself, crying "Mother, mother, please" (Yee and Layton 1982:285). Later the investigation showed that almost all had committed suicide voluntarily.

The incident aroused much psychological research but could scarcely be satisfactorily explained. It was compared by some with another instance of mass death for the sake of religion, in Münster in 1533, during the Protestant Reformation. There the city was taken over by a crazed religious leader, John of Leyden, whose sanity gave way under the pressure of events. But he had control of the city, and most of the inhabitants. When the city was captured, most of the defendants were butchered. In that case, however, the deaths were due to outside intervention, not to mass suicide (Gay and Webb 1973:144–145).

Modern Totalitarianism and Brainwashing

The rise of the totalitarian regimes in the twentieth century has led to an intense interest in the methods of brainwashing that have been used to subject their own peoples and their enemies. Brainwashing involves the change of a person's identity to almost its exact opposite within the space of a few weeks or months, something that ordinarily would never be expected to happen. Robert Lifton has carried out a most intensive study of men brainwashed by the Chinese communists after the revolution, and I shall first summarize his data, based on interviews with the various persons involved.

Four general methods were used: coercion, exhortation, therapy, and realization. Ideological totalitarianism utilizes all four, but leans most heavily on the first two.

The message of coercion is: you must change and become what we tell you to become—or else. The threat embodied in the "or else" may be anything from death to social ostracism, any form of physical or emotional pain. The goal of naked coercion is to produce a cowed and demoralized follower. It is directed at the most primitive of human emotions and stimulates the desire to flee, or fight back, to freeze in fear, or submit completely. A good example is the Nazi concentration camp. There the intent was to break the persons as individuals and to change them into docile masses who could be useful subjects to the Nazi state.

The message of the exhortative approach is: you should change, if you are a moral man, and become what we (in the name of a higher moral authority) tell you to become. Exhortation seeks to create converts and disciples, people who have been changed in accordance with the specific ideological convictions of the mentor. It appeals to preexising tendencies toward experiencing guilt and shame, including existential guilt.

The message of the therapeutic approach is: you can change from your sickly state and find relief for your suffering, if you have a genuine urge to become healthy; and if you are willing to follow my (or our) method and guidance. Its goal is physical and emotional health, freedom from incapacitating disease and defect.

Finally, the message of realization is: you can change, in such a fashion that you will be able to express your own potential, if you are willing to confront yourself with ideas and approaches that challenge your present ways of knowing and acting. Its goal is to produce a person who expresses his creative potential to the full, one who extends his faculties to their utmost in the effort to appreciate and produce at the highest level at which he is capable. This is often called after Maslow self-actualization.

In the Chinese brainwashing experience all four of these methods were used, but particularly the first two. It was noted by Lifton that invariably a certain number of persons were executed, and that the fact of these executions was made known to those undergoing thought reform. The lesson was clear: if you do not change your basic personality in a hurry, that might be your fate too. Yet the authorities always left a lingering doubt about whether the subject would be executed or not. Had they wished to do so they could simply have executed the refractory elements, but evidently they wished to rely on persuasion as well. In this atmosphere of intimidation many did really change their minds, confess the error of their past ways, and promise a rebirth to a new type of person conforming to the new ideology. Again a loss of the old self in a record time.

Self-Aggrandizement: Three Instances

In contrast to persons who give up their selves for the sake of some social order (whether by persuasion or in the context of coercion), we can look at three individuals who lived by accentuated self-aggrandizement. In them the sense of self and its meaning in the world and in history was exaggerated beyond any reasonable measure, and at the expense of those who were near and dear to them. I shall cite some data from published biographies.

Ervil LeBaron: Mormon Prophet of Blood

Ervil LeBaron was a Mormon, born in 1925, at a time when polygamy had been outlawed. Associated with a dissident band of Mormons, he emigrated to northern Mexico, where he succeeded in marrying fourteen women. Breaking off from the Mormons, his brother Joel founded a church known as the Church of the First Born. Ervil maneuvered to get control of the church.

There was another brother, Ben, who early showed signs of mental illness. Ervil's psychosis only came to light gradually. He sought power. Soon he declared himself the Patriarch who would establish God's rule on earth by exterminating all his enemies. He took this literally, first murdering his brother Joel, then another dissident Mormon, Rulon Allred. Eventually, this second murder led to a fuller investigation and he was convicted in 1980. This of course destroyed the church he had founded. While waiting for the appeals to run their course, he died in 1981 (Bradlee and Van Atta 1981).

Isaac Merritt Singer: The Dramatic Polygamist

To most people the Singer sewing machine, which revolutionized the life of the average housewife, is a household word. The life story of its chief promoter (for he did not invent the machine, merely promoted it) is a tale of extraordinary self-aggrandizement.

Singer was born in 1811. His life reads like a Horatio Alger story. At the age of twelve he left for Rochester, New York, then a boom town, without money, without friends, without education, and possessed of nothing but a strong constitution and a prolific brain.

Although he was a skilled mechanic, his life dream was to become an actor. At that time acting was not considered a respectable profession. Singer, however, persisted and joined a strolling troupe. At the same time, at nineteen, he married a girl name Catherine; she was then fifteen. But he did not stay home. He wandered around with his acting troupe. In Baltimore he met another teen-age girl, Mary Ann, with whom he lived for many years always promising to marry her once he was divorced, but never doing so.

By 1849 he was sufficiently successful to move back to New York City with his second family; by this time he was thirty-eight years old, with two wives and eight children. Each wife knew all about the other, but seemingly did not object, especially since he was punctilious about supporting the children.

Once in New York he began to exploit the sewing machine. In business he was as ruthless as in his love life. He swindled his first wife, his first partner, and squeezed many others out of the field. By 1867 he was the undisputed head of the sewing machine industry, with an estimated worth of $15 million, an enormous fortune for that period.

But then his romantic escapades became known. By 1860 he had fathered and recognized eighteen children by four women, of whom sixteen were alive, and supporting them all in reasonable style. It was also claimed, and not denied, that he regularly seduced most of his operatives.

As though this were not enough, he then found still another woman, Isabella, half French and half English. With her he settled down and had five more children. But as an actor he yearned for recognition. Unable to secure it in New York, where he had become notorious for his licentious life, he retired to Torquay in England.

There he built an elaborate house and entertained widely. Though he was ostracized by the local gentry, he was happy to entertain the tradespeople. His house even had a private theater. For the people of the town his parties were a most spectacular fare, and he was warmly regarded by all, who knew nothing of his past. Thus, his last years were spent as an actor offering entertainment; he died in 1875. Histrionic to the last, he even left instructions about how his funeral should be conducted. He was buried in three lavish coffins, the funeral cortege was drawn by his own twelve horses, three abreast, and the funeral procession was nearly three-quarters of a mile long, containing between seventy and eighty carriages.

In all, though married only twice, he acknowledged the children of five women as his own, making provision in his will for all. What was astounding for that time was that he publicly admitted all of his illegitimate children. (Brandon 1977).

Yukio Mishima

Yukio Mishima (1925–1970) was one of the leading Japanese writers of his generation, author of forty novels, eighteen plays, twenty volumes of short stories, and numerous essays. He was a popular and flamboyant character, a Renaissance man who went in, apart from his writing, for weight lifting, sword play, and acting. He was a homosexual who was fascinated by physical beauty and violence. Finally, he was an emperor worshiper and death lover, who said in his autobiographical novel *Confessions of a Mask*: "It was in death that I had discovered my real 'life's aim' " (Matson 1980:235).

His family situation was typical: his mother's darling, hated by a father who went so far as to confiscate and destroy his writings.

An outstanding literary success at an early age, Mishima became the idol of a circle of literary men who identified themselves with the death-obsessed Japanese Romantic school that had flourished during the war years. In his mind death and sexuality became interconnected.

His autobiographical novel, published in 1949, revealed himself to the world in details—his homosexuality, his erotic fascination with the well-tanned naked bodies of young men, his adoration of St. Sebastion, the Christian martyr. At the same time he revealed his sadistic fantasies: "There, in my murder theater, young Roman gladiators offered up their lives for my amusement; and all the deaths that took place there not only had to overflow with blood but also had to be performed with due ceremony. I delighted in all forms of capital punishment and all implements of execution" (Matson 1980:239).

But fame, wealth, and worldly success were not enough for him. Identified with the glory of Japan, he decided to sacrifice his life in a bizarre episode, again Japanese style. Perhaps his death gives us a clue to the dynamics of the Japanese suicide pilots. Together with some comrades from what they called the Shield Society, he went to the quarters of the general in charge of the Eastern Army headquarters, seized him, and made a speech to the soldiers, urging them to reconquer Japan's past glories. They jeered him. Undaunted, he then publicly committed suicide. As he put it in his novel delivered that same day: "It was his conduct on the battlefield that he was now to display" (Matson 1980:244).

In all of these examples, both of self-denial and of self-aggrandizement, rage plays a central role. The theoretical inference is clear: if the person does not build up a reasonable self-image, or goes to the other extreme and becomes too grandiose, the life-style will lead to enormous outbursts of rage. These may be directed at other people, or, in some cases, against oneself. Rage and infantile narcissism go together, though they may take different forms.

Anthropological Data

If the self-image varies with the social order, it stands to reason that it would be different in different cultures, especially those most unlike Western civilization. That this is indeed the case is demonstrated by the extensive field work carried out in the past hundred years, especially since the time of the Boasian revolution. Yet many nagging questions remain unanswered.

Geza Roheim, reporting on his field work among the Central Australian natives, wrote:

> Every society has a characteristic feature, something which strikes the eye of a human being who comes from another society. It seems probable that these peculiarities—the outsider's point of view—have their roots in tendencies which are universally human, yet particularly accentuated in the group in question. If we regard each type of society as a distinct neurosis, we might speak of the characteristic or governing symptoms of these social systems. (1932:121)

While this commonsense position evoked responsive research from a wide variety of anthropologists (e.g., Mead, Benedict, Kardiner, Linton,etc.) in the 1920s and 1930s, later it came under severe attack. It was argued (Levine 1973) that men everywhere strive to live rather than die, to maximize pleasure and minimize pain in their lives. Human behavior, it was urged, is shaped by the coercive pressures of "social survival"—the maintenance and enhancement of career, reputation, status, and the esteem of others. Individual behavior reflects environmental contingencies calculated through application of the individual's capacities for perceiving and logically processing information about environmental demands.

Understanding these processes and their outcomes does not require delving into the psychology of the individual apart from recognizing that he, like all other normal humans, has the capacity for appraising and adapting to his environment so as to maximize his rewards and minimize his risks. Further, some have held that how populations differ psychologically is of little social significance. In its most extreme form this position is associated with a superorganic point of view in which some single factor is conceptualized as determinative of behavior in a specific culture. Still another argument heard is that there are such wide variations within any given culture that to speak of "basic personality" or model ideology" is highly misleading.

Levine, summing up these arguments, lists five different attitudes toward the culture-personality hypothesis described above: anti culture-personality; psychological reductionism; personality-is-culture; personality mediation; and two systems (modal personality and sociocultural institutions are two systems interacting with each other). Concluding his discussion of the culture-personality question, Levine (1973:98) states:

Although different positions have generated divergent concepts and methods, there are no serious theoretical disputes among contemporary culture and personality theorists. Most assume that there is some kind of adaptive fit between the personality characteristics of a population and the sociocultural environment of the population. Most also assume that the individual personality, no less than the sociocultural system, is a functioning system with dispositions that manifest themselves in social behavior. The terms of the adaptive fit and the conditions of its manifestations are matters of divergent emphasis; but there is general agreement that empirical research must resolve these questions. The major difficulties and controversies in culture and personality are methodological.

These methodological disputes run through the entire range of all the social sciences. By and large there is the inner psychic orientation of the psychoanalytically oriented investigator, as contrasted with the outer-behavior-dominated orientation of the anthroplogist (or psychologist) who relies primarily on a behavioral-learning theory kind of psychology. This is the same divergence that has bedeviled psychology ever since the advent of psychoanalysis and behaviorism, both of which assumed prominence at roughly the same time (World War I and its aftermath).

The self-image is preeminently an inner psychological concept. Understanding it, measuring it, charting its growth and conflicts, all require considerable amounts of inference from the observed data. Nevertheless, these methodological problems should not lead us to turn away from this fruitful area of investigation. With these caveats we can then turn to some of the anthropological data that is available.

The Zuni

Ruth Benedict (1934) was the first to describe what she called the "Apollonian" style of life of the Pueblo Indians in the United States southwest (the Zunis, very similar to the Hopi). They live in the midst of America, within easy reach of any transcontinental traveler. And they are living after the old native fashion, still there and not disintegrated, unlike many of the other native Indian cultures. Their self-image, fairly clearly dictated by their social order, is that of someone who fits into the community, eschewing excessive ambition, and excessive release of any forbidden impulses. They are a ceremonious people, who value sobriety and inoffensiveness above all other virtues. Their interest is centered upon their rich and complex ceremonial life. Their prayers are formulas, the effectiveness of which comes from their faithful rendition. The amount of traditional prayer forms of this sort in Zuni can scarcely be exaggerated. Their prayers are rarely violent; they are mild and ceremonious in form, asking for orderly life, pleasant days, and shelter from violence.

A typical prayer, emphasizing the well-being of all, is the following:

All my ladder-descending children,
All of them I hold in my hands,
May no one fall from my grasp
After going but a little way.
Even every little beetle,
Even every dirty little beetle
Let me hold them fast in my hands,
Let none of them fall from my grasp.
May my children's roads all be fulfilled;
May they grow old;
May their roads reach all the way to Dawn Lake;
May their roads be fulfilled;
In order that your thoughts may bend to this
Your days are made. (Benedict 1934:67)

Almost all ceremonial activity is for the benefit of the entire pueblo, and even ceremonies to cure a sick person often include rainmaking or fertility features. Their basic personality (or idea, if you wish) is modest, gentle, and cooperative and does not indulge in disruptive psychological states, such as visions and tortures of other Indian tribes in the area. They are temperate, enjoy sobriety to a moderate degree, and avoid the heights of ecstasy as well as the depths of despair.

By and large, according to Benedict (though as so often her description has been disputed by other anthropologists; see Driver 1969), a man sinks his activities in those of the group and claims no personal authority, not is he ever violent. A good man has a pleasing address, a yielding disposition, and a generous heart. He avoids office. He may have it thrust upon him, but he does not seek it. This same lack of personal exercise of authority is as characteristic of domestic situations as it is of reigious.

In this ordered, anti-individualistic, peace-loving society, suicide is incomprehensible to them, homicide almost unkown. they do not culturally elaborate themes of terror and danger, so that our average TV movie would be entirely foreign to them.

Sex, while not well understood, is accepted realistically. Pleasant relations between the sexes are merely one aspect of pleasant relations with human beings. Where we make a fundamental distinction, their phrase of commendation is: "Everybody likes him, He is always having affairs with women." Or "Nobody likes him. He never has trouble over women." Sex thus becomes merely an incident in the happy life. The self-image of our own culture, in which for so many people forbidden sexual activities instill an enormous sense of guilt and sin, would be totally incomprehensible to them.

The Iroquois

The Iroquois (Driver 1969) present a sharp contrast to the Zunis in that their entire lives were centered around violence. They were strongly individualistic, which permitted no one to give orders to another and contributed to the real lack of authority on the part of chiefs and a parallel absence of real cohesion in the League of the Iroquois. Membership in war parties was on a volunteer basis; warriors were never drafted. But there was never any lack of volunteers.

Parents were permissive with their children but lived in fear of child suicide, which actually happened occasionally. They also resorted to sorcery to right wrongs inflicted on them by others. Polite and impersonal forms of speech were used in public lest one's remarks be construed as personal criticism likely to arouse anger. At the game of lacrosse, the player who did not get angry was the ideal, although in practice these hotly contested matches often ended in brawls between the two sides. Their internal rule was by persuasion and reason, but their external rule of subject peoples was direct and backed by the threat of war.

Wallace (1958) describes an interesting dream theory held by the Iroquois, somewhat akin to psychoanalysis. Dreams were regarded as wishes of the soul that must be satisfied lest the dreamer experience sickness or death. A person dreaming that he was bathing got up and took a bath no matter how cold the weather. A man who dreamed that he was a captive being tortured by the enemy insisted that his friends tie him up and burn his flesh the next day in the belief that this would satisfy his soul's desire and prevent him from actually being captured by the enemy and tortured to death.

Sexual dreams created a problem. Premarital relations were permitted, but they were often shy in heterosexual contacts, and chastity in the young as well as marital fidelity in the mature were regarded as virtues. Still, when a certain man had a dream in which the culture hero ordered him to go to a certain village and cohabit with two married women for five days, his dream fulfillment was permitted by the village authorities for fear that the spirit would bring disaster upon them if disobeyed. Such sexual dreams were common.

Dreams of torture at the hands of the enemy were common among warriors. When one man who had had such a dream told it to another, a council was held. The chiefs agreed that steps should be taken to avoid the ill fortune that the dream foretold. They seized the dreamer and tortured him with fire, telling him that they pitied him and that he should take courage in the hour of agony. Finally, the dreamer ran out of the ring of fires, seized a dog, and offered it as a sacrifice to a war spirit. The dog was killed, roasted in flames, and eaten in a public feast, just as they would eat a human captive. This routine was supposed to prevent the defeat, capture, and torture of warriors from the village where the dreamer lived. In one case it took the dreamer six months to recover from the burns his own tribesmen inflicted on him.

The Central Australians

The Central Australians (Roheim 1953) are among the most primitive people known. They live in an inhospitable environment, wear no clothes, and have little defense against either the climate or starvation. Yet somehow they have persisted and maintain a cultural unity.

Particularly important for our thesis here is that the native has two selves: a public and a private one. As a real person, you see him wandering about the bush or doing the white man's work for his rations. But as a *ngantja*, or hidden person, he has never left the ancestral cave and the *churunga* (a totemic object from which children emanate and into which ancestors are transformed when they die or sink into the ground).

There is some difference of opinion as to the exact nature of this *ngantja*, or hidden self (1932:103ff). Sometimes it is identified with the ancestor who has become a *churunga*, sometimes with the soul, but it is really different from both. While the ghost is red all over and a terrifying apparition, the *ngantja* looks like the real man at the prime of his life. The man dies, but the *ngantja* is immortal. Thus, even these people defend themselves against the reality of death by making up an immortal soul that will survive them indefinitely.

Roheim summarizes the psychology of these peoples as follows (1932:119–120): The fathers have added a vagina to their penis; they are offering boys a vaginal father as a safeguard against and substitute for the phallic mother of their infancy. They pay the price of a superabundant symptom formation, but escape the danger of character transformation. Or rather, to put it more precisely, there is far more socialized symptom formation and far less character transformation than in other civilizations. In one respect, however, we do find a truly reactive character development, which is evidently based on the initial traumatic situation. In the original situation we have a great proximity to the mother and a strong emotional fixation. The one thing they seem to be demonstrating in the ritual is that they want to keep the mother at bay, to separate themselves from the mother. And in the marriage custom (in which they take the woman by force) and the generally more or less sadistic attitude of the male, we have a negation of the strongest emotional ties of infancy.

With a superego based mainly on deflected phallic strivings, with a phallic and aggressive ego, and a minimum of reaction formations in character development, the Aranda is a happy man. When Roheim made inquiries about the sanctions against doing things that were forbidden by ritual, he was told that it is very sacred and taboo. Further inquiries showed, however, that the sanction was merely angry talk, so that the idea was really that the old men would be angry and might kill the offender by magic or violence. Roheim learned that laws were obeyed not from any intrinsic desire to do so, or on account of any spirits, but because they were afraid of the old men. Then again when he inquired about the sanctions for illicit intercourse, first he was told that the old men would kill the offender. But on closer inquiry it appeared that the men were having intercourse all their lives. They had simply taken the risk—"And that is the key to their happiness" (1932:120). They certainly have a superego, but not too much of it, and there is more real danger in their lives than intrapsychic danger. The tortures, which in neurosis are inflicted on the ego by the superego, are here really carried out by the old men at initiation, but not introjected by the young. We know them from cradle to grave and can say: they are not wicked because they do not try to be too good.

> When the Lutheran missionaries began to talk about the doctrine of original sin and to tell these descendants of the eternal dream folk that they were all awful, sinful wicked beings, they answered with great indignation: "Aranda inkaraka mara." "The Aranda are all good." And in this we heartily agree. (1932:120)

Yet in this same group, or others closely allied to it, the problem of starvation was sometimes handled by eating the newborn child or even the unborn child. Women abort, or are made to abort, in times of famine in order to feed the rest of the family. In another Australian tribe the smallest baby was killed by knocking its head against the shoulder of an older sibling; its flesh was used to feed the older siblings and also the rest of the family. In spite of this cannibalism they show great affection for their children. In one case Roheim reported that a small child with whom his parents had been affectionately playing during the day was killed and cooked for dinner (Devereux 1980:127).

Devereux comments that while eating children in times of food shortage is far from rare, hungry children do not seem to kill their parents in order to eat them; he states that he has never heard of such a case in either primitive or modern society. However, Turnbull (1972), who studied the Ik, reported that in this society where everybody was on the verge of starvation, children would steal food from their parents or abandon them completely to die.)

The self-image of the Central Australians, reflecting their total cultural position, is that of an impulse-ridden people, with a weak superego, absence of strong personal ties, highly narcissistic ("An Aranda or Luritja has certainly a high opinion of his own physical excellence, and is never troubled by any inferiority complex in this respect" [Roheim 1932:103].), little sense of shame (although the women are careful to walk and sit in such a manner as to cover the vagina, while the men are ashamed to have an erection in public), demonstrating an exaggerated maleness, manifested in using violence against women and in developing an exclusively male society. There is little guilt so that the most common tendency is to do what they wish without regard for the alleged taboos (e.g., with regard to intercourse).

While Roheim's work is rarely cited nowadays because it was done in the period of id psychology, this neglect seems unfortunate. This is the first careful examination of a primitive society by a trained psychoanalyst. His methodology relied heavily on play with children and on an exhaustive analysis of dreams, two techniques with which few anthropologists are familiar. Most important, for the thesis of this chapter, is that there is a psychologically different social order that creates a self-image that is unique and easily differentiated from that of other cultures.

Papua New Guinea

Rituals of Manhood in Papua New Guinea have by now been described by numerous field workers (e.g., Herdt 1982). Although Papua New Guinea is an incredibly diversified culture area, certain features stand out among many of the groups investigated. Almost always a boy becomes a man by some initiatory procedure that is both painful and violent; in some cases the boys die (Tuzin 1982).

Summarizing the data from the various studies, Keesing (1982) offers the following. A first pervasive theme is that males and females are radically different in their physical and psychological being and that the fluids, essences, and powers of women are dangerous and inimical to those of men. There are several recurrent themes that are expressions of this physiological opposition between the male and female powers and essences. One is restrictions of men's contact with the emanations of women's generative powers, and most particularly menstrual blood. Unless boys undergo the rigors of initiation, they will remain soft and weak. An essential element in this ideology of the creation of men is the challenge of physical growth. Boys will be stunted and weak if they do not follow a prescribed regimen, both positive (in eating enjoined foods, in ingesting semen through the mouth or anus) and negative (in avoiding tabooed foods and debilitating contacts). The cosmologies of New Guinea, perhaps most strikingly in those societies where male cults are fully developed, employ elaborate systems of symbols drawn from the natural world.

Initiation into male cults entails both secrecy from those who are excluded and the revelation of esoteric knowledge to initiates. This sequence is a graded progression to the manhood that must be created by acts of nurturance, ordeal, purification, and instruction. Initiates learn how to be men, how to protect themselves from dangers of pollution. The ultimate revelations of mystery, the unmasking of the deception of sacred flute or bull roarer, serve to underline the collective responsibilities and hence solidarity of men.

Another recurrent theme, though one less clear, is the frequency of male institutionalized homosexual behavior in the men's cults. This homosexuality suggests at least that it is a widespread elaboration, perhaps even the original core, of the ideology of sexual separation, female danger, the growth of boys, and the creation of men.

The basic principles of male initiation allow for much variation. The definition of female being as inimical to male growth and physical powers rationalizes, and indeed demands, a residential separation of adult men and women and the existence of a center of men's activities apart from dwelling houses. In some New Guinea societies the dwelling houses, which are primarily the province of women, are nonetheless the focus of a married couple's daily life. At the other extreme are those cultures where initiated men spend most of their time in men's houses or men's company, where there is little conjugal life, where men are strictly segregated when they enter a woman's house and where marital sexual relations in the house are prohibited. The initiatory sequences also vary considerably in terms of age of initiation, the age variation among the novices, and the number of full grades to manhood.

Warfare appears to be a key factor in male cultism in New Guinea; the relationship among warfare, demonology, and competition for land requires comment. In the longer time span competition for niches and the displacement of populations would seem to be an important factor in shaping the distribution of entire language groups as well as of local kin groups. Thus, men are not only defending territory but also through marriage, exchange, peacemaking, and regional military alliance maintaining a wider framework of political order, however fragile and transitory. Men's labor constructed on the foundations of women's labor reproduced not only a social order but a cosmic one: a realm of spirits and powers behind the visible.

The symbolism and actual practices of initiation rituals show in New Guinea an inescapable preoccupation with sexual themes. A psychoanalytically sophisticated view of the dynamics of the unconscious and of oedipal conflict is necessary if we are to understand the sources of the fantasy materials that in these societies are crystallized into myth and ritual.

Keesing also raises the question of the relationship between normative constructs about men and the personal and private orientation of individuals, i.e., their experiential selfhood. Does initiation create a radically new selfhood, as it is supposed to? The paradoxical question is: How are systems of initiation perpetuated, when perpetuation entails men inflicting on boys experiences that in their own boyhood were psychologically traumatic and physically painful?

To this latter question psychoanalytic theory can provide a plausible hypothesis. As long ago as 1936 Anna Freud described the defense of *identification with the aggressor*, in which children who have been cruelly treated by their parents grow up to be parents who treat their own children cruelly in exactly the same manner. This seems to be the case here with the Papuan initiatory rites. It also sheds an illuminating light on the pscyhological experiences of the initiates who, we would suspect, are terrified by their ordeals, then overcome the fear by determining to do the same thing to others when they are in a position to do so.

Once more the self-image of the male fits neatly into the kind of social order into which he is born and in which he is raised. He has to be a strong, macho he-man, contemptuous of "weak" women, seeking to justify his prowess in combats with men. The whole pattern shows a remarkable similarity to the traditional image of men in our own society, except that the cruel initiatory rituals are for the most part absent. Or is warfare, which has been endemic in Western civilization for nearly a thousand years, the ritualistic experience a boy must undergo in order to become a man?

The Anyi

An entirely different kind of culture is described by three Swiss analysts (Parin, Morgenthaler, and Parin-Matthey 1980) in their book on the Anyi, who live in the rainforests of the Ivory Coast in Africa, an ancient warrior people who today grow coffee for the world market. The authors spent several months among the Anyi in 1966 conducting psychoanalytically oriented interviews with individual subjects. Their investigations showed a conflict-laden society, made up of conflict-laden individuals, full of anxieties, depression, paranoid trends, and pessismism about life.

Depressive trends are clearly brought out in the dancing song of the young men of Bebou:

> Everybody knows me now,
> On the day when I die,
> When I lie in my coffin,
> Nobody will know me any more.
> Those who used to call me by name,
> Now that I am dead,
> Don't know my name any more.
> You have forgotten my name!
> On the day when I die,
> They will carry me to my grave
> When evening comes,
> Quickly, when evening comes. (pp. 384–385)

The distrust and "fear of the neighbor" is clearly illustrated in another song:

> There are men
> Who want to kill me.
> I live in loneliness, far, from men.
> But I live.
> A young girl hears my song.
> I should not sing.
> My song can find no favor with her.

I should not sing in her presence.
I am like the honey wasp—
When I am far, far away,
Then people love me.
When I am here,
They have no love for me any more. (pp.310–311)

In their reconstruction of the metapsychology of the Anyi, the authors make the following points: The society of the Anyi is characterized by particularly striking contradictions. The cohesion between brothers and sisters and all other members of the maternal lineage stands in contrast to the power and prestige structure of the masculine world of chiefs and dignitaries. While early infancy is full of gratifications, as soon as the infant can no loner gratify her needs, the mother retires into the background; thereafter the fear of abandonment is strong.

The depressive moods, dreamlike in their intensity, with which nursing mothers try to counter the danger of an unbearably painful loss of their babies, seems to have contributed to the general predisposition to depression that is so typical of this people. The phase, after eighteen months, of the child who can run, but not run away, has lasting consequences for the demarcation and cathexis of the self, for object relations, and for dealing with reality. As a result, the infant engages in a narcissistic withdrawal and precocious autonomy.

Thus, narcissistic regression is the first consequence of the independence forced prematurely upon the child. He creates a fantasy world in which he is omnipotent and in which he manipulates his objects so that he achieves gratification of his needs and, above all, completion of the self. That he can withdraw into this world at will and be protected in it from anxiety, frustration, and loneliness makes the further developmental step possible.

The image of the omnipotent symbiotic mother is augmented by another feature, one that derives from her compelling commands and from the experiences of anal stimulation and violation through the daily enemas. From this time on she appears in the child's fantasies, anxieties, and desires as anal penetrating and sadistically dominating, without, however, forfeiting her reparatory-supplementary qualities or her role in gratifying oral greed.

The development that follows entails such strong frustrations and constant recourse to the primary process that a revival of omnipotence and symbiotic part objects is necessary. The Anyi child does not envy his younger siblings the mother's breast so much as the mother's person; thus, it is understandable that sibling rivalry is not particularly intense.

The phallic phase is marked by the recurrence of the child's attempts to achieve stable narcissistic cathexis of his own person. Moreover, the Anyi child has no real models of phallic masculinity, unimpaired and deserving of admiration, with whom he might identify. As a result, object relations are very unstable.

However, even though object relations are unstable, the ego derives a dual advantage: it does not need to adjust to objects that promise only slight gratification, and it has freedom of action in such contradictory social situations as polygynous marriage, conflicting loyalties toward persons of the mother's and persons of the father's lineage, and homosexual and heterosexual relationships.

Interaction with the social environment provides the ego with stabilizing functions that serve as an effective defense (group ego) and that in turn help to promote adaptation to the environment.

The ego becomes independent, while the self is differentiated and complete. Apart from this, the boundaries of the self remain open, and the ego must rely on a defense that is magical and that can be compared with psychotic mechanisms insofar as gestures, fantasies, and internal reorientations suffice to manipulate reality.

Oral instinctual impulses and the libidinal desires they later engender, especially sexuality in the strict sense of the word, retain a tendency to demand immediate discharge. Consequently, regressions to the "most recent level of satisfying experience" are numerous and persistent.

Other objects now begin to assume more definite shape, e.g., younger siblings. Envy is rarely violently expressed and does not lead to lasting aggressiveness. It is replaced by a constant fear of being robbed or deprived and is absorbed into a general skeptical feeling of distrust, a feeling that other people have or are given (usually by the fates) more money, more food, more luck than they.

The environment, that is, the external world, does nothing to hamper or restrict the maturation and exercise of independent motor activities, the exploration of the environment, or the cathexis of body feelings, which proceed in part under the guidance of the muscular apparatus and in part under that of the urethal and genital erogenous zone and which can be summed up as the developmental process leading to phallicity. In fact, it appears that the environment actually encourages this development. At this point girls and boys are treated just the same.

In the oedipal conflict, ego maturation regularly entails a reorientation toward the persons of the environment. The oedipal mother now acquires the features of the gratifying mother of the nursing period. The external conditions of Anyi life would be conducive to complete disregard of the father as a rival. Yet, since such rivalry is inevitable, the tendency to evade it continues to exist, owing to the symbiotic nuance present in oedipal love. The phallic libido is unmistakably sexual, and only to a small extent aim-inhibited or otherwise transformable. This accounts for the terrifying castration anxieties that now begin to appear.

All object relations colored by the oedipal conflict can be regarded as comparatively unstable. Many toddlers have to change all their related objects quite frequently, and sometimes even have to exchange their own mothers temporarily or permanently for foster mothers. The ideal oedipal father is the one who remains outside, who can either be isolated from or reexcluded from the family. Identification with an active phallic father is never entirely successful. At the conclusion of the oedipal period, the normal attitude toward the father or the male is characterized by rapidly alternating and mutually supplementary partial identifications.

Aggressive tensions and acute anxiety are typical of the culture-specific personality of the Anyi. Their aggressive fantasies are persecutory in character; for this reason the authors speak of the "normal paranoiac character" of the Anyi. The tendency to come to grips with the cruel and hated object in the outside world is slight.

The course of oedipal development in girls is considerably simpler and the outcome is more clearly defined. They enter the phallic phase with just about the same preoedipal experiences as the boys, but they have a number of advantages. They tend to direct violent reproaches and aggressions toward the mother as a rival. Castration anxiety appears in this process only as a fear of being left alone or of being orally abused, devoured by a witch, sold, or poisoned. At the resolution, the girl (unlike the boy) is able to develop sexual identity with the phallic female and mother, and this is doubtless why puberty is less problematic for her.

Strong affects are diverted. Anxiety and shame are concealed. The urgency of emotional defenses is responsible for a typical characteristic of many dreams; within the manifest dream they contain a wish fulfillment that has been divested of any negative emotions—disappointment, anxiety and so on—by a process of splitting.

The evolution of the body image must be regarded as one of the most important, perhaps the most important, bases of ego formation. Among the vast majority of the Anyi the pleasure in good food and above all good drink has remained intact. Yet allied to this is the widespread hypochondria, with its ever-present anxiety that there is too much in the intestines.

The general prerequisites for group ego functions originate in the oral phase of ego formation. Aggressive tendencies can be processed particularly well by the group, whose acting out of aggression, in which the individual concerned participates, contributes to controlling instinctual impulses. For the ego ideal figures in the environment serve as mediators. It may be the large share of the group in important ego functions that enables the Anyi ego to function normally despite the fact that it is equipped with mechanisms that we find almost exclusively in subjects suffering from serious psychological disorders. Not only the Anyi's ego, but also his superego, is dependent on a human environment that is culture-specific in structure and populated by specific figures; it functions, in a sense, as a "clan conscience." The frustrating parent images inspire anxiety and form the superego nuclei. To compensate for the lack of emotional ties they have a number of quite uniform inner rules that they have acquired through identification.

The difference between the Anyi and the European can be observed in its pure form, so to speak, in connection with the content of the ideal self. Whereas our ideal is to achieve, theirs is to enjoy a fortunate lot in life. Instead of striving to become something, their ideal is to be something. For the Anyi, passiveness, which in our culture has predominantly negative connotations, is in itself neither good nor bad, like activeness. The ideal self evolves without any anal focusing of aggressions, without urethral ambition, and without phallic oedipal focusing of the libido on specific objects. An ideal self of this description can seem worthy of emulation to us only if we happen to find the goals of our own social structure questionable. Since their social structure bears no resemblance to ours, those components of the Anyi self that are derived most directly from the environment cannot be the same as ours.

The review of these five cultures justifies accepting Roheim's thesis (which is the general psychoanalytic position) that every society possesses its own distinct neurosis. The Zuni are ordered, cooperative, yet crushing of individuality; the Iroquois are highly violent and narcissistic; the Central Australians impulse-ridden and guilt-free; the male cults in Papua New Guinea accentuate the differences between males and females, see the male as all-powerful, and resort to initiation rituals that are dangerous and yet inevitably important; the Anyi show a large measure of distrust, paranoia, and depression. In all of these certain central aspects of the self-image can be coordinated with distinctive features of the culture. The self-image in other words is a reflection of, or parallel, to the rewards and constraints of the given social order.

To this must be added the caveat that certain features of life are common to all human groups, others are found in some but not all, while still others are virtually unique to one particular culture (e.g., the daily enemas of the Anyi). The self-image must take these into account as well as the common and distinctive characteristics of the group. Yet, while there may be considerable difficulty in describing the specific features of any cultural self-image, that it is there can scarcely be questioned.

In infancy the self-image is largely determined by parental upbringing. In childhood the self-image reflects the educational process; in adulthood the self-image is coordinated with the general cultural milieu. In all cases (which has not been emphasized sufficiently in the preceding) the self-image carries with it an evaluative as well as descriptive comment; every individual feature is seen as good or bad, approved or disapproved.

The objections raised by Levine (1973) and others to portrayals of the self-image of this kind are three: the description applies to only a small portion of the culture; nothing is said about how it is recreated in the child; and nothing is said about how it came about in the culture at large. None of these objections should lead us to abandon this psychologically meaningful way of approaching the human being. What portion of the culture it applies to is a matter for empirical research. How it is recreated is generally formulated in terms of the superego, which is created within the family, and provides a vital link to the larger community. And how such a culture came to be is in itself an interesting question, but one that in most cases defies an exact answer (outside of well-known cultures such as Western Europe) because not enough material is available. Nevertheless it is there, no matter how it might have come about.

A further significant distinction relates to the dominant emotional climate of the concepts of love cultures vs. hate cultures. A love culture is one in which the predominant feelings among its individual members are love, affection, warmth, caring, and other positive emotions. A hate culture would represent the opposite. Pure cultures rarely if ever exist, but the difference between an ordered cooperative culture and the violent ones such as those found in Papua New Guinea are obvious. Further characteristics of love cultures can be described.

1. There are love cultures. This proposition, which has been so vehemently denied (e.g., by Konrad Lorenz), is the most significant of all. How this came about we do not know. But evidently in the haphazard way in which various human cultures have come into existence, some have learned to stress love, affection, tenderness, cooperation, while others have learned to stress hatred, antagonism, harshness and competitiveness. A further obvious conclusion is that if this has happened by accident, so to speak, it can also be brought about by conscious effort.

2. The major characteristic of the love culture is the general feeling of friendliness that is absent in hate cultures.

3. At the same time it must be recognized that some form of aggression is universal. In most of the cultures so described it takes the form of projection to outside elements, other cultures (as among the Arapesh) or supernatural forces (as among the Ifaluk). However, there is a vast difference between projected aggression, which leaves the everyday lives of the people relatively smooth and unconcerned, and constant, or intermittent, violence, warfare, fighting, and murder.

4. Usually love cultures allow wide latitude for sexual expression. Cultures have been described, such as the Mangaia, where no one is left without a love partner and where frigidity, defined as lack of orgasm, in women is unknown. Impotence in men is rare until relative old age. In other cultures, however, sex is less important, as among the Arapesh, who describe it only as an "easy comfortable feeling," or among the Hutterites, who condone it in marriage but forbid it otherwise. The degree to which sexual enjoyment in marriage exists among the Hutterites is unknown.

5. In general persons living in these cultures are fairly happy and contented with their lives. The severe expressions of emotional conflict and mental disorder so characteristic of our own society are rare among them.

6. Within our own culture distinctions can also be drawn between happy families and unhappy ones (Beavers 1977). In general, the descriptions apply to the majority of the people in the culture, or to a strong and dominant minority, not to everybody. There are always and everywhere individual differences that require more detailed examination and more careful explanation.

7. The self-image of the typical individual in a love culture is markedly different from the self-image of the typical individual in a hate culture. The dominant ethos of the culture will be reflected in the self-images of a considerable portion of its population.

Further comments on love and hate cultures will be found in chapter 7.

Does the Concept of the Self Vary with the Culture?

Another important question to which anthropology can provide some clues is whether the concept of the self per se varies with the culture, or is it universal? Certainly some conceptualization is universal (cf. Roheim, above), but is it the same conceptualization everywhere? This question must be answered decidedly in the negative.

The anthropologist Clifford Geertz asserts:

> The Western conception of the person as a bounded, unique, more or less integrated motivational and congnitive universe, a dynamic center of awareness, emotion, judgment, and action organized into a distinctive whole and set contrastively both against other such wholes and against a social and natural background is, however incorrigible it may seem to us, a rather peculiear idea within the context of the world's cultures. (1975:48)

Shweder and Bourne (1984) consider this question in detail and come to a similar conclusion. One of their categories of understanding is "confusion(ism)," which calls for the honest confession that one culture fails to comprehend the ideas of another. There is no doubt that to piece together the concept of the self that prevails in an alien culture is a formidable undertaking.

Even in our own culture, the crystallization of a clear individual autonomous sense of the self, which is what Geertz is referring to, is a late development. As Lea (1973, 1974) showed more than a century ago, such devices as the duel, the oath, the wager, and the ordeal, all of which confuse the individual self with a larger group, survived until fairly recent times. And one need only reflect upon the "peculiar institution" of slavery, especially in the United States (Paterson 1982). In general, it was in the nineteenth century that slavery was abolished by the European powers. The U.S. South was the only slaveholding community that went to war to prevent the freeing of the slaves. In the famous Dred Scott decision of 1857, the Supreme Court officially declared that a black man could not be a citizen of the United States, in complete contradiction to the Declaration of Independence statement that all men are created free and equal. Patterson equates slavery with social death; archetypically, as he shows, slavery was a substitute for death in war. He coded forty-five of the world's slave cultures and found that in twenty-eight, or 62.2 percent, the masters could kill the slaves with impunity, and from time to time, did (1982:193; see also chapter 1). Under such circumstances the slave could not be considered a true human being; in effect he had no self-image. And since slavery has played such an enormous role in the history of civilization, the fact that the slave had no real self-image is most significant for our thesis that the self-image varies from one culture to another, and even within the same culture. Repercussions of the slavery era still reverberate in the United States with the claims of some psychologists that the black is "constitutionally inferior" to the white, especially in his native intellectual capacity.

Psychotherapy: Change in the Self-Image

Another important line of evidence comes from the study of psychotherapy or, more generally, healing (including somatic therapy), for here a conscious effort is made by either the physician or the patient or both to alter the image of the self that is present. Aware of the interactional and culturally significant character of all "healing," numerous investigators have examined the process in considerable detail. Their work deserves more careful attention.

To begin, the reorientation of the notion of psychotherapy that stems from the perspective of the history of psychoanalysis must be evaluated. As Roheim commented above, every culture has its own distinct neurosis. Accordingly, every person has his own distinct problems that he may or may not recognize; they may be ego-dystonic, in which case he does something about them. Everyone has some ego-dystonic symptoms. So everyone engages in some kind of psychotherapy to get over these symptoms. As a rule this psychotherapy is informal and includes all the devices known to man to succeed from escaping anxiety, from taking a drink to suicide. When, why, and how formal psychotherapy enters into the picture requires more careful evaluation.

Kleinman Study

The most meticulous study in the literature of healing in the context of culture is the work of Arthur Kleinman, *Patients and Healers in the Context of Culture* (1980). Kleinman is a psychiatrist trained in anthropology who spent several years in Taiwan studying the dynamics of the healing process, both physical and psychological, in the native culture. The book is an outcome of this research.

Kleinman pictures the healing process as going through three stages. First, the sickness is labeled with an appropriate and sanctioned cultural category. Second, the label is ritually manipulated (culturally transformed). Finally, a new label (cured, well) is applied and sanctioned as a meaningful symbolic form that may be independent of behavioral or social change.

Generalizing from his observations of the Chinese culture, Kleinman makes further comments on how cultures define the self and its behavioral field:

1. Cultures should fall into a typology of beliefs and values concerning the self and its behavioral field that should, in turn, link to typologies of cognitive coping strategies and affective experience (normal and deviant).

2. Through these cognitive and behavioral typologies, cultures may vary systematically in making individuals more or less susceptible to depressive affect and the depressive syndrome. They may also vary systematically in the relative success of the coping strategies they impart to individuals for managing affective experiences. This cultural variation may exert a definable influence on rates and course of affective sickness, and also on the nature and relative efficacy of indigenous healing approaches to affective disorders. Determination of these potential effects will require epidemiological and outcome studies that consider illness as well as disease.

3. Somatic, interpersonal, and naturalistic idioms for articulating dysphoric affects should give rise to affective illness experiences that are clearly distinguishable from that entailed by a psychological idiom. Similarly, treatments that fit specific cultural idioms should demonstrate relatively greater efficacy and relatively fewer management problems.

4. Westernization will have a predictable impact on the cultural idiom of affective experience and typologies of cognitive coping strategies, changing them toward those characteristic of the contemporary West. This change may be associated with changes in incidence, course, and outcome of affective sickness.

5. In contemporary Chinese societies, it is to be expected that women and the elderly, because they are more culturally conservative, will demonstrate the most characteristic traditional patterns of affective experience and disorders. This should hold for other non-Western societies as well.

6. Differences in how specific stressors are ranked in distinct cultures may be registered in comparable differences in rates and patterns of stress-related disorders.

7. The key distinctions between different cultural patterns of affective experience and affective sickness will be better characterized only by more precise studies of different patterns of cognitive processes and illness behavior. Conversely, studies that attempt to measure affects per se will be less productive.

8. Finally, Kleinman emphasizes that what he has been saying about psychiatric and psychophysiological disorders also holds for physical sickness. Culture affects the way we perceive, label, and cope with somatic symptoms as well as psychological ones. The impact may be (and probably is) greater when the focus is behavior rather than physiology, but there still is an important impact on the latter. There may be a sharper distinction between physical disease and physical illness, since the latter always involves behavior while the former sometimes does not. But the main points are that all illness is normative, i.e., socially learned and guided by cultural norms, and that culture shapes illness behavior principally through its effect on cognitive processes.

The notion that illness is a biased evaluation based on the superego and the cultural forces seems well established. Accordingly, all reports of dis-ease (discomfort) as well as claims of well-being must be regarded with a grain of salt. Thus, in our own culture the claim "I am normal" so frequently made with regard to mental illness is a defensive maneuver of the ego to protect the self-image from (potentially) damaging reproach and punishment.

The Michigan Studies of Mental Health (1981)

Since psychotherapy has, unlike the situation in other cultures, become such a vital part of our own society, the details of what happens in psychotherapy assume the greatest degree of interest. Furthermore, since these details refer to matters which professionals deal with every day, the information is certain to be much more reliable than that for a foreign culture.

Fortunately a careful survey of the American mental health scene and referrals for psychotherapy is available in two books issued by the Survey Research Center of the University of Michigan (Veroff, Douvan and Kulks, 1981a). The studies are particularly helpful because two surveys were done about twenty years apart, one in 1957, the other in 1976, so that a comparison of the changes that came about in a quarter of a century can be documented. (See also ch. 4)

Although the researchers do not specifically approach it in those terms, it is clear that psychotherapy involves a self-evaluation—what is wrong with me?—which leads the individual to seek out some other form of living, or some professional help. Consequently, the two studies can be viewed as reflections of the self-image of certain groups of Americans in 1957 and 1976 and a description of the changes in the self-image that occurred between those two periods.

Before presenting their findings in detail, one comment about change in time must be made. The researchers adopted essentially a psychoanalytic point of view. In 1976 they stated:

> In these characteristics—isolation, detachment, intellectual/verbal analysis—psychoanalysis represents quintessential science. Its popularity marks the movement of the scientific revolution to the last frontier—the sphere of human behavior and the thickets of the human soul—and represents, above all, a remarkable faith in and optimism about the power of science. Its emergence as the model of human counsel marks modern sensibility and displaces a religious/moral model. (Veroff, Douvan and Kulka, 1981a:7)

In other words, the change in the self-image has resulted from the greater acceptance, especially by the more educated section of the nation, of the basic principles and tenets of psychoanalysis. But to follow this through, this acceptance has been only partial, limited in many ways by misunderstanding, professional self-interests (e.g., the psychiatrist's stake in drug therapy and organic explanations in order to bolster his professional self-image and importance; likewise the behavioristic denial of any significance to man's inner life), and accidental factors such as being able to afford professional help. What the authors describe then is only one point in a curve of continuing change, so that one could expect considerable differences if the same surveys were conducted twenty years from now. Elsewhere I have put this in the form that the self-image of the average American is moving in a direction toward the analytic ideal (see chapter 9; also Fine 1981).

In gross numerical terms, there was a substantial increase in readiness-for-referral over the twenty-year period from 1957 to 1976 (p.79). The proportion of the adult population reporting actual use of professional help almost doubled (from 14 to 26 percent), and the proportion who felt that they could always handle problems by themselves declined from 44 percent in 1957 to 35 percent in 1976. As indicated above, those who deny any need for professional help are persons who rely on some informal kind of psychotherapy; in their personality structure they also make extensive use of the defense mechanism of denial, and would thus be classified as severely disturbed by all analytic criteria. They share in the American self-image of independence and Emersonian self-reliance.

Three critical changes were noted in the psychological adjustments of Americans from 1957 to 1976: increased concern about an uncertain future; a movement from social to personal integration of well-being; and an increase in the psychological approach to understanding one's own behavior. All of these changes are related to the greater denial of problems in 1957. The people have not changed; their self-image has been illuminated by the teachings of modern psychology. Overall, there were no significant changes in the way men and women responded to questions about their well-being in 1957 and 1976, but obviously by seeking help more often and by recognizing the role of psychology, they were approaching their well-being in an entirely different way.

The factors that led more people to seek help in 1976 are summed up under these headings: general adjustment; self-perceptions; adjustment in marriage; adjustment in parenthood; job adjustment; the recognition of wide areas in which distressing symptoms occur that cannot be wished away or denied. In psychoanalytic terminology this represents a broad shift from an emphasis on symptoms to an emphasis on character structure. Character structure in turn can be coordinated around the axis of the self-image. In other words, people see themselves in much the same way as before, but have become more dissatisfied with the image of themselves that comes to light.

Indicators of distress assessed in a variety of ways, such as general unhappiness, symptoms of physical and psychological strain, the experience of feelings of inadequacy in family roles, and a number of other measures of subjective mental health, are characteristic of people who accept the idea of dealing with personal problems they have experienced or can imagine experiencing by using professional help. There is also some evidence that readiness for self-referral is associated with being introspective about the self and with the tendency to structure unhappiness and difficulties in family roles in interpersonal terms.

An analysis of the sociodemographic characteristics and a readiness for self-referral offered some firm conclusions. Women, young people, and the better educated are consistently high in readiness for self-referral; of these three, urban or suburban residents, people who grew up or live in the Pacific states, Jews, high church attenders, children of professionals, and adult children of divorce and those divorced themselves are all relatively open to accepting professional help. One of their most important findings was that while being of lower socioeconomic status seemed to be an obstacle to seeking help in 1957, that was no longer the case in 1976. This means that efforts to make professional help more available to the disadvantaged have had some limited success.

Breaking down the data further to find out why people were going for help in 1976 yielded the following:

1. Why people go for help: The particular problems for which help was sought were remarkably similar in 1976 to those reported in 1957. The increase in use of professional mental health counselors is particularly striking, moving from 4 percent in 1957 to 13 percent in 1976.

2. How people choose help resources: Of particular note is the substantial increase in the proportion of people who mentioned an outside referral. The proportion of those mentioning a referral source almost doubled (from 26 to 47

percent), significant increases occurred in referrals from family and friends and from civic agencies, while significant decreases in referrals from clergymen were noted.

3. Do people feel they are helped?: Over two-thirds of the respondents in both survey years who received professional counsel felt that it helped them with their problems, and less than 20 percent reported that it had failed to do so.

4. How people feel they are helped: The most dramatic increase was in the proportion of those indicating having been helped by talking or getting advice, which by 1976 accounted for over four out of ten effective help-seeking encounters. Significant, though less dramatic, increases were also evident in the proportions who said they were comforted by the help they received or who spoke in terms of a palliative change in either themselves or in a relationship.

Some sex differences emerged. Men were significantly less likely than women to have referred problems involving a child (particularly in 1976) or a distressing situational problem (death or illness) and were significantly more likely in both years to have sought help for problems related to a job or their own schooling (particularly in 1976). Young women more often than men tended to seek help for marital problems; however, in 1976 older men were more likely to seek help for marital problems than were older women.

The relationship between psychotherapy and religion or church attendance remained similar in both years. By and large, those who adhere to religious beliefs are much less likely to go to psychotherapists, while conversely those who seek out psychotherapists are much less likely to value religion. This confirms the fact that the American superego is changing from an emphasis on other-directed religious punitive sources to inner-directed humanistic dissatisfaction-producing sources. This may also be rephrased as a gradual shift from a hate culture to a love culture (Fine 1985).

Finally, with regard to the help-seeking process per se, people in 1976 who went for professional help with a personal problem characterized the help they sought differently from their counterparts of 1957 in the following ways:

1. They were more likely to have sought help for a situational problem.

2. They were more likely to have selected a specialized mental health resource (psychiatrist or psychologist, marriage counselor, and other mental health professionals) over a general help source (doctor, clergyman or lawyer) although they turned to all resources much more often.

3. They were more likely to be aware of the referral process, being particularly more alerted to referrals by family or friends.

4. They were more likely to see the counsel of psychologists and psychiatrists

as helpful, but were more qualified in their appraisals of help received from the clergy (seeing it less often as either very helpful or unhelpful).

5. They were more likely to view the supportiveness of the counsel they received as the basis of the help that was offered.

In sum, people in our culture are increasingly becoming aware that every culture, as Roheim put it, has its own distinctive neurosis, and that the distinctive neurosis of our culture is making them unhappy. This unhappiness relates to outmoded versions of the self-image (e.g., that men are all powerful, self-reliant, and intolerant of any feelings of any warmth and intimacy), which they then make a determined effort to change with the help of some professional. On the other hand, the older religious orientation, which tied personal problems with guilt, sin, and religious salvation is increasingly fading out of the picture. Most people see psychotherapy as helpful, while a small minority deny any benefit of such help altogether.

Psychotherapy in Other Cultures

Studies of other cultures have generally borne out the thesis that the self-image is intricately interrelated to the social order, so that psychotherapy, which seeks to change this self-image, runs up against all the blocks that the culture can muster to defend itself against change. Some examples will make this clearer.

The Shona (Gelfand 1964) comprise a large group of more than 2.5 million Africans in southern Rhodesia (Zimbabwe). Their conception of disease is not very different from that of most tribes of southern Africa. Every major clan is supposed to have been founded many hundreds of years ago in the region it now occupies, and the successive ruling chiefs are all believed to have been descended from the original founder. In addition, the spirit of the founder still lives as the clan or tribal spirit, to which the clan turns for advice on all matters of communal welfare. The Shona village is essentially a family affair. The grandfather and father are held in the greatest respect.

Among the Shona the belief is that any spirit can bring about any disease. Four important groups of spirits are believed to cause sickness, the two most frequent being the spirits of the parents or grandparents and the witches. Particularly dangerous is the spirit of one who died an unnatural death through murder, e.g. (and of these there are examples, thus filling the people with anxieties).

An African who is depressed will confess to being a thoroughly wicked person and a witch. He has therefore angered the ancestral spirits, and must be punished accordingly. There are special men endowed with the ability to punish them when they have harmed innocent people. Though much is unknown, there is evidence that when a patient becomes difficult to manage or a danger to others, he is tied up in the village precincts against a heavy object like a log so that he is unable to run about and harm others. When he remains difficult to control and is not likely to become more manageable, he is confined to a cave, where he probably perishes from lack of food or water. The well-behaved or manageable patients are tended by their own families until they recover, as many do, aided by the suggestive therapy of the witch doctor. But many do not recover, and there are a large number of mentally disturbed people living alone in the woods or wilds. Thus, the treatment parallels the authoritarian punitive character of the culture—either obey or get out. The analogy with our own system of shock therapy is striking.

The nature and treatment of madness in Bali are described in a paper by Connor (1982), who ties the whole process up with the notion of the self. For the Balinese, madness is potentially at least an inspired and not a degraded state. Lay persons generally name madness in terms of the dominant behavioral manifestations, while specialists are consulted to pinpoint the cause. Some of the terms used to describe disturbance are dizzy, confused, disoriented, running amok, apathetic, dazed, raving, incoherent speech, talking to oneself, frightened, excessively timid, running away, resisting restraint, and wandering. The Balinese specialist (balian) closely integrates physical and mental dimensions of illness by relating both to concepts of spiritual well-being and by attributing the behavior of the individual to supernatural and other forces beyond the immediate control of clients. In all the cases, patients and families understand the fundamentals of traditional therapies, and comprehend the significance of the major symbols in healing ritual.

For the Balinese the "person" is a nexus of interacting forces, macrocosmic and microcosmic, natural and supernatural, always in a delicate balance. Among the notions that make the self "infinitely extensible" (as Connor puts it) are the Sanskrit difference between the "small world" and the "great world" sibling spirits; spirit reincarnation (of a deceased relative); the soul, which is the focus of elaborate mortuary rites rather than meticulous attention to everyday ritual contexts; thus cremation ceremonies release and purify the soul (*atma*) to the point where it may fuse again with the godhead; the *taksu*, or spirit intermediaries.

With these notions the Balinese place great emphasis on the idea of possession, which is invoked in the explanation of a large range of human behavior. These possessions may be negative or positive; many are institutionalized as ritual possession trance. Deities and ancestors possess human vehicles and make their will known to their devotees, usually a congregation or a corporate group having a ritualized identity. During possession the vehicle of everyday personality becomes latent and many change radically. Afterward he or she usually denies any subsequent recollection of the event. Even when the ritual mediation of possession is minimal, the subject of divine edicts or benevolence renounces all responsibility and motivation is projected to the external agent. It is obvious that in such a society where mythical or semimythical external agents are held responsible for the individual's behavior, the self-image must be radically different from what it is in our culture.

Summary

Evidence from a variety of sources has been presented to show that the self-image is intimately related to the total world view of any social order. In totalitarian regimes, the self has no real existence at all, leading to such extraordinary events as the Japanese suicide pilots in World War II and the rapid transformation of the individual as seen, e.g., in Chinese "thought reform."

The self can maintain its cohesiveness only in cultures where the autonomous individual is valued. Unlike the authoritarian regimes, where violence and rage are the essence of society, when the self is autonomous, affection and love will play a more prominent role.

Anthropological data are cited to show that the image of the self is not uniform but varies with the total cultural milieu. In some cases, as in Bali, the individual may seem to be completely dissociated because of the beliefs that he is controlled by external agents of a mythical variety, thereby depriving him of any responsibility for his actions. This close tie between the self-image and the social order has not been adequately valued in psychoanalytic theory.

Psychotherapy always has to stay within the framework of the culture; hence it cannot be expected to produce any dramatic sudden changes. However, studies in our own culture show that over the past twenty-five years the basic conceptualizations of psychoanalysis have been replacing the more traditional religious views and values in such a way that the self-image has undergone considerable reorientation, with a consequent reorganization of the value system of the entire society. This entire process is still going on, and may be expected to produce more significant changes in the next quarter of a century.

CHAPTER 7

LOVE, IDENTITY, AND ALIENATION

Before going on to a more detailed consideration of the role of love (and hatred) in the topics under investigation, it will be well to recapitulate the argument of the book up to this point.

In the first chapter, a historical introduction, it was shown that the idea of a conflict between the individual and society goes back as far as Plato and Aristotle; it is also present in one form or another in all cultures.

Traditionally, in western culture, narcissism has been viewed as "bad"; it was often called the "heresy of self-love." What that meant in reality was that narcissism was reserved for the ruling classes, while the common man (which included the numerous slaves, often an overlooked aspect of history) had to practice submission and obedience. When the Roman dictatorship was replaced by the Christian one, the narcissism of the believer was maintained by the belief in an immortal soul. In all philosophy and psychology before the twentieth century the soul played a prominent role.

In the Italian Renaissance, as Burckhardt showed, rampant individualism (narcissism) occurred, but it was also generally accompanied by great violence. The rulers everywhere remained narcissistic, generally arrogant, sadistic, and reactionary. Louis XIV, with his famous remark: "I am the state," represents another apotheosis of narcissism.

In this sense the American and French revolutions could be looked upon as anti-narcissistic revolutions, which were followed by attempts to liberate everyone that was oppressed. Liberte, égalité, fraternité were to be applied to all. While dictators often trampled down the masses, the ideals remained for all to see.

Many consequences followed these political developments. The women's liberation movement began. Slavery was abolished. The narcissism of the common man was given a fresh outlet in the new autobiographies, which anybody could write. The soul eventually came to be replaced by the notion of the self.

At this point (the nineteenth century) the old question of the tension between the individual and his society reappeared in a new form. Nationalism gained extraordinary new ground, allowing the average man to identify himself with a larger group. In theory, the narcissist was now ruled out of society, and the label was applied to the psychotic in a manner that had never been done before. This represented a strong tendency to favor the group at the expense of the individual, in contrast to the frequent idealization of the psychotic as one with extraordinary powers, which had previously been quite common.

The psychological theory to deal with these new developments now came to the fore (nineteenth century). German and American theories began to diverge. In German thinking the emphasis, going back to Leibniz' monads, had always been on the self-generating forces of the individual; in America the emphasis from earliest days was on the social self.

It is against this historical background that the development of the psychoanalytic theories of narcissism and the self were considered. Prior to Freud's 1914 paper narcissism was discussed in only two areas; the narcissism of the psychotic and the narcissism of the artist. It was an aspect of psychoanalytic theory that received little emphasis in the whole structure.

Freud's paper on narcissism in 1914 changed that entirely and is for that reason rightly considered a watershed in the history of psychoanalysis. There is, however, no easy way to summarize the paper, except to say that Freud is both stimulating and confusing.

In light of what has happened since, emphasis must be placed on the fact that Freud has extensive discussions of the self throughout his writings. Only his references are to the usual hyphenated self—self-esteem, self-hatred, self-reproach, and the like, which is one common meaning. By contrast, Kohut later came to speak of the self as a kind of separate entity, a superordinate notion that unites the entire personality. We can thus speak of the Freudian and the Kohutian views of the self.

Following Freud and until the 1960s, the topic of narcissism, though discussed, was still not in the center of psychoanalytic thought. It was discovered that psychotics were not as narcissistic as had been supposed. Likewise, papers continued to be written about the narcissism of the artist (and scientist). In the meantime the topic of the self was frequently and freely discussed in American psychology, in all its ramifications. Sullivan, whose work on the self was best known to American psychiatrists and psychologists, followed in the footsteps of

Royce, James, Mead, and Cooley. More orthodox Freudians ignored the question.

A new impetus was given to the topic of narcissism and the self by Kohut with *The Analysis of the Self* (1971) and *The Restoration of the Self* (1977). Kohut introduced a number of novel concepts, particularly the "self-object," a new definition of narcissism, the types of transference in the narcissistic patient, the assumption that narcissism and object love develop along different lines, the diagnostic category of narcissistic personality disorder, and many others, which he eventually hoped would create a new kind of psychology, a "self psychology." His views aroused an enormous amount of discussion and controversy.

With the shift to the discussion of the self in the 1970s, the psychoanalytic community again bifurcated. Since the concept had always been an everyday word in the culturalist school, for them little was added except detail. But the more orthodox Freudians, recognizing the significance of the idea, tried to fit it into the tripartite structure of id, ego, and superego. In this they were notably unsuccessful. Schafer quite rightly commented that "self and identity express basic problems in Freudian theory."

The next chapter turns to a consideration of the nature of neurosis. While following Freud (and the Germanic tradition) neurosis (and psychosis) had at first been viewed as intrapsychic disturbances, perhaps organic in nature (Freud held on to this idea for quite a while), in the American tradition, even going back to preanalytic thinkers such as Adolf Meyer and William Alanson White, considerable stress was placed on the social order. One of the reasons for Sullivan's extraordinary success with schizophrenics in the 1920s was that he had the ingenuity to provide a new kind of social environment for them as well as to apply the principles of psychoanalysis to patients who has previously been considered hopeless.

Since psychoanalysis had shown in many ways that all cultures are neurotic, or in Roheim's phrase, that each culture has a distinctive neurosis of its own, the conventional notion of normality came to be questioned. I have suggested that we should accordingly speak of the adjustment neurosis (the average individual in any society) and the maladjustment neurosis (the deviant). Considerable evidence to bolster this proposal is presented.

The next chapter returns to the question of the tension between the individual and society. Current thinking places the greatest weight on the analysis of the mother-child situation, on interaction and the quality of life as the factors that are most predictive of the future. This can be generalized to the various stages of the life cycle. As a result, we can speak of three stages of the self: in infancy, when it can neither be verbalized nor clearly conceptualized; in childhood, when it revolves predominantly around the family; and in adulthood, when the interaction and the quality of life depend most strongly on the surrounding culture. In general, the group tends to, or tries to, suppress narcissism, creating new identities and identifications throughout the life cycle by the different kinds of group membership in which the individual participates.

Chapter 6 continues the discussion of the tension between the individual and the society, this time in terms of the self-image and its relationship to the social order. The individual either loses himself to the group or rebels against the group. When the conflict is sharp, enormous rage results, which is difficult to resolve; in fact, it may then dominate the course of events.

Studies of other cultures show that the concept of the self varies cross-culturally. The Western image of a clearly bounded self, autonomous in nature, striving to "actualize" itself, is rarely found. Psychotherapy is viewed as a conscious effort to change a self-image increasingly found to be ungratifying by modern man, largely because of the reconceptualization forced on him by psychoanalysis.

The problems now remaining are:

1. How do love and hate fit into the tension between the self and the group? (chapter 7)
2. How can we understand culture in light of these considerations? (chapter 8)
3. How should psychoanalytic theory be broadened and deepened to take these various facts into consideration? (chapter 9)

The Nature of Love

Since I have recently completed a full-length discussion of love (Fine 1985), I shall take the liberty of summarizing here the main points from that book.

In general, the modern understanding of love stems from Freud. His entire work prior to 1914 (with a few papers after that) could be considered a treatise on love. But he did not do it systematically. Sometimes he mixed up normal with neurotic love, he left many points untouched, and he gave scant consideration to the relationship of love to the surrounding culture. Our task today is to build on his insights, not to replace them with dubious novelties. The main relevant points are the following.

The Patient

From the very beginning, as early as the Anna O. case (1880), Freud focused on the love life of the patient, in sharp contrast to his colleagues, who were excessively preoccupied with physiology and biochemistry. Anna O. exhibited the classical features of hysteria, but underneath it could be seen that she had never been able to love anyone. This inability to love was combined with nursing the sick, in her case taking care of her dying father.

Freud contributed the current definitions of neurosis to the psychiatric literature (before him the whole question was very obscure). Yet throughout all the diagnoses that have been offered there runs a consistent thread: mental health consists of the ability to love, mental illness involves an excess of hatred. Thus in 1915 he wrote: "Sexual love is undoubtedly one of the chief things in life, and the union of mental and bodily satisfaction in the enjoyment of love is one of its culminating peaks. Apart from a few queer fanatics, all the world knows this and conducts its life accordingly; science alone is too delicate to admit it" (12:169–170).

If the details of the various diagnoses offered throughout the years are examined, it would appear that there is little difference. In his first independent foray, the paper on anxiety neurosis, Freud listed the following as the clinical symptoms (3:87–137): general irritability; anxious expectation; sudden outbreaks of anxiety; almost every accompanying symptom alone can constitute the attack just as well as can the anxiety itself; waking up at night in a fright; vertigo; typical phobias with regard to general physiological dangers and with regard to locomotion; characteristic digestive disturbances; and paresthesias. Several of the symptoms can appear in a chronic form. But, and here is the nub of the matter, the sexual etiology is the most basic factor of all. "This sexual aetiology of anxiety neurosis can be demonstrated with such overwhelming frequency that I venture . . . to disregard those cases where the aetiology is doubtful or different" (1953–1970, 3:99).

Once he went into his self-analysis (Anzieu 1975), the list of symptoms was broadened and deepened, and sexuality eventually was transformed into love and sexuality, but the heart of the diagnostic system was already there. Through the years there have been many variations—obsessional neurosis, psychosis, borderline cases, character disorders, castration anxiety, masochism, narcissistic personality disorders, and many others—yet the disturbance in the love life has always remained fundamental, thereby depriving the numerous diagnostic systems of any real value. Today the ego functions profile of Bellak and his collaborators (1973, 1984), which quantifies the various aspects of the psychoanalytic approach, is probably a better tool than anything else available for classifying human beings, and this too rests on the basic assumption that mental illness involves hatred and regression, while mental health involves love and growth. Much of the analytic literature devotes itself obsessionally to largely irrelevant details of Freud's thought, ignoring the larger goals and the larger implications.

Childhood

As his thought developed, Freud soon drew a close connection between love, sexuality, and childhood. In 1905 he wrote: "The innumerable peculiarities of the neurotic life of human beings as well as the compulsive character of the process of falling in love itself are quite unintelligible except by reference back to childhood and as being residual effects of childhood" (7:222).

This close connection, which was pursued further in the decade from 1900 to 1910, while strongly attacked, has proven to be one of the most profound insights about love ever made. Christianity had indeed attempted to instill a love without sexuality and had given rise to outbreaks of hatred on a mass scale that were quite unintelligible without reference to psychology; Heer (1962), a historian of medieval life, speaks of mass psychoses in this period. Yet there is no other way to explain such phenomena as the Crusades, the Inquisition, the witch hunts of the fifteenth and sixteenth centuries, the sanguinary wars of religion of the sixteenth and seventeenth centuries, and many other phenomena than in terms of the irrepressible rage of the clergy and their supporters. The history of Christianity is a strong indication that the total repression of sexuality it demands is humanly impossible, inevitably leading to outbreaks of rage and numerous forms of mental disorder.

At the same time, as Freud showed, in any love relationship, especially within the family, limits are set by coercive custom to the gratification of sexuality. Incest, a universal taboo in human cultures, requires some explanation. The ultimate explanation has not yet been offered. What is more significant is that incest is the first impulse that cannot be gratified and that cannot be totally repressed. It is this situation of a psychological drive that can never be satisfied that gives rise to the many peculiarities of human existence and its institutions.

Sexuality

Sexuality, like love, does not spring full-blown into existence at puberty, as had generally been thought before Freud. It has a long history, going back all the way to birth; today researchers are even beginning to study its prenatal manifestations. Without reference to this long history human existence again cannot be understood. By now the details of development have, within broad limits, essentially been worked out, following the general scheme laid down by Freud. The normal person is the one who is fully grown, mature, has reached the genital stage in the traditional terminology. Neurosis (and psychosis, as well) is a fixation, a lack of development. The difference between neurosis and psychosis is only one of degree; throughout his life Freud adhered to the continuum theory of mental disturbance. The differences among the various types of neuroses and psychosis are quantitative, not qualitative.

Culture

For love to flourish, the surrounding culture must be favorably inclined. Yet all cultures have found the need to establish some regulations for the management of sex and love. Some are harsh, some permissive; some allow early experience, some force postponement. Many cultures adopt the most extraordinary measures to prevent the full gratification of sexuality, e.g., the numerous pubertal taboos practiced on boys and girls when they reach maturity, which serve no other purpose than to remind the younger generation that it cannot indulge its impulses freely.

Although Freud never formulated it in that way, this is consistent with the division into love and hate cultures. A love culture is one in which the predominant feelings of one person toward another are affection, friendliness, and love; a hate culture is one in which the predominant feelings are hatred. While no pure love or hate culture exists, the ideal types represent a polarity toward which cultures are inclined.

There can be little doubt that we are living in a hate culture and have been living in one for several thousand years. While many aspects of the hate culture have been softened (e.g., slavery, oppression of women and children, terrorization by an autocratic ruling minority, and the like), so much remains to be done that the world faces for the first time in history a nuclear holocaust that may destroy it entirely.

Mutuality

The most characteristic feature of love is mutuality, in which both partners are able to derive gratification from the interaction. Desire leads to infatuation, which may or may not be mutual. The best definition of love is that it has the following characteristics: a friendly feeling; mutual reciprocity; adequate physical contact; the ability to accommodate to the other person's needs; mutual enjoyment; and a loving family in a loving culture. It is impossible to focus the *love feeling* exclusively on one person, even in the mother-child situation. It is, however, possible to regulate life in such a way that the love feeling is concentrated most exclusively on another person. However, such exclusivity creates so many problems that love cultures have been permissive about allowing more than one love relationship. This multiplicity of relationships, while desirable in some ways, creates problems in others. There is no ideal solution other than to pursue the love feelings; if that is done, the specific arrangements can be adequately regulated. Hatred is the great danger in human existence, not love.

It will be argued that this framework is highly idealized. Yet without ideals man cannot live, even if they are only goals toward which he strives without reaching them. Freud wrote in 1932:

> The program of becoming happy, which the pleasure principle imposes on us, cannot be fulfilled; yet we must not—indeed, we cannot—give up our efforts to bring it nearer to fulfillment by some means or other. Very different paths may be taken in that direction . . . . By none of these paths can we attain all that we desire . . . . There is no golden rule that applies to everyone: every man must find out for himself in what particular fashion he can be saved. (21:108–109)

Once the concept of the love culture (as contrasted with the hate culture) has been assimilated, it becomes indispensible to any discussion of what love really is. For in the hate culture the whole love experience takes on an entirely different cast from what it is in the love culture. Since our own society is still predominantly a hate culture, the love experiences that people have (which Freud and other psychoanalysts have analyzed in such depth) can only be understood in light of the surround.

Refuge Love: The Dominant Form in Our Culture

Since the days of Freud every psychoanalyst has devoted a major portion of his time to the analysis of love. The notion that the analytic population is markedly deviant has long since been dispelled; people who come to therapy represent a cross section of the population, in some ways healthier, in some ways sicker, than the average. Clinical experience is therefore of considerable weight in the evaluation of what love in our culture is really like. One must avoid excessive cynicism, which denies that any happy relationship exists. One must also avoid a Pollyannish attitude, which shifts problems to a small deviant minority. By and large, while there are many happy marriages and other love relationships, the dominant form is that of a *refuge love*, in which two people, fearful or disappointed in the outside world, find a refuge in one another for the hurts that they have to endure at the hands of others. Many times this works out well, at least on the surface; in many other cases it engenders after a while so much hatred and bitterness that the couple breaks up. Generalizations are difficult; it is best to turn to historical and clinical instances.

The image of love bequeathed to us by the early Christians has been the dominant one in Western thought ever since. Yet this image is full of conflicts. Jesus' admonition to give unto Caesar that which is Caesar's and to give unto God that which is God's immediately suggests a refuge type of love. And indeed, in the early centuries the Christians quite literally had to take refuge from the harshness of their Roman rulers. Once the Christians assumed the leadership role, the conflicts surrounding love took a different turn, particularly concerning the relationship of love to sexuality and violence. These dissensions, which have never been satisfactorily resolved, still pose severe problems for all religious denominations.

In the theater, Eugene O'Neill's *Long Day's Journey Into Night* presents a graphic portrayal of the misery that a family can live through. Presumably it is an autobiographical record of what happened to his own family. Hardly any love seems to be present. In spite of his greatness as an artist, O'Neill went through tremendous suffering in his personal life. At an early age he attempted suicide. Later he made several unhappy marriages. Two of his sons turned out badly; one actually did commit suicide. The marriage of his daughter Oona to Charlie Chaplin aroused astonishment because she was eighteen to Chaplin's fifty. Yet the marriage seemed to be a happy one. Analytically we would see it as a daughter-father gratification. Oona's life with O'Neill was apparently quite miserable, and she found in Chaplin the supportive, entertaining, caring father whom she had never had.

Love as an antidote to depression is beautifully depicted in one of Shakespeare's sonnets; this may very well have been his own experience, although really little is known about his personal life. Sonnet 29 reads:

> When, in disgrace with Fortune and men's eyes,
> I all alone beweep my outcast state,
> And trouble deaf heaven with my bootless cries,
> And look upon myself and curse my fate,
> Wishing me like to one more rich in hope,
> Featured like him, like him with friends possessed,
> Desiring this man's art and that man's scope,
> With what I most enjoy contented least;
> Yet in these thoughts myself almost despising,
> Haply I think on thee, and then my state,
> (Like to the Lark at break of day arising)
> From sullen earth, sings hymns at heaven's gate;
> For thy sweet love remembered such wealth brings
> That then I scorn to change my state with Kings.

The alternation of love with depression that Shakespeare describes is a frequent clinical phenomenon. Many depressives are also love addicts. When they are in love, the depression lifts; but the relief is only temporary. When the love turns sour or when difficulties arise, the depression returns. In other words, the refuge no longer protects the person.

Ideally, love and marriage are supposed to go together. This too was more of a fantasy than a reality in the past (Shorter 1975; Stone 1969; Gordon 1978). In 1748 the weekly paper of the small Prussian town of Halle attempted a statistical estimate of how many marriages could be considered happy: scarcely ten in a thousand, while in all the others "the spouses cursed and bemoaned their choices" (Shorter 1975:61).

In another study of the German petty bourgeosie, Helmut Möller did an exhaustive survey of the literary and ethnographic sources of the eighteenth and early nineteenth centuries. He was able to discover scarcely a reference to romance within marriage for this class before 1820. In the preceding period he encountered only fathers emotionally isolated from their wives and the rest of their families—men who were brutal, domineering, obsessed with external forms, prudish, and fanatically authoritarian.

Reporting on eighteenth-century Languedoc in France, Shorter (1975:235) states that there were fathers who conspired with the eldest son to deny the younger their inheritance. The younger siblings then banded together against the eldest, and violent quarrels and murders resulted. Or the father, "seized by the devil," murdered his son. In households where the inheriting son would bring his bride in to dwell with the parents, terrible tensions eventuated between mother and daughter-in-law. For seven long years the widow of a laborer in Escazaux lived with her married son "hating her daughter-in-law and driving the son to mistreat her"; one day the neighbors discovered both of them whipping the daughter-in-law with a bunch of willow rods.

Blumstein and Schwartz (1983) have provided considerable survey material on contemporary marriage in America. Many women, resentful of the traditional role of the housewife and homemaker, try to combine work and marriage. How successful is this and how successful has it been? The authors state:

> Most people like to think that their partners will love them no matter what kind of work they do or how successful they become. Ideally, marriage or an intimate relationship functions as a refuge from the world of work—a place where each person is loved and admired for who he or she is, rather than for what he or she achieves. But some social thinkers hold to the view that modern society has become so judgmental that spouses and lovers now evaluate one another according to how well they do at their jobs. In his book *Haven in a Heartless World* Christopher Lasch writes with bitterness that the working world has invaded family life and that personal relationships are no longer immune from being judged by its standards. He goes on to say that unconditional love is no longer possible because partners and relationships are graded in the same way job performance is. (1983:154)

Sexual satisfaction in marriage, while perhaps better than it was several generations ago, is still threatened by the "double standard" and the frequency of what they call "nonmonogamy," i.e., extramarital sex. They found that a substantial minority of the heterosexual couples have had extramarital sex. Yet even when monogamy is not adhered to, it is a strongly held moral ideal, the conflict of this ideal with the reality of how frequent extramarital sex is naturally creates emotional problems for all sides.

There is always the uncertainty about whether the partner will "cheat": "Ten years of monogamy does not mean that the eleventh is safe" (Blumstein and Schwartz 1983:272). Men are less monogamous than women and have more partners. What they do not have are as many emotional attachments. One of their surprising findings was that religious people do express more conservative values, yet in their daily lives they are no more nonmonogamous than the rest. This split between the ideal and the real will again prove to be difficult at some point. Thus, in spite of all the talk about the sexual revolution, there is a continuity of male behavior and a continuity of female behavior. The superego dies hard.

In the third area investigated, that of money, the issues raised by the partners again sound very difficult. All couples face financial choices that usually revolve around demands for equality and autonomy or the sacrifice of one or both to achieve intimacy, trust, interdependence. These are critical for creating commitment but may interfere with the individual rights of the partners. In traditional marriages interdependence is usually achieved at the cost of the wife's autonomy and her participation on an equal basis in decision making.

We are living in a period of rapidly changing values. The confusion displayed by the courts in decisions about marriage, divorce custody, financial arrangements, and the like bear eloquent testimony to the confusion that exists in the society. The notion of being married and living happily ever after seems to apply to only a few marriages.

While these authors do not attempt to probe with any depth into the emotional currents of marriage, what they find is consistent with the idea that refuge love is more the rule than the exception. In a study of upper-class marriages in Ohio a number of years ago, Cuber (1965) found that the most common type of marriage was the utilitarian, i.e., both men and women married for convenience. Love played a minor role. There too he did not consider that since love is supposed to be the basis of marriage, while in actuality it rarely is, the split between the real and the ideal makes for a bitter pill to swallow.

More data could be presented. But enough has been adduced to document the inescapable conclusion that love is a rare commodity, and that when it does occure, it is more a refuge from the dangers of the outside world than a true mutuality.

Identity and Alienation

Identity and identification are justifiably recognized as two of the most important concepts in this area. In particular, it is usually argued that the lack of a sense of identity leads to that alienation which is such a characteristic element in the life of modern man. These concepts require more careful investigation and elucidation.

The glossary of the American Psychoanalytical Association virtually equates identity with self. Their definition of identity reads as follows:

> The experience of the *self* as a unique coherent entity which is continuous and remains the same despite inner psychic and outside environmental changes. The *sense of identity* begins with the child's awareness that he exists as an individual in a world without outer objects, and that he has his own wishes, thoughts and memories, and his own distinctive appearance. *Identification* with both parents gives a bisexual quality to *self-representations* in children of both sexes. Eventually, however, an integrated self-representation (*self-image*) is created out of the multiple former identifications contributing to character traits. In respect to sexual identity, that self-image usually represents a predominant identification with the parent of the same sex. Relative stability of the sense of identity is achieved with the resolution of bi-sexual identification and the completion of adolescence. The sense of identity is the self-image perceived by one's self and entails awareness of some, though not all, physical sensations, emotional feelings, and character traits. (Moore and Fine 1968:50)

These definitions are in accordance with Erikson's classical development of the topic in his numerous works, which indeed directed attention to phenomena never before considered seriously. However, the definitions omit one essential element, the relationship of the individual to his group. They thus represent the most serious weakness in classical Freudian theory, the overemphasis on the individual and the lack of theoretical concern with the groups to which he comes to belong in the course of life.

A moment's reflection will show how important the group is for identity. I say: I am a male American psychoanalyst, seventy years old, living in New York, a member of the American Psychological Association and other professional groups. In all of these the emphasis is on the group: the group of men (gender identity), Americans (nationality), psychoanalysts (occupation), people living in New York (location in the country), and members of the American Psychological Association (identification with professional colleagues). The sentence describing myself is actually a shorthand for participation in a number of different groups. This gives us an entirely different definition of identity: identity is the location of an individual within a group. It is the conceptual tie that unites the individual world with the social world.

Some of the other factors mentioned in the definition of Moore and Fine represent aspects of personality that are rather variable and require some explanation. The "experience of the self as a unique coherent entity" is simply self-awareness, the degree of which depends on many elements, such as age, pathology, and cultural determinants; for as was previously seen, the definition of the self varies with the culture. Further, the individual does not necessarily see himself as a unique concrete entity; he has many memories that lead him to what went on in his past or feelings about himself with regard to distinct others. The sense of identity begins, as can be demonstrated easily enough, with the child's recognition that he is part of a family group, later peers, and other groups; his individuality can only be appreciated in relation to others, otherwise he would be a complete narcissist, lost in the river into which he is about to fall. This image of narcissistic alienation depicts the absense of any groups with which Narcissus could identify.

The groups through which an individual passes in the course of life can be described in various ways. The most common characteristics we look for are gender; age; occupation; nationality, race; native place; and special gifts. All of these require more extensive scrutiny to clarify how the tension between the group and the individual works out in actuality.

For many theoreticians (Erikson would be included here) identity is a good in itself. But common observation indicates that the child is forced into a variety of groups that provide him with his various identities as he grows up. Some of these are loving; some hateful. Initially the child is unable to use any judgment: he must join the groups offered to him; they are as necessary to him as air and water. Later he comes to reflect on them, and at that point he may react either positively or negatively. In our culture this reevaluation usually occurs in adolescence, which accounts for much of the turmoil in that period. For the adolescent must on the one hand rid himself of the parental objects (the second individuation process) and on the other move into new groups (which are full of uncertainties)

Gender Identity

The first stage in which the child learns to verbalize his own gender identity is roughly about one and a half years of age. Numerous studies have shown that this identity is impressed on the child by the parents and is only partly physiological or departs entirely from physiology (Money and Ehrhardt 1972; Stoller 1968).

It is important to note here that orthodox analysts have struggled with the concepts of identity and self since they were first introduced, the struggle, as noted before, centering almost entirely on the difficulty involved in fitting these concepts onto the tripartite structure. In 1966 Glover, always a caustic though well-informed critic, tried to see whether these concepts could be reduced to simpler terms. Disagreeing with Jacobson's definitions in *The Self* (1964), he accused her of compromising the issues by presenting her own idiosyncratic definitions rather than trying to fit them into standard theory (1966:185). Of identity he was even more critical, writing:

> As for the terms "identity diffusion" and "identity disorder," the least said the soonest mended in my opinion. Either they mean little or nothing, or they comprise the whole of psychoanalytic psychology . . . .Here one must call a metaphysical halt. No term that involves such a complicated interaction of factors and phases of development can lay claim to the status of a basic mental concept.
>
> So we may well return the term "identity" to the care of our lexicographers. (1966:188)

Erikson, in his writings on identity, had originally seen the reciprocal relationship between the individual and his society. He wrote: "Identity formation . . . is dependent on the process by which a society . . . identifies the young individual, recognizing him as somebody who had to become the way he is, is taken for granted . . . the community, in turn feels 'recognized' by the individual who cares to ask for recognition" (1959:113).

A panel discussion was held at the American Psychoanalytic Association in 1957 on the problems of identity. Among the discussants were some of the foremost theoreticians of that day, Eissler, Greenacre, Mahler, and Jacobson. Yet nothing was seen except sharp disagreement.

Greenacre made the important point that the sense of identity involves some relation to others—a degree of observation both by the person himself and through another person by comparison and contrast. Instead of pursuing the connection between interpersonal relationships and the sense of identity, however, Greenacre fell back on discussions of which body parts led to a sense of identity and which did not (Rubinfine 1958:134).

In another paper Eissler proposed the following formula: the ego is formed by age five to six, the superego during latency, and the self during puberty in conjunction with genital maturation (Rubinfine 1958:133). No one was willing to agree with him. In the various other points of view presented, no consensus could be reached either.

In another paper some ten years later Eissler wrote that "psychoanalysis as a therapy . . . does not have a bright future" (1969:462). Likewise, Lichtenstein ended his extensive discussion of the dilemmas involved in the concept of identity with a chapter on "psychoanalysis challenged" (1977, chapter 15).

Thus, it is quite clear that these theoreticians have given up trying to reconcile identity (and later self) with the tripartite structure. An approach has to be sought in some other way. My proposal is that this approach must come via the connection between the individual and the social, a connection that again does not come out of mechanical application of the libido theory. But if the libido theory and the tripartite structure do not clarify identity, interpersonal relationships, or group formation, then it is high time to move beyond them, not to give up these invaluable concepts.

The first identity, in the sense of self-image, no doubt occurs in earliest infancy, in the period that is unrememberable and unforgettable. However, it would be a mistake to believe that this identity has a kind of unity that somehow persists throughout life, as is so often the assumption. All identity can be broken down into its component parts, which is the task we have set ourselves here.

The first instance in which an identity asserts itself in the sense of a link between the individual and the social is that of *gender assertion*, a term that has in the past twenty years virtually replaced sexual, from which it is radically different. As Stoller (1968) comments, sexual can be translated into male and female, gender into masculine and feminine. Nevertheless, gender, especially at such as early age, is primarily the reaction to the body image and its social meaning.

Central, of course, to the boy's body image is the penis, which has been the source of innumerable customs throughout human history. In general, these customs have involved some mutilation of the penis, such as circumcision, subincision (cutting the penis underneath from the glans to the scrotum), and superincision (cutting the penis dorsally, again from the glans to the scrotum). These surgical procedures can be carried out at any age; the older the boy, naturally, the more painful and frightening it is. The usual opinion is that the operations represent symbolically the wish of the older generation to assert its power over the younger males and to remind them that they cannot use their penises indiscriminately without fear of the consequences.

In civilized countries the practice of circumcising the boy shortly after birth, which was adopted early in the century as a sanitary measure, has been questioned. It has been viewed, with some justification, as an early attack on the aggression and masculinity of the growing boy.

Concern with the body and with the genitals in particular remains a central preoccupation with the growing child. Three research projects in the recent past have confirmed that the establishment of gender identity (whether the child is definitely a boy or a girl) is the achievement of the first few years of life. Galenson and Roiphe (1981) studied more than seventy infants intensively in the last part of the first year of life and the second year. They found that some incipient sense of sexual identity arises even when the infant is virtually limited to the mother in the first year of life. But genital awareness emerges somewhere between sixteen and nineteen months, and it is only then that differences between the boys and girls can be discerned. The differences in the awareness of the genital difference seemed, above all, to mark the divergent paths each sex would take. This strongly suggests, as do other studies, that the second half of the second year is a critical period for the development of the sense of sexual identity. The difference between boys and girls at this stage was quite striking. In the girls there was a remarkable increase in semisymbolic capacity and functioning in response to an almost universal castration reaction and the reappearance of fears of object loss and self-disintegration. A further distinction was the erotic turn to the father and a definite change in masturbatory patterns. Although the girls appeared to be far more vulnerable than the boys in their development of intense penis envy and castration reactions, they also showed advances in ego functioning.

The boys, in contrast, showed far less overt disturbance as they defended against castration anxiety by a more profound denial and displacement. It was in connection with the development of exhibitionistic pride as well as the urinary technique or posture used by the boy that the degree of the father's availability and his emotional involvement with his son appeared to play an important role. The importance of the father's availability and support for the boy's growing sense of his male sexual identity during the second part of the second year of life is highly stressed by the authors. They believe that it provides the boy with confirmation of his own phallic body image and allows him eventually to acknowledge the absence of a penis in mother.

The intensity of the boy's attachment to his mother diminished gradually during the early genital phase. But this may be overshadowed by the turmoil of the oedipal phase, which in turn depends on the various interactions among mother, father, child, and siblings or even peers. They agree with Mahler that the period of the rapprochement crisis is more troubled for the girl than for the boy.

Money and Ehrhardt (1972) were concerned with genetically and hormonally deviant individuals. Their findings, like those of Stoller, who studied deviant sex at the Institute for Sex Research at UCLA in Los Angeles (1968), showed that the sex of the parent who rears the infant for the first two years of life plays the major role in the establishment of gender identity. Money and Ehrhardt see the eighteenth month as the critical age beyond which successful sex reassignment is impossible. Stoller, in his work with transsexuals, found that the mothers were bisexual, were excessively permissive in that they maintained close bodily contact with the child for a long time, and felt empty inside (which is why they held their son so close). This emptiness results from a bleak relationship with her own distant, angry, empty mother, plus the disappointment that resulted when the father, who was to be both mother and father, abandoned her (without being close and loving) by death or with the birth of a second sibling. In each case there was also evidence that the boys were severely deprived of their fathers' presence. While the fathers remained in the family, they were remote and unapproachable. Sometimes these transsexual boys were able to show considerable ability in creative outlets. Sexual inadequacy was quite compatible with adequacy in other areas.

In short, the biological givens plus the attitudes of the parents play the decisive role in the establishment of the child's gender identity, which is established before two years of age. This represents an important correction to Erikson's epigenetic cycle, in which the major identity crisis is assumed to occur at puberty. It can only be said that at every stage there is an identity crisis.

By two years of age the child is already able to play with other children, i.e., engage in group behavior, a fact generally overlooked by Freudian theoreticians who focus too narrowly on the intrapsychic development. This peer group increasingly becomes an important focus of the child's libidinal desires and ego and superego formation.

What is alienation at two years of age—the absence of security in a loving family, affecting the maturity and gender identity of the child most strongly? Heinecke and Westheimer (1965) studied brief separations in two-year olds. These separations were occasioned for the most part by the birth of a new sibling, which required that the mother go to the hospital. Typical behavior during separation involved: longing for the parents; sleep disturbances; refusal to participate in the nursery routine; seeking a positive relationship with adults in the nursery; increase of sucking; rapid abandonment of favorite objects brought from home; seeking comfort from the observer; and expressions of hostility. Later there was also a breakdown in sphincter control and a decline in the number of different words used. In short, alienation occasioned by separation from the mother involved a regression to an oral phase from which they could not move on to a new group.

As a child grows, he/she is confronted by the insistent demand of the surrounding society that he/she behave in accordance with his/her gender identity, boys like boys, girls like girls. Against this demand many children rebel, creating a sense of failure that warps their entire future development. In the preoedipal period either they move into an inappropriate group (although this is harder to do at that time; yet it occurs) or they regress and remain excessively dependent on mother. Brody (1964) has devoted an interesting study to the determinants of passivity in boys, in contrast to the assertiveness and aggressiveness that is considered "normal" for boys in our culture. She found that insufficient relief of tension, absence of satisfaction and stimulation, and other early traumata do irreversible damage to the body image and the body ego. Marked absence of opportunity for perceptual exercises and libidinal gratification had decisive negative effects upon affect expression, object cathexis, motility and the capacities for delay, independent efforts toward self-satisfaction, and abstract thinking. Instead the boys became excessively dependent on the mother.

In an earlier section I reviewed how the tension between the individual and the group is manifested at various stages in the life cycle. This tension is also a reflection of the firmness and consistency of the gender identity formed earlier.

At this point (oedipal period) the problem of alienation begins to be more strongly affected by the social surround. In our culture, with its strong emphasis on the nuclear family, the conflicts and hostilities present in the family are most often denied. I have elsewhere expressed the hypothesis that much of the strength of the oedipal turmoil derives from an identification with the parent of the opposite sex and her (his) hatred of the other parent. E.g., a boy with a strong desire for mother and hatred of father is identifying with a mother who at a conscious or unconscious level harbors deep resentment against her husband. It may well be that cultures that practice adoption of children on a wide scale (Levy 1964), such as Tahiti, are expressing a friendly interest in the child, allowing him to seek out other pastures and have new experiences, in contrast to the excessive clinging and enmeshment of so many American families.

Fortes (1969) postulated a principle of amity that accounts for the strong bonds of kinship. And Lambert, discussing foster placement in the Gilbert Islands, writes: "The majority of fosterage relationships grew out of long-standing friendships between the natural parents and the future foster-grandparents. . . . Fosterage is a means of transforming the tenuous link that ordinarily connects distant kinsmen into a far stronger and more significant one" (1964:238).

Thus, here the affective quality, of love and hate, is properly brought into the discussion of a social custom. This should be done all along the line, with all questions relating to identity as well as other aspects of social life. Nothing in social life can be properly evaluated without reference to the fundamental distinction between love and hate cultures (Fine 1985).

As the individual grows older, his life cycle moves from one group to another. Entry into each new group is virtually mandatory on the part of the culture. However, the person can react to these group formations, or the new identity required, either positively or negatively.

Alienation results from the rejection of the prescribed group identity. That group identity, as will be brought out more fully in the next chapter, may also be full of pain and disappointment should not be forgotten. Furthermore, if the identity offered contradicts certain fundamental beliefs or leads to actions that are considered inimical to human or individual welfare, alienation will involve a rebellion against the group. This rebellion, or refusal to accept the identity offered, may be positive as well as negative. Thus, those who led the uprising against Hitler in July 1944 are now honored by the German people, while those who were in the majority, with the wholehearted Nazi identity, are despised or at least rejected.

Further, in extension of Erikson's epigenetic schema, identity does not reach completion at adolescence, as he maintains. As seen earlier, growth goes on through the entire life cycle, and at the numerous transition points a new identity is acquired and a new group formation is entered into. In one sense, the identity crisis of adolescence, which Erikson has described so beautifully, comes about in our culture precisely because for the first time in his life the adolescent has a variety of groups to choose from and can easily resist being forced into conventional or, for that matter, an unconventional mold. Again alienation ("far from the madding crowd") at this stage may be either positive or negative. The oft-cited idealism of adolescence could most profitably be looked upon as a positive form of alienation. In time this became the opinion of many who retrospectively evaluate the alienated young men of the Vietnam generation who refused to enlist in a cause that they considered evil. Granted that many other motives are at play, and rebellion against the prevailing mores should not per se be considered alienation.

With regard to gender identity in adult life, a question that has come to the forefront in more recent times is that of women's liberation. In this area emotions have run so high and still do that it is difficult to present an objective picture. But the principle of the tension between the individual and the group can be called upon to clarify problems.

Women's liberation has been seen as a desirable goal for women since the French Revolution (Fine 1985). It became increasingly clear that the woman's identity as a mother and housewife could and in many cases did have deplorable consequences—excessive burdens, dependency on sadistic men, a dullness of mind that Freud called the "housewife psychosis." Many intelligent women rebelled against a fate apparently decreed for them; Freud was the first to show that this fate, or this identity, could and often did produce outright illness. (The senseless attacks against psychoanalysis and the numerous errors that it has given rise to can only be deplored. Psychoanalysis is, and always has been, in favor of the liberation of women.)

But here too the new groups into which women entered once they had left the family behind in many cases were no great improvement on what had gone on before. If the emphasis was on victimization and liberation, the result was all too often a life of resentment and bitterness. Consciousness-raising groups are no substitute for a happy family.

But if the emphasis is placed on the hate culture and all that that implies, then the major effort will be directed toward getting over the hatred, both of men toward women and of women toward men. This point of view seems to be accepted by Betty Friedan in *The Second Stage* (1981). In other words, women can be truly liberated only if men are liberated as well. It is the sadomasochistic character of the man-woman relationship that requires a change, and in the sadomasochism women exploit men as well as are exploited by them.

Age

It is obvious that age plays a vital role in the identity that the individual adopts. From birth to death there are biological and cultural imperatives that account for how the person looks at himself. Each age has its own biological constraints and freedoms and is looked upon differently in different cultures. Common sense in fact would dictate that apart from gender nothing is more central to the identifications formed, and a fortiori to the identities, than age.

Birth itself is surrounded by innumerable myths, beliefs, and prohibitions, depending on the culture. In one culture the souls rest in the wild fig trees where green pigeons roost (Turner 1978). In another, spirit children were thought to hide behind special stones waiting for young, desirable women to pass by. Even in our own culture the accurate description of how children are conceived and born did not come about until the nineteenth century. Up to the seventeenth century it was widely believed, following Aristotle, that the male had the major role in reproduction, while the female merely allowed herself to be directed—

the woman, in other words, developed the child implanted by the man; she had no other function. Sexual misinformation abounded even in scientific circles (Tannahill 1980:344–345). Thus, menstruation was thought of as a disability, and as late as 1878 the *British Medical Journal* ran a six-month correspondence course on whether hams could be turned rancid by the touch of a menstruating woman (Tannahill 1980:352).

With so many mythology and misinformation, the meaning of a child to the woman in any culture has varied. Since the newborn has meaning as yet only in the eyes of his mother, he comes to life in an atmosphere full of various prejudgments. Bibring (1959), as previously mentioned, found that women had all kinds of psychological processes going on during pregnancy, processes that influenced their image of the oncoming child.

Once the child is born, again there are wide differences in what the child means to the parents. A study of five Asian cultures (East-West Center 1975) showed that there were considerable differentials among the cultures in positive and negative values attached to children. The positive values included emotional benefits, economic benefits and security, self-enrichment and development, identification with children, and family cohesiveness and continuity. The negative values included emotional costs, economic costs, restrictions or opportunity costs, physical demands, and family costs. Large-family values included sibling relationships, sex preferences, and child survival. Small-family values included maternal health and societal costs. Within each culture there would of course be wide individual differences.

The child's first identity, at around the age of two, is adopted from the family; essentially his identity is that he is a member of such and such a family. Since the meaning of the child to these families varies so widely, it is already clear at this age that identity will vary accordingly, especially since the child at this age does not as yet have the ego strength to try to be anything different from what he is supposed to be. Thus, the first identity is forced upon the child.

The current view that children should be given special tender loving care and should have all their needs met so far as is humanly possible represents a recent attitude. Up to the beginning of this century (De Mause 1974) the further back in history one goes, the more likely children are to have been killed, abandoned, beaten, terrorized, and sexually abused. Thus, here too the identity assumed by a child in early life depends very heavily on the treatment he receives or has received from his parents or other caretakers. Yet in all this the child at first has no choice but to assume the identity assigned to him by the family and the parents and later to move into the identity assigned by the first school group he enters, the first move away from the family origin.

Anthropologists have presented voluminous evidence about the relationship between the practices of child rearing in any culture and the adult personalities that are produced there. Though there is no one-to-one correspondence, there is always a close correlation between the two, since the adult is the product of his childhood (Mead and Wolfenstein 1955; Whiting 1963).

In the evaluation of the identity formation at different ages, one of the most vital pieces of information is the data on life expectancy within any culture. It is well known that adolescence is a novelty of the present century largely because life has been lengthened long enough to allow for the psychosocial moratorium that age calls for. But the same is true for other ages as well.

Considerable evidence has amassed to show that people with schizophrenia, which may be most fruitfully looked upon as a refusal to join groups beyond the immediate family (Bleuler 1978), have experienced horrible traumatic childhoods, which makes it difficult for them to move away from the punitive parents. The possibility that the biochemical changes so intensively studied are the result of early childhood stress has been discounted too readily; in other words, on the basis of our present knowledge, schizophrenia in its extreme form could just as well be a psychosomatic disorder as a biological abnormality.

The aged, who form a considerable percentage of the population in modern countries, form a group that is treated differently in different cultures (Amoss and Harrell 1981). It is obvious that how they are treated will in turn affect the self-evaluation and identity of younger people who reflect on what they can expect when they reach old age.

Cultures assign different life tasks to different ages. These life tasks lead to groups with different identities. As soon as the child reaches self-awareness, it also becomes aware of the identities of older people, parents, siblings, teachers, and the like. How they are regarded and treated in the culture, and in the family, will in turn influence the child in its own identity, as well as in its estimate of what it can look forward to. In other words, identity will vary with the pleasures and pains attached to different ages. Thus, in our own culture the low value placed on the sick and aged leads both men and women to continue often needless activities much longer than is required. This activity under stress has been associated with many somatic disorders; e.g., the coronary patient with the Type A personality, always hurrying, always tense, always overoriented toward achievement.

Comments about age-inappropriate behavior are common currency; we say: "Don't be a cry-baby," "Be your age," "He acts like an old man," (she like an old woman), and the like. In other words, the association of a different identity with different age groups is widely recognized.

Alienation occurs when the individual is out of step with the appropriate age group. Again, this may be positive or negative, depending on whether we are dealing with a love culture or a hate culture. Thus, the latency boy who refuses to join the other boys in pestering girls may be healthier than the average or the married woman who finds peace, contentment, and satisfaction in her family life may well be ahead of the woman who is constantly striving to be somebody else. What we are emphasizing here, as all along, is that neither identity nor alienation are simply concepts that can be understood without reference to both the individual and the surrounding culture.

Class

Although Americans generally will wince at the idea that ours is a class society, like any other, the facts speak otherwise. It is perhaps true that the class struggle here is not, as Marx had predicted, as sharp as in other cultures and is by no means as bellicose as it once was. It is also true that the class struggle here is mixed up with the racial struggle, since so many members of the lower class are blacks and more recently Hispanics and other foreign nationals. Likewise, it has turned out that the class struggle here shows less bitterness and violence than it does or has shown in other societies. All of these factors must be weighed in the evaluation of classifying a person's identity as a member of the working class.

Previously attention was drawn to the concept of the "culture of poverty" and its drastic implications for the life-style of the people caught up in it. There is little doubt that this is generally true, though again the severity of the onus of poverty weighs differently on different cultures. Nor does this imply that wealth per se confers mental health or an easy life; in the class struggle the wealthy man may be as badly off in some ways as the poor. But, by and large, poverty has a deleterious effect on the indivdual's aspirations and life activities.

This is, of course, an old observation; some will say banal or a cliche. Yet it has never been adequately credited in psychoanalytic theory (e.g., Erikson), which is generally written as though the individual had complete autonomy. At the same time it is widely recognized that psychoanalytic therapy is not suitable for wide segments of the lower classes and that for them psychoanalytic theory has to pay much more attention than it does to the reality circumstances involved.

More than a hundred years ago, in the first careful study of psychosis in this country, Edward Jarvis, then the leading statistician of psychiatry, wrote:

> Poverty is an inward principle, enrooted deeply within the man, and running through all his elements; it reaches his body, his health, his

> intellect, and his moral powers, as well as his estate. In one or other of these elements it may predominate, and in that alone he may seem to be poor; but it usually involves more than one of the elements, often the whole. Hence we find that, among those whom the world calls poor, there is less vital force, a lower tone of life, more ill health, more early death, a diminished longevity. There are also less self-respect, ambition and hope, more idiocy and insanity, and more crime, than among the independent. (1971:52)

A hundred years later, when scientific sociology was fully underway, systematic surveys revealed over and over the class nature of American society. In their classical description of the social situation Warner and his colleagues wrote:

> we finally developed a social-class hypothesis which withstood the later test of a vast collection of data and of subsequent rigorous analysis. By social class is meant two or more orders of people who are believed to be, and are accordingly ranked by the members of the community, in socially superior and inferior positions. Members of a class tend to marry within their own order, but the values of the society permit marriage up and down. A class system also provides that children are born into the same status as their parents. A class society distributes rights and privileges, duties and obligations, unequally among its inferior and superior grades. A system of classes, unlike a system of castes, provides by its own values for movement up and down the social ladder. In common parlance, this is social climbing, or in technical terms, social mobility. The social system of Yankee City, we found, was dominated by a class order (1963:35–36)

While the existence of a class order is well established, less clear are the psychological concomitants of such an order. By and large, it is taken for granted that those at the lowest end of the social ladder are worse off economically, socially, physically, and psychologically than those higher up. With regard to their mental health, which is of most immediate interest to us here, the work by Hollingshead and Redlich (1958) remains a classic. These authors found that the New Haven community was characterized by a distinct class structure, in which each class exhibits definite types of mental illness. Moreover, each class reacts to the presence of mental illness in its members in different ways, and the treatment of psychiatric patients within the various classes differs accordingly, as was seen earlier.

By and large, psychoanalysis and psychotherapy were reserved for the upper two classes, whether in hospitals or in private practice. Again, the element of reality in the life situation and the hope for a change are fundamental elements in the identity formation of all classes. "In contrast to the higher classes, the reality situations of the lower classes are tough, threatening, and, in many respects, hopeless. Lower class patients who have an insoluble reality situation often have little desire to get better. Moreover, they are not able to understand how thinking and talking can help them" (Hollingshead and Redlich 1958:348).

Subsequent investigations have fully confirmed the observations of these pioneer researchers. Figures vary; thus, Hollingshead and Redlich found that schizophrenia was nine times more common in the lowest class than in the upper, while Jarvis had estimated that it was sixty-four times more common. But whatever the true figures, there can be no doubt that the mental and social worlds of the varying classes are poles apart.

Since the evidence is so overwhelming that social class plays a vital role in the etiology, course, and treatment of schizophrenia, it is all the more remarkable that almost all textbooks and other studies ignore this dimension of the illness (Strauss et al. 1980; Bellak 1979). While there is a wide consensus that the catecholamines play a significant role in schizophrenia, there is less awareness of the fact that the catecholamine levels are highly influenced by stress (Welch and Welch 1969). The classic research of Selye and his followers is also of relevance here.

In any case, being a member of the lower classes will generally be expected to induce a negative identity, leading to shame, resentment, and many psychological problems. We can scarcely expect the member of the lower class to have much healthy narcissism; that some do is true, but the great majority do not. What the lower class member longs for more than anything else is the "American dream"—to get our of his class into the higher ones, at least the next highest one.

Yet, while this does happen, probably with more frequency in the United States than elsewhere, by and large, social mobility is limited and always has been (Dowley 1982). In the most recent investigation of this topic, by Jencks and his colleagues at Harvard (1979), it was again concluded that the most important single ingredient that affects economic success is family background.

First, they argue, family advantages affect economic success in at least five conceptually distinct ways (1979:70):

1. Men from advantaged backgrounds have cognitive skills that employers value.

2. Men from advantaged backgrounds have noncognitive traits that employers value.

3. Among men with similar cognitive and noncognitive traits, those from advantaged families have more educational credentials. Employers appear to value these credentials in their own right, even when they are not associated with measurable skills, attitudes, or behavior.

4. Among men with similar skills and credentials, those from advantaged families seek jobs in higher-status occupations than those from disadvantaged families.

5. Even among men with similar skills and credentials who enter the same occupation, employers seem to pay men from advantaged families slightly more than men from disadvantaged families.

Putting this into quantitative terms they conclude: "family background as a whole explained about 48% of the variance in occupational status and 15 to 35% of the variance in earnings among men aged 25 to 64 in the early 1970's. These estimates imply that those who do well economically typically owe almost half of their earnings advantage to family background" (1979:81).

Translated into the terms under examination in this section, this means that the identity of the lower-class man (and woman) in our society is hard to change, but by no means impossible. Thus, a fair number overcome the handicaps of the identity of the lower class into which they are born; a large number do not.

Alienation here can occur in one of two different ways. The person who overcomes his lower-class background denies his origins, either explicitly or implicitly, and assumes a new identity. Then he often feels like a traitor to the cause, especially if other members of his enlarged family have not made it. The second way is more common: the identity of lower class remains but is accompanied by a sense of alienation from the larger, more successful society by which the person is surrounded.

Race

Race in the broad sense (white, black, Oriental, Indian) is such an obvious physical characteristic of the person that it can never be denied. Hence, the identity of a person from a given race is stamped upon him/her from birth. It thus is always a crucial element in the entire self-image; it represents a group from which there is no escape (the few who manage to "pass" as whites need not concern us here, though the wish to do so is important).

In the United States the racial question refers most specifically to blacks, who make up some 10 percent of the population. Their situation is still so critical that the identity of a black is not something to be envied. Since the monumental piece of research carried out by Myrdal almost half a century ago (1944), while many changes have occurred, the plight of the black on the whole remains grim.

Like many other sociologists Myrdal, viewing the situation with a fresh eye, maintains that the United States has a caste rather than a class system. While social relations across the caste line vary considerably from region to region within the country and from class to class within the black group, a man born a black or a white cannot pass from the one status to the other as easily as he can pass from one class to another. Obviously it is only now (the 1980s) that this rigid caste system is being broken into, but the degree to which it has been broken is not great.

Unlike other situations, in the description of white-black relations, sociologists rarely omit the presence of intense hostility and resentment, though they may see too much of it on the black side and too little on the white. What Myrdal and Dollard (1957) saw, and what exists so often, is little short of open warfare. Nor need it come as a surprise that open warfare does erupt with such frequency or that police departments in large cities are ever on the ready for signs of violence. Again, while much has changed, especially since the famous desegregation of schools decision of the Supreme Court in 1954, the deep hatreds remain.

In a call to battle McKay wrote:

> Oh. Kinsmen! we must meet the common foe!
> Though far outnumbered let us show us brave,
> And for their thousand blows deal one death-blow!
> What though before us lies the open grave?
> Like men we'll face the murderous cowardly pack,
> Pressed to the wall, dying, but fighting back! (1937:227)

And the great Dubois, perhaps the most literate black spokesman of modern times, wrote:

> It is difficult to let others see the full psychological meaning of caste segregation. It is as though one, looking out from a dark cave in a side of an impending mountain, sees the world passing and speaks to it; speaks courteously and persuasively, showing them how these entombed souls are hindered in their natural movement, expression and development; and how their loosening from prison would be a matter not simply of courtesy, sympathy and help to them, but aid to all the world. . . . It gradually

> penetrates the minds of the prisoners that the people passing do not hear; that some thick sheet of invisible but horribly tangible plate glass is between them and the world. . . . Then the people within may become hysterical. They may scream and hurl themselves against the barriers. . . . They may even, here and there, break through in blood and disfigurement, and find themselves faced by a horrified, implacable, and quite overwhelming mob of people frightened for their own very existence. (1940:130–131)

This poignant passage is worthy of reflection. What would unhesitatingly be labeled paranoia in a white person is seen here as the inevitable lot of the black. Thus, to identify himself as a black, the individual must struggle with a dilemma, quite near consciousness and quite near social reality, that much of life involves to kill or be killed.

Here too some emendation of psychoanalytic theory is in order. If identity is, as I have argued, derived from the group to which one adheres (or groups), then if one is born into a group virtually at war with another, inevitably violence is connected with the awareness of one's identity. To accept the identity means to accept violence; to reject it may involve total alienation, or a complete psychosis.

This has often been true in the history of the world; e.g., the Jivaro (Harner 1973) in Ecuador, a head-hunting group who trusts no one, have a saying: "I was born to die fighting." Such was also the situation in Europe for most of its history until recently (Fine 1985); the wholesale massacres of World War II were only the culmination of centuries of wholesale massacres.

Occupation

Since the days of Luther, who coined the term *calling* (*Ruf*) for a man's occupation, a man's work has become an essential part of his identity; the alienated either do not work or are completely devoid of any emotional entanglement in what they are doing. Because work became such an essential part of the man and dissatisfaction is so frequent, when industrial psychology came to the fore, after World War II, the first concentration was on what makes the worker dissatisfied. Here is another example where the identity forced on the man by his circumstances becomes a negative component in his personality. Women's rebellion against the role of the housewife may be viewed in the same light: the identity forced on them becomes a source of frustration rather than of pride and is seen to have pejorative connotations.

The most dynamic investigation of job dissatisfaction is represented in the work of Frederick Hertzberg (1966). In his influential theory motivation and hygiene factors are separately identified. The hygiene factors lead to dissatisfaction because of a need to avoid unpleasantness; the motivator factors lead to job satisfaction because of a need for growth or self-actualization. The major motivational factors he found were achievement recognition, work itself, responsibility, and advancement. The major dissatisfiers were company policy and administration, supervision, salary, interpersonal relations, and working conditions. In a sense, improving the working conditions to maximize motivation and minimize dissatisfaction is a way of forging a positive identity out of the vocation.

In their study of the American occupational structure, Blau and Duncan (1967) found some truth in the Horatio Alger myth, in that while relatively few sons of manual workers reach elite status, the percentage in the United States is higher than that in any other country. Thus, the constant striving of many at the lower rung of the ladder to move upward into the elite rich man's class is not entirely divorced from reality, though for most it remains a dream (Chinoy 1955).

Following the studies of job dissatisfaction, the emphasis shifted to the quality of life, of which the job is only a part (Gardell and Johansson 1981). In this framework the identity conferred by the occupation becomes part of a larger question, that of the identity involved in the kind of life the person is leading. When quality of life becomes the focus, the actual job recedes in importance.

However, the fact remains that for a large percentage of the population, the vocation is forced upon them in various ways, it yields an identity that is often negative, and thus it becomes a source of frustration rather than of happiness. Here too psychoanalytic theory has lagged behind, since few analysts have concerned themselves with the dynamics of work (Fine 1983). Identity, in the sense of becoming part of a larger group, cannot be understood properly without reference to the larger social situation. Or, to come back again to one of the major theses of this book, the incorporation of the culture into our theory is essential.

Summary

The first part of the chapter summarized the psychoanalytic theory of love. It involves ideally mutuality, physical (sexual) gratification, and participation in a wider love culture. This ideal is rarely reached. Hence the most common form of love in our culture is a refuge love, in which two people withdraw from the rest of society, either literally or psychologically, and try to find their happiness in one another.

Next I turned to an examination of identity. It is commonly—and erroneously—believed that a person who has an identity has adequate self-love. A review of the literature showed that this erroneous belief stems from the two meanings attached to identity: the self-image and group belonging. It was argued that the concept of the self (and self-image) should be reserved for the intrapsychic process, while that of identity should be analyzed in terms of the groups that a person belongs to.

The notion of a unique identity, which has intrigued and puzzled both philosophers and psychoanalysts as well as many others, upon closer examination breaks down into one of three meanings. It may be factually true, in that each person is in reality unique, differing from all others. But it also represents a strong desire to be different, to stand out from the crowd, to have a special meaning to the world. Still another meaning comes in here, in viewing identity as the heir of the soul, expressing the strong desire to remain immortal; thus, people do all kinds of things to be remembered, often extending their wishes after their death. This third meaning naturally has to be viewed as an illusion, much as the self in the superordinate sense of the soul is an illusion.

Identity then should be reserved for group belonging. A person acquires an identity by means of the groups to which he/she belongs, beginning with the family. Groups were discussed in relation to gender; age; class; race; and occupation. Other groupings could be added, such as those with special interests (e.g., golf players) or those with special talents (musicians or artists).

No individual can escape the imperative that he adhere to groups without isolating himself from the human community. Group existence is just as essential a part of life as individual existence, a fact largely overlooked by classical psychoanalytic theory. In moving from one group to another Van Gennep's rites of passage can always be observed: separation, transition, and reincorporation.

Erikson's well-known view of the identity crisis, in which the position is taken that it is strongest in adolescense and that identity once properly formed there remains the core of the personality for the rest of life, is seen as too limited. There are identity crises all through life, from birth to death, in that the person always feels the tension between himself/herself and the group.

Because identity is an expression of group belonging, social factors will always play a major role in the search for identity. The individual is always faced with a dilemma: if he accedes to the group too enthusiastically, he loses his individuality; if he refuses to join the group, he is too negativistic. Furthermore, a considerable role in whether to join the group or not is played by the nature of the group. Some people are literally born into a group (such as the blacks) that stamps them with a negative identity, which then becomes one of the key concerns for the rest of their lives. Others have more choice about which groups they will join; however, in many cases this choice is likewise an illusory one.

Alienation means withdrawal from the group. It may be positive or negative, depending on the dynamics of the group and the individual. Schizophrenia, e.g., is seen as a refusal to leave the family group, either literally or psychologically. Since the society is so "sick," many (e.g., Laing) have seen the illness as a sign of strength. However, this confuses intrapsychic with interpersonal motivation. The refusal of the schizophrenic to join the ordinary societal groups is due to traumatic features in his childhood, not to a reasoned evaluation of the wider culture.

Some alienated groups, e.g., the Hutterites, may however in many ways be healthier than the larger society. Psychoanalysts are also critical of society and are in many ways alienated from it. So alienation should not be considered bad per se; it depends on the dynamics of the withdrawal and on the nature of the larger groups, whether loving or hating.

To pursue this line of thought further, I must now go on to a consideration of the larger society, the task of the next chapter.

CHAPTER 8
THE ROMANCE OF COMMUNITY

In previous chapters the community was referred to in a number of discussions. Now it is necessary to submit it to a more careful perusal.

Nisbet defines community as:

> relationships among individuals that are characterized by a high degree of personal intimacy, of social cohesion or moral commitment, and of continuity in time. The basis of community may be kinship, religion, political power, revolution, or race. It may be, in fact, any of a large number of activities, beliefs, or functions. All that is essential is that the basis be of sufficient appeal and of sufficient durability to enlist numbers of human beings, to arouse loyalties, and to stimulate an overriding sense of distinctive identity. (Nisbet 1973:1)

This definition requires careful examination. It is not just an objective statement, it carries with it the implication that there is something inherently good about community, an "overriding sense of distinctive identity." Thus, like so many social philosophers, Nisbet fails to distinguish between an identity that is based on mutuality and love and an identity that is based on antagonism and hatred, for both not only are possible but have been seen throughout history. In short, Nisbet does not differentiate sufficiently between love cultures and hate cultures; it is as though the mere fact that human beings aggregate and have something in common is per se beneficial.

Such a point of view is by no means uncommon. It is understandable that social researchers, who look at communities all the time, should see their virtues and overlook their faults, just as those who focus on individuals, such as psychotherapists, see the value of individual change but overlook its limitations in the larger sphere of the culture. This is what I call the romance of community.

Nevertheless, for a complete evaluation, the feelings involved in the community must be given as much weight as its cohesiveness or its continuity in time. Nor can it be assumed that mere continuity is an adequate criterion. The Roman Empire lasted 500 years with its ghastly enslavement and destruction of entire peoples. The slaveholders in the southern United States went to war rather than give up slavery, a fact they still indignantly deny.

At this point psychology and philosophy become intertwined. No examination of communities or groups can be value free; values are inherent in their formation, maintenance, and dissolution (if they dissolve). These values, as will be clarified more fully in the next chapter, likewise apply to the concepts of narcissism and the self and their relationship to society. Psychology can only go a certain distance; thereafter values inevitably assert themselves.

Normality

Within any group, a sharp distinction is drawn between the disciple and the rebel. In the larger society the concern is always with normality. (See also the discussion of neurosis in chapter 4.) Yet, as we have come to see, especially in the twentieth century, superficial normality can cover a multitude of sins. It is no longer unthinkable to state that whole cultures may be seriously disturbed from an analytic point of view, even if they function tolerably well in their own terms.

Offer and Sabshin (1984) have presented a widely appreciated clarification of what normality is. They distinguish four meanings: normality as utopia; normality as average; normality as health; and normality as a transactional system (what is expectable in the midst of change). Of these the first two are the most important from a theoretical perspective; the other two become subordinate.

The word *utopia* means "there is no such place." In effect, then, this makes normality an ideal that should be sought but can never be found. Later I shall have occasion to examine some of the utopias men have offered through the centuries. Here, for the time being, the emphasis will be on the analytic ideal, which has been the utopian vision offered by Freud and other psychoanalysts (Fine 1981).

In the analytic ideal offered by Freud the individual was stressed at the expense of the community. Somehow there was the implication (and still is) that the human being, if he is strong enough, can withstand any calamity inflicted by the outside world. Since this is manifestly untrue, the analytic ideal for the individual must be supplemented, or enlarged, to offer an ideal for the culture as well. Elsewhere I have put it in this form: love can flourish only in a love culture. The goal of analysis is in the larger sense to replace the hate culture in which we have been brought up and live to a love culture.

Both the group utopias and individual utopias suffer from an idealization of the human being. So far as can be seen, there is no group without some tension between the individual and the group. As Roheim has pointed out, even in the most primitive culture ever examined the inhabitants have some concept of themselves as a private person and distinguish between the private and public selves. As cultures become more complex, this distinction becomes ever more pressing.

William Sumner, who coined the terms *in-group* and *out-group*, recognized the intense hostility that grows between these two types of groups. He wrote:

> The relation of comradeship and peace in the we-group and that of hostility and war towards other-groups are correlative to each other. The exigencies of war with outsiders are what make peace inside, lest internal discord should weaken the we-group for war. These exigencies also make government and law in the in-group, in order to prevent quarrels and enforce discipline. Thus war and peace have reacted on each other and developed each other, one within the group, the other in the intergroup relation. The closer the neighbors, and the stronger they are, the intenser is the warfare, and then the intenser is the internal organization and discipline of each. (1959:12)

On the other hand, Sumner was quite oblivious to the hostilities that could arise within the in-group. Cannibalism, he argued, has a basis of affection in the in-group; thus, mothers who eat their babies do so in order to get back the strength they had lost in bearing them (1959:331). Similarly, Cooley, who coined the term *primary groups* says that the sense of a group is stimulated by cooperation within and opposition without (1964:209).

It was one of Freud's achievements to show that the apparent calm of the in-group covered up an enormous quantity of hostility, envy, and other negative emotions. Originally he attributed this hostility to sexual wishes such as incest, which cannot be gratified; later he saw hostility as an instinctual force in its own right. But whatever the theory, it is obvious since his work that in-groups are also characterized by enormous amounts of hostility and that various social devices have to be constructed to keep these hostilities in check. Consequently, there are always intragroup tensions.

Another contribution of Freud's is that the human being has a number of instinctual drives that defy complete gratification. Instead (like incest), they enter into the psyche and help to make up the rich inner world that he opened up to us. But whatever the individual or the society does, there are always intrapsychic tensions present, which evidently defy complete resolution.

Thus, there is always tension between the group and the individual, always tension within the group, and always tension within the individual (intrapsychic). With so much tension present it need cause no surprise that utopia has never been found (and perhaps never will).

This casts a different light on the image of normality as either utopian or average. To consider the normal in any culture healthy has been the traditional assumption, normal vs. abnormal. But our analysis indicates, and of course by now there is a vast experience to confirm, that the normal or average is never free from tension. In fact, he handles his tensions by building up a character structure that receives a minimum of reproach and censure from the surrounding society and a maximum of approval. In this way he builds up an adjustment neurosis (see chapter 4).

Consequently, the individual is given a choice in reality of either an adjustment neurosis, in which he behaves like others around him, or a maladjustment neurosis, in which he seeks some other way out. This inevitable tension cannot be avoided in any discussion of normality.

The elaboration of this point of view in relationship to our culture and involving the analytic ideal and the redefinition of neurosis as distance from the ideal has already been discussed in chapter 4. Here I wish to concentrate on different kinds of communities and their evaluation.

Love Cultures vs. Hate Cultures

Since communities cannot be properly understood without reference to their underlying orientations, a basic distinction must be drawn between love cultures and hate cultures. The love culture is one in which the predominant feeling of one person to another is loving or affectionate; the hate culture is one in which the dominant feeling of one person to another is hateful or resentful. Although the anthropological data is often insufficient to decide what the culture is like from the inside, the more modern accounts, in which the ethnographers are psychodynamically oriented, will often give sufficient information. A discussion of two cultures, Tahiti as representative of a love culture and rural Ireland as representative of a hate culture, will clarify how this distinction can be carried out.

Tahiti

Tahiti is described by Levy (1964). His field work there was done between 1961 and 1964.

Levy's main work was done in the city of Piri. He found that the health of the villagers was excellent. There is plenty of nutritious food, and aside from filariasis, there are no serious tropical diseases.

Tahitians had always been noted for their gentleness, friendliness, and sexual openness. For example, the London Missionary Society in 1797 reported that

> their manners are affable and engaging; their step easy and graceful; their behavior free and unguarded; always boundless in generosity to each other, and to strangers; their tempers mild, gentle, and unaffected; slow to take offense, easily pacified, and seldom retaining resentment or revenge, whatever provocation they may have received. (1964:96)

Several centuries later Levy's report noted similar reactions. Violence and anger were rare; there was in general a note of interpersonal restraint and a lack of hostile aggressiveness. Effective hostility did come out in small ways, such as gossip, teasing, coolness. There were very few physical fights, and those that occurred were not particularly violent. Lack of fighting is particularly striking among children in public settings. When things get more serious in children's conflicts, the fashion of expressing a threat is carefully ineffectual. The village school in Piri had eighty-five children in 1963. The head schoolteacher there says that in his two years at Piri he has never seen a fight among the older schoolchildren (age eight to fifteen) in the schoolyard.

Public hostile behavior was often characterized by a restraint of physically hurting action, by the dependence on and playing to an audience, by anxiety of the audience, and by a later exaggeration in reporting the incident to others. During the New Year's festival at Piri in 1963, which lasted eight days and involved a considerable amount of drinking, there was only one episode that might have been described as violent, and this involved a deviant man. In those fights that do take place between men, they do not hit each other very hard, and it is easy for the bystanders to hold them back. The presence of bystanders seems necessary for these expressions. The lack of serious physical destructiveness is striking just because of the showy dramatic quality of the behavior.

Manifestations of fear about other people are a very much more salient topic than fear of the supernatural. Interpersonal fear is connected with a sense of shyness and a certain kind of discomfort in the presence of others. Yet essentially there is no shame about being fearful; a certain social timidity is a desirable personal quality.

An entirely different picture is offered by the pleasant feelings. The missionaries collected terms for feelings, and among these were twenty-seven terms for "pleasurable states." The pleasurable terms as defined by the missionaries seemed to fall into two groups: "peaceful feelings" and "joyful feelings."

The most salient terms used now in relation to apparently "happy states" are *'oa'oa* and *'arearea*. *Oa'oa* is used in sentences translated as "I am happy." One also uses it about events or people, to indicate that the event or person was caused or associated with a happy feeling.

The common term for having a joyful good time is *'arearea*. It refers to the general situation of a group of people who are doing such things as laughing, joking, dancing, and drinking. The term usually refers more to the kind of activity of the group, the fun of the group, than to the internal response of enjoyment, but it is used to indicate the latter also. 'Arearea is a matter of parties, of festivals, of special occasions that are clearly separate from activities of ordinary life. Engaging in *'arearea* activities is however one of the ideal aspects of the boys' and young men's adolescent period.

In discussions of feelings associated with what we may call friendly or positive interpersonal action, there are four prominent terms. Thus, in speculating on the motives for the formation and maintenance of a heterosexual union, it may be explained that the couple first came together because of desire, but as they remained together, they become accustomed to each other and began to feel love (*here*); they decided not to separate because of *arofa*, compassion for the suffering of the other that a separation would entail.

Levy goes into some detail about the word *here*, which he translates love. He quotes one informant about what is meant by *here*: "Yes, if we didn't love each other, our life would not be going properly. Yes, e.g., if only I *heered* Tetua and she did not *here* me, then she would do the things that she desired, and if it were the case that it was Tetua who *heered* me and I did not *here* Tetua, then I would not pay attention to her, I would only pay attention to the things that I wanted to. But the way it is, she *heres* and I *here*, and that's that. When things are like that, life goes properly for a couple" (1964:318). Thus, Manu (the informant) and Tetua have a love match.

After a rather carefree childhood (to be described more fully below) most adolescents in Piri are said to begin sexual intercourse between the ages of thirteen and sixteen. Previously it was the custom for groups of adolescents to travel around the island from one district to another for adventure or in the hope of meeting sexual partners.

Sexual relationships between young adolescents are usually transient and secretive, although a boy might boast of it to a trusted friend and, after it was over, to a larger circle of male adolescents. A traditional practice, *moto*, still exists, although it seems to be getting less frequent. The young adolescent boy, after summoning up his courage and making sure none of his peers knows what he is up to, waits until everybody is asleep in the household of a girl who attracts him. He will then sneak through an unlocked window or door and, trying not to wake anyone, go to the girl's sleeping area and lie down beside her. This first time usually they talk in whispers and the boy leaves. On subsequent nights he may enter the girl's room again, and if she approves of him they may have intercourse there. Most likely he will ask her to leave the house and meet him somewhere. After he has left through the window, she may get up and, if her parents wake, tell them that she is leaving the house to go to the outhouse and then meet the boy for a brief act of intercourse. This is silent and quick and, in the reminiscences of mature women, often of interest to the young girl mostly as an adventure, not as a sensual experience.

After some time, rarely within months of their first transient sexual experiences and usually not until some years have gone by, individuals will begin to move into a series of more and more stable unions of longer and longer duration. These involve overt living together instead of clandestine meetings and also involve shifts in the qualities of the sexual act. The male is supposed to initiate the various sequences that might lead to intercourse. Boys also ask other boys, sometimes a relative of the girl, to serve as go-between. A woman can always say no and that is the end of it. Rape, even though it existed in previous days, is considered shocking. There are no cases of violent rape in recent years known to the chief of police.

In a stable relationship the woman often more or less covertly initiates the sexual act by signaling her receptivity through her attitude and perhaps dress. There are cultural encouragements for beginning intercourse. It is believed that if the onset of menstruation is not followed within the next very few years by at least one act of intercourse, the girl will suffer from "filled-up sickness." The blood will eventually cause choking sensations in the throat and may lead to insanity and death. In spite of this belief, some girls in the village did remain virgins.

Adult males reporting on themselves and speculating on others say that in the first year or two of a permanent union a couple has intercourse daily, sometimes two or three times a night; after a year of two there are intervals of a day or a week without intercourse; and after several years the frequency goes down to once every two or three weeks or once a month. It is agreed that if the man got a new woman the frequency would go up again.

Intercourse continues during pregnancy until two or three weeks before delivery and begins again, depending on the healing of the women's genitals, in one or two months. Intercourse does not usually go on during menstruation, since menstrual blood is considered dangerous for the male.

The woman's sexual responsiveness is related to the type of relationship. There is an old tradition of women's using the sexual act in a direct and open marketing exchange for goods and services. This is the case in many of the sexual relations between Polynesian women and Europeans. Reports of the women's response in these kinds of relationships often note considerable passivity and lack of responsiveness.

By and large there are no reports of frigidity among adult women, although there are reports of relative lack of feeling during early sexual experiences. Men deny experiencing or having heard about impotence except as a result of physical illness or, more commonly, as a result of a severe chilling after diving for fish. This lack of reported impotence is partially due to the concept of the interrelation of the self and the sexual act. In a casual relationship, if a man starts to caress a woman and finds that he does not have an erection, he will decide that the woman is not attractive to him and make some excuse to avoid proceeding. This is not considered a failure, nor is it considered that in spite of this desire for intercourse he cannot perform. He simply concludes that he does not want to have intercourse.

Both men and women report nocturnal sexual dreams, often accompanied by orgasm. These are always felt to be the result of some spirit activity and are felt to be dangerous.

The various statements about attributes desirable for a sexual partner stress such things as cleanliness, attractive smell, pleasant face, and smooth skin and hair, that is, qualities of softness, blandness, and pleasant surfaces.

Even without the ceremony of marriage most people establish heterosexual relationships and households. Not counting the widowed, who often remarry in later ages, only three men in Piri were living there without a woman. All these people are considered strange in one way or another. At the very least they are said to be "unable to find or hold a woman" and this seems to be considered a mild stigma.

Adultery goes on, although people are rather secretive about it. Nobody in

Piri admits to adultery, although it is one of the things men say they want to do when asked whether they have any wishes they are afraid or ashamed to act on. It seems, however, more or less taken for granted that when a man goes by himself to Papeete, he will try to find a woman with whom to have sex, and a number of men who deny any relationships in the village brag about conquests in Papeete.

A serious settling down, even a relatively limited settling down, means, particularly for a man, a difficult and conflict-laden transition. At the very least it represents a move toward adulthood, which is seen as being wearying and less pleasant than the carefree years of adolescence (though the word is not used). The reasons for settling down are largely convenience. (See also Cuber and Harroff 1965, where the same essential reason was given by upper-class Americans in Ohio.) Manu, one informant, said that he settled down because the woman would wash his clothes, take care of the house, and have food ready for him. Settling down represents the reestablishment of the ordered household of their childhood. Both partners tend to bring to heterosexual relationships a number of expectations, interpretations, and conflicts that make the transition into a permanent state fragile and vulnerable. But somehow problems get solved. There appears to be little divorce, if any. Mostly one sees in settled households respect, equality, and a cooperative working together.

In childhood the mother and father make every effort to make and keep the child secure. Missionaries had already commented in 1797 that as "wives, in private life, they are affectionate, tender and obedient to their husbands and uncommonly fond of their children. They nurse them with the utmost care, and are particularly attentive to keep the infant's limbs supple and straight" (Levy 1964:43).

Aside from cold baths and cosmetic manipulations the infants and young children seem to have had indulged and easy lives. Levy says he almost never heard babies crying in Piri. As a baby becomes active, the people around him begin to respond to him as an amusing small adult, with an individuality and will of his own. Babies sleep next to their mothers. Toilet training is low key and matter of fact—the child teaches himself. The child nurses a long time, is toilet trained late and easily, and runs around without clothes until fairly late (by our standards)—five or six. Not surprisingly, babies and young children appear to be happy, active, flourishing creatures. People are pleased and amused as a baby develops motor and verbal skills. Discipline is mild—verbal threatening, mild physical punishment, mild mocking and shaming. The usual phrase for actively dealing with children is "to steer."

The most traumatic experience undergone by all the boys in the culture is supercision (also written as superincision). This is longitudinal dorsal cutting of the penis. It takes place somewhere between eleven and fourteen. It stands out as being violent and unnatural, quite out of keeping with the normal rhythm of Tahitian life and is seen by Levy as a relic of some of the ancient, more violent themes that have otherwise disappeared. Although the standard answer to questions about the purpose of the operation is cleanliness, a few adults add that the operation increases sexual pleasure for both participants. An unsupercised man is supposed to have a quick and ungratifying orgasm. Boys will generally play down the pain and discomfort involved.

Although there are some negative features I have skipped over, for the sake of conciseness, all in all Tahiti presents a picture of a love culture. The families are reasonably happy, husband and wife enjoy and love one another, and sexually both partners find gratification; if they cool off, there seems to be little opprobrium attached to an occasional fling with someone else. Children are desired and made to feel warm and welcome. Food is plentiful. There seem to be no great economic crises. After a period of enjoyable sexual experimentation in adolescence, almost all people settle down to an orderly life (with or without the actual ceremony of marriage). Violence is rare; when it does occur, it is quickly brought under control. There seem to be almost no instances of murder, suicide, rape, or other acts of violence. The people lead a contented happy life, though it is devoid of great adventures and extraordinary peak experiences.

Rural Ireland

In sharp contrast to the carefree, easy-going contented life of Tahiti is the sorrow-driven unhappy character of rural Ireland, which has been described by a number of anthropologists. Our description here is based primarily on the work of Nancy Scheper-Hughes, *Saints, Scholars, and Schizophrenics* (1979), for which she received the Margaret Mead award in 1981. Her field work was done in 1976, and there was a return visit to Ireland in 1981. (Some comments on rural Ireland can also be found in chapter 5.)

Virtually all authors (Murphy 1982) agree that the incidence of schizophrenia in rural Ireland is the highest in the world. Scheper-Hughes also expresses the belief that rural Ireland is dying and its people are consequently infused with a spirit of anomie and despair. As will be seen, in almost every respect the description of rural Ireland is the exact opposite of the descriptions of Tahiti. The anomie of Ireland is expressed in the decline of the traditional industries (agriculture, sheep grazing, fishing) and the ubiquitous dole. The flight of young people, especially women, from the desolate parishes of the western coast, drinking patterns among the stay-at-home class of bachelor farmers, and the general disinterest of the local populace in sexuality, marriage, and procreation are further signs of cultural stagnation. The relative ease with which a growing proportion of the young, single, male farmers are able to accept voluntary incarceration in the mental hospital as a panacea for their troubles is another indication that western Ireland, once one of the oldest and most continually settled human communities in Europe, is in a virtual state of cultural decline. Evidently the only real remedy the people see is to leave. Messenger cites figures showing that the population of the area he studied (he calls "Inis Beag") dropped progressively from 532 persons in 1861 to 409 in 1926 and 350 when he and his wife were there in 1958. Yet this is a people that has given the world many great writers and leaders (one president of the United States was of recent Irish descent, and a leader of Chile's fight for independence in the nineteenth century was an Irishman named O'Higgins). The high morale and stunning accomplishments of the Irish abroad are in marked contrast to their demoralization at home. Obviously life in Ireland must have a very depressing effect.

Scheper-Hughes calls her village "Ballybran" and I shall use this designation throughout. Ballybran is an isolated parish, so isolated in fact that they were even spared the worst horrors of the Black Famine (1845–1849). It is an insulated community, intensely familistic and tightly endogamous, who view their terrain as a holy geography, their past as a religious history, and their language as a sacred tongue. Thus, it is a cohesive community, but what is the nature of this cohesiveness?

The ethnohistory of the area is full of stories of rebellion, persecution, tragedy, and death. There are five historical periods known to virtually everybody: the bloodbath that crushed the rebellious Earl of Desmond; Penal Times and the persecutions of Oliver Cromwell; the Black Famine; the "troubles" and horrors of the English "Black-and-Tans"; and the shipwreck in Brandon Bay of a California frigate, the *Port Yarok*. The continuing violence in Northern Ireland is recorded daily in the newspapers. The "war" for Irish liberation was particularly savage in southwest Kerry and Cork. Heroes were made and burned alive in Tralee. Thus, the people have for centuries learned to adjust to adversity.

As the title of her book indicates, there is considerable evidence of sexual frustration in Ballybran. The average age at marriage for couples in the area is thirty-four for men and twenty-eight for women, much later than elsewhere in Ireland. Only one of every three adult males is married. As marriage becomes increasingly uncommon, the majority of middle-aged adults live alone or with one or more of their family of origin.

The flight of girls and marriage-aged women from the small villages of the west of Ireland is at once the cause and result of rural decline. There is a virtual absence of eligible females in Ballybran. Similar tendencies exist in the rest of the country as well. A tabulation showed that in 1961 Ireland had the highest excess of males in rural areas in Europe, 24 percent (Scheper-Hughes 1979:38).

For most of its history the problem of sheer physical survial has dominated the lives of Ballybran villagers, who are situated between rough sea and eroded mountain. The average-sized farm is between five and twenty acres, much of it fragmented and with poor yields. In the process of modernization undertaken by the Common Market, the Irish were the last to receive any substantial benefit. There was widespread dissastisfaction with what was offered.

Low fertility and decreased productivity have resulted in a gradual constriction of the major social institutions in the community. Thus, the Ballybran secondary school must fight annually for the meager government funds needed to keep its doors open. There are still a number of shepherds, an isolating occupation that exudes a "maleness" that is antagonistic to the opposite sex. The traditional trades have been dying out, while the main occupations are threatened by emigration and lack of heirs.

As a result there is a contagious spread of a spirit of despair and anomie. The majority of village bachelors find some kind of adjustment to their lot in life by excessive drinking at the village pub. Depression is common to all.

The high incidence of mental illness has already been mentioned. On any given day two out of every hundred males in western Ireland were in a mental hospital. Of these 89 percent were lifelong celibates. In out-patient care almost 5 percent of the population was registered at the hospital or clinic. Two-thirds of these patients were men, and all but one were single. All kinds of myths about mental illness abound, and as might be expected, treatment is given only at the most rudimentary level. As in the United States, the bias was in favor of an organic basis and organic treatment, even though most psychiatrists were ready to admit the role of sexual repression and religious guilt. The community generally reacts with panic to mental patients; as a result, most patients become resigned to long periods of institutionalization.

It is not hard to trace the childhood roots of this depression, antisexuality, and life frustrations. To begin with, new children are not even produced in sufficient quantity. The dearth of children and new births is aired by the community as its greatest continuing tragedy, and village folklore and proverbs are mighty in their condemnation of sterility and barrenness. Envy of married couples with children is a strong overtly expressed theme by the many bachelors, spinsters, and childless couples of the parish, who lavish attention upon, "borrow," and fill with sweets the available village children. Yet village parents in their turn often express resentment at having more children than they want or need: "I am a prisoner in my house and my children are my jailers," said one woman (Scheper-Hughes 1979:137).

As a result of the strict Catholic prohibition of abortion and contraception, a paradox results: Ireland has the greatest amount of postponed marriages and permanent celibacy, as well as the highest marital fertility rate in the world. Conflicts abound all along the line (Scheper-Hughes 1979:137). Pregnancy is a private matter and is kept a secret by women from their relatives, neighbors, and children for as long as possible. Until very recently pregnancy was shrouded with an aura of danger and fears of magical and supernatural influences over or through the mother and fetus. During labor the woman is expected to be self-possessed and stoical.

These fearful attitudes toward pregnancy and birth mirror the deep-seated sexual inhibitions of the community. In fact, child training sounds like a rehearsal of techniques designed to keep both men and women in total sexual repression. Although mothers bestow considerable affection and attention on their offspring, especially on their sons, physical intimacy is rare. The profile of the infant and toddler is remarkably low. Small children, reports Scheper-Hughes, were neither heard nor seen (1979:143).

Even breast feeding is uncommon because of its sexual connotation. By late infancy verbal affection comes to replace contact affection. Any form of direct or indirect sexual expression, such as masturbation, mutual exploration of bodies, use of either standard or slang words relating to sex, and open urination and defecation, is severely punished by word or deed. Care is taken to cover the bodies of infants in the presence of siblings and outsiders, and sex is never discussed before children. Messenger (1969) reports that several times his wife inadvertently inquired whether particular women were pregnant, using that word before youths, only to be hushed up or to have the conversation postponed until the young people could be herded outside. The adults were so embarrassed by the term that they found it difficult to communicate with her after the children departed. She once aroused stupefaction among men on the strand when she attempted unsuccessfully to identify the gender of a bullock about to be shipped off.

In the home the separation of sexes is inaugurated among siblings in early childhood (by contrast, in Tahiti such a separation does not occur until shortly before puberty). Boys and girls in the family remain apart not only when interacting with the parents of the same sex at work but also when playing in or near the cottage and when traveling to and from school. Parents and their older offspring read popular religious journals, found in most homes, which admonish them severely not to have anything to do with sexuality, or they will suffer the consequences.

Sexual misconceptions are myriad. They believe that men by nature are more libidinous than women. The latter have been taught that sexual relations with their husbands are a "duty" that must be "endured," for to refuse coitus is a mortal sin. A frequently encountered assertion affixes the guilt for male strivings on the enormous intake of potatoes. There is much to indicate that the female orgasm is unknown. Men too feel that sexual intercourse is debilitating. They will desist from sex the night before they are to perform a job that will require the expenditure of great energy. Women are not approached sexually during menstruation or for months after childbirth, since they are considered dangerous to the man at such times. "Yanks" have been denounced from the pulpit for describing American sexual practices to island youths, and such "pornographic" magazines as *Time* and *Life*, mailed by kin from abroad, have aroused clergyman to spirited sermon and instruction.

The separation of the sexes started within the family is augmented by separation in almost all segments of adolescent and adult activity. Boys and girls are separated to some extent in classrooms and completely in recess play and movement to and from school. During church services there is a further separation of adult men and women, as well as boys and girls, and each of the four groups leaves the chapel in its turn. The pubs are frequented only by men or by women tourists and female teachers who have spent several years away from home and thus are "set apart." Women occasionally visit the shops to procure groceries, but it is more common for them to send their children to do so, since if they go out, they will meet men. Even on the beach during the summer male tourists tend to bathe at one end and women at the other (Messenger 1969:16–17).

Messenger stresses that such extreme sexual frustration is handled by the ubiquitous drinking, alcoholism, disputes, and pugnacity (1969:17). According to Messenger, premarital sex was unknown, and marital sex was limited as to foreplay and the manner of consummation. Courting never seemed to go on in public (1969:17).

Allied to this severe sexual repression is the extreme sense of embarrassment about the body in general. Nudity is abhorred, and even infants have their entire bodies sponged only once a week (1969:18). Adults do not wash or bathe often. Clothing is always changed in private, and it is usual for people to sleep in their underclothes. There is not even a "dirty joke" tradition, offering some outlet for the repression, while the style of dancing allows for very little bodily contact. Even so some girls refuse to dance.

Most observers of the Irish scene have agreed that the particular school of thought that dominates the rural Irish church is one that is monastic, ascetic, Augustinian, Jansenist, and puritanical. All these terms simply represent through various historical phases the continuity of a penitential version of Chritianity, a tradition emphasizing sin, guilt, the innate weakness of human nature, the need for purification and rituals of self-mortification, a distrust of reason, a fear of sex, and a high regard for fasting and sexual abstinence. The moral education of the infant born into the disgrace of original sin and believed to possess an innate proclivity toward evil begins early. It is in such a psychological atmosphere that the numerous bodily restrictions are inculcated.

Paul Blanshard, in *The Irish and Catholic Power*, states: "When all the reasons for a flight from Ireland have been mentioned, there still remains a suspicion that Irish young people are leaving their nation largely because it is a poor place in which to be happy and free. Have the priests created a civilization in which the chief values of youth and love are subordinate to Catholic discipline?" (1954:154)

It may be objected that rural Ireland, as described by Scheper-Hughes, Messenger, and others, should be called a depressed culture, not a hate culture. But psychoanalytic theory teaches us to see the combination of depression, schizophrenia, and hatred. Most of the hatred in rural Ireland seems to be internalized, but a considerable amount is expressed in overt ways.

When Scheper-Hughes returned to Ballybran after her book had been published, she came under a severe attack from many. One person said: "It's not your science I'm questioning, but this: don't we have the right to lead unexamined lives, the right *not* to be analyzed?" (Scheper-Hughes 1979:317). Another said quite simply: "She should be shot" (1979:viii). Others, however, were relieved that some of their misery had been exposed: "A kind of great burden has been lifted. There's no need to hide it and worry over it alone—it's part of the public record now, anyway" (1979:x).

There are naturally many elements of hostility in Tahiti and many positive areas of affection and love in rural Ireland. Love and hate cultures are ideal types, in Weber's sense, and only approximations can be found on earth. Yet the distinction makes a great deal clear. The two examples chosen, with their sharp contrasts in virtually all areas of living, show that the distinction is a useful one and can be applied to other cultures as well as to smaller groups.

This raises a question that will have to be asked many times, that of values. Love is the basic psychoanalytic value (Fine 1985). To deny it is to make a mockery of the whole science. Naturally it can be misapplied, or misinterpreted, but that does not detract from its fundamental importance. As many have pointed out, value-free science is also in the long run valueless. Thus, when I come to examine other groups or communities, their fundamental values can never be disregarded.

Group Experience

With this distinction between love cultures and hate cultures firmly in mind, I can examine some of the ways in which humankind has tried to organize its group experiences. Four types of communities in particular will be looked at: utopias; intentional love communities; healing communities; and self-help groups in our own culture.

Utopias

From time immemorial, and in all cultures men have dreamed of a different kind of society, either here or in an extraterrestrial place (heaven) where people could live in peace and harmony. Such fantasies, or imaginary creations, are obviously a reflection of the degree of unhappiness the persons are experiencing now, or here on earth. (The depression song went: There'll be pie/in the sky/ when you die/it's a lie.) Almost invariably the decline of religion has been set off by the unrefutable observation that if God is so good and all-powerful, why does he allow so much evil and misery on earth? Thus, the study of utopias is useful primarily because it sheds light on whatever was troubling individuals in those times when *Utopia* was written.

Utopias are almost always group experiences. They describe a thinly veiled idealized family in which the parents (usually the father) retain their great power, allowing the others to be protected children. This comes out very clearly already in Augustine's *The City of God* (426):

> Now the point about Eden was that a man could live there as a man longs to live, but only so long as he longed to live as God willed him to live. Man

in Eden lived in the enjoyment of God and he was good by a communication of the goodness of God. His life was free from want, and he was free to prolong his life as long as he chose. There were food and drink to keep away hunger and thirst and the tree of life to stave off death from senescence. There was not a sign or a seed of decay in man's body that could be a source of any physical pain. Not a sickness assailed him from within, and he feared no harm from without. His body was perfectly healthy and his soul completely at peace. And as in Eden itself there was never a day too hot or too cold, so in Adam, who lived there, no fear or desire was ever so passionate as to worry his will. Of sorrows there was none at all and joys none that was vain, although a perpetual joy that was genuine flowed from the presence of God. (pp. 317–318)

This paradise that Augustine describes is clearly the bliss of the newborn infant with mother. What disturbs it? He then goes on to consider how lust can take place. As a solution to his antisexual dilemma, he postulates that somehow the semen can "reach the womb with as little rupture of the hymen and by the same vaginal ducts as is at the present the case, in reverse, with the menstrual flux" (1958:318). Even if this has never been experienced, he argues, it is possible.

Clearly here bodily sexual contact is the great fear, and that this natural function should be classified as evil has remained one of the greatest dilemmas of Christianity through the centuries.

The history of Christianity is full of communes in which human beings separate themselves from their surroundings, go off into another part of the world, and find paradise in some blissful group experience. Sometimes this has been merely fantasy, but many times it has been tried.

The monastic orders represent one such attempt. *Monos* is Greek for "alone," yet monasteries always involve a social utopia. At least two of the early utopian fantasizers were deeply involved with the images of the monastic life. Thomas More longed for it but considered himself incapable of fulfilling its vows. Campanella was made a novice of the Dominican order in his early youth and spent the rest of his life in rebellion against the requirements of obedience. Were we to trace the history of the monastic orders in detail, these two kinds of experience, too sinful to enter or too rebellious once entered, would be seen as paradigmatic of much that happened. In any case, Christianity now has reached the point where same-sexed orders where men and women exclude themselves from the world can no longer attract enough believers because of the severe sexual repression involved (Greeley 1982).

Thomas More. The first great utopia of modern times is described by Thomas More (1478–1535) in *Utopia*. More rose to be lord chancellor under Henry VIII, but when he refused to abjure his Catholic faith, he was executed for treason. His work was a description of an ideal state guided by reason, quite different from the blissful paradise of the garden of Eden in the Christianity of St. Augustine.

More's book is in large part a monologue by a wild-eyed Portuguese mariner Raphael Hythloday, who knew many of the courts of European lords, secular and ecclesiastic, was a member of Vespucci's expedition to America, and became the leader of a party of even more intrepid explorers who had left Vespucci and ventured as far as the domain of King Utopus. Thus, the pattern was set for many other utopias: it was far away and hard to reach.

The second book describes all aspects of utopian life, social, moral, political, religious, intellectual, setting a pattern fro authentic travel literature for centuries to come. The whole world of the utopians is seen only through the fierce eyes of Hythloday, who is so carried away by his description of their calm happiness that in the recital he becomes as mild and gentle as they are.

More's book depicts an earthly society and an urban society; it is not a heavenly paradise. The society is ruled by persons best fitted for public office, outstanding in goodness and learning, thus establishing a nonhereditary aristocracy that enjoys virtually no privileges beyond esteem. There is equality among citizen heads of large family units, within which order and degree depend upon age and sex. The order of society is patriarchal, ruled by the father, women and the young obediently accepting their subordinate position.

War is not excluded. Great warrior nobles and their retainers are the barbaric enemies. The cities will manage to defend themselves with mercenaries and through the bribery and subversion of foreign courts.

Continuing his down-to-earth philosophy, More describes the complete equality of property for all free inhabitants and an intricate hierarchy of pleasures. The root of all evil is seen as the lust for possessions, a passion that leads men to behave like beasts toward one another. Existing society, he argues, is nothing but a conspiracy of the rich to defraud the poor. In contrast, in utopia nobody will go hungry. Provisions are made for all, including care of the sick and security in old age.

There are lawbreakers, criminals of various kinds. These are punished severely, though ordinarily not put to death. Instead they are burdened with golden chains as symbols of their shame and forced to work at hard labor. To deprive society of their work by executing them would be pointless.

Though egalitarian, the community tolerates slavery. Most of the slaves are war booty, men whose lives have been spared after their defeat in conflicts they unjustly provoked. It is inconceivable that the utopians would get involved in an unrighteous war, and it is always victorious.

A surprisingly modern tone is set by the doctrine that the chief part of man's happiness lies in pleasure, honest moderate enjoyments leading to contentment, not wild and maddening orgies. There is general consensus about the rank of the pleasures, those of the mind having clear superiority over those of the body and those of the body being sharply divisible into true, honest pleasures and false adulterated ones. There are two limitations set on pleasure: no pleasure is permitted if it brings pain in its wake or is harmful to others, and no lower pleasure is chosen in preference to a higher one. But many pleasures are allowed: eating, drinking, sex, even scratching, as long as there is no overindulgence.

The key economic utopian questions revolved around the amout of labor required to fill the need of the society and a definition of the character and extent of these needs. More concluded that men should work just enough to provide an ample supply of basic necessities plus a substantial surplus for defense purposes and as insurance against drought. Nevertheless work is an unavoidable necessity, not a real pleasure. Thus, people work for the good of society.

Throughout the history of Christianity, once it became an established Church with all the appurtenances of authority, there were innumerable revolts against the clergy, especially by the poor. Before the successful reformation of the sixteenth century, which established Protestantism all over northern Europe, there were many unsuccessful attempts at reformation that ended in failure and severe punishment, including extermination of the rebels, by the Church. The cry was always the same: "The ecclesiastical organization, with its hierarchy, its rites and sacraments, is nothing but a monstrous imposition to purloin for the benefit of a few what should be the property of all." One such movement that is worth closer examination is Catharism, which spread over much of Europe in the eleventh and twelfth centuries.

Catharism. The Cathars claimed to be the true Christians, preserving the purity and simplicity of the early church. Their missionaries were men and women vowed to a totally ascetic way of life. They traveled about in pairs, on foot, in black habits, carrying St. John's Gospel in a leather wallet, rating this gospel above the others. They lived on the charity of the faithful, and when they were not on the move, they lived in houses that were rather like convents for men and women. They never ate meat, first, because this food might arouse carnal passions and, second, because they believed in the transmigration of souls and to kill even an animal was strictly forbidden. They observed total chastity and condemned the sexual act in all circumstances, but especially in lawful marriage, for this risked having as a consequence the imprisonment of further souls within the jail of the human body. They forbade all violence and also the taking of oaths (which was fundamental in the society of that day) for it led to taking the name of God in vain.

The Church in the twelfth century was in poor shape. By contrast, the Catharist teaching was very simple and perfectly accessible to less cultivated minds. Evil and injustice abounded. How was it possible to believe that this repulsive world was the work of a supreme all-loving God? So they held that the creator of so obviously imperfect a world was an evil spirit. From him came all material things. But as for our souls, they were created by the good God and imprisoned within their fleshly bodies. What the Cathars brought was the secret of deliverance, and this they had from Christ himself.

Understandably, with such theology, they refused any kind of legitimacy to the Roman Church. They argued that the Church had taken a wrong turn in the fourth century, after the Edict of Milan (313), when its position had been officially altered from the persecuted church to the official church. They claimed to be going back to the position preceding the establishment of an official church. Furthermore, they rejected most of the Old Testament.

Their crucial ceremony was the "consolamentum," which in essence was the reception of the Holy Spirit. For them, however, the Holy Spirit was the principal spirit, the prince of the heavenly army whom God had sent forth from himself, like Christ, but who was inferior to Christ. When the angels fell, according to their doctrine, each fallen angel became a soul imprisoned within a human body. But the immaterial body of this captive soul remained in heaven, watched over by a holy spirit. The effect of the consolamentum was to restore to the fallen soul its holy spirit, which would lead it, after death, toward its heavenly body of light and save it the ordeal of successive reincarnations.

The novitiate preceding the reception of the sacrament was called the *abstinentia*, because one of its features was to subject the postulant for about a year to the diet of the ancients. But the novice was also instructed in the Catharist doctrine, and great importance was attached to this since some people were refused the consolamentum on the grounds that their doctrinal knowledge was faulty. The novice was also trained in absolute obedience, not only to the minister assigned to him but also to the church as a whole (Maudale 1967, chapter 2).

When he was finally judged worthy of it, the recipient was given the consolamentum. This ceremony took place in public in a very well-lit room, for light was the symbol of good. As the Cathars had no regular places of worship, they chose any suitable locality for the celebration of their rites, and this was usually a friendly castle. All impurities had to be avoided, to the extent that everybody washed their hands before the ceremony. Eventually the novice received his consolamentum and was a full member of the Church.

Although it seems harmless enough on the face of it, Catharism aroused the ire of the official Church. For above all it denied any validity to the Church, so that the official structure would have collapsed and did collapse. Accordingly, in the beginning of the thirteenth century a crusade was launched against the Cathars. They either had to repent or be murdered. Most of them chose to be murdered ("executed for heresy" is more polite), and by the middle of the thirteenth century the heresy had been "vanquished." In this respect the Cathars again repeated the history of the Church, which in the early years refused to condone any kind of violence at all against the Romans and was mercilessly slaughtered. Paradoxically it was a military victory (Milvian Bridge, 312) that led Constantine to adopt Christianity as an official religion.

Just what would have happened to the Cathars without the persecution by the Church we have no way of knowing. Similar organized groups have appeared from time to time, some also attempting to regain the purity of the early Christians, but as will be seen, internal discord always leads them to fall apart. The lesson to be drawn is that a group that does not pay adequate attention to psychological factors is bound to collapse sooner or later as a result of rebellion and internal friction.

Auguste Comte (1798–1856). Comte, widely regarded as the father of sociology (he coined the term), spent his life developing a utopia along what he considered scientific lines. In this respect he could be seen as the forerunner of Marx and later theoreticians and even of the contemporary psychologist B. F. Skinner (Walden Two, 1961), whose utopias are also in theory constructed on scientific principles and governed by scientifically trained administrators.

Born at the end of the French Revolution, when Bonapartism was taking over, Comte in his own way visualized himself as implementing the ideals of the revolution. But first his utopia needed a scientific basis. This he tried to supply in his master work *Cours de Philosophie Positive*. In this and other works he set forth first of all a scientific approach to society, which he called positivism, a universal religion of love, called the Religion of Humanity, and a systematic method for reorganizing society by means of numerous hierarchies of administrators who would operate along scientific lines. He himself was to be the high priest of this new religion that was to bring about a utopia.

The earlier part of Comte's life was filled with poverty and tragedy. He could not make a living at anything he liked. Attached to the utopian socialist St. Simon for a short while, he left him in a quarrel; but St. Simon was also an apostle of a utopia based on love. Then Comte married a prostitute on whose earnings he lived for quite a while. For years he sustained himself as a teacher, but he could not get along with the authorities. Later in life he met a woman whom he worshipped and idealized, making her the high priestess of his utopia, ranking her above him. Fame and some comfort came to him only toward the end of his life.

Comte was a typical prophet, full of a historic sense of his mission in the world. Toward the end of his life he wrote:

> Living in an anticipated tomb, I must henceforth speak a posthumous language to the living, a form of speech which is free from all manner of prejudices, above all the theoretical ones, as our descendants will be. Up to now I have always had to speak in the name of the past, though I was continually aspiring toward the future. Now I must interest the public of the West in the future state—which irrevocably follows from the various anterior modes—in order to discipline them at the same time as I consecrate them. (Manuel and Manuel 1979:723)

Comte's works are a curious mixture of extraordinarily obsessional detail and high-flown phrases that can be interpreted in a hundred different ways. Thus, just as he regulated his own diet and arranged hours for prayer and work for himself, so he multiplied ritualistic details for the Religion of Humanity. The positive sacraments became the manifest symbols of the new education process: the presentation of the infant, initiation at fourteen, admission at twenty-one, destination at twenty-eight, marriage before thirty-five, maturity at forty-two, retirement at sixty-two, and finally the sacrament of transformation (Manuel and Manuel 1979:723). In the end the evil ones, the suicides and the executed or those who had failed in their duty to humanity, were relegated to the field of the forgotten, while those upon whom the final judgment of incorporation was favorable were transferred to the Holy Wood, which surrounded the Temple of Humanity.

But then again in his *Cours de Philosophie Positive*, when he is discussing the study of social phenomena, we find paragraphs like the following:

> Defining according to this conception the static laws of the social organism, we shall find that their philosophic principle is a general consensus, such as characterizes any and all phenomena of living bodies, and which social life

> manifests in the highest degree. Thus understood, the social anatomy which constituted static sociology must have as its permanent object the positive study, at once experimental and rational, of the various parts of the social system in their action and reaction upon one another, abstracting for the time being as much as possible the movement which is always modifiying them. Sociological predictions, founded on the exact knowledge of these interrelations, are thus destined to derive the various static indications of each mode of social existence in conformity with further observation, in a manner analogous with what habitually takes place in individual anatomy. (Andreski 1974:149)

Perhaps thinking of passages like the above, Andreski, who edited the writings of Comte in contemporary form, writes that "in this respect he is the true father of contemporary sociology with its bombastic proclamations of methodological purism, accompanied by pseudoscientific practices which often descend to the level of folly or charlatanry" (1974:16).

Although Comte was not read in France during his lifetime (Manuel and Manuel 1979:724), ultimately positivism, like many of the other great dogmatic structures of modern times, exerted its greatest influence in those countries that were comparatively backward in their cultural and economic development. In Europe, for a long time ridicule was heaped upon him as another of the many religious messiahs who had come forth with panaceas for universal peace and happiness.

Yet there is another side of the picture. The image of a utopia organized along the lines of scientific knowledge, with capable administrators at the head, and inspired by a philosophy of love as an ideal lies at the base of many of the revolutionary movements of modern times. Marx could be read in this light, and the disillusionment that set in about Russia in the Stalinist period and subsequently comes from the destruction of this image of utopia.

B. F. Skinner. Still another follower of Comte in modern times could be considered the psychologist B. F. Skinner (1904–), the only psychologist that ever put an image of utopia on paper, in *Walden Two* (1948). Skinner's utopia follows pretty much the same lines as Comte, except that he seems to have no use for love, dismissing it as "positive reinforcement." What is more vital for Skinner is survival, i.e.,group cohesiveness. Thus, in *Beyond Freedom and Dignity* he writes:

> The social environment is what is called a culture. It shapes and maintains the behavior of those who live in it. . . . A major step is the emergence of

> practices which induce members to work for the survival of their culture. Such practices cannot be traced to personal goods . . . the evolution of a culture introduces an additional kind of good or value. A culture which for any reason induces its members to work for its survival is more likely to survive. It is a matter of the good of the culture, not of the individual . . . . If there is any purpose or direction in the evolution of a culture, it has to do with bringing people under the control of more and more of the consequences of their behavior. (1971:143–144)

Here Skinner is explicitly denying any role to values. In fact, he does not hesitate to ridicule the values of freedom and dignity, which are so vital to the humanism of Western culture. All he seems to care about is the survival of the group and mastery of the contingencies of reinforcement that lead to such survival. With such a denial of basic values, it is not surprising that Skinner's utopia has been the subject of endless controversies. Its alleged umbrella of "scientific psychology" is little more than a smoke screen for control by some powerful individual who can, if you wish, according to Skinner, be a benevolent despot (Fine 1975a).

Many of the utopian schemes have been tried in one form or another and are still being tried. According to Zablocki (1980), who made an intensive study of the topic, for at least three centuries there has not been a single year without the formation of a communitarian organization in the United States. Wilson (1973) has depicted numerous millenarian movements among tribal and Third World peoples. Almost all of these efforts are consciously or unconsciously motivated by the desire to form a new society that will be governed by love and harmony. The yearning for love is universal, as is the attempt to establish what has been called intentional love cultures. Usually these have had religious overtones, but many have been far from religion of any kind.

Love Communities

Like most observers, Zablocki was concerned with the stability of the communes that he was studying. In this respect his findings were paradoxical, since he found that love is both the bond and bane of communal life.

The most powerful single predictor of leaving is defined at the relational level of analysis: the amount of love received from fellow commune members. By "love" Zablocki refers to the number of times that a person is mentioned by fellow commune members as an object of love; he seems to mean popularity rather than love. The more popular a person is, the less likely he or she is to leave the commune.

But then comes what seems to be the opposite finding: the more sociometric love relations existing at any time in a commune as a whole, the more likely it is that the commune will disintegrate or, if the commune should survive, the higher its annual membership turnover is likely to be. This appears to mean that when many individuals feel strong love relationships for a number of others, the tensions aroused are too great and many people simply leave.

But matters are even more complicated: this very strong relationship between dyadic love and communal instability is almost completely suppressed by the physical presence in the commune of a charismatic leader. Among the communes in the sample, only under direct daily charismatic influence is it possible for very high densities of dyadic love relationships to coexist with very low membership turnover rates. On the other hand, charismatic leaders themselves are just as likely to leave their communes in any given year as ordinary members.

To translate these sociological findings into more ordinary language, especially as it relates to the central examination of intentional love cultures, when the group members like one another, the group stays together, but if there is too much of a demand for intimacy, then the group begins to fall apart. Both of these propositions are contradicted if there is a strong charismatic leader; then whatever he says goes.

In the nineteenth century numerous attempts at communal living were made, especially in the United States where plenty of room was available. One of the best known is the Oneida Community founded and guided by John Henry Noyes (1870). He describes the essentials of this community as follows (1966, ch . 46).

The Oneida Community. Noyes was born at Brattleboro, Vermont, in 1811. The revival movement of that day exposed him to new experiences and new views of the way of salvation, which took the name of Perfectionism (cf. the Cathars, whose chief exemplars were called perfecti—the perfect ones). This was in 1834. The next twelve years were spent in studying and teaching salvation from sin. Gradually a little school of believers gathered around him. Started at Putney, Vermont, a new community was eventually organized and settled at Oneida, New York, in 1847.

Among the innovations introduced by Noyes were a freer regulation of love and sex: "There must be a restoration of true relations between the sexes" (1966:629). He divided sex into two branches, the amative and the propagative, and regulated both by the principle of *stirpiculture*, a forerunner of modern eugenics. However, Noyes denied that he was preaching free love.

The three community families (in all, 277 persons) were financially and socially one unit. They worked diligently and prospered. But Noyes was essential to the welfare of the community. When he left in the 1870s, the community was dissolved. One of the reasons for its dissolution was that the members could no longer defend themselves against the free love charges. However, looked at objectively, a more compelling reason is that without the charismatic leader, the members take to quarreling with one another too much.

The tension between the group and the individual, which is held in check by the charismatic leader, is nowhere more clearly illustrated than in a song of the Oneida community (Nordhoff 1915:299–300):

We have built us a dome
On our beautiful plantation
And we all have one home
And one family relation

Then later a man sings, looking at a woman near him:

I love you, oh my sister
But the love of God is better;
Yes, the love of God is better—
Oh, the love of God is best.

To this she replies:

I love you oh my brother,
But the love of God is better;
Yes, the love of God is better—
O the love of God is best.

An even more emphatic rejection of close ties is found among the Shakers, who forbade all sexual relations. One of their songs was (Kanter 1976:167)

Of all the relations that ever I see
My old fleshly kindred are furthest from me.
How ugly they look, how hateful they feel,
To see them and hate them increases my zeal.

Hare Krishna. Similarly, the group experience is stressed as most fundamental in all of these intentionally formed groups, urging the individual to adhere to their rules. Thus, in the Hare Krishna movement, one group gathered at their central farm in 1972 to chant in celebration of Lord Krishna, who lived nearly 5,000 years ago (Kanter 1976). Over 1,000 devotees lived together in city houses serving as temples. Clothed in saffron robes and carrying simple instruments, they gathered on street corners to chant Hare Krishna and spread the message. Their faith was demanding: they ate no fish, meat, and eggs, engaged in sex only under strictly regulated marital conditions, and turned over all their worldly goods to the sect. They believed that purity of mind and body is the path to spiritual awakening. Their similarities to the Cathars are striking.

Kanter (1976) has delineated six commitment-building processes she found in contemporary communes: 1) sacrifice; 2) investment; 3) renunciation; 4) communion; 5) mortification; and 6) transcendence. By transcendence she means the experience of higher power and meaning residing in the group, the felt connection with forces and events outside of and beyond the life of a single person. While she mentions the charismatic figure, she fails to mention obedience to this figure as one of the essentials of every group. One of her interesting comments is that communal movements partly achieve communion by having enemies (1976:170), just as they gain activity and purpose by facing dangers and challenges from unconverted multitudes.

Summing up this material on intentional love communities: all have a charismatic figure whom they obey implicitly. The members make various sacrifices to remain in the group but get little individual gratification. Intimacy is both encouraged and discouraged—too little or too much, both destroy the group. Survival of the group is the essential demand.

However, looking at these groups from the outside leads one to question the value they really do attach to love and what they mean by it. Rather, it looks as though here, as throughout history, groups of people dissatisfied with their original families get together and form a new family. The head of this new family, usually a man, is revered as a father figure. Outsiders are regarded as enemies and fought (or submitted to). The individual is lost in the crowd; in psychological language, the member has to abandon his self-identity in order to join and remain in the group. The prime value is regression to an earlier stage of development, mainly childhood when the sexual demands and the demands for autonomy could be warded off. Sooner or later these demands and the pent-up hostilities, which cannot be fully repressed, burst through and destroy the group. Persecution, which forces the group members to defend one another, is more likely to preserve the group than simple acceptance. If accepted, the internal conflicts surface; if persecuted, these internal conflicts can be held back.

It is noteworthy that these empirical findings agree with Freud's theoretical arguments in *Group Psychology and the Analysis of the Ego* (1921). Man, as he put it there, is a horde animal, not a herd animal.

Healing Communities

In previous chapters mention has been made of various kinds of primitive psychotherapy, i.e., psychotherapy in primitive communities. We know today that all cultures practice therapy in one form or another, as indeed do all human beings, since informal therapy, in which the individual learns to cope with his or her anxieties, always goes on. Such informal therapy must be distinguished from formal therapy. Here we wish to examine the concept of the *healing community* used by many groups, including our own. This represents the idea that group experience of certain kinds can exercise healing powers or that group experience as such is of healing value (Almond 1974). Almond describes healing communities in three cultures: the Zuni, Ethiopia, and Hawaii (the Tensho sect).

Zuni. The Zuni present a complex network of permanent treatment groups, that meet both the moral exigencies of the belief system and the requirements of social order. These groups are made up of lifelong memberships devoted to the management of chronic behavior disorder. Furthermore, the ethnologist (Carmen Acosta) alleges, incorporation of such behavior has been accomplished without show of force or hardship to individuals.

Individual Zuni medicine men and women do a thriving business in the pueblo, setting the bruised feelings, chocked emotions, and tight stomachs to rights again with herbal preparations, massage, prayers, and other techniques. These problems appear to be transitory and are accepted as cases by private practioners, often priests of the medicine societies, who charge fees in goods or services.

However, sometimes illness worsens or the treatments that are successful in acute cases do not rectify the difficulty, even when repeated over a long period of time. In such instances of more severe chronic behavioral disorders, the family will call in a medicine society to perform a series of ceremonies on behalf of the sufferer. Arrangements must then be made for him to be initiated into the same society in order to preserve the healing secrets of the group and maintain the sufferer's improvement. In this way many deviant individuals are treated by integrating them into an appropriate medicine fraternity. There problem behavior is subjected to patterning as the new member learns and rehearses the required prayers, rituals, and public performances of this fraternity. Once he is an initiate, he may be required to spend the major portion of his waking time for the rest of his life in programmed activities with his fraternity.

There are twelve Zuni healing societies. Each derives its power from an animal god, usually a beast of prey. These gods are considered the source of disease and death. They also give man medicines and magical powers that members of healing societies can use to control maladies. Each cult has a special area of disorder; some treat injuries, some infections. If an individual is considered seriously ill, he may be "given" to the society. Then, if he is cured he will be initiated into the group that saved him. This will make the cure permanent and also secure secrets he has observed during his treatment. Each of the twelve medicine fraternities carries on a cycle of fasts, retreats and prayers, rituals, and public dance dramas that dovetail into one another and into the other ritual activities of the tribe.

The Zuni supernaturals, like the Greek gods, have interesting and distinct stylized personalities. There is e.g., the great and handsome lover, the fool, the rascal, the glutton, the good-natured one, the pretender, the blunderer, the stingy one, the angry man, and the one who is "kindly yet grave, with a look of endless contentment on his face and anger gone forever from his heart." Each fraternity guards a group of masks and costumes representing its patron supernaturals. An impersonator, through years of apprenticeship, prepares himself to care for the mask and costume and to wear them on ritual occasions.

A cluster of medicine fraternities act as clowns, or delight makers, for the Zuni community. In short, these prayers concern all phenomena that make up the beloved world of the Zuni. The delight makers are distinctly curative in their avowed purpose, for vigorous, regenerating life is health indeed. Each fraternity is legitimized by its place in the ancient origin myths and stories of the peregrinations of the tribe.

Almond comments that the most impressive aspect of Zuni medicine societies is the positiveness of the processes that go on (1974:210–212). Problem behaviors in Zuni have a variety of potential benefits. First, there is relief for the problem. Second, the sufferer becomes a member of a new group, where he is trained as a priest. And third, membership can lead to advancement that goes beyond overcoming the initial problems.

The only trouble with this analysis is the rosy hue in which the healing communities are perceived. In our own society the effects of psychotherapy have been attacked, dissected, questioned, elaborated, studied, and disputed. Shall we do less with the alleged effects in other cultures? What the ethnologists have done is to describe how persons who call themselves sick are treated in this culture, that is, shifted into groups where they remain the rest of their lives. This sequence of events is familiar to us from many other sources, e.g., the intentional love cultures and the self-help groups in our own society (see below). But how much and what kind of therapeutic effect is achieved? This question is very difficult to answer; on the basis of the available material it impossible to answer. What does seem to happen is that the individual finds an institutionalized outlet for his particular complaints, or series of complaints, attaches himself to a new family or familylike structure where he can function somewhat more adequately, and represses or ignores the rest of his troubles. Without the availability of formal psychotherapy, which provides insight and character change, this seems to be one device very widely adopted.

Zar. The Zar cult of Ethiopia is another healing community, originating in Ethiopia but found as well in other countries in Africa. This is the major treatment modality for what Western medicine identifies as psychiatric disorders. These illnesses are attributed to Zar spirits, or "Zars," which are analogous to, but of a different species from, the demons treated with amulets. Zar treatment is most specifically for "hysterical" symptoms, meaning immature, childlike behavior, withdrawal, miscarriage or barrenness, change of personality, and bizarre behavior like self-injury and running amok. The psychiatric version of Zar is also known as "group therapy Zar."

Messing, the chief authority on the Zar, comes to the following conclusions (1959:331):

1. The Zar is a catchall for many psychological disturbances ranging from frustrated status ambition to actual mental illness.

2. Healing is in context of a culture that is socially much more organized than commonly found under the shaman type.

3. Since no patient is ever discharged as cured, the Zar cult functions as a form of permanent group therapy. The chronic patients become devotees, "nice psychopaths" in some cases, who form a close-knit social group in which they find security and recognition.

4. The Zar cult is not actually a deviant cult. Its significance lies in that it maintains the status quo. The patient must confess neglect not only of the Zar but also of his other social duties. The Zar spirit in turn becomes protective and helps the patient carry out his normal role in the outside community.

5. Recently the motivation is shifting (1959) toward employment of cult membership for upward social mobility. This can be observed from the epidemiology of possession itself. In the past a neglected wife could punish her husband through having her Zar extort economic sacrifices from him on threat of relapse. Now, ex-slave and low-class persons are increasingly being chosen by the Zar. Both seek escape from their social confinements in the Zar cult.

Messing also comments that in the traditional form of the Zar cult, the chief beneficiary was the Zar doctor. Since most of the devotees are women, the transformation (sometimes direct gratification) of sexual wishes plays a prominent role. The patient goes into a trance, and the Zar doctor uses various magical devices to discover what Zar has possessed her. In a group of chronic cases the women start dancing. The patient in turn twirls like a top, faster and faster, until she drops in a heap. This "gurri" dance is described by Messing as on the one hand the frantic death throes of an animal about to surrender its individual existence and on the other the climax of the magical coitus, much like the bride who is "conquered" on her wedding night.

A closer examination of this cult reveals it as not so much a healing cult as a group of women who use magical and symbolic means to improve their sexual and social position in a community in which they have traditionally had low status. Again there is no way of knowing how successful this maneuver is; the mere fact that it has gone on for 100 years or so does not prove anything.

Tensho. The Tensho sect of Hawaii is a religious group that grew up around the inspirational leadership of a Japanese farmer's wife named Ogamisama and spread to Hawaii in 1952. By 1965 it had about 500 members; by 1974 it claimed 326,000 members led by Kiyokazu Kitamura, the granddaughter of the founder. She is known as Himegamisama (Honorable Princess God) and was selected successor by her grandmother, who died in 1968. Healing is not the prime purpose of the sect but is cited by most members as evidence of benefit.

Joining Tensho frequently begins with the individual searching for a religious solution to his subjective situation. Tensho members may then provide nurturant care, such as massage for chronic ailments, or professional aid. These forms of aid evoke a sense of obligation, or *on*, a powerful motive in Japanese psychology.

That the Tensho sect is another variation of a mother religion seems obvious. One devotee said: "I wanted to be with Ogamisama every moment, I could not think of anything else. Whenever I was not with her, I missed her like my mother. In fact I missed Ogamisama more than my parents" (Almond 1974:186).

At the same time all the members are equal: "We comrades are all equal, regardless of class differences in the outside world (Almond 1974:189). And every Friday night I feel revitalized. I gain power from that nightly prayer by so many members all at once. If I prayed alone, the power of the prayer would be much less" (1974:189).

Three sorts of meetings are held: 1) a two-hour meeting, which all are required to attend, is held every Friday evening; 2) study groups also meet weekly, but attendance is voluntary; 3) once monthly all sect members on each island gather at a public park for consolation day, which is dedicated in gratitude to Ogamisama. This meeting consists of dancing with eyes closed to the singing of one member and of group chanting of Tensho prayers. In addition to the specific group religious activities, there is social life with other members. Many members report a dramatic, almost magical improvement in their financial condition after joining. On the spiritual level Tensho membership creates a sense of "symbolic salvation," which invests life with meaning and supplies an evaluative framework for events. Magical devices and protection also abound; thus, one member reported that when things went wrong with her car some spirit had possessed the car.

The Tensho is again a typical religious group inspired by a charismatic leader. What is less usual is that the leader (Ogamisama) was not always present in Hawaii; still her influence was felt. Again the member is shifted into a childlike position in a new family with a powerful mother. What happens sexually is not made clear in the report but is obviously of less concern to the devotees. Once more the nature of the "healing" is something that has to be examined more closely. There has never been a shortage of religious sects that promised salvation, but delivery is something else.

Self-Help Groups in Our Own Society

Group therapy led by professionals became popular in the years after World War II, partly because of the shortage of trained therapists and partly because of the inherent benefits in the group situation. Soon many learned that groups could also function without expert leaders. So the self-help movement was born and has continued to flourish vigorously ever since (Rosenbaum and Snadowsky 1976).

A national self-help clearing house has been set up at the City University of New York. According to this source, there were in 1982 fifteen million Americans who belonged to some 500,000 self-help groups of all kinds, ranging from illness to finances to mental health. The main motive was to bring together people who had conquered or were trying to solve the same problem (Naisbitt 1982:150) and to tackle it without help from the outside.

Initially the impetus for self-help groups came from the field of psychotherapy. After World War II, when the demand for psychotherapy was high and the number of practitioners low, some persons began to experiment with seeing patients in groups. Wolf (1962) pioneered in practicing psychoanalysis in groups; he has always insisted that what he does is psychoanalysis in the group, not group psychoanalysis. Wolf trained a whole generation of group therapists and group analysts.

One of Wolf's innovations was the *alternative session*, in which the members met without the leader. From here it was but a short step to the formation of groups without leaders and the mushrooming of self-help groups from the 1960s on. One variation was the *encounter group* (Solomon and Berzon 1972), in which groups of various kinds meet, sometimes with a clear-cut goal, sometimes with no set purpose other than self-exploration. The rationale of what went on and the results achieved by these methods were always open to numerous questions. As Rosenbaum, one of the leaders in the field, has said, "The *practice* of group psychotherapy has been considerably in advance of its *theoretical* understanding and conceptual clarity" (Rosenbaum and Snadowsky 1976:17).

Many of the leading practioners of group therapy and self-help groups are highly enthusiastic, writing in an inspirational tone. Thus, Carl Rogers says:

> The intensive group experience has a more general philosophical implication. It is one expression of the existential point of view which is making itself so pervasively evident in art and literature and modern life. The implicit goal of the group process seems to be to live life fully in the here-and-now relationship. I think the parallel with an existential point of view is clearcut. (Solomon and Berzon 1972:x)

In this passage, as in so many others in the group literature, a wide gulf is drawn between classical psychoanalysis and group experience. What is overlooked is that the goals that Rogers describes are the goals set up by Freud and other psychoanalysts. The techniques are different, but the goals remain the same.

It is difficult, if not impossible, at the present time to achieve any objective evaluation of how much help the encounter group or any other group experience does offer. As in the Zuni medicine fraternities, you "do it and feel better." This difficulty, however, is part of the general problem of determining how much benefit psychotherapy per se offers.

Clinical observation indicates that sooner or later groups that start without a leader will choose one. As in the social-historical experience the charismatic leader is an essential.

Further, while most self-help groups start with a positive orientation to life, many of them very quickly become dumping grounds for the latent hostilities of the members. As in Sumner's observation about in-groups and out-groups, the inner cohesion of the therapy group is accompanied by hostility directed against external enemies (such as psychonalysis). And within the group deep-seated rivalries quickly come to the fore. Bion (1961) classified the reactions of the members into three categories: fight, flight, and pairing-off. Fight and flight are both obviously expressions of hostility. Pairing-off is an example of the refuge love characteristic of our society (discussed earlier in this chapter).

Thus, as with healing groups in primitive communities, no clear-cut appraisal can be undertaken without a knowledge of the members of their groups, their motivation(s) in joining, and their general attitudes to life (love-hate continuum). The group experiences could become an outlet for hatreds, as they often have been in the past, or for love. A discussion of their philosophical bases and how these work out in practice is indispensable.

Summary

Humankind has always been intrigued by community and group experience. The hope has been that if people merely get together, the most marvelous consequences will result. Despite this hope and the universal drive toward group formation, the effects of groups are quite variable.

To begin with, there is always some tension between the individual and the group. If the person submits to the group entirely, he loses his or her individuality. On the other hand, if the person rebels against the group, there is always a considerable release of hatred and aggression.

Second, it turns out that groups have to have a leader. Groups that are formed without one sooner or later gravitate toward finding one. In the most primitive human communities ever investigated, there is a chief who dominates the situation. In a way, this is merely a continuation of the trait in the animal kingdom, where it has also been found that social animals are held together by finely sensitive bonds of dominance and submission.

The ideology of the leader will govern the group, by fair means or by foul. For this reason the group must be evaluated along the love-hate continuum. It has been shown that cultures as a whole can be analyzed in this way, even if no pure love cultures or hate cultures exist. But the management of these basic feelings of love and hatred will lie predominantly in one direction or the other.

Advocates of groups speak and write with a good deal of inspirational enthusiasm. This has been called the "romance of community." Looked at more closely, it is an effort to restore the original blissful family of childhhod. Since adults form the group, this regression to childhhood, with a powerful parent figure, usually father but occasionally mother, is bound to run up against serious obstacles.

Nevertheless, group formation is such a powerful drive in human beings that it cannot be disregarded in any scientific psychology. Traditionally psychoanalysis has been an individual psychology, treating the group as a vehicle in which instinctual needs can be projected and met. This view is an error. Group formation has to be given adequate weight in any complete psychological system based on psychoanalysis.

CHAPTER 9

AN INTEGRATIVE APPROACH: TOWARD A BROADENING OF PSYCHOANALYTIC THEORY

The task that I have set myself in this book is that of conceptual clarification. To this end the data from all the various points of view present in the field have been considered. It is now time to integrate them into one consistent whole. That this is the attitude adopted by the leading analytic theoreticians (in spite of the ever-present cries of "dogmatism") is shown in the following quotation from Hartmann:

> The empirical foundations of analysis are manifold, its theories are complex, verification is difficult and time consuming: therefore the actual interrelation of its various parts on (chronologically speaking) the same level has not always been clearly realized. Despite incomplete attempts toward a more or less systematic presentation, we may say that even at present an understanding of analysis is hardly possible without a detailed knowledge of its history. When working on some analytic proposition without such knowledge, one is likely to find one's way encumbered by hypotheses which actually belong in quite different stages of its development. This state of affairs is troublesome . . . . The endeavor to promote architectonic adjustments, a better coordination of factual and theoretical aspects, may also help us gain some new insight into certain problems which are either neglected or incompletely understood. (1964:69–70)

Our historical reconstruction must go back first to the 1914 paper on narcissism and then to the 1923 paper establishing the tripartite theory, the structural view that replaced the old topographic view. The paper on narcissism represented an attempt to grapple with the problems of psychosis and object (interpersonal) relationships, as well as with the concept of narcissism. As was seen, it was a transitional attempt, successful in some ways, sadly deficient in others. If there seems to be an excessive concentration on its deficiencies here, that is only because my effort is to undo the current confusion surrounding the concepts of narcissism and the self and to see how Freud's theories led up to this confusion.

It was seen that Freud's theory of narcissism, viewing it as a developmental stage, primary in earliest childhood (the first developmental stage in fact) and either primary or secondary later in life, has had to be discarded. The notion of primary narcissism is untenable either in the form in which Freud presented it or in Mahler's version of the autistic stage. The voluminous data on the first year of life has knocked both of these ideas into a cocked hat. We know now that from birth on the infant is intricately involved with the mother, that it has a well-functioning sensory apparatus but an undeveloped motor apparatus, and that its development can be charted with some confidence but that what happens to the infant depends very heavily on how it is treated by its caretakers. The younger the infant, the greater this dependency on the caretaker (mother).

On the one hand it can be said that the infant is cognitively immature, which accounts for much of its cognitive functioning. On the other hand its emotional reactions are in the beginning limited to love and hate (good mother, bad mother). Later they become more varied, yet they always hold on to this basic distinction between love and hate.

Within this framework, narcissism can be either healthy or unhealthy. The healthy narcissist develops on the basis of a secure attachment to the mother, thus the introjection of a loving mother, also referred to as the internalized object (but it is wise to remember that the object is always originally the mother—sometimes the terminology covers this up). The unhealthy narcissist develops on the basis of an insecure relationship with the mother, which leads either to withdrawal or excessive clinging (dependency).

Narcissism as such can be most simply defined as self-involvement (the definition contained in the Moore and Fine Glossary of the American Psychoanalytic Association). It can be excessive, in which case we have the classical Narcissist, like the Greek mythological character Narcissus, or a dependent clinging infant who finds it very difficult to separate from mother.

Freud began his 1914 paper with the question, a burning one at the time, of whether the phenomena of narcissism could be fitted into his psychosexual theories as he had always thought, but which Jung denied. It was seen that in order to fit into his psychosexual theories, Freud resorted to some extreme and far-fetched positions there and in subsequent papers over the next ten years. A rash of metapsychological disquisitions that had never been there before entered the picture. Concepts such as psychic energy, fusion and defusion of instincts, ego libido, and the like were introduced in order to keep the theory consistent. This consistency was purchased at the expense of a theoretical structure that moved so far from clinical realities that more and more analysts began to question it. Eventually a point was reached, as of today, where many openly expressed the opinion that the entire metapsychological scaffolding created by Freud in the years 1914–1924 is excessively cumbersome and should be either simplified or discarded.

A further diminution of the significance attached to sexuality in the early days came with the introduction of a dual instinct theory in 1920 (*Beyond the Pleasure Principle*). Freud's assumption of a death instinct has been almost universally rejected, even by his most loyal followers (Jones 1957). However, the notion that there are two basic instincts, sexuality and aggression, has maintained itself.

The assumption of two basic instincts has gone along with the extensive changes in the libido theory introduced in the 1914 paper and later. It was argued that these changes were neither necessary nor desirable and had the net effect of weakening the force of the early propositions deriving from the psychosexual theory of 1905. A return to the earlier theory was urged, while the tendency of many modern analysts to disparage the importance of sexual motivation in favor of hostility was deplored.

In his subsequent formulation of the tripartite structure in 1923 (*The Ego and the Id*) Freud drew upon a number of different sources. The id-ego conflict is a potent reformulation of his first psychoanalytic observation in 1894 that the neurotic defends himself against unbearable impulses. The id also embodied Groddeck's notion that we "are lived" by our impulses whether we acknowledge it or not. The ego represents reality. The superego is the internalization of the parents. Powerful as this formulation has proved to be, it nevertheless has exhibited a number of flaws, as subsequent psychoanalytic history has shown.

Neither the id nor the ego are unitary entities. Both stand for a number of functions, though both have something in common among all these functions.

The id in the 1923 formulation embodied both libido and aggression, sexuality and hostility. But while these two drives have much in common, they also have distinctive differences. In particular, the analytic scheme Freud adopted for the analysis of sexuality in *Three Essays* (1905) turned out to be much less fruitful when turned on hostility. Unlike sexuality, there appears to be no organic basic for hostility, nor does it exhibit the same or a similar developmental scheme. Hence the notion of an id combining these two drives has to be questioned.

A second objection raised is that insufficent attention is paid to anxiety in this formulation. Although Freud later (1926) provided a comprehensive analysis of anxiety, tracing it back originally to separation and reversing his earlier belief that anxiety is repressed libido (so that now it is anxiety or fear of the parents that leads the child to repress its libido), he still refused to allow anxiety the status of an instinctual drive. It was argued that, as is more usually the case in psychological theory, the basic instincts should be viewed as three: love, hate, and fear, or sexuality, hostility and anxiety.

Still a third difficulty arises with the id concept in that no distinction is made between impulses held over from childhood and impulses deriving from present-day physiological pressures. It seems evident that while the impulses deriving from childhood can eventually be overcome or outgrown, that is not the case with current physiological drives. Hence id pressures will always exist, will always create tension, and will at best be held in check by the ego by the various defense mechanisms.

A fourth problem comes up when the force of the id impulse is reconsidered. Part of this force derives from its unconscious roots, part from the impulse proper. As time has gone on, the unconscious has become increasingly prominent, the impulse as such less peremptory. A resolution of this difficulty was suggested by differentiating sexuality from hostility more sharply.

The concept of the ego was considerably expanded subsequent to Freud's work. The defense mechanisms he described vary somewhat but have not changed noticeably since Anna Freud's historic work in 1936, *The Ego and the Mechanisms of Defense*. This part of the theory was so thoroughly worked out that it has been incorporated into all subsequent formulations.

In his 1923 work Freud departed from his earlier postion that there are two classes of instinct, the sexual and the ego, by assuming that everything originates with the id, that the ego is an offshoot of the id, and that the superego is an offshoot of the ego. This rather schematic systemization, rather typical of Freud, led to many difficulties; in particular, it embodied the assumption, which he had always previously rejected, that everything originally comes from the id.

A change came about with the classic book by Hartmann, *Ego Psychology and the Problem of Adaptation* (1939). Here Hartmann postulated the existence of an undifferentiated ego-id state at birth and shortly thereafter, followed by separate lines of development for the ego and the id, though they always remain related. He also assumed a conflict-free sphere of the personality, which Freud had initially also assumed in 1905 but then forgotten in his synthesis of 1923. The notions of a conflict-free sphere of the personality and of different lines of development for the ego and the id have become firmly entrenched in all psychoanalytic theory. The assumption of an undifferentiated ego-id state at birth runs up against the same difficulties mentioned in connection with the id, that is, it ignores the extensive data now available on how the infant really develops in the first year of life.

Following Hartmann's work, the autonomous ego functions could now be conceptualized and analyzed. Extensive work has been done along these lines. Since these functions are autonomous, they can also be approached via the nonanalytic sciences of man, cognitive psychology, sociology, linguistics, anthropology, and so on. As a result, a highly fruitful area of collaboration between psychoanalysis and the social sciences was opened up. This collaboration has served to buttress another of Hartmann's important convictions, which Freud touched upon but did not pursue, that psychoanalysis is really a general psychology and should be treated as such.

The superego proved to be one of Freud's happiest insights. It serves in contemporary theory in many different ways. First, it helps in the understanding of all the major psychological disturbances: all display a harsh superego dominated by hatred rather than love. The patient fears punishment and rejection, essentially by the superego (or introjected object, as it is frequently referred to today), which can then be projected to other figures in the environment (e.g., the analyst in the therapeutic situation).

Second, in the normal course of events, the superego replaces the parental commands and prohibitions at the period of the passing of the oedipus complex, thereby substituting an internal censor for an external one. This increasing internalization (for it need not be assumed that the superego is fixed once and for all at the age of five or six) explains much of human behavior. It also becomes the theoretical basis for the practice of psychotherapy. Character reconstruction involves greater awareness of the id, strengthening of the ego, and replacement of the superego by rational consideration.

Third, the superego forms a vital link between the family and the larger culture (Parsons 1964). The superego represents the commands and prohibitions of the culture; if the family is too deviant, the culture will be forced to take measures against it. Furthermore, every culture has its own superego structure, also frequently referred to as the ethos, or values, of the culture. Incorporated by each individual, its strength derives from its unconscious roots as well as from external reinforcement. The greater the variability of individual superegos, the more disorganized the community.

Finally, the superego is the repository of the individual's values. Here Freud took a leaf from his admired American follower James Putnam. Psychoanalysis does pay adequate attention to the higher strivings of man, which are embodied in the superego. They may vary all over the lot, from bitterness and harshness to affection and love. But values are always present and always forceful.

Unlike the id and the ego, the superego is a unified entity, deriving from the parents. It is the internalization or representative of the parents. Hence it becomes most directly a link with other persons as well.

In sum, the tripartite structure, while full of extremely fruitful ideas, does not as yet offer a complete analysis of the human personality. Id, ego, and superego all require further dissection and specification for fuller understanding.

However, the most severe challenge to the Freudian formulations came from the culturalist school, which stressed that man is driven by his culture to behave in various ways, just as much as he is driven by inner instinctual drives. This assertion, while in many ways self-evident, led to an inordinate amount of quarrel and dissension in the analytic community. It eventually led to a split between two rival groups of analysts, the Freudians and the culturalists, with two different organizations, the American Psychoanalytic Association and the American Academy of Psychoanalysis.

The Self and Identity

Meanwhile two new concepts, the self and identity, forced a reexamination of traditional theories. In part these concepts were stimulated by the extension of psychoanalytic therapy to the psychotic population, in part by the application of psychoanalytic principles to the broader understanding of culture, and in part by the simple growth of psychoanalytic thought. In any case, once formulated, they have stimulated a whole new series of theoretical and clinical discussions.

Self

The self was first explicitly mentioned by Freud in the 1914 paper on narcissism. However, he used the self in its hyphenated form; self-regard or self-esteem. He was unfamiliar with both the superordinate notion of a self as seen in such thinkers, deriving from the Germanic philosophical tradition as Jung, Heidegger, and Husserl, and the American commonsense notion of the self, discussed by such savants as Mead, Cooley, and William James. Freud even diregarded one of the most brilliant papers on the self, by his pupil Roheim, who, as both anthropologist and psychoanalyst, could integrate a wide body of anthropological knowledge into a coherent psychoanalytic theory. For Freud the self remained a commonsense notion used in everyday language, primarily in hyphenated form, without further theoretical significance. I call this the Freudian self.

An entirely different body of knowledge, later to be incorporated into psychoanalysis, was developed in the United States. From the earliest days the emphasis on individuality in the United States, given the most theoretical formulation by such thinkers as Emerson in his famous essay on self-reliance, has been strong. All the American thinkers stressed that the self began and continued in contact with other selves: it was primarily a social self. Cooley formulated this with his looking-glass self, Mead his generalized other, and James his social self. By contrast, the German philosophical tradition had led to such concepts as Jung's superordinate self, Husserl's *Wesen* (being), Heidegger's *Dasein* (being here), and earlier Hegel's self-consciousness (equivalent to Freud's primary narcissism). It was obvious that the American tradition went back to the tabula rasa of John Locke, while the Germanic went back to the independent monads and their preestablished harmony of Leibniz. It was also clear that all of these thinkers had something to offer.

Still a third view of the self, this time sharply differentiated from classical theory, was offered by Kohut in the 1970s. His position quickly grew into a movement, some said dominated by a charsmatic leader. Like the bandwagon effect around other prominent analysts (e.g., Kernberg; cf. Calef and Weinshel, 1979, as well as Abend, Porder, and Willick 1983) it led to a sharp polarization and numerous contradictory arguments.

Kohut postulated the existence of a superordinate self from birth onward. Although he refused to define the self with more precision, he did speak of the bipolar self, which involved the relationship to both parents. He attempted a restructuring of the notion of neurosis and psychosis around the concept of the cohesive self with normality and a strong cohesive self at one end of the spectrum and psychosis and disintegration of the self at the other. Another central notion is that of the self-object. In his last work, published posthumously, Kohut emphasized that the cure in psychoanalysis takes place by working out the transference of the self to the self-object.

These three views of the self have to be integrated to one coherent position, accepting what is valid in each and discarding what is invalid. In addition, the developmental process reveals three different stages of the self; earliest childhood to about one and a half years, when the self cannot be verbalized but is nevertheless present in varying measure; childhood, when the self is a shadow or mirror of the family; and the adult self, which is a reflection of the larger society.

The early assumption that personality is competely fixed at age five has had to be given up; though early influences are of vital importance, they maintain themselves because the environment does not change and are subject to all kinds of influences from outside sources. In particular, the adult part of the life cycle cannot be considered an uneventful period: numerous investigators by now have described the changes that go on throughout life, including the feelings about the dead.

In light of these conceptions, the self must be seen as going through a developmental process throughout the life cycle. More than other psychic instances, it matures later and is more susceptible to influences and pressures in later life. The differences among the various theoretical positions have to be evaluated in light of this ongoing change.

Further consideration reveals several important features of the self-image. It is vital not to confuse the self with the older notion of the soul, which was its virtually universal meaning up to the beginning of the twentieth century. And it is equally important to realize that the self is intimately bound up with the ethos of the culture, to such an extent that the self is defined in various ways depending on the culture. While the topic is heavily discussed in the current analytic literature, no consensus has been reached among analysts.

Identity

Another post-Freudian concept is that of identity. Sometimes identity is used as synonymous with self, sometimes as a shorthand for group membership. It is urged that self should be reserved for the individual meaning of identity, while the term itself should be used for the various groups to which an individual belongs in the course of life. The introduction of this concept by Erik Erikson in the 1950s again brought out a wide variety of opinions both pro and con, leading to a lively ferment in analytic theory. If identity is seen as group formation, its opposite, *alienation*, can be seen as the absence of group adherence in the individual. The extreme of alienation is found among persons who have no groups to which they adhere.

When the concepts of self and identity were introduced, Freudian analysts made valiant efforts to incorporate them into the tripartite structure. These efforts proved to be useless. This casts doubt on the all-inclusiveness of the tripartite structure, which must instead be seen as a heuristic device to describe certain important features of the personality while leaving out others. In other words, self and identity must be added to id, ego, and superego to have a complete psychology. It is particularly in the areas of social life and interpersonal experience that these concepts have proved especially illuminating; they have in fact been explored as much by social psychologists and anthropologists as by analytic psychologists.

Group Experience and Interpersonal Relations

While interpersonal relations (object relations) were always given careful consideration in psychoanalysis, for a long time Freud was dominated by the idea that everything had to be reduced to libidinal terms. When he came to consider object relations in the 1914 paper on narcissism, he distinguished three stages: narcissism, anaclitic dependency, and object relatedness. Later Hartmann modified this scheme somewhat by substituting need gratification for anaclitic dependency. However, as time went on it became increasingly obvious that the treatment of interpersonal relations in classical Freudian theory was far from adequate. Added to this observation was the increasing polarization of the largest psychoanalytic groups into the Freudians and the culturalists. Almost in reaction to the charge that they were too exclusively instinctual, many Freudians (e.g., Fenichel) reasserted the fundamental significance of the drives, assuming that persons are chosen in order to gratify the drives. Culturalists in their turn deemphasized the drives and stressed cultural forces, seeing in them the capacity to override the drives. Obviously both of these positions have some merit, but much more integration is needed. It is also regrettable and damaging that, in part, the argument has been carried along on politically partisan grounds rather than in terms of an attempt to reach theoretical agreement. Since writers like Kohut attempt to bridge the two positions, it can be said that one of his major contributions is to have brought to light the assets and liabilities of each.

Freud's three stages of interpersonal relations were eventually replaced in two ways: first by the careful examination of actual interpersonal relations in the family, in human experience, in different cultures, and second in the course of therapy. If anything of general meaning came out of this, it could be put as the fundamental importnce of *interactions*, in that whatever the individual drive or desire was, it had to be modeled to suit the interaction with another person.

Within Freudian theory, his description of object relations was eventually replaced by Mahler et al.'s (1975) delineation of the separation-individuation process. Mahler first distinguished two stages: autistic (which replaced the older term narcissistic) and symbiotic (which replaced the older term anaclitic). The symbiotic relatedness to the mother in turn was outgrown by a process she divided into hatching, practicing, reapprochement, and object constancy, with appropriate time periods for each. Others tried to generalize her fourfold division to a similar process in all later relationships, yielding reverberations of these schema throughout the life cycle.

However, criticism of Mahler's schema can be offered on a number of grounds. First, it allows too little leeway for the environment, although in other papers she does consider what happens if the mother does not go along or does not understand the individuation process. Second, it does not give sufficient consideration to the well-known psychosexual libidinal development. Third, the final stage of object constancy is placed by her at three years of age, then (1975) left open. At this stage, where there is a firmly introjected image of the mother (the internalized object), the child is seen as being "autonomous," as in later stages where the individual outgrows one relationship to move to an autonomous position.

This can be questioned on two grounds. First, common observation indicates that the child moves from one person to another, not from person to independence, although greater maturity does ordinarily imply greater independence. And second, it pays insufficient attention to the group, for common observation again indicates that no sooner released from family ties, the child gravtates toward group situations as much as toward individual, if not more so.

Mahler's stages are a variation of the well-known stages described by the anthropologist Van Gennep in 1909: separation-transition-reincorporation. Since Van Gennep's stages have a wider bearing on the human condition, it would be preferable to use them in both theoretical and clinical discourse. They cast illuminating insights on the different stages of the life cycle.

Thus, with this theoretical structure in mind, we can say that in the course of life the individual moves through the maturation of a number of different drives—oral, anal, phallic, genital. In many cases, if not most, these drives can only be partially gratified. Their gratification depends as much on the relationship to the mother or other significant persons as on the drive per se. However, there is an irreducible minimum in all these drive configurations beyond which the individual cannot go without suffering severe consequences.

Thus, in the traditional modes of bringing up children in Western culture, the emphasis has been on deprivation rather than gratification—no breast feeding (before bottles, infants were sent out to wet nurses, even when it was known that sending them to a wet nurse was often a sentence of death), early toilet training, no masturbation, no sex, no aggression, no exhibitionism-voyeurism. It was one of Freud's major achievements to show that the deprivations inflicted on children in his environment were excessive, leading to neurotic and psychotic illness. Since then the Freudian revolution has sanctioned a much greater degree of permissiveness in the training of children, with consequent positive benefits for their mental health.

However, two qualificaions must be added to this attitude of permissiveness. In some cases it was read to mean let the child do anything (Neill 1960). This led to a wild release of all kinds of id impulses in which the ego and superego were unable to develop; the results were often disastrous. It was then realized that the permission to gratify the impulses must be kept within certain limits. Ego and superego growth are as important as id release. And now self and identity cohesiveness have likewise to be seen as vital as the release of the id. For the sake of his relationship with others, the child is willing to abandon some of his instinctual demands.

The frustration of instinctual demands leads to consequences that differ, depending on the instinct and depending on the relationship with the caretakers. The child with a healthy ego will be able to tolerate more frustration than the child with a defective ego; hence, with instinctual release we never know whether we are dealing with an organically determined quantitative demand or with the ego's incapacity to modulate and control the drives. As time has gone on, the earlier emphasis on the drives and the need to satisfy them has given way increasingly to the position that beyond a certain irreducible limit the child with a healthy ego can learn to give up a great deal. However, it is also true that the ego grows in an atmosphere where there is more and more adequate stimulation of the instinctual apparatus. Thus, no easy formula is available. Instinctual gratification and interpersonal satisfaction go together.

At the same time, there has been a strong and deplorable tendency to "desexualize" psychoanalysis. This is but another example of the move from one extreme to another: either make impulse release the desideratum of a good life or replace it by a kind of ascetic ego control. If anything of a general nature can be said on this point, it is only that extremes must be avoided.

In the classical Freudian position, the significance of interpersonal relationships tended to be underestimated—not ignored, as some have contended, but allowed less weight than the id. For this there are good and adequate historical reasons; as Freud once put it, he had to call men's attention to the vital significance of sexuality, even if in the process he had to exaggerate. The assumption that objects are sought out in order to gratify drives has had to be abandoned, although this might occur in some cases for neurotic reasons (actually in many cases the process is referred to as acting out).

Instead, it has to be assumed that people are biologically as important as impulses, a position consonant with general evolutionary theory, as seen today. With this assumption, life can be seen as moving from one person to another. Initially there is the mother, then the turn to the father. This is followed by peers, then homosexual relationships followed by heterosexual. The next step is parenthood and entrance into the world of work as delineated by adulthood. Within the adult period there are the stages of moving into a vocational field and eventually settling down, accompanied by settling down into the new family situation. Then comes middle age and the midlife crisis. Again, once this bridge is crossed, the person moves on to old age, decline, and death. Even here, however, the attitudes in the culture prevalent toward the old and the ancestors have to be given full consideration.

A third line of development, and again just as important as the other two, is that of the group experience. A consideration of history shows how vital groups are and always have been in human experience. Again the group experience is fundamental; it cannot be "inferred" either from libidinal wishes or from individual personal relationships. Humans live in groups and have always done so.

What theory has to do is to delineate the various stages through which the group exeriences pass. Here too there is room for additions to the classical Freudian description of development. No individual relationship can actually be properly understood without reference to the group in which it occurs. Thus, even the mother-infant dyad is by no means independent of the father, and how the father feels about the dyad in turn has a strong influence on what the child will derive from the nursing period.

In the study of cultures it was found that a basic division into love and hate cultures is plausible. Hence, in all groups a basic division into love and hate or, less strongly, into positively toned and negatively toned groups must be drawn. There is and always has been a strong tendency to romanticize the group as such, but without some specifications as to whether it embodies loving or hating relationships, no group can be properly understood.

In the normal course of development in our culture the moves from one group to another can easily be charted. From the family the child moves on to peers, then to the school, then (from eight years on or so) to unisex groups (such as the Boy Scouts), then to heterosexual groups in adolescence, then to a new family, and then to work groups, social groups, and a recapitulation with the children of the kinds of groups that the parent went through when he or she was a child.

Narcissism and the self must both be contrasted with the group as well as some other single person. The narcissistic individual who cannot enter into a group is worse off than the narcissist who joins a group and projects his narcissism to it, the more usual case.

Yet closer investigation shows that there is always some tension between the individual and the group. If he does not want to submit, rebellion results; if there is submission, there is loss of individuality. Just as the impulses allow no ideal solution, group belonging allows none either. In particular, the roles of the leader must be given great weight; people are either leaders or followers. Groups always have a leader, often a charismatic one to whom allegiance takes precedence over everything else.

The independent development of interpersonal relations and group experience help to explain why the concepts of self, narcissism, and identity could not be fitted into classical psychoanalytic theory. These concepts do not fit in too well with the drives, but they can readily be assimilated into the known facts about interpersonal relationships and groups.

Through all this there is also an independent line of development of somatic factors and of cognitive processes. The brilliant investigations of Piaget and others have shown how cognitive processes function in their developmental aspects. Cognitive psychology can likewise not be explained in terms of classical analytic theory. Again the newer knowledge has to be integrated with the older to form a complete theory.

Sickness and Health: The Diagnostic Categories

The problem of mental health (in itself a neologism introduced by psychoanalysis) had traditionally been approached via psychiatry and is approached in that way today. For various reasons, psychoanalysts from Freud on have been critical of this approach and have attempted to replace it in a number of different ways.

The main trouble with the conventional psychiatric classification inherited from Kraepelin is that it lacks an adequate reference point. From the very beginning analytic experience indicated that the average human in our society is much more disturbed than had been thought; hence to use him as a reference point is bound to be misleading. Subsequently, as was seen, in all epidemiological studies those that were analytically oriented always came out with a much higher degree of disturbance in the general population than those that were organically or Kraepelinian oriented.

Allied to this recognition of a deeper degree of disturbance is the continuum theory, which holds that all neuroses and psychoses are quantitatively, not qualitatively, different, a position Freud took at an early stage and never abandoned. When he formulated his differentiation between the transference and narcissistic neuroses in 1914, he did seem to make a qualitative distinction, but then a few years later he reasserted that the differences are only ones of degree.

While much of the contemporary psychiatric literature makes the claim that schizophrenia is a hereditary organic illness, this is disputed by many others. What has to be determined, even if schizophrenia has an organic component in some patients, is what percentage of patients can be described in this way. At the present time no definite test is available. It is beyond dispute that many schizophrenics recover from their illnesses, some of them completely, others only partially. Thus, that some patients have an organic disturbance does not change the continuum theory but merely requires an insubstantial modification in some cases.

It has also been pointed out that the various diagnostic categories in which the "mentally ill" have been divided are continuations of the older belief in demons (Reider 1955). Thus, in practice the diagnostic system in use in the United States and other modern countries does not differ so much from the belief in "malevolent spirits" that is so widespread in primitive communities.

Within the neurotic range, the various diagnostic categories stem largely from Freud and his followers. His original division of neurosis into hysteria and obsessional neurosis was immediately modified by his admonition that in practice the mixed cases are by far the most common. As psychoanalytic theory developed, different neurotic categories were fitted into the theoretical knowledge; e.g., when the theory of masochism was explored in the 1950s, the masochistic patient was emphasized. When narcissism became the topic of inquiry in the 1970s, the narcissistic patient was stressed. It should not be thought, however, that these different classifications, reflecting theory rather than difference in clinical observations, vary so much from one another.

The reference point to which the classification was finally directed was the image of the analytic ideal. Psychoanalysis has always stressed the ideal character of its categories of health, contrasting them with what is actually found in either the clinical or the cultural situation. Looked at in this light, neurosis involves a lack of love, sexual frustration, lack of pleasure, domination by hatred rather than love, irrational behavior, lack of a secure family, lack of sense of identity, absence of a satisfying role in the social order, difficulties in work, inability to communicate, blockage of creative outlets, and finally (and as a consequence of one or all of the above) psychiatric symptomatology. This is what I have called the analytic ideal; average (normal), neurotic, and psychotic behavior must all be evaluated in light of this analytic ideal.

In this way psychoanalysis becomes a trenchant critic of the established order. Following the division of cultures into love and hate cultures, our own culture would be seen as a hate culture (this does not detract from the fact that other cultures on the world scene at present could be equally hateful, or even that the American culture could be less filled with hatred than any other culture at present available). But that the deep-seated hatreds that divide people at present set one group against another, condemn millions of people whose economic circumstances are basically satisfactory to lives of endless misery, and leads to wars and other social evils should not be overlooked.

If neurosis is defined as the distance from the analytic ideal, then a natural division into adjustment neuroses and maladjustment neuroses suggests itself. The average person in our culture would present an adjustment neurosis. Part of the tremendous growth of psychoanalysis and of the great interest attached to it is that now for the first time this adjustment neurosis can be properly understood and suitable measures to change it have been made available (psychoanalysis and psychoanalytic therapy).

Initially Freud, as he himself once put it, hugged the coastline. He defined neurosis as a conflict between the ego and the id, and psychosis as a conflict between the ego and reality. However, once the concepts of the self and identity entered the picture, and their full import grasped for theory as well as practice, theory extends and proliferates in many different directions. Not limited to the maladjustment neurosis, the traditional domain of psychiatry, psychoanalysis can become a powerful lever for bringing about significant changes in the entire culture.

Technically these considerations virtually do away with the conventional diagnostic nomenclature. We find that people are unhappily married, that they have poor sex lives, that they express hatred much more than love, etc., and we call these manifestations "neurotic." But this gives the term "neurotic" an entirely different meaning from the more traditional usage of neurotic as deviant from the average. The mixture of a philosophical approach to the culture and a medical litany of psychological and somatic symptoms deleterious to the individual (though he may not realize it) has created endless confusion on the current scene. Thus, psychoanalysis is an indispensable corrective to the understanding of man.

Therapeutic Implications

To understand where and how psychotherapy fits in, it is first necessary to distinguish between formal and informal psychotherapy. All people have anxieties—some more, some less. Anxiety is part of the human condition. If a person suffers from anxiety, he tries to do something about it. These measures to ward off anxiety may take a hundred different forms—repression, projection, drinking, hostility, ambition, and many other devices the person thinks will diminish the anxiety, leaving to one side (although they are still important in our culture) such primitive beliefs as astrology, numerology, superstition, denial, and the like. Thus, all people, whether they realize it or not, engage in some form of informal therapy.

This informal psychotherapy may and does have a number of consequences. Since anxiety is inherently unpleasant, most people arrange their lives in such a way as to avoid or minimize the sources of anxiety to the extent that they can. This results in a concentration on ego-dystonic symptoms, i.e., symptoms that are subjectively uncomfortable. In accordance with this wish to avoid symptoms, people will accept any measure that promises to relieve immediate anxiety. This may be done by taking drugs, by altering the sex life, by working too much or too little, by marrying or by not marrying, or any one of a large number of other devices.

In this process the ego-syntonic symptoms will necessarily be disregarded by the individual. Even to face them requires the ability to tolerate a certain amount of anxiety, an ability which few have. Hence the ego-syntonic symptoms enter into and form the main component of the character structure. Thereafter the character structure will interact with the various pressures, both internal and external, brought to bear on the individual to determine the course of each individual's life.

Formal psychotherapy enters this picture in one of two ways. First, the informal therapy may not work adequately, so that too much anxiety results. The person will then seek help, although very often this help may be of a nonpsychological kind, such as drugs or acting out of various kinds. But with sufficient sophistication many people recognize that their symptoms have a psychological component and can be treated psychologically.

The second route by which psychotherapy enters is the educational. In this route the ego-syntonic devices are seen to be screens that serve to mislead or befuddle the individual into thinking that he is all right, when in reality there are many problems underneath, some of a quite serious nature. This educational approach helps to explain the vast number of books and records on self-help systems of all sorts. Unfortunately it also tends to encourage brief and superficial therapy, in which symptoms may rapidly disappear as a result of the positive transference.

By now the effects of formal psychotherapy can be predicted reasonably well on a *statistical* basis, not on an individual basis. Psychotherapy works best with those who are closest to the YAVIS image—young, alert, verbal, introspective, and sexual. It works worst with those who are deficient in one or more of these qualities. And it does work. Even in those who are not such good candidates, the amount of improvement that can be obtained with psychotherapy is often quite impressive.

There is a vast literature on the results of psychotherapy, including classical psychoanalysis. On the whole most researchers now grudgingly admit that psychotherapy does lead to some benefit (Smith, Glass, and Miller 1980). But these statistical results should not be used in a misleading way. By and large, the researchers take an ego-dystonic view of symptomalogy, inasmuch as they have no real technique for evaluating the ego-syntonic symptoms, which are far more important in the total picture.

Psychological propositions do not lend themselves to easy verification or easy quantification. In the main, it can be said that when one human being talks to another, reveals his or her innermost thoughts, secrets, and wishes, and is given some insight and guidance in how to understand them and handle them, benefits will result. The notion of a "cure" was abandoned by psychoanalysis a long time ago; the goal is to obtain some improvement in understanding and functioning, not a cure in the somatic sense, although that may sometimes come up as an incidental question. On the whole, in the light of everything that has been done, it can be said that there is reason to believe that the basic proposition of psychotherapy, that people will benefit when they talk to others in a reasonably professional atmosphere, has considerable validity. Much more could be said, but this is as much as can be reasonably demonstrated at the present time.

Philosophical Implications

In this final section I wish to pull together all the previous arguments into a coherent evaluation of psychoanalysis as it stands today. The concepts of self and narcissism were introduced because of a dissatisfaction with the prevailing theory of that day. While these concepts, together with allied ones such as identity, alienation, culture, and so on, are themselves the subject of considerable controversy, they have stirred up many analysts to look to a broader image of their science and their profession. It is this broader image that I wish to concentrate on in this section.

Psychoanalysis as a Psychology

It is essential to emphasize that psychoanalysis is a system of psychology. This point has been stressed by all the leading psychoanalysts from Freud on but has largely been overlooked by nonanalytic psychologists who continue to regard psychoanalysis as simply another kind of personality theory or another technique of psychotherapy. Many theoreticians regard psychoanalysis as too narrow or too jumbled a system to advance to a full psychology; many others, however, have tried to formulate what psychology would look like if approached from a psychoanalytic point of view. To do that, frequently the word *psychodynamic* is substituted for psychoanalytic, since the connotations of the word psychoanalysis are more apt to be confusing than enlightening because of the bad publicity the field has generally received. In any case, whichever term is used, that a psychoanalytic psychology is possible along scientific lines has been argued by many authors (e.g., Rapaport 1960; Rosenblatt and Thickstun 1977; Hartmann 1959; Hook 1959; Fine 1975b). I have elsewhere suggested the following definition:

> Psychoanalysis is a scientific systematic approach to psychology which is based on man's affective and unconscious experience, offers a theory of happiness in line with the analytical ideal, and combines these with the results of other rational inquiry to build a complete science of man. (1981:494)

There is, however, considerable difference of opinion about how to convert psychoanalysis into a more systematic psychology; each of the authors enumerated above and many others not mentioned take a different tack. The old criticism that psychoanalysis is completely unscientific has virtually gone out of the window completely, but there is as yet no unanimity on how to pursue its scientific purpose further. Since psychoanalysis represents both a philosophy of living and a psychology, both must be taken into account.

In an interesting paper Piaget (1973), whose influence on psychology continues to grow, drew some fascinating parallels between the affective unconscious and the cognitive unconscious—the former has been explored by the analysts, the latter by cognitive psychologists, among whom Piaget was foremost. For example, he says that in the affective unconscious the situation is in many ways remarkably comparable to the cognitive unconscious: relative consciousness (though it, too, is impoverished) of the result, along with what must be a practically (or initially complete) unconsciousness of the innermost mechanisms which produce their end products. However, he does not deny that the affective unconscious has a dynamic content that is absent from the cognitive, since the affective is repressed because of anxiety while the cognitive is repressed (if is can be called that) because of incapacity.

Still, he argues, the technique he suggests could be applied more generally and fruitfully; thus, "multiple problems remain to be resolved, and today is not too soon to start thinking of formulating a general psychology which would bear simultaneously upon the mechanisms discovered by psychoanalysis and the cognitive processes; the kinds of comparison which we have made here are but a beginning and appear to be rich with promise" (1973:261).

What Piaget is suggesting is that the psychoanalytic data should be coordinated with other data to help resolve the problem or problems under discussion. This is the approach I have adopted in this book; e.g., with regard to the concept of the self and the various propositions associated with it, data have been cited from sociology, social psychology, anthropology, and experimental and developmental psychology, as well as from psychoanalysis. A complete picture of the self in all its functions cannot be obtained from any one discipline currently on the horizon.

In this way psychoanalysis becomes an integrative discipline that unites disparate material from many different sources as well as a critical discipline that casts a revealing light on the nature of the data obtained by any investigator. Thus, again coming back to the self, it was noted that the 4,500 experimental studies cited by Ruth Wylie in her book on the self yielded no definitive results. The only conclusion to be drawn from that is that the methodology adopted was not adequate to the problems posed.

Psychoanalysis provides or has provided conceptual clarification in a number of important topics in psychology, e.g., the theory of dreams and fantasy life in general. Such conceptual clarification would necessarily affect the manner of research and the kinds of data any investigator would seek to unearth. In this respect it would of course be sharply critical of any behavioristic approach that omits the inner life of the subject (Fine 1975a). For example, the widespread analytic criticism of the Kinsey studies (1948, 1953) when they appeared was that the mere enumeration of sexual outlets without a concomitant evaluation of what these meant to the subject leads nowhere.

Specific propositions elicited by psychoanalytic research have been offered many times. By and large, they can be tested by the usual methods of scientific investigation, with due regard to the nature of the material under investigation. When that is done, much is confirmed, much rejected, just as in clinical psychoanalysis (Masling 1983; Fisher and Greenberg 1977).

One point about the psychoanalytic approach to psychology is especially noteworthy; unlike other systems, it does not shrink from an empirical investigation of happiness and misery. Since these are among the most important feelings in human existence, psychoanalysis makes a contribution in this area that is not matched by any other psychology.

Finally, it should be borne in mind that no psychology on the present scene lays a serious claim to being a "complete scientific system." At one time learning theory was widely believed to have that potential, but after its failure to explain such human behavior in any but a most general way ("aggression is the result of a social learning process"), there has been a widespread feeling of disillusionment about the possibilities that it offers. Thus, psychoanalysis enters a field where there is no one science universally accepted. Its own efforts to establish scientific truth have to be evaluated in light of this situation.

Psychoanalysis as a Philosophy

The domination by philosophy of the diverse spheres of knowledge has long since ended, yet philosophy and philosophers still lay a claim to a degree of wisdom beyond that of any one science. Such a claim is not made by psychoanalysis. What it does maintain is that it offers a basis for happiness in a philosophy of living that is consistent with a democratic society and with the humanist ideals that have been the hallmark of many Western thinkers since the French Revolution.

In *The Idea of Happiness* (1967) McGill frankly concedes that the search for what happiness is has to be turned over by the philosophers to the psychologists on the current scene. He writes:

> The disciplines that are obliged, more than any others, to say what they *mean* by an improvement of the individual's general condition, and hence what they mean by a satisfactory or ideal life, are personality theory and psychotherapy. Both are concerned with undesirable symptoms and their removal, but their interest often goes beyond this negative result to a positive conception of "mental health," which is close to what we have been discussing under the name of "happiness." The fact that this conception is logically connected with the medical therapy or with objective tests and controlled studies gives it a significance lacking in earlier theories. (1967:322)

With regard to the other traditional problems of philosophy, metaphysics, epistemology, ethics, esthetics, and logic, the situation is different for each. Metaphysics has become a branch of astronomy or history, and speculations about the origin of the world are no longer taken seriously. Epistemology represents the interface between the physical world and human cognition. Thus, depending on each for its data, Piaget originated the influential and profound school of genetic epistemology. Neither ethics nor esthetics can be pursued without reference to psychology. Logic and mathematics have become one; each could be considered a part of the other.

Thus, in philosophy too there are widespread historical changes which per se have nothing to do with psychoanalysis. Levi wrote: "It is a paradox faced by all of those who attempt to write the history of philosophy that the 'philosophy' whose history they write probably would not have been defined by any two of the major figures whom they judge it fitting to include in their account in the same way" (*Encyc. Brit.*, 15:613).

Another consideration is that the reflections on the good life that have come from the minds of speculative philosophers through the ages have not been very different from the reflections of wise men among the most primitive of peoples. Radin, in presenting primitive man as philosopher, wrote:

> [The] higher natures among primitive people can have a true moral sense and an intuitive insight into right and wrong. That they can also possess true wisdom, that they can envisage life in a critical and half-pessimistic manner, that they can face fortune and misfortune objectively and with equanimity, that they can in fact accept life in all its realities and still enjoy it, for that the reader is not prepared any more than the ethnologist who discovers it. And yet there is no escaping recognition of the fact, for it is borne in upon him in numerous songs, speeches, myths and proverbs, and is to be encountered in every tribe in the world. (1955:98)

Through the ages there have been many philosophical or religio-philosophical systems that have attempted to help men with their numerous dilemmas. Sometimes these philosophies had a rather sophisticated form of psychotherapy. Thus, the Sophists in ancient Greece would talk to people, attempting in this way to help them with their problems. The two Greek mottos "Know thyself" and "All things in moderation" could be considered two of the cornerstones of analytic theory. The world *sophist* has persisted in our language, with the dual meanings of "sophistry," or fraudulently persuasive arguments, and "sophisticated," or more cultivated than the masses—the kind of ambivalence that our patients display toward us today. Stoicism, which flourished for several centuries before and after Christ, elevated itself to a position above the rest of mankind, attempting to offer consolation, composure, and fortitude to many in times of trouble and despair.

Epicurus, another Hellenistic philosopher, presented a philosophy of defense in a troubled world and attracted a large following (not unlike that of existentialism today). The major Epicurean principle was to pursue pleasure and avoid pain, again similar to some underlying psychoanalytic ideas.

There have been other attempts in the past and present to combine psychotherapy with some kind of world religion or a more philosophical orientation. Within psychoanalysis many ideas that are philosophical in the sense of a possible choice among many alternatives are offered instead of having "therapeutic" value. Thus, Maslow's notion of self-actualization has aroused a wide resonance, even though its meaning is by no means entirely clear, nor is it clear how it is to be achieved.

On the current scene, and especially since World War II, the philosophy that has attracted the widest attention has been existentialism; for many people it has proved to be the most attractive alternative to psychoanalysis. However, as usual its definition is obscure. Rollo May, its leading American spokesman, defines it as "the endeavor to understand man by cutting below the cleavage between subject and object that has bedeviled Western thought and science since shortly after the Renaissance" (May et al. 1958:10). Beyond that, existentialism, which preaches living in the here-and-now because there is nothing else, is widely seen as a philosophy of despair. It also makes minimal demands on the subject.

By contrast, the philosophy of psychoanalysis derives from a rational optimism about the human condition and the possibilities of improving it. Opposed to it is the emphasis on irrational demonic forces in human nature and the world, beyond the capacity of any one individual or even one country to combat. With the added threat of a nuclear holocaust, which many believe will occur in this century, the sweet reasonableness of psychoanalysis becomes too much for many people to take.

Summary

This book began with an attempt to clarify the concepts of narcissism and the self, especially in their relationship to society. In the historical introduction it was shown that these concepts go back a long way, antedating the technical considerations of psychoanalysis. Freud brought them into the psychoanalytic purview in his 1914 paper on narcissism.

However, this paper, while revolutionary in some respects, was sometimes in serious error. The revision of the libido theory that was introduced there, with its attendant metapsychological distinctions, was quite unnecessary; the notion of an ego-libido is contradictory in terms and should be abandoned, as it has been by many. Likewise, though narcissism is considered really for the first time in analytic history, it is given a rather peculiar twist, especially with the notion of primary narcissism. This confuses cognitive incapacity with emotional incapacity and has remained a stormy petrel ever since.

A major distinction not sufficiently emphasized by Freud is that between healthy and unhealthy narcissism. Likewise, the basic emotional split in the infant, between love and hate, while not given prominence by Freud, was stressed by a number of his followers. Narcissism must, therefore, if it is to be healthy, be based on self-love, which in turn derives from the love received in earliest infancy. Secondary narcissism, based at some level on hatred, is another defensive posture to be understood like any other defensive mechanism.

Although the notion goes back all the way to the beginning of psychoanalysis, the concept of an introject, or introjected object, later the superego, is commonly traced back to the 1914 paper. This object then becomes an important, if not vital, driving force within the individual. Later Klein was to clarify the further breakdown into the good object and the bad object, split apart for neurotic reasons. Splitting, projection, and projective identification have been essential aspects of psychoanalytic theory ever since.

Narcissism leads inevitably to the notion of the self. Here three strands were traced: first, the commonsense notion of the self, which was used freely by Freud and others in his immediate following; second, the exploration of the social self, peculiarly the product of the American School of philosophers and psychologists; and finally, the self psychology Kohut introduced in the 1970s, which totally disregarded the other two. Whatever is of value in each of these conceptualizations has to be integrated into the modern knowledge of the self.

In reviewing the development of the self, it was seen that again three stages can be distinguished. First, there is the early preverbal self, in the infant up to about one and a half years of age. This self has been most extensively explored and investigated by Freudian psychoanalysts, although more orthodox Freudian analysts have tended to disregard the self altogether. Second, there is the self-image of the growing child, which is intimately tied up with the family. This self has been described most fully by developmental and social psychologists. Finally, there is the self of the mature individual, which continues to change and develop throughout the entire life cycle. The material here derives from many different sources, including history and all the social sciences, as well as philosophy and religion.

It was also seen that when the self-concept was first introduced into psychoanalysis in the 1950s, the efforts of Freudian analysts were devoted to incorporating it into the tripartite structure of id, ego, and superego. In this effort they were singularly unsuccessful, so that the self and its concomitant identify remained a riddle for them. By contrast, the culturalist school could easily absorb the concept and all its corollaries.

Next, attention was focused on the social structure, particularly as it relates to the prevalence and understanding of neurosis. The old definitions of neurosis, such as an ego-id conflict, have all gone by the board in the growing recognition that whole cultures can and have become "neurotic," or emotionally disturbed, sometimes to the point of psychosis, at times even to the point of self-destruction. The analytic ideal was described as the philosophical doctrine most congenial to psychoanalytic thinking. Neurosis can best be defined as distance from this analytic ideal. Review of some contemporary literature indicated that this broadened image of neurosis has spread to considerable segments of the population.

The next few chapters considered the question of the group more intensely. In an examination of the relationship between the group and the individual, it was seen that the group plays an important role at every stage of the individual's life. Hence, the mere description of development without relating it to the group is incomplete. This applies especially to narcissism and the self, which is one reason why the efforts to incorporate the concepts of self and narcissism into the classical tripartite structure failed.

One chapter was devoted to a detailed consideration of the relationship between the self-image and the larger social order. It was seen that the self cannot be properly defined without considering this larger social order. In fact, the self differs considerably with different cultures, making it just as much of a cultural concept as an individual one.

Next, the connections between love, identity, and alienation were explored. Identity is used in a double sense, as the innermost individual aspects of a human being (his "true identity") and as an index of the groups to which he belongs. Since these two meanings are confusing, it was urged that the first ("the true identity") be reserved for the self-image, while the term identity should be used to describe the various groups to which the individual belongs. In consideration of the developmental process, the crucial role of love was again stressed. In the course of life the person moves from one group to another. Whether these groups are loving or hateful in their basic emotional attitudes is of central importance.

At a broader level, the romance of community was then investigated. There seems to be a virtually universal longing for an ideal community that would live in peace and harmony. Many have tried to reform their own society in this direction; others have tried to set up isolated artificial communities in which they could find what they were looking for. Inevitably frictions set in that disrupted the idealized notions of how human beings ought to behave. In examining the artificial communities it was found that virtually all seek love as a prime goal. Hence again whether the community is loving or hateful becomes crucial.

Finally, the implications of these considerations for psychoanalytic theory were examined. The major new concept introduced after Freud is that of culture or the group. The human being functions intrapsychically in terms of instincts, drives, and defenses. He also functions interpersonally in terms of the family and other human contacts. Finally, he functions as a member of a larger community, moving in life from one group to another. All three of these aspects of human life must be considered.

Thus, the careful scrutiny of the concepts of narcissism and the self leads to a broadening and deepening of psychoanalytic theory. Psychoanalysis must be viewed as the basis of a complete psychology and the foundation of a philosophy of living. In this process of broadening and deepening, all past formulations must be given due consideration, but no one is decisive. Freud's formulations remain basic but require considerable extension to accommodate the new findings.

BIBLIOGRAPHY

Abend, S., M. Porder, and M. Willick. 1983. *The Borderline Patient*. New York: International Universities Press.

Abraham, K. 1953. *Selected Papers on Psychoanalysis, 1927*. New York: Basic Books.

Abrams, S. 1979. "The psychological normalities." *Journal of the American Psychoanalytic Association* 27:821–835.

Adler, A. 1928. *The Practice and Theory of Individual Psychology*. New York: Humanities Press, 1951.

Ahlstrom, N. M. and R. J. Havighurst. 1971. *400 Losers*. San Francisco: Jossey-Bass.

Alexander, F. and T. French, eds. 1946. *Psychoanalytic Therapy*. New York: Ronald Press.

Alexander, F. 1950. *Psychosomatic Medicine*. New York: Norton.

Alexander, J. F. and R. E. Maloof. 1983. "Intervention with children experiencing problems in personality and social development." In Mussen, ed. *Handbook of Child Psychology*, 11:913–981.

Allport, G. W. 1954. *The Nature of Prejudice*. Cambridge, Mass.: Addison-Wesley.

Almond, R. 1974. *The Healing Community*. New York: Aronson.

Amoss, P. T. and S. Harrell, eds. 1981. *Other Ways of Growing Old*. Stanford, Calif.: Stanford University Press.

Amsterdam, B. 1972. "Mirror self-image reactions before age two." *Developmental Psychobiology* 5; 297–305.

Amsterdam, B. and M. Levitt. 1980. "Consciousness of self and painful self-consciousness." In A. J. Solnit et al., eds., *Psychoanalytic Study of the Child* 35:67–83. New Haven: Yale University Press.

Andreski, S., ed. 1974. *The Essential Comte, 1830–1842*. New York: Barnes and Noble.

Annual Review of Psychology. 1979. Palo Alto, Calif: Annual Reviews.

Anzieu, D. 1975. *L'Autoanalyse de Freud.* Paris: Presses Universities de France.

APA. 1975. *A Psychiatric Glossary. 4th Rev. Ed.* Washington, D.C.: American Psychiatric Association.

APA. 1981. *Diagnostic and Statistical Manual* (DSM III). Washington, D.C.: American Psychiatric Association.

Aptheker, H. 1971. *Afro-American History.* New York: Citadel Press.

Arieti, S. 1974. *Interpretation of Schizophrenia.* New York: Basic Books.

Arieti, S., ed. 1974–75. *American Handbook of Psychiatry.* 6 vols. New York: Basic Books.

Arlow, J. 1983. "Review of A. Goldberg, ed., *Advances in Self Psychology.*" *Psychoanalytic Quarterly* 52:445–452.

Arlow, J. and C. Brenner. 1969. "The psychopathology of the psychoses: a proposed revision." *International Journal of Psychoanalysis* 50:5–14.

Astin, A. W. 1977. *Four Critical Years.* San Francisco: Jossey-Bass.

Augustine. *The City of God.* New York: Image Books, 1958.

Bach, S. 1977. "On the narcissistic state of consciousness." *International Journal of Psychoanalysis* 58:209–233.

Bandura, A. 1977 *Social Learning Theory.* Englewood Cliffs, N.J.: Prentice-Hall.

Basch, M. F. 1981. "Selfobject disorders and psychoanalytic theory: A historical perspective." *Journal of the American Psychoanalytic Association,* 29:337–351.

Bayley, N. 1955. "On the growth of intelligence." *American Psychologist* 10:805–818.

Beach, F. A. 1976. "Sexual attractivity proceptivity and receptivity in female mammals." *Hormones and Behavior* 7:105–138.

Beavers, W. R. 1977 *Psychotherapy and Growth.* New York: Brunner/Mazel.

Becker, H. S. 1970. *Sociological Work: Method and Substance,* Chicago: Aldine.

Becker, H. et al., eds. 1968. *Institutions and The Person.* Chicago: Aldine.

Beckwith, L. 1979. "Prediction of emotional and social behavior." In J. Osofsky, ed., *Handbook of Infant Development,* pp. 671–706.

Beebe, B. and P. Sloate. 1982. "Assessment and treatment in mother-infant attunement in the first three years of life: a case history." *Psychoanalytic Inquiry* 1:601–624.

Beebe, B. and D. Stern. 1977. "Engagement-disengagement and early object experiences." In N. Freedman and S. Grand, eds., *Communicative Structures and Psychic Structures,* pp. 35–55.

Bell, R. A. et al. 1971. "Newborn and preschooler: Organization of behavior and relations between periods." *Monographs of the Society for Research in Child Development* 36:1–2 (Series 142).

Bellak, L., ed. 1979. *Disorders of the Schizophrenic Syndrome.* New York: Basic Books.

Bellak, L. and L. Goldsmith, eds. 1984. *The Broad Scope of Ego Function Assessment.* New York: Wiley.

Bellak, L., M. Hurvich, and H. Gediman. 1973. *Ego Functions in Normals, Neurotics, and Schizophrenics.* New York: Wiley.

Belsky, J., ed. 1982. *In the Beginning: Readings on Infancy.* New York: Columbia University Press.

Benedek, T. and E. J. Anthony, eds. 1970. *Parenthood: Its Psychology and Psychopathology.* Boston: Little Brown.

Benedict, R. 1934. *Patterns of Culture.* Boston: Houghton Mifflin.

Benedict, R. 1946. *The Chrysanthemum and the Sword,* Boston: Houghton Mifflin.

Berkovitz, I. H., ed. 1972. *Adolescents Grow in Groups.* New York: Brunner/ Mazel.

Bibring, E. 1947. "The So-called English school of psychoanalysis." *Psychoanalytic Quarterly* 16:69–93.

Bibring, G. L. 1959. "Some considerations of the psychological processes in pregnancy." In Ruth Eissler et al., eds., *Psychoanalytic Study of the Child* 14:113–121. New York: International Universities Press.

Biddle, B. J. 1979. *Role Theory: Expectations, Identities and Behaviors.* New York: Academic Press.

Bing, J. F., F. McLaughlin, and R. Marburg. 1959. "The metapsychology of narcissism." In Ruth Eissler, et al., eds., *Psychoanalytic Study of the Child* 14:9–28. New York: International Universities Press.

Bion, M. R. 1961. *Experiences in Groups.* New York: Basic Books.

Blanchard, P. 1953. "Masturbation fantasies of children and adolescents." *Bulletin of the Philadelphia Association for Psychoanalysis* 3:25–38.

Blanchard, P. 1954. *The Irish and Catholic Power.* London: Derek Verschoyle.

Blau, P. M. and D. D. Duncan. 1967. *The American Occupational Structure.* New York: Free Press.

Bleuler, M. 1978. *The Schizophrenic Disorders.* New Haven: Yale University Press.

Bloch, H. and A. Niederhoffer. 1958. *The Gang.* New York: Philosophical Library.

Bloch, S. and P. Reddaway. 1977. *Psychiatric Terror.* New York: Basic Books.

Blos, P. 1979. *The Adolescent Passage.* New York: International Universities Press.

Blumberg, H. H. et al. 1983. *Small Groups and Social Interaction* vol. 1. New York: Wiley.

Blumstein, P. and P. Schwartz. 1983. *American Couples.* New York: Morrow.

Bornstein, B. 1951. "On latency." In Ruth Eissler et al., eds., *Psychoanalytic Study of the Child,* 6:279–285. New York: International Universities Press.

Bornstein B. 1953. "Masturbation in the latency period." *Psychoanalytic Study of the Child,* 8:65–78. New York: International Universities Press.

Bott, E. 1971. *Family and Social Network.* London: Tavistock.

Bowen, M. 1981. "The use of family therapy in clinical practice." In R.J. Green and J.F. Framo, eds., *Family Therapy,* pp. 263–311.

Bower, T. 1971. "The object in the world of the infant." *Scientific American* 225:38–47.

Bower, T. 1976. "Receptive process in child development." *Scientific Amer.* 235:38–47.

Bowlby, J. 1969–80. *Attachment and Loss,* 3 vols. New York: Basic Books.

Boyer, L. B. 1979. *Childhood and Folklore.* New York: Psychohistory Press.

Boyer, L. B. and P. L. Giovacchini. 1980. *Psychoanalytic Treatment of Characterological and Schizophrenic Disorders*. New York: Jason Aronson.

Bradlee, B. and D. Van Atta. 1981. *Prophet of Blood.* New York: Putnam.

Brandon, R. 1977. *A Capitalist Romance.* New York: Lippincott.

Brazelton, T. B. 1973. *Neonatal Behavioral Assessment Scale.* (National Spastics Society Monograph). London: Heinemann.

Brazelton, T. B. 1976. "Discussant's comments." In T.D. Tjossem, ed., *Intervention Strategies for High Risk Infants and Young Children*, pp. 325–334.

Brenner, C. 1982. *The Mind in Conflict.* New York: International Universities Press.

Bridger, W. 1961. "Sensory habituation and discrimination in the human infant." *American Journal of Psychiatry* 118:991–996.

Brody, S. 1964. *Passivity: A Study of Its Development and Expression in Boys.* New York: International Universities Press.

Brody, S. 1981. "The concepts of attachment and bonding." *Journal of the American Psychoanalytic Association* 29:815–829.

Brody, S. and S. Axelrad. 1978. *Mothers, Fathers and Children.* New York: International Universities Press.

Brody, E. B. and F. C. Redlich, eds. 1952. *Psychotherapy with Schizophrenics.* New York: International Universities Press.

Broussard, E. R. and M. Hartner. 1971. "Further considerations regarding maternal perception of the first born." In J. Hellmuth, ed., *Exceptional Infant,* vol. 2. New York: Brunner/Mazel.

Brown, B. E., ed. 1983. *Great American Political Thinkers,* 2 vols. New York: Avon Books.

Brunswick, R. M. 1928. "A Supplement to Freud's "A History of an Infantile Neurosis." *International Journal of Psychoanalysis* 50:317–333.

Burckhardt, J. 1860. *The Civilization of the Renaissance in Italy.* 2 vols. New York: Harper, 1958.

Burr, A. R. 1909. *The Autobiography.* New York: Houghton Mifflin.

Buxbaum, E. 1980. "Between the oedipus complex and Adolescence: The quiet time." In S. Greenspan and G. Pollack, eds., *The Course of Life* pp. 121–136.

Caddux, C. J. 1982. *The Early Christian Attitude to War.* New York: Seabury Press.

Calef, V. and E. M. Weinshel. 1979. "The new psychoanalysis and psychoanalytic revisionism: Book review Essay on Borderline conditions and pathological narcissism." *Psychoanalytic Quarterly* 48:470–491.

Call, J. D., E. Galenson, and A. L. Tyson, eds. 1983. *Frontiers of Infant Psychiatry.* New York: Basic Books.

Cath, S. H., A. R. Gurwitt, and J. M. Ross, eds. 1982. *Father and Child.* Boston: Little, Brown.

Cancro, R. 1983. "The treatment of the severe schizophrenic patient." In A. Gralnick, ed., *Treatment of the Seriously Ill Psychiatric Patient.* pp. 113–128. Port Chester, N.Y.: High Point Foundation.

Chapman, J. R. and M. Gates. *The Victimization of Women.* Beverly Hills, Calif.: Sage, 1978.

Chattah, L. 1983. Reporter. "Metapsychology: Its cultural and scientific roots." *American Psychoanalytic Association,* 31:689–698.

Cheetham, N. 1982. *Keepers of the Keys.* New York: Scribner.

Chess, S. and A. Thomas. 1977. *Temperament and Development.* New York: Brunner/Mazel.

Chiland, C. 1982. "A new look at fathers." In A.J. Solnit et al., eds., *Psychoanalytic Study of the Child* 37:367–379. New Haven: Yale University Press.

Chilman, Z. S. 1983. *Adolescent Sexuality in a Changing American Society.* New York: Wiley.

Chinoy, E. 1955. *Automobile Workers and the American Dream.* Boston: Beacon Press.

Chisholm, J. S. *Navajo Infancy.* 1983. New York: Aldine.

Clarke, A. and A. D. B. Clarke, eds. 1976. *Early Experience: The Myth and the Evidence.* New York: Free Press.

Cohler, B. J. and H. U. Grunebaum. 1981. *Mothers, Grandmothers, and Daughters.* New York: Wiley.

Cohen, R. S., B. J. Cohler, and S. H. Weissman, eds. 1984. *Parenthood: A Psychodynamic Perspective.* New York: Guilford Press.

Cohen, Y. 1964. *The Transition from Childhood To Adolescence.* Chicago: Aldine.

Colarusso, C. A. and R. A. Nemiroff. 1981. *Adult Development.* New York: Plenum.

Coles, R. 1970. *Erik Erikson: The Growth of His Work.* Boston: Little Brown.

Collins, G. 1983. "U.S. social tolerance of drugs found on rise." *New York Times* March 21:B1–5.

Committee on Public Information. 1975. *A Psychiatric Glossary.* 4th ed. New York: Basic Books.

Compton, A. 1983a. "The current status of the psychoanalytic theory of instinctual drives. I: Drive concept, classification and development." *Psychoanalytic Quarterly* 52:364–401.

Compton, A. 1983b. "The current status of the psychoanalytic theory of instinctual drives. II: The relationship of the drive concept to structures, regulatory principles and objects." *Psychoanalytic Quarterly* 52:402–426.

Condon, W. and L. Sander. 1974. "Neonatal Movement is synchronized with Adult speech." *Science* 183:99–101.

Connor, L. 1984. "The unbounded self: Balinese therapy in theory and practice." In Marsella and White, eds. *Cultural Conceptions of Mental Health and Therapy,* pp. 257-268.

Conway, F. and J. Siegelman. 1982. *Holy Terror.* Garden City, N.Y.: Doubleday.

Cooley, C. H. 1902. *Human Nature and the Social Order.* New York: Schocken Books.

Cuber, J. and P. Harroff. 1965. *The Significant Americans.* New York: Appleton-Century.

Curtis, M., ed. 1981. *The Great Political Theories.* 2 vols. New York: Avon.

Davenport, M. 1979. *Mozart.* New York: Avon Books.

Demos, J. and S. S. Boocock, eds. 1978. *Turning Points: Historical and Sociological Essays on the Family.* Chicago: University of Chicago Press.

De Mause, L., ed. 1974. *The History of Childhood.* New York: Psychohistory Press.

Dennis, W., ed. 1948. *Readings in the History of Psychology.* New York: Appleton-Century-Crofts.

Deutsch, H. 1945. *The Psychology of Women,* 2 vols. New York: Grune and Stratton.

Devereux, G. 1980. *Basic Problems of Ethnopsychiatry.* Chicago: University of Chicago Press.

Dewey, J. 1939. *Intelligence in the Modern World. John Dewey's Philosophy.* New York: Random House Library.

Dohrenwend, B. P. et al. 1980. *Mental Illness in the U.S.: Epidemiological Estimates.* New York: Praeger.

Dollard, J. 1957 *Caste and Class in a Southern Town.* Garden City, N.Y.: Doubleday.

Dowley, A. 1982. *Class and Community: The Industrial Revolution in Lynn.* Cambridge: Harvard University Press.

Driver, H. E. 1969. *Indians of North America.* Chicago: University of Chicago Press.

Dubois, W. E. B. 1940. *Dusk of Dawn: An Essay Toward an Autobiography of a Race Concept.* New York: Harcourt, Brace.

East-West Population Institute. 1975. *The Value of Children: A Cross-National Study,* 5 vols. Honolulu: East-West Center.

Ehrenreich, B. 1984. *The Hearts of Men.* Garden City, N.Y.: Doubleday Anchor Books.

Ehrenreich, B. and D. English. 1978. *For Her Own Good.* Garden City, N.Y.: Doubleday.

Eidelberg, L. A. 1945 "A contribution to the study of the masturbation fantasy." *International Journal of Psychoanalysis* 25:127–137.

Eisenstein, V., ed. 1956. *Neurotic Interaction in Marriage.* New York: Basic Books.

Eissler, K. 1968. "Irreverent remarks about the present and the future of psychoanalysis." *International Journal of Psychoanalysis* 50:461–471.

Emde, R. N. 1981. "Changing models of infancy and the nature of early development: remodeling the foundation." *Journal of American Psychoanalytic Association* 29:179–219.

Emde, R. N. and R. J. Harmon, eds. 1982. *The Development of Attachment and Affiliative Systems.* New York: Plenum Press.

Emerson, R. W. 1841. In Carl Bode and Malcolm Cowley, eds., *The Portable Emerson.* New York: Penguin Books. 1981.

Erikson, E. 1950. *Childhood and Society.* New York: Norton.

Erikson, E. 1959. *Identity and the Life Cycle.* New York: International Universities Press.

Erikson, E. 1968. *Identity Youth and Crisis.* New York: Norton.

Erikson, E. 1974. *Dimensions of a New Identity.* New York: Norton.

Escalona, J. K. and G. M. Heider 1959. "Prediction and outcome." *Menninger Clinic Monograph Series, No. 14.* London: Imago.

Escalona, S. K. 1968. *The Roots of Individuality: Normal Patterns of Development in Infancy.* Chicago: Aldine.

Fairbairn, R. 1954. *An Object Relations Theory of Personality.* New York: Basic Books.

Federn, P. 1929. *Ego Psychology and the Psychoses.* New York: Basic Books, 1952.

Federn, P. 1934. "The analysis of psychotics." *International Journal of Psychoanalysis* 15:209–214.

Fenichel, O. 1945. *The Psychoanalytic Theory of Neurosis.* New York: Norton.

Field, T. M. et al, eds. 1982. *Review of Human Development.* New York: Wiley.

Fine, R. 1973. *The Development of Freud's Thought.* New York; Jason Aronson.

Fine, R. 1975a. *Psychoanalytic Psychology.* New York: Aronson.

Fine, R. 1975b. "The bankruptcy of behaviorism." *Psychoanalytic Review,* pp. 131-151.

Fine, R. 1979a. *A History of Psychoanalysis.* New York: Columbia University Press.

Fine, R. 1979b. *The Intimate Hour.* New York: Avery.

Fine, R. 1981. *The Psychoanalytic Vision.* New York: Free Press.

Fine, R. 1983. *The Logic of Psychology.* Washington, D.C.: University Press of America.

Fine, R. 1984. "The analytic triad." *Current Issues in Psychoanalytic Practice* 1 (3):3-34.

Fine, R. 1985. *The Meaning of Love in Human Experience.* New York: Wiley.

Fine, R. 1986. *The Forgotten Man.* New York: Haworth Press.

Fingarette, H. 1963. *The Self in Transformation.* New York: Basic Books.

Finley, M. I. 1983. *Economy and Society in Ancient Greece.* New York: Pelican Books.

Fisher, S. and R. G. Greenberg. 1977. *The Scientific Credibility of Freud's Theories and Therapy.* New York: Basic Books.

Flavell, J. 1963. *The Development Psychology of Jean Piaget.* New York: Van Nostrand.

Fortes, M. 1969. *Kinship and the Social Order.* Chicago: Aldine.

Fortes, M. 1977. "Custom and conscience in anthropological perspective." *International Review of Psychoanalysis* 4:127–154.

Foucault, M. 1973. *Madness and Civilization.* New York: Random House.

Fox, R. W. 1978. *So Far Disordered in Mind: Insanity In California 1870–1930.* Berkeley: University of California Press.

Fraiberg, S., ed. 1980. *Clinical Studies In Infant Mental Health. The First Year of Life.* New York: Basic Books.

Franklin, B. 1790. *The Autobiography of Benjamin Franklin.* New York: Macmillan, 1962.

Freedman, J. L., D. O. Sears, and J. M. Carlsmith. 1981. *Social Psychology.* 4th ed., Englewood Cliffs, N.J.: Prentice-Hall.

Freedman, N. and S. Grand, eds. 1977. *Communicative Structures and Psychic Structures.* New York: Plenum Press.

Freud, S. *The Standard Edition of The Psychological Works of Sigmund Freud.* 24 vols. James Strackey, ed. London: Hogarth Press; New York: Macmillan, 1953-1970. All references to Freud, unless otherwise indicated are to volumes in the Standard Edition.

Freud, S. and C. Jung. *The Freud-Jung Letters.* William McGuire, ed. Princeton, N.J.: Princeton University Press, 1974.

Freud S. and O. Pfister. *Psychoanalysis and Faith: The Letters of Sigmund Freud and Oskar Pfister.* Heinrich Meng and Ernst Freud, eds. New York: Basic Books, 1963.

Friedan B. 1963. *The Feminine Mystique.* New York: Dell.

Friedan, B. 1981. *The Second Stage.* New York: Simon and Schuster.

Fries, M. E. 1977. "Longitudinal study: Prenatal period to parenthood." *Journal of the American Psychoanalytic Association* 25:115–132.

Frondizi, R. 1971. *The Nature of the Self.* London: Feffer and Simons.

Frosch, J. 1983. *The Psychotic Process.* New York: International Universities Press.

Gabbard, G. O. 1984. "Further contributions to the understanding of fright: Narcissistic issues." *Journal of American Psychoanalytic Association* 31:423–442.

Gagliardo, J. G. 1969. *From Pariah to Patriot.* Lexington: University Press of Kentucky.

Galenson, E. and H. Roiphe. 1981. *The Infantile Origins of Sexual Identity.* New York: International Universities Press.

Gardell, B. and G. Johansson, eds. 1981. *Working Life.* New York: Wiley.

Gay, P. and R. K. Webb. 1973. *Modern Europe.* New York: Harper and Row.

Gear, M. C., M. A. Hill, and E. C. Liendo. 1981. *Working Through Narcissism.* New York: Aronson.

Gecas, V. 1982. "The self-concept." *Annual Review of Sociology,* 8:1–33. Palo Alto, Calif.: Annual Reviews.

Gecas, V. and M. L. Schwalbe. 1983. "Beyond the looking-glass self: Social structure and efficacy-based self-esteem. *Social Psychology Quarterly* 46:77–88.

Geertz, C. 1975. "On the nature of anthropological understanding." *American Scientist* 63:47–53.

Gelfand, M. 1964. "Psychiatric disorders as recognized by the Shona." In A. Kiev, ed., *Magic, Faith, and Healing,* pp. 156-173.

Gergen, V. J. and M. M. Gergen. 1981. *Social Psychology.* New York: Harcourt, Brace, Jovanovich.

Gesell, A. L. and L. B. Ames 1937. "Early evidence of individuality in the human infant." *Scientific Monthly* 45: 217–225.

Gilman, C. P. 1975. *The Living of Charlotte Perkins Gilman: An Autobiography*. New York: Harper Colophon Books Books.

Gittins, D. 1982. *Fairsex: Family Size and Structure in Britain, 1900–1939*. New York: St. Martin's Press.

Glick, J. and K. A. Clarke-Stewart 1978. *The Development of Social Understanding*. New York: Gardner Press.

Glover, E. 1966. "Metapsychology or metaphysics. A psychoanalytic essay." *Psychoanalytic Quarterly* 35:173–190.

Goffman, E. 1959. *The Presentation of the Self in Everyday Life*. Garden City, N.Y.: Doubleday.

Goffman, E. 1967. *Interaction Ritual*. New York: Doubleday Anchor.

Goldberg, A. 1980. *Advances in Self Psychology*. New York: International Universities Press.

Goldfarb, W. 1974. *Growth and Change of Schizophrenic Children: A Longitudinal Study*. New York: Wiley.

Goode, W. J. 1956. *Women in Divorce*. New York: Free Press.

Goode, W. J. 1982. *The Family*. Englewood Cliffs, N.J.: Prentice-Hall.

Goodman, G. 1972. *Companionship Therapy*. San Francisco: Jossey-Bass.

Goody, J. 1983. *The Development of the Family and Marriage in Europe*. New York: Cambridge University Press.

Gordon, M. M. 1963. *Social Class in American Sociology*. New York: McGraw-Hill.

Gordon, M., ed. 1978. *The American Family in Social-Historical Perspective*. New York: St. Martin's Press.

Gorer, G. 1948. *The American People*. New York: Norton.

Goslin, D., ed 1969. *Handbook of Socialization Theory and Research*. Chicago: Rand McNally.

Gottfried, A. W., ed. 1984. *Home Environment and Early Cognitive Development*. New York: Academic Press.

Goubert, P. 1970. *Louis XIV and Twenty Million Frenchmen*. New York Vintage.

Gould, R. L. 1978. *Transformations: Growth and Change in Adult Life*. New York: Simon and Schuster.

Greeley, A. M. 1982. "American Catholics going their own way." *New York Times Magazine*, October 10.

Green R. J. and J. L. Framo eds. 1981. *Family Therapy: Major Contributions*. New York: International Universities Press.

Greenspan, S. I. 1980. "Analysis of a five-and-a half-year old girl: Implications for a dyadic-phallic phase of development." *Jounal of the American Psychoanalytic Association*, 28:575–603.

Greenspan, S. I., 1982. "The second other: The role of the father in early personality formation and the dyadic-phallic phase of development." In S.H. Cath, A.R. Gurwitt, and J.M. Ross, eds., *Father and Child*, pp. 123–138.

Greenspan, S. I. and G. H. Pollock, eds. 1980. *The Course of Life: Psychoanalytic Contributions Toward Understanding Personality Development*, 3 vols. Washington, D.C.: U.S. Department of Health and Human Services.

Gunnar, M. R., K. Senior, and W. W. Hartup. 1984. "Peer presence and the exploratory behavior of eighteen and thirty-month-old children." *Child Development* 55:1103–1109.

Guntrip, H. 1973. *Psychoanalytic Theory, Therapy, and the Self*. New York: Basic Books.

Hallowell, A. I. 1955. *Culture and Experience*. Philadelphia: University of Pennsylvania Press.

Handlin, O. and M. F. Handlin. 1971. *Facing Life: Youth and The Family in American History*. Boston: Little, Brown.

Hanly, C. and J. Masson. 1976. "A critical examinations of the new narcissism." *International Journal of Psychoanalysis* 55:49–66.

Harner, M. 1973. *The Jivaro*. Garden City, N.Y.: Doubleday Anchor Books.

Harris, M. 1968. *The Rise of Anthropological Theory*. New York: Crowell.

Harrison, J. F. C. 1969. *Quest for the New Moral World*. New York: Scribner.

Harticollis, P. 1983. *Time and Timelessness*. New York: International Universities Press.

Hartmann, H. 1939. *Ego Psychology and the Problem of Adaptation*. New York: International Universities Press.

Hartmann, H. 1959. "Psychoanalysis as a scientific theory." In H. Hartmann, *Essays in Ego Psychology*, pp. 318–352.

Hartmann, H. 1964. *Essays in Ego Psychology*. New York: International University Press.

Hartmann, H., E. Kris, and R. Loewenstein. 1946. "Comments on the formation of psychic structure." In Ruth Eissler et al., eds., *Psychoanalytic Study of the Child*, 2:11–38. New York: International Universities Press.

Hartog, J., J. R. Audy, and Y. A. Cohen, eds. 1980. *The Anatomy of Loneliness*. New York: International Universities Press.

Haskell, T. L. 1977. *The Emergence of Professional Social Science*. Urbana: University of Illinois Press.

Haas, A. 1979. *Teenage Sexuality*. New York: Macmillan.

Heer, F. 1962. *The Medieval World*. New York: New American Library.

Hegel, G. M. F. 1807. *The Phenomenology of Spirit*. New York: Oxford University Press, 1977.

Heinicke, C. M. and I. Westheimer. 1965. *Brief Separations*. New York: International Universities Press.

Herdt, G. H., ed. 1982. *Rituals of Manhood: Male Initiation in Papua, New Guinea*. Berkeley: University of California Press.

Hermann, I. 1936. "Sich-Anklammern, Auf-suche-Gehen. (To cling and to go in search)." *Internationale Zeitschrift Fuer Psychoanalyse* 22:349–370.

Hertzberg, F. 1966. *Work and the Nature of Man*. New York: World.

Herzog, J. M. 1982. "On father hunger: The father's role in the modulation of aggressive drive and fantasy." In S.H. Cath, A.R. Gurwitt and J.M. Ross *Father and Child*, pp. 163–174.

Hillery, G. A., Jr. 1972. *Communal Organizations: A Study of Local Societies*. Chicago: University of Chicago Press.

Hinchliffe, M. K. et al. 1978. *The Melancholy Marriage*. New York: Wiley.

Hollingshead, A. B. and F. C. Redlich. 1958. *Social Class and Mental Illness*. New York: Wiley.

Honzik, M. P. and D. W. MacFarlane. 1963. "Personality development and intellectual functioning from 21 months to 40 years." In L. F. Jarvik, C. Eisdorfer, and J. Blum, eds., *Intellectual Changes From Childhood Functioning in Adults: Psychological and Biological Aspects*. New York: Springer.

Hook, S., ed. 1959. *Psychoanalysis, Scientific Method, and Philosophy*. New York: New York University Press.

Hopkins, K, 1978. *Conquerors and Slaves*. New York: Cambridge University Press.

Horney, K. 1928. "The problem of the monogamous ideal." *International Journal of Psychoanalysis* 9:318–330.

Horney, K. 1937. *New Ways in Psychoanalysis*. New York: Norton.

Hosken, F. P. 1979. *The Hosken Report: Genital and Sexual Mutilation of Females*. Lexington Mass.: Womens' International Network News.

Howitt, A. W. 1904. *The Native Tribes of Southeast Australia*. New York: Macmillan.

Hoyt, E. P. 1983. *The Kamikazes*. New York: Arbor House.

Hsu, F. L. K. 1961. *Psychological Anthropology*. Homewood Ill.: Dorsey.

Ickes, W. and W. Knowles, eds. 1982. *Personality, Roles, and Social Behavior*. New York: Springer.

Inglis, F. 1981. *The Promise of Happiness: Value and Meaning In Children's Fiction*. New York: Cambridge University Press.

Inkeles, A. and D. J. Levinson. 1968. "National character: The study of modal personality and sociocultural systems." In G. Lindzey and E. Aronson, eds., *Handbook of Social Psychology*, 4:418–506. 2d ed. Cambridge, Mass.: Addison-Wesley.

Jacobson, E. 1964. *The Self and the Object World*. New York: International Universities Press.

Jaffe, Y. and Y. Yinon. 1983. "Collective aggression: The group-individual paradigm in the study of collective antisocial behavior." In H.H. Blumberg et al., eds., *Small Groups and Social Interaction*, pp. 267–275.

Jaher, F. C., ed. 1975. *The Rich, the Wellborn, and the Powerful*. Secaucus, N.J.: Citadel Press.

James, W. 1890. *Principles of Psychology, 1890*. New York: Dover. 1950.

James, W. 1902. *The Varieties of Religious Experience*. New York: Random House, Modern Library

James, W. 1971. *The Essential Writings*. New York: Harper Touchbooks.

JAPA. *Journal of the American Psychoanalytic Association*. New York: International Univerities Press.

Jarvis, E. 1971. *Insanity and Ideology in Massachusetts, 1855*. Cambridge: Harvard University Press.

Jencks, C. et al. 1979. *Who Gets Ahead?* New York: Basic Boods.

Jensen, A. R. 1980. *Bias in Mental Testing*. New York: Free Press.

Jersild, A. T. 1960. *Child Psychology*. Englewood Cliffs, N.J.: Prentice-Hall.

Jespersen, O. 1922. *Language, Its Nature, Development and Origin*. London: George Allen and Unwin.

Jones, E. 1920. "A linguistic factor in English characterology." In: E. Jones, *Essays in Applied Psychoanalysis*, pp. 88–94. London: Hogarth Press and The Institute of Psychoanalysis, 1951.

Jones, E. 1929. "Psychoanalysis and psychiatry." In E. Jones, *Collected Papers on Psychoanalysis*, pp. 365–378. 5th ed. London: Bailliere Tindall and Cox, 1948.

Jones, E. 1953–57. *The Life and Work of Sigmund Freud*, 3 vol. New York: Basic Books.

Jones, H. E. 1960. "The longitudinal method in the study of personality." In I. Iscoe and H. Stevenson, eds., *Personality Development in Children*. Austin: University of Texas.

Juel, N. N. 1980. *Individual and Environment. Monozygotic Twins Reared Apart*. New York: International Universities Press.

Jung, C. G. 1935. *Analytical Psychology: Its Theory and Practice*. New York: Pantheon, 1968.

Jung, C. G. 1938. *Basic Writings*. New York: Modern Library, 1959.

Jung, C. G. *Abstracts of The Collected Works of C. G. Jung*. Rockville,Md.: Information Planning Associates 1976.

Kagan, J. 1971. *Change and Continuity in Infancy*. New York: Wiley.

Kamerman, S. B. and C. D. Hayes, eds. 1982. *Families That Work: Children In A Changing World*. Washington, D.C.: National Academy Press.

Kamter, R. M. 1976. "The romance of community: International communities as intensive group experiences." In M. Rosenbaum and A. Snadowsky, ed., *The Intensive Group Experience*, pp. 146–185.

Kanter, R. S. and B. A. Stein, eds. 1979. *Life in Organizations*. New York: Basic Books.

Kaplan, J. 1980. *Walt Whitman: A Life*. New York: Bantam Books.

Kardiner, A. 1939. *The Individual and His Society*. New York: Columbia University Press.

Kardiner, A. 1945. *The Psychological Frontiers of Society*. New York: Columbia University Press.

Karon, B. and G. Vandenbos 1983. *Psychotherapy of Schizophrenia: The Treatment of Choice*. New York: Jason Aronson.

Katz, M. M. and M. S. Konner. 1981. "The role of the father: an anthropological perspective." In M. Lamb, ed., *The Role of the Father in Child Development*, pp. 155–186.

Keesing, R. M. 1982. "Introduction: Toward a multidimensional understanding of role initiation." In G.H. Herdt, ed., *Rituals of Manhood*, pp. 1–43.

Kegan, R. 1982. *The Evolving Self*. Cambridge: Harvard University Press.

Kelly, A. 1981. *Eleanor of Aquitaine and The Four Kings*. Cambridge: Harvard University Press.

Kernberg, O. F. 1969. "A contribution to the ego-psychological critique of the Kleinian school." *International Journal of Psychoanalysis* 50:317–333.

Kernberg, O. f. 1975. *Borderline Conditions and Pathological Narcissism*. New York: Aronson.

Kernberg, O. F. 1976. *Object Relations Theory and Clinical Psychoanalysis*. New York: Aronson.

Kernberg, O. 1981. "An overview of Edith Jacobson's contributions." In S. Tuttman, C. Kaye and M. Zimmerman, eds., *Object and Self*, pp. 103–128.

Kiev, A., ed. 1964. *Magic, Faith, and Healing*. Glencoe, Ill,: Free Press.

Kinsey, A. C. et al. 1948. *Sexual Behavior in the Human Male*. Philadelphia: Saunders.

Kinsey, A. C. et al. 1953. *Sexual Behavior in the Human Female*. Philadelphia: Saunders.

Klein, M. 1948. *Contributions to Psychoanalysis 1921–1945*. London: Hogarth Press.

Kleinman, A. 1980. *Patients and Healers in the Context of Culture*. Berkeley: University of California Press.

Knutson, J. N., ed. 1973. *Handbook of Political Psychology*. San Francisco: Jossey-Bass.

Kohn, N. 1977. *Social Competence, Symptoms and Under-Achievement In Childhood: A Longitudinal Perspective*. New York: Wiley.

Kohut, H. 1966. "Forms and transformations of narcissism."*Journal of the American Psychoanalytic Association* 14:243–272.

Kohut, H. 1971. *The Analysis of the Self*. New York: International Universities Press.

Kohut, H. 1977. *The Restoration of the Self*. New York: International Universities Press.

Kohut, H. 1984. *How Does Analysis Cure?* Chicago: University of Chicago Press.

Krieger, L. 1970. *Mothers in Poverty*. Chicago: Aldine.

Kris, E. 1975. "The study of variations of early parental attitudes: A preliminary report." In E. Kris, ed., *Selected Papers*, pp. 114–150.

Kris, E. 1975. *Selected Papers*. New Haven: Yale University Press.

Kubie, L. and H. Israel. 1955. "Say you're sorry." In Ruth Eissler et al., eds., *Psychoanalytic Study of the Child* 10:289–299. New York: International University Press.

Labarre, W. 1961. "Psychoanalysis in anthropology." In J. Masserman, ed., *Science and Psychoanalysis*, 4:10–20. New York: Grune and Stratton.

Laing, R. D. 1969. *Self and Others*. New York: Penguin Books.

Lamb, M. E., ed. 1981. *The Role of the Father in Child Development*. New York: Wiley.

Lambert, B. 1964. "Fosterage in the Northern Gilbert Islands." *Ethnology* 3:232–f258.

Landauer, K. 1924. "Passive technik: Zur analyse narzissisticher erkrankungen." *Internationale Zeitschrift fuer Aerztliche Psychoanalyse* 10:415–422.

Langbaum, R. 1982. *The Mysteries of Identity: A Theme in Modern Literature*. Chicago: University of Chicago Press.

Laplanche, J. and J. B. Pontalis. 1973. *The Language of Psychoanalysis*. New York: Norton.

Lasswell, H. 1939. *Psychopathology and Politics*. Chicago: University of Chicago Press.

Lasswell, H. 1948. *Power and Personality*. New York: Norton.

Lea, H. C. 1866. *The Duel and the Oath*. Philadelphia: University of Pennsylvania Press, 1974.

Lea, H. C. 1866. *The Ordeal*. Philadelphia: University of Pennsylvania Press, 1973.

Le Bon, G. 1903. *The Crowd: A Study of the Popular Mind*. London: Unwin.

Lederer, W. J. and D. D. Jackson. 1968. *The Mirages of Marriage*. New York: Norton.

Levi, A. 1978. "A History of western philosophy." *Encyclopedia Britannica* 4:261–275.

Levine, R. A. 1973. *Culture, Behavior, and Personality*. Chicago: Aldine.

Levinson, D. J. et al. 1978. *The Seasons of a Man's Life*. New York: Knopf.

Levy, D. 1943. *Maternal Overprotection*. New York: Norton.

Levy, R. I. 1964. *Tahitians*. Chicago: University of Chicago Press.

Lewis M. and J. Brooks-Gunn, 1979. *Social Cognition and the Acquisition of Self*. New York: Plenum Press.

Lewis, O. 1966a. "The Culture of Poverty." In O. Lewis, ed., *Anthropological Essays*, pp. 67–80.

Lewis, O. 1966b. *La Vida*. New York: Random House.

Lewis, O. 1970. *Anthropological Essays*. New York: Random House.

Licht, H. 1932. *Sexual Life in Ancient Greece*. London: Abbey Library.

Lichtenberg, J. D. 1981. "Implications for Psychoanalytic Theory of Research on the Neonate." *International Review of Psychonalysis* 8:35–52.

Lichtenberg, J. D. 1983. *Psychoanalysis and Infant Research*. Hillsdale, N.J.: Erlbaum.

Lichtenberg, J. D. and S. Kaplan, eds. 1983. *Reflections on Self Psychology*. Hillsdale, N.J.: Analytic Press.

Lichtenstein, H. 1977. *The Dilemma of Human Identity*. New York: Aronson.

Lifton, R. J. 1963. *Thought Reform and the Psychology of Totalism*. New York: Norton.

Lifton, R. J. 1970a. *History and Human Survival*. New York: Random House.

Lifton, R. J. 1970b. *The Life of the Self*. New York: Simon and Schuster.

Linton, R. 1939. "Marquesan culture." In A. Kardiner, *The Individual and his Society*.

Linton, R. 1945. *The Cultural Background of Personality*. New York: Appleton-Century-Crofts.

Lippman, S. et al. 1983. "Using pulse rate to assess the severity of psychosis." *Hospital and Community Psychiatry* 34:739–741.

Liss, M. B., ed. 1983. *Social and Cognitive Skills: Sex Roles and Children's Play*. New York: Academic Press.

Lynd, R. S. and H. M. Lynd. 1929. *Middletown*. New York: Harcourt Brace.

Lyons, J. O. 1978. *The Invention of the Self*. New York: Feffer and Simmons.

Maas, H. S. and J. A. Kuypers. 1974. *From Thirty to Seventy*. San Francisco: Jossey-Bass.

MacAndrew, C. and R. B. Edgerton. 1969. *Drunken Comportment: A Social Explanation*. Chicago: Aldine.

McClelland, D. C. 1961. *The Achieving Society*. Princeton: Van Nostrand.

Maccoby, E. E. and C. N. Jacklin. 1974. *The Psychology of Sex Differences*. Stanford, Calif.: Stanford University Press.

Macfarlane, A. 1975. "Olfaction in the development of social preferences in the human neonate." In *Ciba Foundation Symposium 33*, pp. 103–117. Amsterdam: Elsevier.

MacFarlane, J. 1964. "Comments." In *Parent-Infant Interaction: CIBA Foundation Symposium 33*, pp. 103–118. New York: Elsevier.

McFarlane, N. R., ed. 1983. *Family Therapy in Schizophrenia*. New York: Guilford Press.

McGill, V. J. 1967. *The Idea of Happiness*. New York: Praeger.

McGlashan, T. H. 1984. "The Chestnut Lodge follow up study." *Archives of General Psychiatry* 41:573–601.

Mack, J. E. and S. L. Ablon. 1983. *The Developing and Sustaining of Self-Esteem in Childhood*. New York: International Universities Press.

McKay, C. 1937. *A Long Way From Home*. New York: L. Furman.

Mackenzie, N., ed. 1967. *Secret Societies*. London: Aldus books.

McNeill, W. H. 1976. *Plagues and Peoples.* Garden City, N. Y.: Doubleday.

McNeill, W. H. 1982. *The Pursuit of Power*. Chicago: University of Chicago Press.

Madaule, J. 1967. *The Albigensian Crusade*. New York: Fordham University Press.

Maetze, G., ed. 1970. *Zehn Jahre Berliner Psychoanalytisches Institut*. Meisenheim, Federal Republic of Germany: Anton Hain V.G. (reprint of 1930 book with additions.)

Mahler, M. et al. 1975. *The Psychological Birth of the Human Infant*. New York: Basic Books.

Manuel, F. 1979. *A Portrait of Isaac Newton*. Washington, D.C.: Republic Books.

Manuel, F. E. and F. P. Manuel. 1979. *Utopian Thought in the Western World*. Cambridge: Harvard University Press.

Marcus, I. M. 1973. "The Experience of separation and indivduation in infancy and its reverberations through the course of life. 2. adolescence and maturity." *Journal of the American Psychoanalytic Association*, 21:155–167.

Marcus, I. M. and J. Francis, eds. 1975. *Masturbation; From Infancy to Senescence*. New York: International Universities Press.

Marsella, A. J. and G. M. White, eds. 1984. *Cultural Conceptions of Mental Health and Therapy*. Boston: D. Reidel.

Marshall, D. S. and R. C. Suggs, eds. 1971. *Human Sexual Behavior*. New York: Basic Books.

Masling, J., ed. 1983. *Empirical Studies of Psychoanalytical Theories*. Hillside, N.J.: Analytic Press.

Massie, H. 1978. "The early natural history of childhood psychosis: Ten cases studied by analysis of family home movies of the infancies of the children." *Journal of the American Academy of Child Psychiatry* 17:29–45.

Masters, W. and V. Johnson. 1966. *Human Sexual Response*. Boston: Little, Brown.

Mathers, E. W. and T. A. Guest. 1975. "Anonymity and group antisocial behavior." *Journal of Personality and Social Psychology* 31:881–886.

Matson, N. 1980. *Short Lives: Portraits in Creativity and Self-Destruction*. New York: Morrow.

May, R. et al., eds. 1958. *Existence*. New York: Simon and Schuster.

Mayman, M. et al., eds. 1982. "Infant research: The dawn of awareness." *Psychoanalytic Inquiry*, vol. 1, no. 4.

Mead, F. H. 1936. *Movements of Thought in the Nineteenth Century.* Chicago: University of Chicago Press.

Mead, M. 1935. *Sex and Temperament in Three Primitive Societies*. New York: Morrow.

Mead, M. 1949. *Male and Female*. New York: Morrow.

Mead, M. 1964.*Continuities in Cultural Evolution*. New Haven, Conn.: Yale University Press.

Mead, M. and M. Wolfenstein, eds. 1955. *Childhood in Contemporary Cultures*. Chicago: University of Chicago Press.

Meissner, W. W. 1981a *Internalization in Psychonalysis*. New York: International Universities Press.

Meissner, W. W. 1981b "Metapsychology who needs it?" *Journal of the American Psychoanalytic Association*. 29:291–938.

Menaker, E. 1960. "The self-image as defense and resistance." *Psychoanalytic Quarterly* 29:72–81.

Mendel, W. M. 1976. *Schizophrenia: The Experience and its Treatment*. San Francisco: Jossey-Bass.

Menefee, S. P. 1981. *Wives for Sale*. New York: St. Martin's Press.

Menninger, K. et al. 1963. *The Vital Balance*. New York: Viking Press.

Messenger, J. C. 1969. *Innis Beag*. New York: Holt, Rinehart.

Messing, S. D. 1959. "Group therapy and social status in the Zar cult of Ethiopia." In M. K. Opler, ed., *Culture and Mental Health*, pp. 319–332.

Meyers, S. J. 1981. "The bipolar self." *Journal of the American Psychoanalytic Association, 1981*, 29:143–159.

Minar, D. W. and S. Greer. 1969. *The Concept of Community*. Chicago: Aldine.

Misch, G. 1951. *A History of Autobiography in Antiquity*, 2 vols. Cambridge, Mass.: Harvard University Press.

Mischel, T., ed. 1977. *The Self: Psychological and Philosophical Issues*. Oxford, England: Basil Blackwell.

Mishima, Y. 1958. *Confessions of a Mask*. New York: New Directions.

Mitscherlich, A. 1971. "Psychoanalysis and the aggressions of large groups." *International Journal of Psychoanalysis* 52:161–168.

Modell, A. H. 1975. "A narcissistic defence against affects and the illusion of self-sufficiency." *International Journal of Psychoanalysis* 56:275–282.

Moller, H. 1969. *Die Kleinburgerliche Familie Im 18.Jahr Hundert: Verhalten und Gruppen Kultur*. Berlin: De Gruyter.

Mommsen, T. 1854. *The History of Rome*. New York: World. 1958.

Money, J. 1980. *Love and Love Sickness*. Baltimore: Johns Hopkins University Press.

Money, J. and A. Ehrhardt. 1972. *Man and Woman, Boy and Girl*. Baltimore: Johns Hopkins University Press.

Moore, B. F. and B. D. Fine, eds. 1968. *A Glossary of Psychoanalytic Terms and Concepts*. New York: American Psychoanalytic Association.

More, T. 1516. *Utopia*. New Haven: Yale University Press, 1965.

Morison, S. F. 1972. *The Oxford History of the American People*. New York: New American Library.

Moss, C. 1982. *Portraits in the Wild*. Chicago: University of Chicago Press.

Moss, H. A. and J. Kagan, 1964. "Report on personality consistency and change from the Fels longitudinal study." *Vita Humana* 7:127–138.

Mueller, C. G. 1979. "Some origins of psychology as science." *Annual Review of Psychology* 30:9–30.

Murdock, G. P. 1949. *Social Structure*. New York: Macmillan.

Murphy, H. B. M. 1982. *Comparative Psychiatry*. New York: Springer.

Murphy, L. 1973. "Some initial contributions of psychoanalysis and child development." In *Psychoanalysis and Contemporary Science*, 2. New York: International Universities Press.

Mussen, P. H., ed. 1983. *Handbook of Child Psychology*, 4 vols. New York: Wiley.

Myrdal, G. 1944. *An American Dilemma*. 2 vols. New York: Harper Torchbooks.

Nagera, H. 1967. *Vincent Van Gogh*. London: Allen and Unwin.

Naisbitt, J. 1982. *Megatrends*. New York: Warner Books.

Neill, A. S. 1960. *Summerhill*. New York: Hart.

Neilon, P. 1948. "Shirley's Babies After Fifteen Years." *Pedagogical Seminary and Journal of Genetic Psychology* 73:175–186.

Neisser, V., ed. 1982. *Memory Observed: Remembering in Natural Contexts*. San Francisco: Freeman.

Neugarten, B. L. et al. 1964. *Personality in Middle and Later Life*. New York: Atherton Press.

New York Psychoanalytic Institute, 1983–1984. *Bulletin*.

Nichols, M. 1984. *Family Therapy: Concepts and Methods*. New York: Gardner Press.

Nisbet, R. 1973. *The Social Philosophers. Community and Conflict in Western Thought*. New York: Crowell.

Nordhoff, C. 1875. *The Communistic Societies of the U.S.* New York: Schocken Books, 1915.

Noyes, J. G. 1870. *History of American Socialisms*. New York: Dover, 1966.

Oakes, J. 1982. *The Ruling Race*. New York: Knopf.

Offer, D. and J. B. Offer. 1975. *From Teenage to Young Manhood*. New York: Basic Books.

Offer, D. and M. Sabshin, eds. 1984. *Normality and the Life Cycle: A Critical Integration*. New York: Basic Books.

Olney, J., ed. 1980. *Autobiography: Essays Theoretical and Critical.* Princeton: Princeton University Press.

Opler, M. K. and J. L. Singer. 1956. "Ethnic differences in behavior and psychopathology: Italian and Irish." *International Journal of Social Psychiatry* 12:11–23.

Opler, M. K., ed. 1959. *Culture and Mental Health.* New York: Macmillan.

Ornstein, P. 1974. "A discussion of the paper by Otto F. Kernberg on further contributions to the treatment of narcissistic personalities." *International Journal of Psychoanalysis* 55:241–247.

Osofsky, J., ed. 1979. *Handbook of Infant Development.* New York: Wiley.

Page, C. H. 1969. *Class and American Sociology.* New York: Schocken books.

Pagels, E. 1981. *The Gnostic Gospels.* New York: Vintage Books.

Paige, K. E. and J. M. Paige. 1981. *The Politics of Reproductive Ritual.* Berkeley: University of California Press.

Parin, P., F. Morgenthaler, and G. Parin-Matthey. 1980. *Fear Thy Neighbor as Thyself.* Chicago: University of Chicago Press.

Parsons, T. 1964. *Social Structure and Personality.* New York: Free Press.

Paterson, D. 1982. *Slavery and Social Death.* Cambridge, Mass.: Harvard University Press.

Pearsall, R. 1975. *Night's Black Angels: The many faces of Victorian Cruelty.* New York: McKay.

Peller, L. 1958. "Reading and daydreams in latency boy-girl differences." *Journal of the American Psychoanalytic Association,* 6:57–70.

Perry, H. S. 1982. *Psychiatrist of America.* Cambridge: Harvard University Press.

Piaget, J. 1923. "La pensee symbolique et la pensee de l'enfant." *Archives de Psychologie* 18:273–304.

Piaget, J. 1973. "The affective unconscious and the cognitive unconscious." *Journal of the American Psychoanalytic Association,* 21:249–261.

Piaget, J. 1977. *The Essential Piaget.* H. Gruber and J. J. Voneche, eds. New York: Basic Books.

Pine, F. 1981. "In the beginning: Contributions to a psychoanalytic developmental psychology." *International Review of Psychoanalysis* 8:15–33.

Psychiatric Glossary. 1975. American Psychiatric Association, Washington, D.C. New York: Brunner/Mazel.

Pulver, S. 1970. "Narcissism: The term and the concept." *Journal of the American Psychoanalytic Association* 18:319–341.

Putnam, J. J. *Letters.* Nathan Hale, ed. Cambridge: Harvard University Press, 1971.

Quen, J. M. and Carlson, E. T. 1978. *American Psychoanalysis*. New York: Brunner/Mazel.

Radin, P. 1927. *Primitive Man as Philosopher*. New York: Dover, 1955.

Randall, J. H. 1965. *The Career of Philosophy*. New York: Columbia University Press.

Randall, J. H. 1926. *The Making of the Modern Mind*. New York: Columbia Univeristy Press, 1976.

Rangell, L. 1982. "The self in psychoanalytic theory." *Journal of the American Psychoanalytic Association* 30:863–891.

Rank, D. 1914. "Der Doppelgänger; Eine Psychoanalytische studi" (The Double: A Psychoanalytic Study). *IMAGO*, 3:97–164.

Rapaport, D. 1960. *The Structure of Psychoanalytic Theory*. New York: International Universities Press.

Redican, W. K. and D. M. Taub. 1981. "Male parental care in monkeys and apes." In M. Lamb, ed., *The Role of the Father in Child Development*, pp. 203–258.

Reider, N. 1955. "The Demonology of modern psychiatry." *American Journal of Psychiatry* 3:851–856.

Reik, T. 1919. *Ritual: Psychoanalytic Studies*. New York: International Universities Press, 1976.

Ridley, M. 1978. "Paternal care." *Animal behaviour* 26:904–932.

Riesman, D. 1961. *The Lonely Crowd*. New Haven: Yale University Press.

Roberts, R. 1925. *The Social Laws of the Koran*. London: Williams and Norgate.

Robinson, D. N. 1982. *Toward A Science of Human Nature*. New York: Columbia University Press.

Robitscher, J. 1980. *The Powers of Psychiatry*. Boston: Houghton Mifflin.

Roche de Coppens, P. 1979. *Ideal Man in Classical Sociology*. University Park: Pennsylvania State University Press.

Rodgers, I. E. 1982. "Roots of madness." *Science* 82:3–85.

Roheim, G. 1921a. "Das Selbst." *Imago* 7:1–39; 142–179; 310–348; 453–504.

Roheim, G. 1921a. "Primitive man and environment." *International Journal of Psychoanalysis* 2:157–178.

Roheim, G. 1932. "Psychoanalysis of primitive cultural types." *International Journal of Psychoanalysis* 13:2–224.

Roheim, G. 1959. *Psychoanalysis and Anthropology*. New York: International Universities Press.

Roheim, G. 1955. *Magic and Schizophrenia*. New York: International Universities Press.

Rosen, G. 1968. *Madness in Society*. New York: Harper Touchbooks.

Rosenbaum, M. and A. Snadowsky, eds. 1976. *The Intensive Group Experience*. New York: Free Press.

Rosenberg, M. 1979. *Conceiving the Self*. New York: Basic Books.

Rosenberg, M. and H. B. Kaplan, eds. 1982. *Social Psychology and the Self-Concept*. Arlington Heights, Ill.: Harlan Davidson.

Rosenblatt, A. G. and J. T. Thickstun, 1977. *Modern Psychoanalytic Concepts in a General Psychology*. New York: International Universities Press.

Rosenfeld, H. A. 1965. *Psychotic States*. London: Hogarth Press.

Ross, J. M., S. H. Cath, and A. R. Gurwitt, eds. 1982. *Father and Child: Developmental and Clinical Perspectives*. Boston: Little, Brown.

Rossi, A. J., ed. 1973. *The Feminist Papers*. New York: Bantam Books.

Rothman, S. M. 1978. *Woman's Proper Place*. New York: Basic Books.

Rothstein, A. 1980. *The Narcissistic Pursuit of Perfection*. New York: International Universities Press.

Rubinfine, D. L. 1958. "Problems of identity." *Journal of the American Psychoanalytic Association*, 6:131–142.

Saadawi, N. E. 1982. *The Hidden Face of Eve*. Boston: Beacon Press.

Sagan, E. 1979. *The Lust to Annihilate*. New York: Psychohistory Press.

St. Augustine. 426. *The City of God*. Garden City, N.Y.: Image Books, 1958.

Sarbin, T. 1967. "On the futility of the proposition that some people be labelled mentally ill." *Journal of Consulting Psychology* 31:447–453.

Sarnoff, C. *Latency*. 1976. New York: Aronson.

Schacht, R. 1971. *Alienation*. Garden City, N.Y.: Anchor Books.

Schachtel, E. 1947. "On memory and childhood amnesia." *Psychiatry* 10:1–26.

Schafer, R. 1976. *A New Language for Psychoanalysis*. New Haven: Yale University Press.

Schaie, K. W., ed. 1983. *Longitudinal Studies of Adult Psychological Development*. New York: Guilford Press.

Scheper-Hughes, N. 1979. *Saints, Scholars, and Schizophrenics*. Berkeley: University of California Press.

Schneir, M., ed. 1972. *Feminism: The Essential Historical Writings*. New York: Vantage Books.

Schur, M. 1972. *Freud Living and Dying*. New York; International Universities Press.

Searles, H. 1965. "Review of E. Jacobson: The self and the object world." *International Journal of Psychoanalysis* 46:529–532

Selye, H. 1976. *The Stress of Life*. New York: McGraw-Hill.

Senn, M. J. E. and C. Hartford, eds. 1968. *The Firstborn: Experiences of Eight American Families*. Cambridge: Harvard University Press.

Sherover, C. M., ed. 1974. *The Development of the Democratic Idea*. New York: New American Library.

Shirley, M. M. 1933. *The First Two Years of Life: A Study of 25 Babies*. Minneapolis: University of Minnesota.

Shweder, R. A. and E. J. Bourne, 1984. "Does the concept of the person vary cross-culturally?" In Marsells and White, eds., *Cultural Conceptions of Mental Health and Therapy*.

Shorter, E. 1975. *The Making of the Modern Family*. New York: Basic Books.

Shorter, E. 1982. *A History of Women's Bodies*. New York: Basic Books.

Silverman, L., E. Lachmann, and R. Milich. 1984. *The Search for Oneness*. New York: International Universities Press.

Simmel, E. C., M. E. Hahn, and J. K. Walters, eds. 1983. *Aggressive Behavior: Genetic and Neural Approaches*. Hillsdale, N.J.: Erlbaum.

Simon, B. 1978. *Mind and Madness in Ancient Greece*. Ithaca, N.Y.: Cornell University Press.

Skinner, B. 1948. *Walden Two*. New York: Macmillan.

Skinner, B. F. 1971. *Beyond Freedom and Dignity*. New York: Knopf.

Skultans, V. 1975. *Madness and Morals*. London: Routledge and Kegan Paul.

Smeriglio, V. L., ed. 1981. *Newborns and Parents*. Hillsdale, N.J.: Erlbaum.

Smith, J. E. 1974. *The Spirit of American Philosophy*. New York: Oxford University Press.

Smith, M. L., G. V. Glass, and T. I. Miller, 1980. *The Benefits of Psychotherapy*. Baltimore: Johns Hopkins University Press.

Solomon, L. N. and B. Berzon, eds. 1972. *New Perspectives on Encounter Groups*. San Francisco: Jossey-Bass.

Sorensen, R. C. 1973. *Adolescent Sexuality in Contemporary America*. New York: World.

Southwick, C. 1963. *Primate Social Behavior*. New York: Van Nostrand.

Spielrein, S. 1983. *A Secret Symmetry*. New York: Pantheon Books.

Spiro, M. E. 1961. "Social systems, personalities and fuctional analysis." In B. Kaplan, ed., *Studying Personality Cross-Culturally*. Evanston, Ill.: Row, Peterson.

Spiro, M. E. 1965. *Children of the Kibbutz*. New York: Schocken Books.

Spiro, M. E. 1967. *Burmese Supernaturalism: A Study in the Explanation and Reduction of Suffering*. Englewood Cliffs, N.J.: Prentice-Hall.

Spiro, M. 1980. *Gender and Culture*. New York: Schocken Books.

Spiro, M. E. 1982. *Oedipus in the Trobriands*. Chicago: University of Chicago Press.

Spitz, R. 1957. *No and Yes*. New York: International Universities Press.

Spitz, R. A. 1965. *The First Year of Life*. New York: International Universities Press.

Spitzer, R. L. et al. 1981. *DSM-III Case Book*. Washington, D.C.: American Psychiatric Association.

Spree, R. 1981. *Soziale Ungleichheit Vor Krankheit und Tod: Zur Sozialgeschichte des Gesundheits Bereichs Im Deutschen Kaiserreich*. Göttingen: Vandenhoek und Rupprecht.

Spurr, R. 1981. *A Glorious Way to Die*. New York: Newmarket Press.

Standing, E. M. 1962. *Maria Montessori: Her Life and Work*. New York: New American Library.

Stern, D. 1977. *The First Relationship*. Cambridge: Harvard University Press.

Sternberg, R. J., ed. 1982. *Handbook of Human Intelligence*. New York: Cambridge University Press.

Stevens-Long, J. 1979. *Adult Life: Developmental Processes*. Palo Alto, Calif.: Mayfield.

Stoller, R. J. 1968. *Sex and Gender*. New York: Aronson.

Stolorow, R. D. 1975. "Toward a functional definition of narcissism." *International Journal of Psychoanalysis* 56:179–185.

Stone, A. E. 1982. *Autobiographical Occasions and Original Acts*. Philadelphia: University of Pennsylvania Press.

Stone, L. 1979. *The Family, Sex, and Marriage in England 1500–1800*. New York: Harper.

Strain, P. S., ed. 1981. *The Utilization of Classroom Peers as Behavior Change Agents*. New York: Plenum.

Strasser, S. 1982. *Never Done: A History of American Housework*. New York: Pantheon.

Stratton, P., ed. 1982. *Psychobiology of the Human Newborn*. New York: Wiley.

Strauss, J. S. et al. 1980. *The Psychotherapy of Schizophrenia*. New York: Plenum.

Strauss, A. L. 1959. *Mirrors and Masks: The Search for Identity*. New York: Free Press.

Strauss, A. L. 1968. "Some neglected properties of status passage." In H. J. Becker et al., eds., *Institutions and the Person*, pp. 265–271.

Suggs, R. C. 1971. "Sex and personality in the Marquesas: A discussion of the Linton-Kardiner report." In D. S. Marshall and R. C. Suggs, eds., *Human Sexual Behavior*, pp. 163–186.

Sullivan, H. S. 1931. "The modified psychoanalytic treatment of schizophrenia." *American Journal of Psychiatry*88:519–540.

Sullivan, H. S. 1939. *Conceptions of Modern Psychiatry*. New York: Norton.

Sullivan, H. S. 1962. "The relation of onset to outcome in schizophrenia." In H. S. Sullivan, ed., *Schizophrenia as a Human Process*, pp. 233–255.

Sullivan, H. S. 1962. *Schizophrenia as a Human Process*. New York: Norton.

Suls, J., ed. 1982. *Psychological Perspectives on the Self*, 1. Hillsdale, N.J.: Erlbaum.

Suls, J. and A. G. Greenwald, eds. 1983. *Psychological Perspectives on the Self*, 2. Hillsdale, N.J.: Erlbaum.

Sumner, W. G. 1959. *Folkways, 1906*. New York: Dover.

Sze, W. C., ed. 1975. *The Human Life Cycle*. New York: Aronson.

Tacitus. *The Annals of Imperial Rome*. New York: Penguin Books, 1977.

Talbott, J. A., ed. 1984. *The Chronic Mental Patient: Five Years Later*. New York: Grune and Stratton.

Tannahill, R. 1980. *Sex in History*. New York: Stein and Day.

Teicholz, J. G. 1978. "A selective review of the psychoanalytic literature on theoretical conceptualizations of narcissism." *Journal of the American Psychoanalytic Association*, 26:831–861.

Thomas, A. et al. 1963. *Behavioral Individuality in Early Childhood*. New York: New York University Press.

Thomas, A., I. Chess, and H. Birch. 1968. *Temperament and Behavior Disorders in Children*. New York: New York University Press.

Thrasher, F. 1936. *The Gang*. Chicago: University of Chicago Press.

Tissot, R. 1977. "Long-term drug therapy in psychoses." In C. Chiland, ed., *Long-Term Treatment of Psychotic States*, pp. 89–216. New York: Human Sciences Press.

Tjossem. T. D., ed. 1946. *Intervention Strategies for High Risk Infants and Young Children*. Baltimore: University of Maryland Press.

Torrey, E. F. et al. 1984. "Endemic psychosis in Western Ireland." *American Journal of Psychiatry* 141:966–969.

Tracy, P. C. 1980. *Jonathan Edwards, Pastor*. New York: Hill and Wang.

Treurniet, N. 1983. "Psychoanalysis and self psychology: A metapsychological essay with a clinical illustration.", *Journal of the American Psychoanalytic Association* 31:59–100.

Turnbull, C. M. 1972. *The Mountain People*. New York: Simon and Schuster.

Turner, A. W. 1978. *Rituals of Birth*. New York: McKay.

Turner, V. 1977. *The Ritual Process*. Ithaca, N.Y.: Cornell University Press.

Tuttman, S. 1981. In Tuttman, Kaye, and Zimmerman, eds., *Object and Self*.

Tuttman, S., C. Kaye, and M. Zimmerman, eds. 1981. *Object and Self: A Developmental Approach*. New York: International Universities Press.

Tuzin, D. F. 1982. "Ritual violence among the Ilahita Arapesh." In G. H. Herdt, ed., *Rituals of Manhood*.

Untermeyer, L. 1959. *Lives of the Poets*. New York: Simon and Schuster.

Vaillant, G. E. 1977. *Adaptation to Life*. Boston: Little Brown.

Van Gennep, A. 1909. *The Rites of Passage*. Chicago: University of Chicago Press, 1960.

Vanggaard, T. 1972. *Phallos: A Symbol and Its History in the Male World*. New York: International Universities Press.

Van Lawick-Goodall, J. 1968. "The behavior of free-living chimpanzees in the Gombe stream area." *Animal Behavior Monographs* 1, 3:161–311.

Van Lawick-Goodall, J. 1972. *In the Shadow of Man*. New York: Houghton Mifflin.

Veroff, J., E. Douvan, and R. A. Kulka. 1981a. *The Inner American: A Self-Portrait from 1957 to 1976*. New York: Basic Books.

Veroff, J., R. A. Kulka, and E. Douvan. 1981b. *Mental Health in America*. New York: Basic Books.

Viederman, M. 1979. "Monica: A 25-year longitudinal study of the consequences of trauma in infancy." *Journal of the American Psychoanalytic Association*, 27:107–126.

Waelder, R. 1924. "The psychoses, their mechanisms and accessibilities to influence." *International Journal of Psychoanalysis* 6:254–281.

Waelder, R. 1964. *Basic Theory of Psychoanalysis*. New York: International Universities Press.

Wallace, A. F. 1958. "Dreams and the wishes of the soul: A type of psychoanalytic theory among the seventeenth century Iroquois." *American Anthropologist* 60:234–248.

Wallace, A. F. C. 1970. *Culture and Personality*. New York: Random House.

Wallerstein, R. S. 1978. "Perspectives on psychoanalytic training around the world." *International Journal of Psychoanalysis* 59:477–515.

Wallerstein, R. S. 1981. "The bipolar self: Discussion of alternative perspectives."*Journal of the American Psychoanalytic Association* 29:377–394.

Warner, D. and P. Warner. 1982. *The Sacred Warriors: Japan's Suicide Legions*. New York: Avon.

Warner, R. 1983. "Recovery from schizophrenia in the Third World." *Psychiatry* 46:197–212.

Warner, W. L. et al. 1960. *Social Class in America*. New York: Harper.

Warner, W. L., ed. 1963. *Yankee City*. New Haven: Yale University Press.

Wasser, S. K., eds. 1983. *Social Behavior of Female Vertebrates*. New York: Academic Press.

Weil, A. P. 1970. "The basic core." In Ruth Eissler et al., ed., *The Psychoanalytic Study of the Child* 25:442–460. New York: International Universities Press.

Weiner, H. 1977. *Psychobiology and Human Disease*. New York: Elsevier.

Welch, B. L. and A. S. Welch. 1969. "Aggression and the biogenic amines." In S. Garattini and E. B. Sigg, eds., *Biology of Aggressive Behavior*. Amsterdam: Excerpta Medica.

Westley, W. A. and N. B. Epstein. 1969. *The Silent Majority*. San Francisco: Jossey-Bass.

Whiting, B. 1963. *Six Cultures*. New York: Wiley.

Whiting, J. W. M. and L. L. Child. 1953. *Child Training and Personality: A Cross-Cultural Study*. New Haven: Yale University Press.

Whyte, W. 1956. *The Organization Man*. New York: Simon and Schuster.

Williams, B. 1973. *Problems of the Self*. New York: Cambridge University Press.

Wilson, B. R. 1973. *Magic and the Millennium*. New York: Harper and Row.

Winnicott, D. W. 1975. *Through Pediatrics to Psychoanalysis*. New York: Basic Books.

Winslow, R. W., eds. 1980. *The Emergence of Deviant Minorities*. San Ramon, Cal.: Consensus Publishers.

Wolf, A. and E. N. Schwartz. 1962. *Psychoanalysis in Groups*. New York: Grune and Stratton.

Wundt, W. 1861. *Lectures on Human and Animal Psychology*. E. Creighton and E. B. Titchener, trans. London: Swan and Somenschein, 1894.

Wylie, R. 1961. *The Self-Concept*. Lincoln: University of Nebraska Press.

Wylie, R. 1974. *The Self-Concept*. 2d ed. Lincoln: University of Nebraska Press.

Yablonsky, L. 1970. *The Violent Gang*. New York: Penguin.

Yablonsky, L. 1971. *Synanon: The Tunnel Back*. New York: Pelican Books.

Yankelovich, D. 1981. *New Rules: Searching for Self-Fulfillment in a World Turned Upside Down*. New York: Random House.

Yarrow, L. J., J. L. Rubenstein, and F. A. Pederjen. 1975. *Infant and Environment: Early Cognitive and Motivational Development*. New York: Wiley.

Yee, M. S. and T. N. Layton. 1982. *In My Father's House*. New York: Berkley Books.

Zablocki, B. 1980. *Alienation and Charisma: A Study of Contemporary American Communes*. New York: Free Press.

Zigler, E. and J. Valentine, eds. 1979. *Project Head Start: A Legacy of the War on Poverty*. New York: Free Press.

Zweig, P. 1980. *The Heresy of Self Love*. Princeton: Princeton University Press.

Zuñi People. 1972. *Self-Portrayals*. Albuquerque: University of New Mexico Press.

Zurcher, L. A. 1981. *Social Rules: Conformity Conflict and Creativity*. Beverly Hills, Calif.: Sage.

Index